MANAGING ZARI INDUSTRY IN SOUTH GUJARAT

FEBRUARY - 2005

PREFACE

Zari is a historic product of surat. The glitter of zari attracted British, French and Dutch people to Surat. The golden/silver thread is produced from solid pure gold and silver metal. The skilled craftsmen produce hair thin zari thread, which is a state of the art product. The zari thread has been an attraction for everybody. Today the precious metal gold and silver has become too costly and hence pure zari is beyond everybody's reach. Metallic Yarn Zari (imitation zari) has come as an able, ideal and most suitable substitute to all types of pure zari.

The zari industry in Surat is marked by division of processes between enterprises. Theoretically speaking, this gives scope for specialization, efficiency and innovation, essential for competing beyond local markets. Surat based zari has not been able to build on these advantages of clustering, due to mutual suspicion, distrust and lack of unity, coupled with agreed and exploitative labour practices, prevalent among the manufacuters.

The industry caters to the end product made in different parts of the country by supplying three distinct classes of products viz. real zari, imitation zari and plastic zari. It is unfortunate that despite surat being a major synthetic textiles production centre, the zari produced in surat cannot be interwoven with synthetic textiles due to technical inadequacies having their roots in lack of innovation in products and processes. Our study has brought out this as a major constraint as well as a major opportunity if the challenges is overcome. In the absence of local demand and due to severe and unhealthy competition in catering to the limited and stagnant distant markets of zari products, the industry has wounded up with adverse terms of trade. Our recommendations based on view of historical experiences of small manufacturing units and our understanding of the current scenario of the surat zari industry, naturally follow similar lines.

An attempt has been made in the present study about 'managing zari industry in South Gujarat'. The primary objective of the study was to revive the sagging zari industry so as to improve the employment potential of the industry. Due to peculiar nature of traditional industry working with a stagnant market in a very competitive atmosphere, it became necessary to give up formalise empirical research method. The study had to be based on informal interviews, and discussions at various levels and field visits to a few units in several parts of surat.

The present study is divided into five chapters. Chapter one, which is introductory in nature, inclusive of historical background. It also reflects the products of zari industry, the process of different zari's, the types of patterns of organization, marketing, export, the growth and the developmental situation of the industry.

Second chapter focuses on the issues of zari industry. It also includes SWOT analysis. The infrastructure facilities, prospectus ahead, role of co-operative societies, role of government as well as environmental aspects have been analysed in the second chapter.

The third chapter reflects the research methodology, scopes and objectives and limitation of the study.

Chapter four shows the characteristics of respondents, analysis of the data as well as summarized findings.

The fifth chapter enlightens the challenges in time to come, recommendations and further research avenues.

ACKNOWLEDGEMENT

The present study has been made possible through the co-operation, assistance and encouragement of many individuals to whom I wish to express my gratitude. I sincerely express my gratitude to my guide Dr. Vinod B. Patel, Professor, Department of Business and Industrial Management, Veer Narmad South Gujarat University, Surat, for his invaluable guidance. His constant encouragement and tireless assistance helped me to complete my study so successfully.

I owe lot to Dr. Satyendra Kumar - Professor and Head, Department of Business and Industrial Management for his precious guidance and assistance. I fall short of words to express my deep sense of gratefulness to Shri J. B. Shah, Principal, Arts & Commerce college, Amroli, for his constant motivation and direction throughout my study. I wish to express my thanks to Shri Champakbhai Gandhi, Shri Ranjitbhai Gilitwala, Shri Shantilal Jariwala, Shri Ramanbhai Jariwala and all other office bearers as well as members of Zari Goods Producers' Co-operative Credit Society, South India Zari Merchant and Manufacturer's Association, Andhra-Karnatak Zari Manufacturing Association, Varanasi Zari Mandal to provide me all the necessary information. I also wish to express my thanks to Chamber of Commerce, Surat for providing me the details.

I would like to express my sincere gratitude to all my colleagues who besides encouraging me to go deeper into the subject helped me in more than one way. Yet specific mention must be made of Prof. Ritu Agarwal, Professor in English, who carefully reviewed the manuscript and gave helpful comments. I express my deep gratitude to my dearest friends Shri Navin Chapadia, Ex-member of Handicraft and Handloom Board, Government of India, New Delhi (Surat), Shri Kapil Puri (Guru), Prof. B. N. Patel who have provided me constant inspiration and helped me a lot in the successful completion of my study. I am grateful to Hon'ble Kashiram Rana, the then Textile Minister, Government of India and his staff of ministry who have provided me the required information and also extend needed co-operation.

During my research work, The computerised and printing work was handled by my student, Kasim M. Varsi, and thereby I express my heart felt thanks to him.

Last but not the least, specific mention must be made to my parents, and above all my wife, Aruna, daughter Heta as well as Ashuthosh, my son, whose inspiration and assistance at various stages not only goaded me on but boosted my self confidence while relieving me of my odd domestic chores. Lastly, I thank one and all, who inspired and helped me directly or otherwise, in providing the necessary form of the study.

SURAT   **(GIRISH N. RANA)**

MANAGING ZARI INDUSTRY IN SOUTH GUJARAT - A STUDY

CONTENTS

CHAPTER NO.	TITLE	PAGE NO.
1	**INTRODUCTION AND HISTORY**	
	1.1 INTRODUCTION	1
	1.2 HISTORY	7
	1.3 PRODUCTION OF ZARI INDUSTRY	37
	1.4 PROCESS OF CRAFT	79
	1.5 PATTERNS OF ORGANISATION	96
	1.6 MARKETING OF ZARI	101
	1.7 EXPORTS OF ZARI	105
	1.8 GROWTH AND DEVELOPMENT	120
	1.9 PICTORIAL PRESENTATION OF ZARI AND ZARI PRODUCTS.	128
2	**BASIC ISSUES OF ZARI INDUSTRY**	
	2.1 SWOT ANALYSIS.	213
	2.2 INFRASTRUCTURE FACILITIES IN SURAT.	224
	2.3 PROSPECTS AHEAD IN INDIA FOR ZARI.	226
	2.4 ROLE OF PUBLIC REPRESENTATIVE i.e. MEMBER OF PARLIAMENT / MEMBER OF LEGISLATIVE ASSEMBLY.	230
	2.5 ROLE OF CHAMBER OF COMMERCE.	233

CONT...

CHAPTER NO.	TITLE	PAGE NO.
	2.5.1 ROLE OF GOVERNMENT IN THE DEVELOPMENT OF ZARI INDUSTRY.	234
	2.5.2 ROLE OF ELECTRICITY COMPANIES IN THE DEVELOPMENT OF ZARI INDUSTRY.	235
	2.5.3 ROLE OF BANKING AND TERM LENDING FINANCIAL INSTITUTION IN THE DEVELOPMENT OF ZARI INDUSTRY IN SURAT.	236
	2.5.4 ROLE OF MUNICIPAL CORPORATION.	245
	2.6 NEED OF MARKETING CO-OPERATIVE SOCIETY.	246
	2.7 ENVIRONMENTAL ASPECTS.	247
3	**RESEARCH METHODOLOGY**	
	3.1 SCOPES	256
	3.2 OBJECTIVES	260
	3.3 SAMPLING PLAN	263
	3.4 METHOD OF DATA COLLECTION	264
	3.4 LIMITATIONS	268
4	**ANALYSIS AND OUTCOME**	
	4.1 CHARACTERISTICS OF RESPONDENTS	270
	4.2 ANALYSIS	272
	4.3 DATA ANALYSIS	284
	4.4 SUMMARIZED FINDINGS	316
	CONT...	

CHAPTER NO.	TITLE	PAGE NO.
5	**RECOMMENDATIONS AND SUGGESSTIONS**	
	5.1. CHALLENGES IN TIMES TO COME	322
	5.2 RECOMMENDATIONS	325
	5.3 FURTHER RESEARCH AVENUES	333
I	**REFERENCES**	340
II	**BIBLIOGRAPHY**	343
III	**APPENDIX**	369

LIST OF TABLES

TABLE NO.	TITLE	PAGE NO.
1.4.1	Zari Units In Surat - 1970.	87
1.5.1	Spatial Distribution Of Surat Based Zari Units.	96
1.5.2	Distribution of Family and Hired Workers in Units.	100
1.7.1	Exports of Zari and Zari Goods.	107
1.7.2	Statement of Exports of Handicrafts.	110
1.8.1	Zari Industry - 1980.	125
2.5.3.1	Statement of Surat Zari Goods Producers Co-op.Soc.	237
2.5.3.2	Profit - Surat Zari Goods Producers Co-op.Soc.	243
4.3.1	Types of Firms.	284
4.3.2	Types of Zari Products.	286
4.3.3	Tenure of Production.	288
4.3.4	Investment.	290
4.3.5	How many Machines Utilized in Production.	292
4.3.6	Any Technical changes done or not.	294
4.3.7	Supply of Finished Goods.	297
4.3.8	Availability of Raw-Material.	300
4.3.9	Training received or not.	303
4.3.10	Finance for Business.	306
4.3.11	Management Applied in Business.	309
4.3.12	Any reasonable Research done for Business.	312
4.3.13	Offering Study or not.	312

LIST OF CHARTS

CHART NO.	TITLE	PAGE NO.
1.4.1 (A)	Zari Units In Surat - 1970.	87
1.4.1 (B)	Zari Units In Surat - 1970.	88
1.4.2 (A)	Workers in Various Units.	88
1.4.2 (B)	Workers in Various Units.	88
1.7.1 (A)	Exports Value in Crores of Rupees.	108
1.7.1 (B)	Exports Value in Crores of Rupees.	108
1.7.2	Exports of Handicrafts.	111
1.7.2 (A)	Artmetalware - Exports.	112
1.7.2 (B)	Artmetalware - Exports.	112
1.7.3 (A)	Woodware - Exports.	113
1.7.3 (B)	Woodware - Exports.	113
1.7.4 (A)	Handprinted Textiles and Scarves - Exports.	114
1.7.4 (B)	Handprinted Textiles and Scarves - Exports.	114
1.7.5 (A)	Embroidered & Crocheted Goods - Exports.	115
1.7.5 (B)	Embroidered & Crocheted Goods - Exports.	115
1.7.6 (A)	Shawls as Artware - Exports.	116
1.7.6 (B)	Shawls as Artware - Exports.	116
1.7.7 (A)	Zari and Zari Goods - Exports.	117
1.7.7 (B)	Zari and Zari Goods - Exports.	117
1.7.8 (A)	Imitaion Jewellery - Exports.	118
1.7.8 (B)	Imitaion Jewellery - Exports.	118
1.7.9 (A)	Miscellaneous Handicrafts - Exports.	119
1.7.9 (B)	Miscellaneous Handicrafts - Exports.	119

CHART NO.	TITLE	PAGE NO.
2.5.3.1(A)	Membership.	238
2.5.3.1(B)	Membership.	238
2.5.3.2(A)	Share.	239
2.5.3.2(B)	Share.	239
2.5.3.3(A)	Other Funds.	240
2.5.3.3(B)	Other Funds.	240
2.5.3.4(A)	Reserve Funds.	241
2.5.3.4(B)	Reserve Funds.	241
2.5.3.5(A)	Dividend.	242
2.5.3.5(B)	Dividend.	242
2.5.3.6(A)	Profit.	244
2.5.3.6(B)	Profit.	244
4.3.1 (A)	Types of Firms.	284
4.3.1 (B)	Types of Firms.	285
4.3.2 (A)	Types of Zari Products.	286
4.3.2 (B)	Types of Zari Products.	287
4.3.3 (A)	Tenure of Production.	288
4.3.3 (B)	Tenure of Production.	289
4.3.4 (A)	Investment.	290
4.3.4 (B)	Investment.	291
4.3.5 (A)	How many Machines Utilized in Production.	292
4.3.5 (B)	How many Machines Utilized in Production.	293
4.3.5 (A)	Any Technical changes done or not.	294
4.3.5 (B)	Any Technical changes done or not.	295

CHART NO.	TITLE	PAGE NO.
4.3.7 (A)	Supply of Finished Goods.	297
4.3.7 (B)	Supply of Finished Goods.	298
4.3.8 (A)	Availability of Raw-Material.	300
4.3.8 (B)	Availability of Raw-Material.	301
4.3.9 (A)	Training received or not.	303
4.3.9 (A)	Training received or not.	304
4.3.10(A)	Finance for Business.	306
4.3.10(B)	Finance for Business.	307
4.3.11(A)	Management Applied in Business.	309
4.3.11(B)	Management Applied in Business.	310
4.3.12(A)	Any reasonable Research done for Business.	312
4.3.12(B)	Any reasonable Research done for Business.	313
4.3.13(A)	Offering Study or not.	313
4.3.13(B)	Offering Study or not.	314

ABBREVIATIONS

SGCCI	:	Southern Gujarat Chamber of Commerce and Industry.
ZMA	:	Zari Merchants' Association.
ZGPCOS	:	Zari Goods Producers Co-operative Societies.
IRMA	:	Institute of Rural Marketing Association.
SMC	:	Surat Municipal Corporation.
DIC	:	District Industrial Centre.
AIHB	:	All India Handicrafts Board.
C.A.	:	Current Anthropology
G.O.I	:	Government of India.
IETJ	:	Indian Export Trade Journal
EFCS	:	Ethnographic and Folk Culture Society.
JIAI	:	Journal of Indian Art and Industry.
TTPR	:	The Town Planning Reveiw
Z.I.IC.	:	Zari Industry Inquiry Centre.
A.I.Z.F.	:	All India Zari Federation

CHAPTER 1 :

INTRODUCTION AND HISTORY

		Page No.
1.1	INTRODUCTION	1
1.2	HISTORY	7
1.3	PRODUCTION OF ZARI INDUSTRY	37
1.4	PROCESS OF CRAFT	79
1.5	PATTERNS OF ORGANISATION	96
1.6	MARKETING OF ZARI	101
1.7	EXPORTS OF ZARI	105
1.8	GROWTH AND DEVELOPMENT	120
1.9	PICTORIAL PRESENTATION OF ZARI AND ZARI PRODUCTS.	128

CHAPTER 1 : INTRODUCTION AND HISTORY

1.1 INTRODUCTION:

From Rigvedic times, we have been hearing of several varieties of textiles, among which cloth of gold-hiranya , figures as a distinguished type. Gods in their grandeur wear it, as they ride in their stately chariots. Hiranya cloth has usually been considered the earliest equivalent of present-day zari work of kimkhwabs (brocades).

India has long been known for its golden thread, for Zari. Well-known products of the Indian Zari industry, besides gold and silver thread (Zari kasab) are the embroidery materials like stars and spangles, chalak, champo, kinari, salma and badla. The zari craft includes making zari thread and other materials, as well as thread. The latter covers zari embroidered saris, evening-bags, foot-wear and belts, zari textiles and the world-famous brocades.

Surat is the biggest zari thread-making centre in the country, followed by Varanasi. Both imitation and real zari threads, zari embroidery material and zari lace and borders are manufactured in Surat. Varanasi, on the other hand, is a big centre for the manufacture of superior quality real zan thread (kalabattu) zari textiles and zari brocades. Other centers of production are Jaipur and Ajmer which specialise in zari gota and zari thappa work.

The other centres of zari embroidery products are Agra, Bareilly, Varanasi. The items of zari are handbags, belts, shoe uppers, etc. Other popular items of export are zari badges all produced manually by skilled craftsmen in Bareilly and Varanasi. Zari threads are used extensively in handloom (and powerloom) saris which are manufactured all over India, especially in Varanasi, Bangalore, Dharmavaram, Kanchipuram and Paithan.

Zari is a historic product of Surat. The glitter of zari attracted British, French & Dutch people to Surat. The golden/silver thread is produced from solid pure gold & silver metal. The skilled craftsmen produce hair thin zari thread, which is a state of the art product. This zari thread has been a center of attraction for everybody. Today, the precious metal gold & silver has become too costly & hence pure zari is beyond everybody's reach.

Metallic yarn zari (imitation zari) has come as an able, ideal & most suitable substitute to all types of pure zari. Due to upgradation of technology, polyester film was metallised & coated, bringing into to existence the basic raw material for producing metallic yarn zari. France & Japan were the first to flood the market with zari made from polyester film in the year 1970. Since then, due to continous research & development metallic yarn zari has gained more market compared to all other types of imitation zari (made from copper) and pure zari.

Considering the cost aspect metallic yarn zari has done a great service to the nation by saving precious metal like gold & silver & also copper. Metallic yarn zari costing Rs.350/kg has become an easy & affordable luxury for common man. Pure zari costing Rs.4000 per kg has become a product beyond common man's reach.

Metallic zari industry today is an industry giving employment & self employment to more then 4000 families in Surat & to families at other centres like Ajmer, Maunathbhanjan. Salem, Coimbatore, Bangalore, Delhi, Malegaon, Nadiad. The process involved in making zari is very simple. Metallised coated film in desired colours are available in the market. This metallised coated film is first slitted with the help of a razor blade to pancake of small widths (normally 50 mm to 72 mm). The pancake produced are passed from the thin cutters, size of which depends upon the thickness of required zari. The zari so produced is wound on spools with the help of winder.

Major centers using metallic yarn zari are Surat, (used in

making various products viz kasab tilla, champo, gotta, zalar, etc.), Ahmedabad, (used in making borders for various gift applicatious), Bombay (used in ornamentation of fabrics meant for exports & used in decoration items), Bhivandi (used in fabrics & tapestry), Bangalore (used in handlooms), Salem, Coimbatore (handloom), Madras, Banaras, Maunathbhanajan (making sarees traditionally worn in marriage).

The questionnaire planned to be administrated to the zari workers broadly related to collection of information on:

(a) socio-economic conditions

(b) working environment

(c) employment and income distribution

(d) technology and extension services, and

(e) marketing pattern

This was done as the zari industry is predominantly owned by the zari merchants without whose active cooperation and willingness, access to information from the workers and fellow merchants would not have been possible.

Right from the beginning, zari merchants were extremely reluctant to part with any information relating to the zari industry. The stock answer provided by them was that since the industry was operating from the houses of the workers and merchants, and there existed no mechanism for collection and analysis of data on the industry, they would not be in a position to provide any information.

Further, on account of a possible suspicion on the part of the zari merchants about possible misuse of any information against their own interests, they systematically discouraged direct interaction with the workers and with fellow-merchants. In view of the impossibility of administering the questionnaires prepared by me, it became necessary to abandon the collection of primary data through structured interviews/questionnaires. It was considered advisable to elicit information through a process of unstructured dialogue, provided the zari merchants saw some purpose which would benefit them from the study.

After a lot of persuasion with the past and present office bearers of the Surat Zari Merchants' Association, a few meetings and visits could be organised. The meetings and visits, conducted in an informal and unstructured way, brought to fore many issues surrounding the zari industry of Surat. The report discusses these issues with reference to the structure of the zari industry in Surat and makes certain recommendations on the basis of the field observations. While it may be argued that strict research methodology by administration of questionnaires and collection and analysis of data could have provided statistically significant results, the study had to assume the course it had taken owing to the structure of the industry and the results had to be arrived at on the basis of unstructured interviews and informal observations. Further, visits of several zari units engaged in different processes and magnitudes of operation brought out the commonality of the pattern of issues in all units.

1.2 HISTORY:

1.2.1 ZARDOZI AS A CRAFT

Fabrics ornated with gold suggest regal opulence evoking historic splendour. In any artefact and culture, the use of gold tends to symbolise wealth and power, the fabrics with zardozi are no exception. The oldest documentary evidence to what might have been the earliest artefacts embroidered in precious metal is to be found in the Vedic age. However, zardoz[1] as a class of artisans along with other artisans followed the footsteps of the sultanate conquerors in the twelfth century down the mountain passes of the Khyber on to the plains of Indian sub-continent. A popular myth is found among the zardoz of Delhi, relating to the origin of this craft. This runs as follows:

Once a mosquito found entrance to a king's head. The fluttering of this mosquito caused the king severe headache. Every kind of treatment had failed. Finally Paigamber himself advised the head hakim in his dream that the king would be cured of his headache if he is hit by a shoe in the area of pain. The hakim narrated his dream to his associates. They executed a plan. A shoe decorated with pure gold and silver threads was ordered to be made for the purpose. The king was hit with the shoe. This killed the mosquito, curing the king of his ailment. He appreciated the artistic outlay on the shoe and desired to patronise the work. Other emperors and nobles followed him.

Retracing the history we come across the mention of hiranyan atkan which emphasises that the garments in the Vedic age were often embroidered with gold. Marut is often described as wearing mantles adorned with gold. Usha is described as wearing shining clothes, which were resplendent with gold. Apart from the unsewn garments which were general in those days, the Rigveda also refers to some words atka,[5] drapi, pesas indicating sewn garments. The term atka means a garment embroidered with gold thread. Another word hiranyair vyutarn signifies dresses worked with gold, reflecting like the sun. Rigvedic texts make innumerable allusions to such dresses which were worn by both men and women of high social ranking. References indicate this continuity in the epic period as well. Swarnatantu nirmita, the word occurring in Valmiki Ramayana, means adorned by gold wire.

Adiparva and Sabhaparva of the Mahabharata give interesting accounts of costly clothes embroidered with gold. Maharhavasthambra is a variety of costly robe mentioned at the time of marriage of the five Pandavas with Draupadi. The king of Kamboja is said to have presented Yudhishtara with many kinds of animal skins and woollen blankets all inlaid with threads of gold during the rajasuya sacrifice ceremony (jiftarupa-parishkitari), During this ceremony the kings of Chola and Pandya countries also presented fine clothing studded with shining precious stones. Even the gifts from Sinhal Desh were studded with precious stones. All these accounts are indicative of the fact that royal courts were making frequent presentations of fabrics with gold and precious stone work.

Valmiki's Ramayana speaks about maharajatvasas, the clothes embroidered with gold and silver. Rama and Sita were attired in yellow clothes (ratnambar) embroidered with gold thread and jewels when they went into exile. Dress of Ravana is described as maharhvastra sambaddh and mahamjatvasas indicating that the kingly costumes were expensive. Maharshaum sanvit is another reference in the same text implying the embroidery of fine expensive clothes. All these references indicate beyond doubt that embroidered costumes worked in gold, silver and precious stones were part of opulent tradition during the epic period. Vyasa also makes this observation in his accounts. This tradition seems to have extended to greater India.

No textual reference is available in support of the existence of this craft during the lull after the epic period. Panini, however, refers to a kind of silken cloth named koseyya signifying possibly the fabric adorned with gold. Buddhist literature provides very little evidence of embroidered clothes. It is possible that in the new stage of economy, when urbanism was in the process of emergence, and people were trading in exchange of gold bullion, there was less demand for gold decoration on fabric. But that the skill was present in some form could be known from the Jatakas where the stories refer to golden turbans used by kings and golden trappings used for state elephants. Sona-Nanda Jataka gives an elaborate description of the use of a heavily embroidered turban in gold in connection with king Manoja's entering the hermitage of Bodhisattva who in this blaze of glory comes, with turban cloth of gold", Such evidences would clearly indicate that the lavish use of gold and silver threads on turbans was in fashion among the nobility.

Jain literature provides interesting information about the silver or gold work on clothes, the text categorically banned the acceptance of such precious clothes by the monks and nuns, when they were begging for clothes. The sacred text says, 'no monk or nun should accept golden plaids, glittering like gold, embroidered with gold'. This description in Acharanga Sutra clearly spells out the evidence of the use of such clothings either by the royal courts or moneyed people. Kanakakhachiya was a kind of cloth embroidered with golden thread.

Several references, however, have been found in the accounts of Greek travellers throwing light on the existence of the gold embroidery tradition of the 4th century B.C. onwards. Describing the Indian ways of living as seen by Megasthenes, Strabo writes, "Contrary to their simplicity in general, they like to adorn themselves with apparels embroidered with gold." Strabo on another occasion says, 'the variegated garments spangled with gold' were in fashion. Curtius Rufus Quintus says that a king rides in a golden palanquin, garnished with pearls which dangle all round it and he is robed in fine muslin embroidered with purple and gold. Ptolemy speaks about the manufacture of muslin adorned with small pearls. These references distinctly reflect that gold and precious stone embroidery on various fabrics including muslin was much in vogue amongst the nobility. It is difficult to find out a corroboration of the texts with the contemporary life pattern of the Indians. But one may make a good attempt at it, if one tries to analyse the contemporary art pieces which depict men and women wearing draperies and jewellery.

Starting with Bharhut which in the true sense illustrates human figures in all poses and postures for the first time, we find a tradition of textiles which is usually plain without much decorations, except for a narrow decorative band made to hang between the legs attached to the kamarband. Unlike the other parts of dress, which are plain and simple, one would notice that this strip was beautifully decorated and perhaps also embroidered. This is found in Sanchi as well.

There is reason to believe that this piece of cloth attached to drapery later on came to be known as patka. Barua observed that kamarband, the belt around the waist, was also embroidered. The painting from Ajanta shows three women attendants wearing kamarband heavily embroidered in gold colour. One may perhaps speculate that the use of gold and silver thread was in currency during the period.

With the Kushanas, the socio-cultural and economic life of India seems to have taken a new turn. During this period India witnessed two cultural forces, one from central Asia and the other through the coast because of Indo-Roman trade. Indian economy not only reached a stable stage, but a new socio-historical phenomenon called urbanism swept practically the whole of India. The contemporary texts such as Divyavadana and Lalitavistara refer to a word hiryani or hirivastra indicating a cloth of gold. For the first time in a historical text we find reference to a cloth embroidered or woven with gold. It is not known whether hiryani was changed into kinkhab of later time. But on the testimony of Divyavadana, we may say that the shawls richly embroidered and brocaded with precious stones and gold became popular during this period. This is inferred from the mention of the term ratna-swarna-pravaraka. Here pravamka possibly means a dupatta, the head veil and ratna-swarna refers to precious stones and gold, hence meaning a dupatta adorned with gold and precious stones.

Much like the earlier sculptures, the Mathura sculptures of the Kushana period also show embroideries of various kinds. The seated image of Surya as illustrated by Vogel is shown wearing a short sleeved tight tunic fitting closely to the body and the arms. The tunic, having a semi-circular neck, has embroidered borders made of a scale pattern running down the middle of the chest. The cap which he is found to have worn is also heavily embroidered.

Another figure which by its beard and frizzled hair seems to be Persian or Saka, is shown wearing what appears to be a heavily embroidered tunic. The patterns seem to be embroidered in arched panels with simple beading and rope-like designs on both sides. The hem of the hemispherical cap is embroidered and decorated with the figures of sun and moon on the left. The decorative designs found on these sculptures may be claimed to be in gold and silver thread, as these are very similar to objects found on the grave goods of the Scythian burials. But one is also not very sure whether these designs developed later into what we understand as the zardozi embroidery of a later period.

The second phase of Ajanta painting, which is contemporary to the Guptas, provides a better picture in this regard. It is interesting to notice that the costumes of the local kings, their guards etc. represented in the Ajanta paintings are very plain and do not show any ostentatious decorations on their garments. But while representing foreigners, the painters are very particular about emphasising designed costumes. In Cave No. XVII, where a number of foreigners, apparently of Iranian descent, are depicted, they are shown wearing dresses heavily embroidered in gold colour, indicating gold thread. On top of the left side of the painting, an Iranian is shown riding on an elephant wearing a tunic with sleeves, the cuffs and the front portion of which are beautifully embroidered. Another fat attendant apparently of foreign origin, with a humorous face wears an embroidered dress with design consisting of bands decorated with solid triangles and circles. The tunic is tied around the waist with folds of a kamarband.

The women in Ajanta are also represented wearing embroidered clothes showing profusion of gold colour. In Cave XVII, a woman (otherwise without much clothing) wears an embroidered scarf covering her hair. In Cave II a woman is represented wearing a striped and embroidered cap. The colour and intricate design shown in the painting suggest embroidery done by gold thread. The Champiya Jataka represented in Cave No. I illustrates small stars worked in silk and gold or silver thread on a dull yellowish texture over the cushions and backrests. The black spaces visible underneath indicate the embroidered portion. Plate (b) shows the cushion for an arm rest embroidered with golden stripe in the centre, on the blue base. One may apprehend perhaps that the stuff of the cloth was possibly tash, embroidered with gold and silver wire. The patterns shown in the plate are so well marked that one may consider these as specimens of zardozi workmanship. There are a number of other paintings in Ajanta, where similar evidence is available. But the texts of the contemporary time are not very explicit about embroideries done in metal thread. An interesting evidence is however noteworthy in Harshacharita though late in date, referring to a dazzling muslin robe embroidered with hundreds of diverse flowers and birds gently rippled by the motion of the breeze, bahuvidha kusuma sakunisata sabhisatta.

Indeed, the descriptions found in Harshacharita and Kadambari, the popular works of Banabhatta, speaking eloquently about embroidery work in metal, leave no room for doubt that silk clothings of different colours (indrayudhajala-varnamsuka) were embroidered with gold and jewels, muktamsuka, meaning studded with fine pearls. The expression tara mukta phalopachiyamanas referred to the couches whose gay coverlets cast the hamsa tribes into shade as the bodies were overlaid with star-like pearls. Verse 243 of Harshacharita however mentions kararange meaning leather buckles having charming borders adorned with bright gold leaf work. We are not sure whether this gold work on leather followed the zardoz technique, but in view of the myth found among the zardoz living in Delhi, it is highly probable that gold work on leather might have been in practice during that time. We may however recall in this context that leather objects found in the Scythian burials have designs embroidered in gold and contemporary designs of leather upper and leather shoes.

A text called Kuttanimatam belonging to a later period gives an important information about the craft. Damodar Gupta, the minister of Jaypida, categorically speaks about this work, when he refers to the shoes worn by Bhattasuta Chintamani, a person of affluent position. His shoes were embroidered with gold thread and decorated with a floral meander (kusumadana). His lower garment also shows work done in gold thread (uchanda-kanaka-garbhita).

On surveying the contemporary lexicons, Sanskrit and Prakrit texts, we come across the word khalikachitavastram as some kind of embroidered clothes. Incidentally during the voyage of Marcopolo through India in the early 13th century, he found that gold working was at an opulent stage both in leather and textile. While describing the robes received by the twelve thousand barons from the emperor on the great festivals of India, he commented that "these robes are garnished with gems and pearls and other precious things in a very rich and costly manner. A fine golden girdle of great richness and value and likewise a pair of boots of camut, i.e., of Borgal" curiously wrought with silver thread.

At another place, while mentioning the prices of the commodities found in the coast of Gujarat, he observed that the Indians living in this part of country decorated cushions with gold embroidery. He writes, "they also work here beautiful mats in red and blue leather, exquisitely inlaid with figures of birds and beasts and skilfully embroidered with gold and silver wire. They also embroidered cushions in gold thread, so fine that they are worth six marks of silver apiece." In the explanatory note, Marcopolo observes that in places like Gujarat, Kathiawar and Rajasthan inlaid gold and stone working on leather for making bed covers and palanquin mats were in great fashion during this time. The accounts are very important, as these tell us how silver embroideries were practised on objects like dress materials, furnishing and other items of use particularly of leather.

The historical references cited above from Vedic times to thirteenth century enumerate several references pointing to ornamentation with gold and silver along with precious stones on a variety of fabrics including wool and leather.

Although repeated mention of gold embroidery in variegated forms occurs at several places in early history, absence of material indicating elaborate production of such embroidery leads us to believe that the craft had marginal existence in relation to the main cultural stream in terms of manufacture or production. However, definite evidences are found for large scale manufacture of zardozi textiles after the advent of Sultanate rule in India. It is difficult to accept that zardozi work found in this period was really a continuation of the earlier tradition. Instead one would find that the craft reached new heights at this stage. One may remember in this context that the Persian vocabulary uses a term zarkas during this period, which means zari embroidery. The practice of offering a robe of honour embroidered with gold and silver thread to the noble guest was in vogue during the period. Accounts are also available regarding the master craftspersons coming from Persia for teaching skills to local craftspersons in the production centres which were known as tiraz factory. It may be mentioned here that such references of manufacture are found during Tughlak dynasty, which seems to be the earliest evidence in so far as India is concerned.

Quluqshandi, a writer of the contemporary times, provides a detailed account of state-owned factories under the rule of the Tughlaks. He writes, " therein, of these who are master craftsmen are.. .makers of embroidery (zarakisa). The Sultan of Delhi has a tiraz factory (dar-al-tiraz) in which there are four thousand manufacturers of silk making all kinds of textiles for robes of honour (khilla), robes (kasawa) and presents (itlakat)." Al-Umari while speaking about the dress of the nobles of Delhi during the reign of Sultan Muhammad Tughlak writes, "No Indian but the Sultan and those whom he permits could use saddles with gold embroideries. The rest according to him could use only silver embroideries." Regarding the costumes of the Indians, he wrote, "most of their tartar (tartari) robes are embroidered with gold (muzarkasa-bi-dhahab). Some wear garments with both sleeves having a tiraz border of gold embroidery (zarkas). Giving an account of Sultan Muhammad (1320-51 A.D.), Barani writes that "Sultan Muhammad decided to recognise the Abbasid caliphate." He paid allegiance to the representatives of the family, who were in Egypt in the year (1343-44 A.D.) and in return he received a robe of honour (khilla) (dar tiraz-i-djamsha-yi-zarbaft-u-kimati) meaning that on the tiraz inscription of gold embroidered robes of value, they should inscribe the name of Caliph and nothing else. These are said to have been the specific orders given by Muhammad Tughlak.

Making an overview of the accounts left by Quluqshandi, Umari and Barani, there is no doubt that the Sultanate period was the time when there was a preponderance of gold/silver embroidery on dresses and on saddles and other leather works. The precious embroideries were affixed either on the arms or on the shoulders or in front or even at the skirt edges of garments. The use of such decoration by the Muslim aristocrats came into fashion at this time. One interesting custom noticed during this time was embroidering of the writings from holy scriptures with metal thread, indicating perhaps that this work was well absorbed in the mainstream of culture by that time. Gold embroideries in India seem to have reached a new phase in history. This could be known from frequent references to costumes of different kinds embroidered with gold and silver by several workers. But what is important to note in this context is that initially the tiraz inscription in the name of Caliph started to be made in zarkas. The makers of such embroideries were called zarkisa.

The other sources of information of this period are translations of the works of Ibn Batuta, who travelled through India during the Sultanate period (1287-1290). He has given interesting details of gold embroidery. Giving an account of a robe of honour which probably came from the Delhi tiraz factory, Ibn Batuta writes, "after the maghrib prayer they brought to Amir Ghadda a silk robe of blue colour embroidered with gold and studded with precious stones with a cap to match. The precious stones were so many in number that even the colour of the cloth was hidden from view." Describing the same robe R.B. Serjeant opines that it was presented to him by the king of India Muhammad Shah.

Ibn Batuta goes on to say: In the year 743 H (1342 A.D.) the king of China sent to the Sultan of India at Delhi a present containing, among other things, five garments studded with jewels and five gold embroidered quivers (tarakis muzarkasa). These beautiful exquisite zari works were found not only on the dresses and draperies, but Batuta has left a picturesque description about the majestic pavilion, with five parasols, where Sultan Kaiqubad celebrated Navroz festival. During the festival time, the white parasol was embedded with gold; the curtains were made of velvet and silk and these were of different colours. The most popular colours were violet, purple and blue. These were all decorated with embroideries in gold. According to the description, the king used to wear a long coat and belt interwoven with high workmanship of gold. It seems that when the Sultans after the initial invasions settled down in Delhi, they adapted this embroidery from the Tartar and Khotan. Thus by the time Muhammad Tughlak ascended the throne, zardozi became the dress of the court and courtly nobles.

Amir Khusro, the Persian poet who came during the time of Iltutmish, has also left a narration of this. He has given a list of foreign stuffs which seems to have had gold embroidery.

Among these one was nasiz translated as a kind of silken stuff with gold embroidery. According to him Sultan Kaiqubad sent an embroidered cloth to Bughra Khan's camp.

During the Sultanate time saddles were elaborately embroidered. Ibn Batuta tells us that these were decorated with gold embroideries. The text narrates that during the Id morning, the elephants were adorned with saddles embroidered with silk and gold threads and these were kept reserved for the Sultan's use only. Each elephant was decorated with a silk parasol studded with jewels and pure gold. On the back of each elephant was placed a seat, which was again studded with most precious jewels. The narration tells us how in front of the royal elephant marched the servants and slaves, each wearing a gold cap and a gold belt, which were studded in some cases with jewels. Ibn Batuta further describes that during the Id festival, the entire palace was decorated with jewels and gold: A throne was placed for the Sultan, over which there was a parasol studded with jewels.[71] The banners and standards which were used by the footmen in the processions were said to have been embroidered in gold.

The narration also tells us how the number of tents in the city of Cambay were made not only of expensive pieces of cloth, but these were embroidered with gold and bedecked with jewels. A confirmation of this statement is found from the travel accounts of Marcopolo, who himself had seen some of these gold embroideries.

Ibn Batuta tells us that Khudawandzada Ziya-ud-din, who was appointed as lord of justice (amir-i-dad), was offered a robe of silk, embroidered with gold called surat-i-sher (i.e. image of lion) by the Sultan. The robe which included the lion motif was done with intricate stitches in gold thread. Ibn Batuta further writes that when he attended the court of Ala-ud-din Tarmashirin of Transoxiana which was situated between China, India, Iraq and Uzbek, he found that the king who was sitting inside the tent was draped in a silk dress decorated with embroidery in gold. This information is very interesting, as it suggests that zardozi work was popular as a form of royal dress even as far as this region, which might have been the result of direct or indirect trade contacts between India and Trans-Asia. The travel account of Ibn Batuta clearly reveals that embroidery in gold on both silk and velvet was very popular among the nobility and royalty.

The next literary source which is of immense importance in regard to this craft is the Futuhat-i-Firozshahi, the autobiography of Firozshah Tughlak, where for the first time the word zardozi appeared. This gives an elaborate description of the dresses of the Sultans which were made with this form of embroidery.

According to this account, the Sultan is said to have worn kulah (turban) on his head, which was studded with precious stones. In public meetings the Sultan used to wear barani (either of wool or of silk) with its shoulders beautifully embroidered. The textiles which were presented to people from the courts were always embroidered with gold. Delhi being the centre of the Sultanate power became an important centre of zardozi work as well. Simultaneously several new centres came up in places like Gujarat, Rajasthan and Bengal. Needless to say, these centres grew up because of the patronage extended by the provincial Sultans and the Hindu kings of the respective regions.

The Futuhat-i-Firozshahi gives us elaborate information about this craft. We are told that Firozshah Tughlak classified this exotic embroidery into various types. According to clause 13, the objects prepared for giving as presents by the kings or royal nobles should be the best ones; in other words these should be beautifully embroidered. But at the same time a restriction was imposed on figurative motifs on the robes. Firoz ordered that only those symbols could be used for decoration which were allowed in the Shariyat. In clause 14, Firoz writes prior to this, clothes of the rich people were made of silk, embroidered with gold or zaridar. But from this time these have been banned as there was prohibition for such clothes in the Shariyat. Firoz says, "I have been empowered that only such garments should be worn as have been approved by the Prophet as lawful."

Thus all embroidered costumes were banned allowing only small-sized embroidered banners and caps. In clause 51, he reminds his readers once again about the prohibition of the use of embroidered clothes.

Apart from imposing general restrictions on gold embroidery, he restricted designs also. It is clear from his account that a Sultan can easily be distinguished by his dress, which was lavishly embroidered by gold, from other persons of noble birth. This is also evident in some of the paintings of the period.

Thus we see that during Firozshah's time, either for Firoz's own bigotry or for some other reason, the craft faced a setback. With him thus ended the climax of the zardozi work of the Sultanate period.

Ziya-ul-din Barani has left an interesting account of the

regulations imposed by Ala-ud-din for control of prices of such luxury goods. By regulation, the Sultan controlled the prices of five stuffs i.e. tasbin, tabrizi, zamaizarbaft wazarnigar (embroideredbrocades) and khaz-hia Delhi (Delhi alike). According to the court instructions, these objects could not be sold at Sarai Adl (main business centre of the city) without the order of the superintendent.

There is thus no doubt that the turning period of zardozi craft may be observed during the time of Firozshah Tughlak, who in his official capacity imposed restrictions and curtailed the production of the craft. This left a deep impact on the gold embroidery craft in general.

We may also recall here Marcopolo's mentioning of a kind of stuff which was among the articles sent from Baghdad to Okkodai Khan. The material is called dardas (a stuff embroidered with gold). Motichandra correctly observed that these terms were indications of their origin, which were definitely not of indigenous nature.

Spies in his translation of Subh-ul-asa mentions an authority namely Ash-Shauf Nasir-al Din al-Husayuial-Adami, who writes that during the 14th century the nobility used to wear gold embroidered tartaric gowns, having embroidered sleeves and an embroidered cloth between the shoulders.

Here we may compare the Sanskrit literature of the 14th and the

15th century, which throws light on the existence of gold and silver embroidery. As narrated in the Prabandhachintamani, the king of Kolhapur received sandals inlaid with jewels. Two words svarnopadan and svarna valaksagumphita refer to shoes embroidered with gold and inlaid with jewels. These words occur in the Pumtana-prabandha-sangmha. The Varnamtnakara, a 14th century work written by Jyotirisvara Thakura, cites two words: sonapalika manikanti. Jyotirisvara has written his work in Maithili and the area he talks about is North Bihar or present-day Mithila. It mentions Sonasuchika karao ekadevagiria pachitta eka phanda badhane, implying a gold embroidered dhoti on deogiri stuff. His list of stuffs includes varieties of silks manufactured in the country either indigenously or imported from outside. Suchisona as implied by the name indicates that the silk was embroidered with gold. Similarly kanakpatra probably refers to gold leaf on silk.

Dr. B.J. Sandesara has compiled a list of textile stuffs (varnakas) which refers to traditional stuffs and imported items prevalent in Gujarat during the 14th and the 15th century. The compilation called varnakasamuchaya mentions terms Tikejarabapha referring to Persian zarbaft; karmadana the sanskritised form of the Persian word kamdanitiie gold embroidered stuff; pataniya sachopa, where sachopa implies gold embroidery and pataniya indicates the centre of manufacture of such stuff, which is Patan, probably in Gujarat. The Prithvichandracharita written in 1421 also gives reflections of textiles with work in gold and precious stones. Phudadiya indicates a rich silk stuff with jewel setting. The Jain miniature paintings of Kalpasutra also show use of gold.

The Kanhadade Prabandha of Padmanabha refers to the word sonapana which may be the same as kanakapatra. All these imply a rich silk stuff decorated with gold leaf. Such textiles were worn by the merchants of Kalavagudra, Anagundi which were located in present-day Bidar and Telengana. It means that the zardozi had already started penetrating the South. Phaudadi was some kind of rich stuff in which gold and gems were used. The study of several texts from Gujarat, Bihar and Andhra-Telengana mentioning textile stocks, clearly reveals that in spite of all the restrictions and temporary setbacks imposed by Firozshah Tughlak at the main seat of Sultanate power i.e. Delhi, the zardozi with its intricaties was fully imbibed in the Hindu mainstream. The rich and the aristocrats both Hindus and Muslims had been using them as a special form of distinction. The cultural absorption of the zari embroidery was so deep that the original Persian names were suitably adopted in the local dialects of Gujarat, Bihar and Andhra. We may mention here that silk handkerchiefs and caps embroidered with gold were reported to be manufactured in Bengal also. But this seems to have been connected with the emergence of the Muslim nobility in Bengal.

During the 16th century, the zardozi craft seems to have reached a flourishing stage in Vijayanagar under the Hindu rule of Krishnadev Rai

(1509-1530). Robert Sewell mentions the visit of a Portuguese traveller named Christana de Figueiredo to the court of Krishnadev Rai, where he found the king wearing expensive dresses made with gold and jewels.

The king was clothed in certain white clothes embroidered with many roses in gold and to each Portuguese he gave such embroidered cloth designed with many pretty figures as tokens of friendship and love. This account is important, as it throws an interesting light on the design of the gold embroidery work, which was in practice in Vijayanagar during the 16th century. This seems to have been also a popular commodity of export craftwork in Europe. The influence of gold embroidery in the Vijayanagar empire continued during the time of Achyuta Rai (1530-1542). Fernao Nunex, another Portuguese traveller, mentions that king Achyuta Rai's clothes were all made of precious silk stuff worked with gold.

The above two narrations indicate very clearly that gold embroidery was very much a part of the court culture in the Deccan during the 16th century and the Portuguese naturally became attracted to this prestigious craft. It was probably at this stage that the Portuguese influence started making an impression on the craft.

A new revival is noticed in this craft during the Mughal period. The court costumes of the Mughal emperors were all made in zardozi work. Consequently, there grew up important centres of this craft, as the centre of court karkhana shifted with the change in capital by different Mughal emperors. Akbar's court was at Agra, which was shifted to Delhi by Shahjahan, the epicentres of the Mughal culture. But court-run workshops were organised in several other places to cater to the requirement of the court, small or big. The craftsmen grew in number and came over to these places from all parts of the country. But their centre of attraction was the Mughal court where they could take advantage of the court-run workshops and could sell their objects at high prices. In a separate section we have dealt with in detail how these karkhanas provided economic stability to the artisans by offering theoretical and practical knowledge to the craftspersons on the one hand, and negotiating market facilities on the other. The Mughal paintings from the time of Akbar provided an illuminating picture of zardozi work prevalent during this time. Not only were the royalty and nobility represented richly attired in gold and jewels; the horses, camels, the elephants are all depicted with richly embroidered saddles. Thus while appearing in public a king not only tied pearl-strings around his neck but used to wear dresses like achkan embroidered with pearls. Such gold embroidered pieces became popular with the Mughal kings as gift items as well. The gifting of such items to the non-Muslim nobles, rulers etc. extended this craft to the non-Muslim courts, particularly in Rajasthan and Gujarat, where the opulent traditions already existed. Slowly the Hindu elite also started using gold embroidered dresses as a form of aristocracy in contemporary India.

The Ain-i-Akbari gives a rich account of zardozi work in various items, particularly the shawls. The text elaborately speaks about the production of the embroideries under the karkhana system. It further refers to people generally wearing tus shawls without altering its natural colour. His majesty had them dyed. The emperor paid much attention to craftsmanship and the genuineness of the materials. He took care that pure gold and silver was used. All embedded textured fabrics used to give the finished product a subtle aura.

Besides garments, the Mughals adopted this craft in various other items. One of the most important objects which seems to have been decorated with zardozi work was the tent materials. In describing the camp furnishing of the tents Abul Fazl commented about various types of tent structures viz. chubin, rawati, do-ashiyana manzil, zarhindoz, ajaibi, mandal shamiyana, all having inner linings of velvet brocade. It is to be noted that he did not specifically mention gold embroidery, but he referred to zardozi tent in some places in connection with the servants. It is thus clear that the temporary structures for the emperors also had works in gold embroidery on the inner side. Looking at the rich assemblage of zardozi material, and on the basis of the information giving Akbar's patronage, there is no doubt that the zardozi craft reached its highest peak during this time.

Monserrate also corroborates this view. It is said that the emperor used to wear garments of silk, beautifully embroidered in gold with pearls and gold jewellery. The list of the official records presenting the state of things at the death of Akbar was included in De Laet and Manrique's Itinerario Itenerten ts. These were published in 1531 and 1640. Abdul Aziz reproducing these facts states that there were 5,000,000 items with gold and silver decorations, which included tents, kanats etc. decorated with gold and silver; covering clothes for horses and elephants, cloak of every kind etc. Also various kinds of coats and equestrian ornaments, worked and embroidered with gold, silver and precious stones, including the arms borne and insignia carried before the imperial persons and those of the royal house.

The zardozi embroidery which was firmly established by then in the large production system, continued to maintain its excellence during the regime of Jahangir. His memoir Tuzuk-i-Jahangiri mentions at several places such expensive, gorgeous robes of honour. At one place he mentions, "on Tuesday, the 17 zi-gada, he (Shahjahan, his son) was free to go, I presented him with a special gold embroidered robe of honour. Describing the Nauroz festival, Jahangir has mentioned a tent erected at divan-i-am having canopies of the richest and most finely embroidered velvet, silk and cloth of gold. These were inlaid with pearls, jewels and diamonds."

The glory of zardozi as a craft in Mughal period was noticed by Tavernier in his Indian Travels. He says that "The great Mughal has seven thrones, some set all over with diamonds, others with rubies, emeralds and pearls. But the longest throne is erected in the hall of first court of palace. The underpart of the canopy is embedded with pearls entirely, fringe of pearls round the edge, upon the top of the canopy which is made like an arch with four panes, stands a peacock with its tail spread consisting entirely of sapphires and other precious coloured stones. At the distance of 4 feet upon each side of throne are placed two umbrellas, the handles of which are about 5 feet high covered with the diamonds, the umbrellas themselves, being of crimson velvet, embroidered and fringed with pearls. This is the famous throne which Timur began and Shahjahan finished and is really reported to have costed a hundred and sixty millions and five hundred thousand and time of our money."

The author of the Khulasat-ut-tawarikh while giving an account of craft and industries of different provinces writes, "Agra was famous for its gold and silver embroidery on turbans and Gujarat for stuffs of gold embroidered velvet."

Shahjahan's period may be called the golden period in regard to sophistication of this craft. With the shifting of his political seat from Agra to Delhi, the court-based karkhanas spread up in and around Delhi; the karkhanas then worked in full swing, and the craftsmen got patronage from all sections of rich people. As the seat of Mughal rule was shifted to Delhi, a large number of craftsmen moved to Delhi from Agra as well as other parts of the country.

But the period of Aurangzeb shows a turning point in zardozi work. Due to incessant warfare, royal resources became scarce. Besides, Aurangzeb was in favour of austere living. The court no longer patronized this art and as a result many craftsmen left the Mughal metropolis and took shelter around provincial courts. Many craftsmen were then recruited by the Rajput rajas, who by this time had not only become conversant with Mughal luxuries, but in their respective ways had become quite powerful independently. Quite naturally they wished to emulate Mughal sophistication in their own courts. In the south, at Srirangapatam and Hyderabad the zardozi craft got a fresh swing under Tipu Sultan's and the Nizam's rule respectively. The comparative study of the items manufactured in these places reveals that zardozi craft of these places was influenced by the contemporary Mughal tradition. In spite of the overwhelming influence of the Mughal style, the period saw the emergence of several regional centres with their distinctive quality. The craftsmen who dispersed to the provincial courts, got a new boost by the introduction of riyasati karkhanas which replaced the earlier court karkhanas. The system of karkhanas which was introduced during the Mughal period was a vital economic system and after a lapse of time this became rejuvenated in the provincial courts under the riyasati karkhana system. The zardozi craftsmen working at Delhi and Agra at this stage shifted to the provincial centres. Thus, while the traditional karkhana system was losing its roots in Delhi, it was gaining in strength in the provincial areas.

This new socio-economic and political factor provided some impetus for the continuation of this craft. The artisan group during this time got some opportunities from the newly created urban elite class, who by that time inherited some of the tastes and preferences of their rulers. Though the work was not on an opulent scale, there was more or less a steady market, as there was an increase in demand for smaller work. Most of the objects were small domestic articles but the court tradition was not lost totally.

Meanwhile the discovery of the Cape route at the end of the 15th century provided a major change in the structure of Euro-Asian trade. The Portuguese participated in intra-Asian trade. They naturally became interested in this luxurious product for export to European markets.

It is, therefore, clear that before the East India Company, Europe had become a market for the zardozi craft. Lotika Vardarajan has rightly observed that "there was an opulent tradition of couch work based on the usage of metallic thread, and interspersed on occasions with precious stones." The Portuguese were great patrons of this craft, and as a result, the European market to which the Portuguese were attached was flooded with this prestigious handicraft.

The popularity of zardozi craft in Europe in the 16th century gave a boost to the craft, when the East India Company set its foot on the

Indian soil. Also this opened channels for marketing of the zardozi craft in later periods.

Having survived the vicissitudes of time and fortune, Delhi in the latter half of the 19th century came to acquire again a new look under the British rule. The new political power provided a fresh impetus for the revival of the city culture. On January 1,1877, Delhi celebrated the great occasion of the assumption of the title Kaisar-i-Hind or Empress of India by Queen Victoria. The activities were arranged in grand Mughal fashion. Durbar was once again organised, first by Lord Lytton and then 26 years later on January 1,1903 by the Viceroy Lord Curzon to coincide with the proclamation ceremony of Edward VII as the King Emperor. This durbar was planned on the model of the King Durbar of 1877 but it was on a vastly larger and more gorgeous scale. Lord Curzon took great pains to plan the whole show himself. During this time, the special durbar issue, India Durbar, London reported of this unique situation. The main streets of Shahjahanabad again witnessed an imposing spectacle of splendid processions in the finest tradition of Mughal rule. The third durbar was held on 12th December, 1911 in the presence of Emperor George V, who on that occasion announced the transfer of the capital of India from Calcutta to Delhi. The insignia worn by the emperor is exhibited. This was borne out by the tremendous increase in the population of Delhi. Ghurye observes, "Delhi's great growth began after it became capital of the country registering an increase of population of 30.7% in 1921."

With the gradual inception of British rule, the zardozi craft underwent changes at two levels. Firstly, as there was no longer royal patronage, both the karkhana and riyasati karkhana systems completely crumbled down. Secondly, the craftspersons felt the need of finding a market to sell the finished products. The expensive nature of the craft restricted its use. But fortunately a new group of patrons emerged as there was a substantial section of the administration, rich traders among the European population who seemed to have shown their appreciation for the skills of the zardozi craftspersons. New types of articles were manufactured to cater to the needs of this new group of elite. This was the time when the craftspersons started doing new items like uniforms, table covers, etc. Naturally a remarkable change in the sizes and hence in the forms of the objects could be noticed at this time. We propose to take up this aspect in detail in the chapter on design and forms. But one important socio-economic phenomenon arose during this time. Formerly this work had been restricted to Muslim artisans, but now with the change in fashions and requirements the skill was found to have penetrated into the cultural stream of the Hindu society as well.

The brief historical background indicates that this noble craft adapted itself suitably to every political change. The craft spread to the European market and later sought American, Middle East and Japanese outlets. Overseas patronisation provided a backbone to the crumbling market outlets for the craft. These economic networks had direct influence on the design, form, social and production pattern. The material about its history is indeed most inadequate. We are not yet sure about the origins of the craft, but there is enough evidence to indicate that the craft was in existence in the pre-Islamic period. During the Sultanate and Mughal periods due to the patronage extended by the rulers, the craft seems to have established firm roots in India. But the fall of the Mughal empire resulted in complete dislocation of the craft tradition, forcing it to shift its activities from Delhi and Agra to several provincial courts. During this period new centres like Hyderabad, Jaipur, Patiala, Rampur, Bhopal and Banaras emerged as active centres of this craft. The next stage of development was the result of patronage offered by the Portuguese and other European traders. Lately, it is being patronised by several eastern countries, America, Japan and European nations.

1.3 PRODUCTION OF ZARI INDUSTRY :

From Rigvedic times, we hear of several varieties of textiles, among which cloth of gold "hiranya" figures as a distinguished type. Gods in their grandeur wear it, as they ride in their stately chariots. Hiranya cloth has usually been considered the earliest equivalent of present day zari work of kimkhabs (brocades).

India has long been known for its golden thread, for Zari. Well known products of the Indian Zari industry, besides gold and silver thread (Zari Kasab) are the embroidery materials like stars and Spangles, Chalak, Champo Kinari, Salma and badla. The Zari craft includes making Zari thread and other materials as well as thread. The latter covers Zari embroidered saris, evening bags, foot wear and belts. Zari textiles and world famous brocades.

Surat is the biggest Zari thread making center in the country, followed by Varanasi in both imitation and real Zari threads. Zari embroidery material and Zari lace and borders are manufactured in Surat. Varansi on the other hand is a big center for the manufacture of superior quality real Zari thread (kalabattu), Zari textiles and Zari brocades. Other centers of production are Jaipur and Ajmer which specialize in Zari gota and Zari thappa work.

The other centers of Zari products are Agra, Bareilly, Varansi. The items of zari are handbags, belts, shoe uppers etc. Other popular items of export are zari badges all produced manually by skilled craftsmen in Barreily and varansi. Zari threads are used extensively in handloom (and powerloom) saris which are manufactured all over India, especially in Varansi, bangalore, Dharmavaram, Kanchipuram and Paithan.

The principal products of the Zari Industry in Surat are the gold and Silver threads alias Zari Kasab and Zari embroidery materials like Badla alias Lametta etc. but the Industry has produced with amazing skill and techniques other allied zari products in response to the demand of the loving people of our great country related to fashion, dress, costumes and tradition.

PRINCIPAL PRODUCTS:

(i) Real and Imitation zari threads or kasab or gold and silver threads.

(ii) Real and Imitation Badia or Lametta.

ANCILLIARY PRODUCTS:

(i) Real and Imitation Zari Embroidery materials like stars, Spangles, Ring katori, Sadi, Salma, Zik, Tiki, and Kangri etc.

(ii) Laces, Fifth-kinari and Borders.

(iii) Gota Thappa, Ful, Champo, Chatai etc.

(iv) Zari embroidered sarees and Ornis, Evening Bags, Money Purses, Latest hand Bags, Table Clothes, Foot Wears and Shoe Uppers,

Zari belts Spectacle cases, Picture plaques, Photo designs, caps and such artistic zari embroideries.

(v) Zari textiles like the welknown kinkab or Gold cloth, Brocades, Lungies, Tissue, and Banarsi Sarees.

Of the above mentioned products of zari industry, Gold Thread(Zari) and Badla are mainly used in the manufacture of the welknown Kinkab, Tissue and Banarsi sarees, Scarfes, Laces and Borders. Badla which is also generally used for embroidery purposes also forms raw materials like chalak.

The allied products like stars, Spangles, Zik, Tiki, Salmo, kangri, Ring Katori etc. are used as embroidery work on Sarees, Evening Bags, Money Purses and such works of handicraft like zina caps.

All these different zari products have different markets in India and in foreign countries. For example Zari threads find its principal market in South Indian States particularly in the states of Chennai and Mysore, Banaras in U.P. Embroidery materials like salmo, Zik, Tiki, Ring, Katori etc. are consumed in the states of Gujarat and Maharashtra while Gota thappa and full champo in the states of Rajasthan, U.P and Delhi. All these products have also captured markets in all the principal cities of the world though the west Asian Countries, Indonesia, Malasiya, Pakistan and ceylone are leading consumers of Gold Thread and other zari items. Enchanting and artistic zari textiles and emboroidered zari goods like purses, bags etc. are sold mostly in the shophisticated markets like the U.K and U.S.A.

The industry produces all these items in its two principal sectors viz. The real and the Imitation It is indeed a noteworthy feature that looking to the needs and aspirations of the "Janta Class" the wonderful zari artisans have succesfully manufactured imitation zari or say "Jantajari Cheap zari" for the lower strata of its customers. The difference is only in the basic raw material which is silver for Real Zari and Copper (Silver Electroplated Wire) for imitation or Janta zari.

Furnishing Items and Accessories:

Tent hangings, kanats, covers, spreads, trappings, umbrellas, parasols, etc. form an important part of the furnishing itineraries. The cultural scene which was oriented to the floor required a variety of carpets, pillows of assorted types and sizes as home furnishings and court furnishings. The large bolsters generally known as masnads were used for back support. As my discussions have basically developed from the literary and illustrative sources, time and again I have referred to the illustrations in the miniature paintings as the source of reference. Very few examples of pre-Mughal work have come down to us. The illustrative examples have been taken from various museums and private collections. During the Sultanate period, the enclosures or tents were called seracheh. These were made with separate pieces of fabric, suitably embroidered with gold. Sivan is the pandal proportionate to the court furnishings. Ibn Batuta is full of such accounts. Sayabans, the ceiling covers of gold embroidery, are referred to in Ain-i-Akbari. The beautiful wall-hangings decorating the walls also recall at once the typical courtly Mughal form of style.

Hangings and Kanats :

The earliest examples of gold work represented in furnishings are seen in the folios from Kalpasutra dating back to circa 1475-1500 A.D. Calico Museum and Victoria and Albert Museum, London have in their collections a number of tent-covers or hangings which have been published elsewhere. An interesting hanging illustrates a group of human figures in a garden scenario. A noble woman is shown holding a branch of the tree. A lady musician is playing on veena near her with another lady accompanying her on tanpum. Two other lady attendants are shown standing on sides. The noble woman by her features and costume appears to be a Mughal lady. She is followed by a female attendant holding a tray. A variety of Indian birds are chirping on the tree. Two bucks with their young ones are seen in the foreground. Everybody is enchanted by the musical notes, which is clearly depicted by the postures of gazelles and deer in the scenery. The conventional flowering tree is covered by a semi-circular arch. The outer border is filled with continuous floral stems interspersed with birds. Thematically this embroidered panel is more in the fashion of a miniature painting. The design shows metal wire couched in basket pattern on the background. The figures are embroidered with silk thread in satin stitch. A two-dimensional effect has been given to the human figures, as is usually found in miniature paintings. But in rendering the stags, the vision and execution of the roundity is presented in almost a sculpturesque manner. The movement of the stags contributes to the dynamism of otherwise static composition. The intrusion of the Iranian element is clearly visible, in the manner of using the semi-circular arch, at times encircled by creeper blossoms. There is no doubt that the zardozi work through the compositional scheme is reminiscent of Mughal court painting.

It is known that zardozi embroidery became popular in Gujarat during the late Mughal period with arrival of Dara Shikoh and his court. A new class of patrons grew up during this time, who by their profession were traders and Jains in their religious affiliation. A wall-hanging embroidered with silver gilt thread on velvet. By and large, the designs and motifs and even the workmanship of embroidery referred to above are courtly in character. The hangings behind the Jain abbot were in reality the enlargement of the puthias which were meant to be hung for religious purposes. Interestingly, here too one finds an illustration of a throne in the centre, over which is placed a decorated canopy. It may be mentioned here that the cushion on the throne exhibits lavish decoration in couching technique, a tradition which was very popular during the Mughal period. Two creepers with leaves, buds and flowers are found placed on opposite sides of the throne.

The highly stylized art found in this embroidery is a characteristic hieratic type of the Jain miniature. This is shown in the facial and physiognomical features in the dresses and headgears of the two chauri-bearers standing opposite to each other across the throne and in high boots. Indeed the type seems to have been imitated from such paintings which were presumably available in the Jain manuscript painting and in the courts of Muslim nobles. This may be compared with the Jain miniature paintings of the Kalpasutra. It is also well-recognized that the trees and plants which are represented in these paintings are more symbolical than elements of natural life. It is noteworthy about the embroidery on these hangings that the general direction of the decorative devices is on the vertical plane rather than a horizontal spread.

A kanat on red velvet again rendering a vertical design shows star patterns encircled in medallions. Two roaring lions are seen holding hoisted flag each with the front paws above a lotus motif encircled in a pan-shaped device. This composite design is the insignia of the princely court to which the kanat belongs. This kanat is from Rajasthan, probably late 19th century. The style of execution is mainly karchobi.

Carpets and Covers :
The next group of furnishings discussed are the carpets or floor spreads, ceiling covers, bed covers, etc. All these items have more emphasis on spread-out patterns. The span of designs varies from all over spread to concentration in centre and four corners.

Carpet was more or less a generic name for a variety of floor spreads. In the Mughal court each covering had a distinctive term based on its individual usage or function. Zaminposh, the cover for the floor; takhtposh, the cover for the takht or raised rectangular, square or circular wooden platform with supporting legs; palangposh, the bed spread; dastarkhan, the spread used for dining purposes; janamaz, the prayer mat; khanposh, the cover for food trays; saazposh, the spread for the musical instruments and so on. The design orientation in each variety was specifically related to its usage. Janamaz, the prayer mat, would depict a mehrab, an arch with pillars signifying the mosque or a rectangular niche in a wall with the tree of life. Inscriptions from the Kuran were often embroidered. The central area in all coverings was deliberately left plain to suit the purpose of sitting while offering prayers. Dastarkhan would again be devoid of any embroidery in the areas meant for sitting and keeping food. Saazposh often in the form of the particular instrument had embroidery only along the borders. Similarly zaminposh which is used for general or occasional purpose of sitting would have embroidery restricted to the borders.

Covers like the takhtposh and khanposh, however, infrequently used the entire surface of the fabric for decoration. Patterns with gold and silver composed the motif defining and giving the textured surface a uniform tone. Such covers gave the embroiderer ample opportunity to demonstrate his skills. Such orientation of the spread of design in accordance with its usage is typical of zardozi artefacts.

The folios of the miniature painting in Persian style describing the story of Sheikh Sanah and Christian maiden dated circa 1595 A.D. show resplendent use of gold decorations in hangings and carpets. Similarly, a painting describing darbar of Shah Alam at the end of 18th century depicts usage of furnishings with decorations in zardozi style. Bernier in his travel accounts has mentioned fine coverings with delicate silk embroidery interspersed with gold and silver. The folios from Ragini Kangra circa 1785-90 A.D. show geometrical pattern in gold on the rolled curtain, whereas the borders of the carpet show gold embroidery, the all over spread design of creepers in the centre may be in silver wire and silk thread. The actual specimens studied include a takhtposh, which is presently in the Indian Section at the Victoria and Albert Museum, London bearing Acc. No. 0762. The base fabric of this takhtposh is red and green velvet and white satin. The picturesque embroidery here is comparable to any painted narrative. The name of the zardoz as evident from the signage was Sherendazka, a Muslim embroiderer.

This splendid takhtposh has an outer border of repetitive floral motifs depicting alternately ath dane ki nargis and khairu ke dam ka chaugula. Nargis and khairu are two Indian flowers often repeated in metal embroidery. The space between the floral motifs is filled by chakle walijali and sitare ki bharat. Sequins are liberally used to bring lustre to the design. The impenetrable undersurface is visible. The border is edged with a gold and silver braid, ending in tassels.

The body of this takhtposh is divided into three panels. The undersurface is mainly red velvet. The two panels on either side have an octagonal wheel with eight spokes as the central motif. Half replicas of the wheel are repeated at the corners. The wheels are embroidered with gold and silver kalabatoon in ari bharat. The spaces between the spokes depict foliage. Repetitive motifs of pairs of peacocks, four pairs in all, each holding a beaded necklace in its beak, are excellent examples of the meenakari effect in embroidery. The body of each peacock is embellished with alternate rows of blue silk and silver thread. The creeping foliage surrounding the peacocks renders traditionally prevalent motifs of zardozi embroidery, for example, karan ka phul, karan ki kali and the patti design.

The central panel is the main scene of the narration. The portion is divided into two sections by a canal or river. Over the water, linking the two banks, is a bridge embroidered in gold and silver wire. The canal is highlighted by appliquing a white stripe in the satin fabric, thus matching the colour and ripple of flowing water. This water intersection seems to be an important channel linking the two banks for trade and communication. Navigational activity is illustrated by varieties of small boats, nine in number, floating in the canal. These are palinav, decorated boats, mayur pankhi (a boat with a peacock head) and a steamer. Apart from these, four fish and a large number of floating ducks represent marine life. The surface of the land, marked by the red velvet background, illustrates the city and the forest on the same plain, without confusing periphery demarcations. A city in the vicinity of the forest is marked by several buildings in Hindu and Muslim architectural styles. Most of the fortifications run along the outer border away from the water source except for one structure, which is centrally placed close to the river. This is perhaps a Hindu temple. A large tree with a thick growth on one side suggests a forest in the background. Stylistically the citadel is more prominent but it is devoid of any rhythm or movement indicating the presence of life. The area portraying the forest is adorned with creeping foliage with repetitive motifs of karan ka phul, lot ka phul and patti. Life here is represented by a tiger hunting a deer on one side. Details of the animals' bodies have been traced in the ent ki jail and nakhuni jali motifs. The blood-stained mouth of the tiger is represented by stitches in red silk, while the eyes, nose, ears and tail have a black silk filling. A leaping deer in the farthest corner suggests a large forest area. A palm tree has been embroidered against the backdrop of the building on this side. On the other side of the river, forest life is represented by a deer hunt.

A hunter, holding a large bow, is seen sitting on a galloping horse on the other side of the temple-like structure. Apparently, the hunter is chasing the two deer who are running for their life. The outlines of all the figurative and architectural forms as well as the leaves, branches and stem of the tree and other floral motifs are indicated by silver wire of the kora variety. The wire is laid according to the conventional method of zari embroidery whereby it is attached to the surface of the fabric with the help of silk and cotton thread. The body of the horse has an embossed pattern which appears to be khardar bharat. The hoofs, eyes, ears, tail are all filled with black silk thread. The finer details on the body of the horse, like the hair on the neck, saddle and rein are again depicted with kora wire. The embroidery here is important in the context that each anatomical and subject detail has been exemplified by using varieties of gold and silver wire, kalabatoon and silk thread in variegated thickness. This elevates the rhythm and movement of the figurative forms as well as the structural specifications of the architecture. The door, windows, dome, flag and so on are all individually and specifically highlighted. Another interesting representation is of a two-wheeled locomotive placed amidst the floral foliage near the river bank. The depiction of this mode of road transport highlights as to how industrialisation has influenced the embroiderer. The locomotive, which appears to be more like a cycle, has a short front wheel and a large back wheel.

The central panel is more like a painted canvas where life, in water and on land, has been manifested. The delicacy of each motif, which is rather difficult to achieve in non-pliable metallic wire, is clearly visible. The takhtposh distinctly reveals that gold embroidery styles had strong links with the tradition of floor coverings commonly called carpet in the courts of upper India.

A takhtposh from Bharany's collection in Delhi in red velvet shows repetitive floral motifs, dense in the border and much apart in the centre.

Another zaminposh from the Victoria and Albert Museum collection in red velvet has resplendent embroidery, gold and silver gilt wire, spangles and sequins only on the borders with repetitive flower and geometric patterns. Four turanj i.e. corner motifs inside the border are in kairi shape.

These can be compared with the private collections of Bharany in India, where the border and the body are in two colours i.e. green and red velvet. The joint of the two fabrics has been skilfully hidden with continuous couching stitch in metal wire. Here the base colour of the fabric, particularly in the border, forms part of the repetitive patti wall buti design. The outer border has continuous tcclc wall jali along with guldaudi floral motif. Here the under-surface is totally invisible. The turanj depicts champa, ded khar ki patti buta.

Another zaminposh also has similar execution of design. In both these coverings couching technique has been employed. However, this double colour scheme is not seen in another cover from the same collection.

Khanposh, the cover for food, has very elaborate embroidery on the four borders, which is extending to almost half the width of the total fabric. This again reflects the decoration of the parts more visible to the eyes. The cover when put on the large food tray hangs down, when the bearer carries the tray. The cover is rectangular but the central part is squarish. Black and red velvet form the border and the centre. The border has splendid bharat work with only deliberate spaces of the outlines of the buta and patti motifs. Silver wire has also been used to depict champa ki buti. Thus the whole design is composed in gold, interspersed with silver and black hues. The central part has a running border in gold gilt wire with turanj in kairi motif. Such massive embroideries were done on long rectangular strips which were joined later. The style is karchobi. The finer embroidery is however rendered on bed spreads.

A saazposh is the spread for keeping the string instruments like sitar. The shape of the spread eloquently speaks of the purpose for which it is used. The blue velvet is the circular form to which a tapering rectangular fabric is joined. The silver and gold wire embroidery in repetitive guldaudi buti adorns the continuous border of the spread. The centre of each buti has red silk embroidery, border designs are used to fill the inter-spaces. Two buta designs again in floral pattern adorn the inner borders of the extended arm. The central part both in head and the arm is devoid of any embroidery.

Asmangir or the canopy is another furnishing accessory which was abundantly used inside the palace, courtyards, terraces, gardens and other outside locations. The famous peacock throne of Shahjahan, which was installed in the diwan-i-khas (hall of private audience) of the Red Fort, Delhi, has been described as the major symbol of Mughal wealth.

A painting from National Museum showing Raja Prithvi Singh of Datia with his sons dating circa 1736-1752 A.D. depicts a beautiful canopy in green colour having resplendent gold work which may be embroidery. A specimen of asmangir is said to have belonged to the time of the last Mughal Emperor Bahadur Shah Zafar. This asmangir of silk fabric shows an element of decorative device during the decline of Mughal art. Earlier very often the richly illuminated border decorations composed of conventional trees, stylised flowers, galloping stags, running lions, revealed clearly a very skilful manipulation of a number of central Asian/Iranian decorative designs. The trends in conception and execution were more towards large and heavy proportion, which was presumably the requirement of the objects.

The red asmangir, however, has a border design of conventional repetitive floral motifs in gold gilt thread, which appears to be ath dane ki nargis along with neem ki patti and ded khar ki patti. The span of design is on the running borders, the corners and the central spaces.

The outer covering of this asmangir is of thick cotton. The piece is important since it shows the technique called vasli, where a thick cardboard is put beneath the motifs; to give the desired raised effect, gold gilded wire is used. Also such work was generally done on velvet for kanats etc. but since asmangir hangs below the ceiling or acts as a sky cover, the light weight fabric was preferred, since silk cannot carry very heavy embroidery.

Another asmangir of early 20th century from Rajasthan. The base fabric is maroon velvet and gold gilded wire is used for couching. The embroidery depicts a jungle scene where a lion is hunting the deer. Similar depiction was found in the carpet of Victoria and Albert Museum of 18th century. However, here the jungle scene includes variety of flowers, birds and insects. Such designs became popular in the provincial courts after the decline of Mughal court and many of the zardoz from Delhi remember such designs.

We may say that after the decline of the Mughal rule, there was a perceptible decrease in the gorgeousness of zan-workon tents, kanats, etc. With the slow decline in patronage from the Mughal courts, the zardoz faced a major setback. At this juncture the artisans sought patronage from the provincial courts and carried the design prevalent in Mughal courts to the provincial courts. A lady at bath under the canopy, a miniature from National Museum, highlighting the transitional influence in provincial courts. Another miniature painting from the same collection portrays Maharaja Anup Singh of Jodhpur seated under an asmangir which has resplendent gold work.

Other furnishing accessories include various types of cushion covers, pillow covers (takiya cover) of different sizes and shapes. A painting of circa 1759-1806 A.D. shows Shah Alam seated on the throne with an elaborately gold-embroidered masnad (bolster) cover on the back in red fabric. This painting is from National Museum collection.

Another painting describing raga Hindola from the same collection Uniara circa 1770-80 A.D. also shows delicate gold embroidery on masnad cover. During the examination of the actual specimens, it was uniformly observed that the kalabatoon wire was used instead of pure metallic wire for embroidering the bolster covers. The soft and supple kalabatoon wire was not injurious to the body on touch. The pillows were in all sizes and shapes, square, semi-circular, circular. The designs on the covers of these supports matched the design of the floor spread.

Plate 46 shows a rectangular masnad in green velvet. This is from the Red Fort Museum in Delhi and belongs to the court of the last Mughal Emperor Bahadur Shah Zafar. The worn-out condition of the velvet is indicative of the regular use of this masnad. Here the design is kamal ki bel (lotus creeper) repeated all along the patti i.e. the strip joining the two sides of the masnad. Four turanj motifs are embroidered on the four corners. The central space is left bare.

A cushion cover in semi-circular shape from Salarjung Museum, of late 19th century. Here the central motif, a floral pattern, radiates in butis and pattis. Such are the conventional buta designs which were very popular during the 18th-19th century. Later on such designs were embroidered on purses etc. These cushion covers are further decorated with sequin.

The oval masnad cover in green and red velvet from Bharany

collection is similar in design depiction to the jaminposh described earlier; the design of the gold embroidery is confined to the ends of the red velvet, the green velvet has silver sequins placed graphically. The masnad covers were tightened by fastening the string; for this purpose a red cotton tape is stitched on the end.

India has a long tradition of offering presentations to the nobilities. The presentation or exchange of items was done in the thai which was normally circular in shape. The goods were arranged in containers or otherwise in the thai and were covered with a fabric cover. Zardozi embroidery was extensively used on these covers. Generally the ends of these covers had gold or silver-braided tassels. Although no illustrative example is shown here, but the palanquins were also covered with such gorgeously embroidered cover. Tray covers or thai posh were eloquently adapted by the Britishers in their day-to-day utilitarian items.

Two thai posh from Victoria and Albert Museum collection bearing Acc. Nos. 4756/3667 and 4757/3487. The red and black base is embroidered with gold silver wire.

It is customary for the royal entourage to have a large number of accessories known as insignias. Flags, qur, alam, parasols, umbrellas, trappings are included in these items. There are descriptive accounts in the Rehla of Batuta. He speaks of horses bearing the insignias of khilafat, which according to his description were girdles of silk, woven with gold.

There were others which were ornamented with white silk embroidered with gold. Batuta has specifically mentioned that these decorated horses were not used by anyone but the Sultan himself. Batuta has made here a very clear distinction between gold weaving and gold embroidery. It is apparent that the Sultan had this insignia beautifully embroidered for his personal use on his horses, the other senior members of the royalty could use the horses with woven girths. At another place Batuta mentions, "out of these sixteen elephants the Sultan rides one, in front of which the saddle-cover studded with the most precious jewels is carried." Here although the specific symbolisation in the form of the design is not mentioned, it is clearly stated that the elephant used by the Sultan could be easily distinguished from others. Describing a royal procession Batuta narrates, "and before him was carried the ghasia which is a saddle-cover studded with gold and precious stones."

Ghasia is a term which is not found to be used elsewhere, but Mehdi Hussain, the commentator of Ibn Batuta, says, "Ghasia was carried before the king being the equerry as a sign of majesty among the Egyptian members." Here ghasia is referred to as an insignia of the royalty and not the trapping. In spite of these elaborate descriptions and specifications of items in the text, we have no extant example of the objects belonging to the Sultanate period. But information regarding trappings, insignias etc. during the Mughal period seems to be more complete due to the availability of textual and pictorial materials. Shahjahan Nama of Inayat Khan has referred to the presentation of horses and elephants received and given to the honoured guest. "On the 16th of Shawwal 1061 (2 October, 1651) Muhyi-al-din, the ambassador, presented to His Majesty a saddle cloth sewn with pearls."

The miniature paintings of different schools show various kinds of animal trappings. It was customary to adorn the horse, camel, donkey or an elephant. A folio of the miniature painting of Persian tradition narrating the story of Sheikh Sanah and Christian Maiden, circa 1595 A.D., shows the Sheikh visiting the maiden. He is seen riding on what looks like a donkey. Although the gait of the animal is horse-like but long ears and elongated face place it closer to a donkey. The borders of the red trapping are adorned with gold embroidery. Another painting from Mughal school belonging to Jahangir period (1605-1629) depicting a scene of camel fight interestingly shows both the camels wearing black girdles with gold embroidery in geometric pattern. These are from National Museum collection.

The saddle cloth was also known as zinposh. John Irwin has illustrated two of them, which are said to be in the collection of the toshkhana of the Nizam of Hyderabad, Deccan, belonging to the 17th century. While describing this zinposh, Irwin writes, "The foundation is a double thickness of loosely woven cotton fabric, upon which is an applique pattern in pieces of red, green and yellow velvet and a ground embroidered in twisted silver gilt thread." This saddle cloth is in line with the design of the zardozi style prevalent during the 17th century, where the ground is extensively embroidered in metal embroidery and the patterns are done with silk thread; here, however, the patterns are in velvet which is appliqued. Stylistically there is a difference between zinposh and jhool. The former as described above remains tightly fitted on the body of the animal whereas jhool elaborately hangs down the sides.

A ragini painting from Malwa School of circa 1680-90 A.D. shows zinposh on horse and jhool on elephant. The painting describing raga Nata depicts a battle-scene. The gold work on the body of the jhool and zinposh is elaborate. Another painting of Ragmala series circa A.D. 1785-90 shows an elephant jhool with orange body and green border. The design here is more specific on the borders and the corners while the depiction of Nat Ragini of circa 1680 A.D. shows the horse trapping covering the body of the horse upto the neck.

An actual specimen of a camel trapping depicts the buti pattern in gold gilded wire on the maroon velvet body. The design is repetitive. The zinposh has a hole in the centre which suitably fits the hood of the camel. A Sikh style miniature painting showing Krishna hurling the wheel is a scene from the Mahabharata. Two horses in the forefront show the trappings with gold work.

A camel saddle in accoutrement from Jodhpur also shows gold embroidery. Later references to the trappings are available in the

Imperial Gazetteers, where brief accounts of various animal trappings with metal embroidery testify to the continuity of the tradition till the abolition of princely states. Delhi, Patna, Murshidabad, Agra, Banaras, Lucknow, Gulbarga and Aurangabad were some of the important centres of metal embroidery where animal trappings were adorned with gold embroidery. We come to know from the contemporary records that Deccan was an important centre where animal trappings with heavy karchobi on velvet were manufactured. These massive forms of animal decorations were adapted by provincial courts. Later the same opulence was seen to impress the British emperor. So on their visit to Delhi when the Delhi Durbars were held in 1903 and 1911, the British Highness rode on the elephant, the jhool for which was worked upon by the zardoz of Delhi. The memories of the two Delhi durbars were recounted by the senior members of few zardoz families in Delhi who had worked frivolously for these durbars. They emphasized that apart from royal processions, it was customary in Delhi even for the religious processions and marriage processions to adorn the animals with tastefully embroidered covers. These massive forms of decorations were mostly composed of floral and geometric devices often accompanied with elaborately embroidered insignias of the state court. This important item of metal embroidery has totally disappeared from the scene.

Parasol:

The umbrellas and parasols (aftabgir), which formed essential part of the noble regalia, right from the Sultanate period, were also profusely embroidered in metal; unlike the trappings, these were often studded with precious and semi-precious stones. Although such parasols might have formed an important part of noble processions, they have not been well preserved. The main reason perhaps being the possible looting of the precious stones used in the embroidery.

The earliest references to parasols are again found in 'Rehla of Batuta', where he has described sixteen elephant seats reserved for the use of the Sultan, having over each of them a silk parasol.[16] The elephants in front of the Sultan were adorned, the standards and sixteen parasols being attached to them. The latter were hoisted, some of these were embroidered with gold and some bejewelled. One of the parasols was raised over the Sultan's head.

We find a brief account of parasols which were also termed as chatars in Ain-i-Akbari where a number of jewels were affixed to adorn a chatar.

Tavernier, while describing the famous peacock throne, also spoke about two umbrellas. These umbrellas were placed at a distance of about four feet on each side of the throne, and were of crimson velvet, embroidered and fringed with pearls. A late example is from Bharany's collection showing karchobi work on an umbrella.

Birdwood has left a detailed description about gorgeous gold embroideries on the velvet cloth of the umbrellas, which were made in

Lucknow, Gulbarga, Aurangabad and Hyderabad. Hunter also referred to embroidered umbrellas. All these clearly indicate that the contemporary provincial courts continued to display the same adornment on umbrellas, which were popularly known as chatar. After the abolition of these courts, umbrellas were found to have been used in religious processions alone. But by that time the adornment had lost much of its gorgeousness.

The embroidery on parasols was done for the temples. These were placed above the idols. The religious proceedings also earmarked the use of metal embroidered parasols. Crafts Museum has such examples in its collection [Ace. No. 84/6740 shows figures of Krishna and his cow, child Krishna amidst dense foliage]. In the late fifties craftsmen of Delhi were commissioned to embroider such parasols in bulk for various religious institutions. Although the use of velvet umbrellas for deities is still popular, the fashion of embroidering with metal thread has now declined altogether.

Badges, Banners, Uniforms etc. :

The articles falling under this category mainly refer to decorations, presentations and identifications related to social and religious institutions. The items embroidered generally have well-defined designs which may be affixed on any dress, material or may be carried independently.

Their history goes back to as early as the Sultanate period. Ibn Batuta mentions, "He conferred on him a silk robe embroidered with gold called surat-i-sher i.e. the image of a lion which it bears on its front and back." Batuta has also mentioned another robe which he has classified as mahairibi robe. Mahairibi is derived from the Persian word mihrab meaning an arch. Thus the robe has on its front and back the embroidered design of an arch. Batuta has also written about the standards made of silk embroidered with gold.

The Futuhat-i-Firozshahi [clause 48] says that Allaudin Khilzi gifted to Allaul-Mulk a golden zardozi robe which had a figure of lion. In the same text [clause 14] he mentions embroidering of banners with golden thread which are not more than four fingers. Here the imposition is in terms of the design restricting it to a minimum width of four fingers. Accounts regarding the motifs given by Batuta and Firozshah refer to zari embroidered robe with lion, which was perhaps the insignia during the Sultanate period. During the Mughal period a specific terminology was used for items falling under royal insignias. These devices were called qur. The Ain-i-Akbari has described qur as a collection of flags, arms and other insignias which follow the king wherever he goes. It is therefore clear that these insignias embroidered with metal thread were very significant during this period. The forms of insignias at times were different, but the symbolic meaning of depicting insignia was universally accepted. The lion shown in also depicts insignia of provincial courts.

Coming to the next period, we find that the tradition of symbolic designs in various forms continued even in the provincial courts. Salarjung Museum, Hyderabad, has a good collection of mehtabgiri procession fans or standards which accompanied the Nawabs of Hyderabad. These standards were also embroidered with metal embroidery.

It is understandable that adornment of military dress with metallic embroidery was a tradition from the earlier period. But lack of evidence both pictorial or written restrains us from corroborating it. However, such adornments are continuing even today. A flag staff in the -miniature painting showing Raga hindola. Ace. No. 567A/1952 from Victoria and Albert Museum, London, depicts the insignia of the English Crown. This is said to have been worn around the neck so that the insignia hangs in front. This is simple embroidery on white satin. It was used by royal personages visiting the Delhi durbar as mentioned earlier. The Imperial Gazetteer also mentions uniforms with metal embroidery. T. N. Mukherji while describing the Glasgow exhibition writes, "Gold and silver embroidered banners were made both at Lucknow and Banaras." Many articles for use in the church were also embroidered with gold and silver. These were exported to Europe from various parts of India. The Shia flag from Victoria and Albert Museum collection is another religious flag taken out during the Moharram procession.

After independence, when the provincial courts were abolished, the symbolic meaning of the insignia was lost, and thus there was very little demand for these objects. The zardozi community then faced a massive setback. But a new channel was opened. A large number of zardozi craftsmen from the walled city of Delhi took up assignments of embroidering small badges, insignias etc. mainly for foreign market, particularly for Europe and America. As described in the socio-economic section, a major part of the zardozi community now produces such articles in their domestic karkhanas. There are large varieties of designs pertaining to this category. The designs show no specification for floral, faunal or geometrical devices, instead the new motifs are a blend of all the three. The articles, whether small or large, are worked with fine karchikan work.

Costumes and Related Accessories:

The rich costume tradition of India has been exemplarily decorated with gold embroidery. A variety of unstitched lengths of fabrics worn in different ways were gorgeously worked with zardozi. The discussion in this section starts from the unstitched fabric used as costume or accessories like the belt, patka, kamarband, shawl, misir, chunri, dupatta, sari. The variety of unstitched lengths have different purposes. Sometimes used for covering the upper body like shawl or else used as head veil (chunri, dupatta, scarf), a dress like sari or just a belt used for tightening the costume.

Raja Dhirajpal of Raghogarh (Madhya Pradesh) of circa 17th century highlights the costume details. The magnanimous size of the patka with beautiful gold design is seen to be held around the waist of the king as well as his attendant. Several words like prota, pota mean an embroidered or patterned cloth. Another word futa which was found to occur in the travel accounts of Ibn Batuta represents a belt for tightening the dress. If we accept/Ufa as a piece of cloth to be tied around waist, it is then similar to patka. But the latter has sometimes dual function of serving as a waist-band as well as a turban. With the emergence of the Sultanate power in India during the 12th and 13th century A.D., when the zardozi craft occupied a very important position, this embroidered cloth used for tying around the waist or sometimes head locally called as patka became very popular.

Another miniature painting, where Raja Bhav Singh is visiting the court of Bahadur Shah I, depicts the waist-girdle also known as kamarband with elaborate gold work. Examples from Crafts Museum collection depict that thinner fabric like muslin, tash, brocade cloth is generally used as the base material. A variety of floral motifs are done with silk, silver gilt wire, flat wire (badla) using simultaneously sequin, sitaras and beetle wings. Lucknow Museum has a patka embroidered in gold gilded silver kalabatoon wire on red velvet. This patka is dated around 18th century. The design here seems to have affiliation with the zardozi objects found in the Red Fort Museum collection. The nobles from the Mughal court in the later period started favouring belt which could be used as the arms borne for keeping their swords. An example is reported from the Red Fort Museum. It shows a bel and patti motif on red silk fabric in gold gilded wire. These belts were adapted commercially with modified designs and forms in European and American market and continued to be commercial success.

Shawl is the particular article of dress, which could well signify a scarf, a mantle or at times a turban and which could be square, rectangular, triangular or even circular. Generally the style of wearing a shawl guided the flow of design. We get graphic descriptions of shawls with zardozi work in the Ain-i-Akbari.

There are references, as cited by Manrique in 1630, to borders ornamented with fringes of gold, silver and silk thread, indicating that shawls were embellished with gold and silver thread in the early Mughal period. However, there are no extant examples illustrating presence of such shawls prior to the late 18th century. Khwaja Yusuf, while promoting embroidery on woven shawls, encouraged use of zari wire for decoration. The main industry was located in Punjab and Delhi. A shawl from Victoria and Albert Museum collection. This is a black woollen rectangular fabric left plain in the centre. The tanzir or the side border has narrow stripe of repetitive floral motif in gold gilded wire. The pallu on both ends has two bands of red wool fabric interspersed with black bands. Each of these has dense embroidery in gold colour. The joints are skilfully concealed with the embroidery.

Another example from Bharany collection shows dense

embroidery in silk, wool and kalabatoon wire on the whole body of the fabric, making the base invisible. The pallu has repetitive paisley motifs. Red wool fabric with gold gilded wire embroidery. Here again the concentration is to decorate the sides and borders. Plate 81 depicts a shawl bel which is stitched on another fabric. A doshala, again a woollen shawl in which multicolour stripes are joined together with gold kalabatoon embroidery infused with floral designs. The stripes are already worked with zardozi motifs.

Satbanteli, odhani, chunri, dupatta are other varieties of unstitched garment adorned with gold embroidery. A satbanteli depicts elaborate medallion design in gold, silver zari wire and spangles on the centre of the side border in the area which covers the head when this is worn. The side borders have the running design. Satbanteli is worn by the proud mother of a first-born baby among the Rabari community of Kutch, Gujarat.

In other parts of the country chunri, much like patka, is made of a thinner fabric, generally transparent. There are several representations of chunri in the miniature paintings, showing exemplary use of the beetle wings, precious stones and gold wire in ornating this piece of garment. Plate 84 depicts a chunri worn by the bride. Here the blue-coloured centre is followed by the red yellow and red stripes of continuous border, which are joined to each other with fine embroidery stitches. The body design is in ari bel, while border has repetitive floral motifs and bharat design.

Sari, one of the most important untailored dresses, has been replenished with metal embroidery for a long time. The pallus and border of the sari continue to be decorated with zari embroidery representing floral and creeper designs. Among the Parsi community it is customary to have velvet border embroidered with zardozi design stitched on the sari border. Plate 85 shows a fine tissue sari from Victoria and Albert Museum having embroidery with gold tinsel sitara and goldgizai wire. The design is floral depicting karan ka phul motif. Red silk thread is used to embroider the centre of the phul which appears like vermilion mark on fair body. Resplendent embroidery with beetle wings and metal wire on red fabric.

A purple neck scarf which is in the collection of Victoria and Albert Museum. This is an illustrative example of the small unstitched costume accessory embroidered in zardozi technique. Here the span of the design is the same as in the Kashmir shawls but in smaller dimension.

The evidence of earliest embroidered clothes for the upper and lower garments of men and women of high social status is found in historical texts. During Maurya and Sunga periods antariya and pattika are seen to have been embroidered with floral motifs. Though this is conjectural, these embroideries were possible in gold and precious stones. Gold embroidered fillets are mentioned to be used by richer classes of women during the Satavahana period. Antariya, the upper garment worn by men, is reported to have gold embroidery. The Gupta period also makes mention of few costumes embroidered in gold and silver.

The custom of embroidering clothes by profuse use of gold and silver became very popular. Batuta in his writings has mentioned that Sultan Muhammad Shah granted Nasir-ud-din a gilded robe of black abfasi colour embedded with precious stones together with a turban to match the robe. At another place, he has described among the presentations to amir Ghadda a silk robe of blue colour embroidered with gold which was studded with precious stones, together with a cap to match. Batuta has also described presentation of linen embroidered in gold by the Sultan to newcomers on the 4th of Shawwal (8th June, 1334). Miniature paintings of the Sultanate period also show Sultans dressed up in robes decorated ostentatiously.

During the Mughal period, dresses with gold and silver embroidery were much in fashion with the royalty and the nobility. The treasure of Akbar included a vide range of stitched garments which were embellished with metal embroidery. Bernier while describing Shahjahan's appearance in the court in his accounts wrote, "The king appeared seated upon his throne at the end of the great hall in the most magnificent attire, which was of white and delicately flowered satin with a silk and gold embroidery of fine texture." He also mentioned other stuffs striped with gold and silver and also turbans embroidered with gold.

A folio from the story of Sheikh Sanah and Christian maiden depicts the Sheikh sitting with the holy men. The Sheikh is seen wearing a choga with gold ornamentation. The canopy on the top also has a gold fringe. This miniature painting is from the National Museum collection and stylistic costumes of Mughal and provincial courts.

Various texts of the 19th century mention different types of dresses embroidered with zardozi work. As regards the nature of embroidery on dresses and costumes, the work is reported to have been of fine variety of karchikan for female costumes, whereas the karchobi for male costumes. The distinction in the fineness of embroidery for women and men perhaps characterises the delicacy and roughness of the two sexes.

Various museums in India and abroad are credited with having a good collection of costumes with zari embroidery from the late 18th, 19th and 20th centuries. Several kinds of male robes like choga, achkan, angarkha, jama, bugal-bandi, coat have various spans of ornamental embroidery. A variety of majestic robes in woollen fabric have dense or sparse embroidery. In bugalbandi and the coat the embroidery travels along the tailored cut on the front, the edges of the sleeves, the slits and the hem. In achkans and chogas, the front and the back yoke, the shoulder, the cuff, the border and the edges of the front opening are heavily embroidered. The rest of the body is either left plain as in Pl. 91 where the base fabric is kani style woven material or the design moves along the boundaries of the flowered pattern on the fabric. At times the body is covered with repetitive pattern of lobes or designs along trailing stems.

Sometimes the design on the body is in ari bel (slanting creepers) at intervals. Generally kalabatoon wire is employed by a hath ari, the hand-operated awl, which became very popular in the late 19th century. The bugalbandi has kamdani work. Here the embroidery in gold wire and precious stones was done on the satin fabric. This was stitched on the desired parts along the seams and edges. Flowering scrolls and paisley motifs are repeated. Among the desert clans of western India, the zardozi skills are amply found to occur on white cotton robes. The abhor have thick minakari work in silk and zari wire with repetitive medallion design.

Under the British influence, the Indian nobility slowly started abandoning their traditional attires and adopted the British costumes. Among the men's robe, coat was one of the important upper garments which was adopted all over the country. However, since it was a prerogative with the nobility to have their garments embroidered in zari wire, the coats were also tastefully embroidered. The back of the coat tastefully embroidered much in the same span as the choga.

Coming next to the women's costume, it is observed that there was more emphasis on adorning the lower garments such as lahenga, sharara, ghaghra, garara. These garments provided vast span for the embroiderers to show their skills. The work profusely remained in the kamdani style. Plate 108 depicting ragini Vinod shows the nayika wearing a lahenga probably with gold work. A sharara i.e. a lower garment with two legs but having a very broad circumference at the lower end; the waist end remaining generally near the waist size. The width in the lower part is achieved by adding tapering strips of cloth. Sometimes it requires about 9 to 12 metres of fabric to make a sharara. This is a popular Muslim dress and is worn even today by elite on auspicious occasions. The sharara described here is from the Crafts Museum collection mainly in green crepe satin. The lower portion or the gher has alternate stripes of green, blue, pink and mauve crepe satin fabric. There is continuous band of zardozi embroidery along with gota kinari to conceal the joint. The body of the garment is embroidered in jail pattern with buti motifs in each jali on the upper part. This pattern is intercepted by the vertical bands at intervals. There is repetitive creeper (bel) design on the gher.

The lahenga is green satin fabric restricting embroidery to the gher. The embroidery is the floral pattern mainly in the gold gilded wire intercepted at places with silver cups placed in shapes of a flower. A ghaghra from Gujarat in plain dark maroon silk fabric shows small kairi butis placed in squares in gold gilded wire. The lower end has a gold braid. Another lahenga worn by the bride.

Kurti, kurtani, kameej, choli, jumper, angiya are the upper garments for women. These have different lengths and are worn with salwar, sharara, ghaghra or lahenga. Kurtani is worn together with lahenga and kurti. A choli in orange silk fabric with bands of green silk on the sleeves and the waist. This exquisitely embroidered choli is worn with white muslin lahenga. Ornately embroidered kanchali in red silk fabric has ari bel design on the back and the front part shows creepers. The borders on the sleeves, the waist and the back have repetitive floral patterns.

A stylishly cut jacket in the European tradition - a combination of green and red velvet. This jacket with full sleeves shows stripes running with neck line, shoulder seam, arm joint where the green and red fabric are joined at sleeve ends. This tight-fitting jacket was perhaps worn with a skirt. Another jacket from the Victoria and Albert Museum collection having profuse gold work on front and back yoke.

Vaskets worn both by men and women are customarily worked with zardozi. Several museums including the National Museum in New Delhi have vaskets in their collections. A mauve-coloured vasket with polyester fabric as the base. This is worked with hath ari. The base cloth is removed from the area with dense jali work in the front and back portion. These parts reflect the colour of the garment over which the jacket is worn. There is running floral pattern on the waist, arm, front opening and neck border and certain portion of the back, which appears as appliqued work.

Having discussed the costumes we come next to the related accessories. Headgears, shoes, purses, belts are the important accessories, which have zardozi work. A variety of turbans and caps from several Indian provincial courts reflect usage of zardozi work.

The tradition of gold embroidered accessories was in vogue during the Sultanate and Mughal period. Though there are no exact references in the texts but the miniature paintings give vivid references. Shiraj painting from the folios of Sheikh Sanah and Christian Maiden shows the nobleman and his visitor wearing turbans with gold work. This painting is of circa 1595 A.D. There are ample evidences of a variety of headgears and footwear in the Mughal miniature paintings and paintings from the provincial courts. A portrait of Shah Shuja, son of Shahjahan, circa 1680 A.D. The stylish turban and jutis show zardozi work.

A crown-like cap in red velvet cardboard bands, gold, silver wire and sequins. A six-petalled blooming bud is shown emerging from the tight-fitting circular band. This type of cap which was similar to the European crown became popular in Oudh court.

From the 18th century to the middle of the 20th century, caps with zardozi embroidery were used by both Muslims and Hindus belonging to all social strata. The base fabric was mainly velvet or satin. These were made in vasli technique i.e. a cardboard was always used between two layers of fabric. Circular caps were worn by upper caste Hindus, particularly Brahmins, Baniyas and Jain community. The caps used by the Nawab of Hyderabad were conical in shape. The embroidery on the cap is done by laying a lining on the under-surface. A cardboard piece is placed between the two fabric layers for stiffening.

Such caps were functional and elaborate. These were worn with the formal dress. This cap seems to have emerged from dopalri where two circular halves are stitched together. Elaborate use of beetle wings along with sequins lends indigenous charm to this cap.

The traditional footwear such as jutis continued to be embroidered with gold silver wire. During the Mughal period the paintings show the royalty in elegant footwear with zardozi work. The upper part of juti known as uparla is worked on a velvet pasted on cardboard. These uppers are then stitched with the sole or tala.

A variety of uparla worked in zardozi karkhana and the collection of the Indian Museum. This kind of juti has a burzi or curved extension of uparla, which depicts the high status of the wearer. Such jutis were worn in Bengal. A knee high shoe from the Victoria and Albert Museum shows stylistic adaptation of Indian skill on European design. The blue and red velvet is covered with couched floral patterns in badla wire along with sequins.

Ladies juti has more delicate form. Here the uparla has red and gold base, worked with semi-precious stones, beetle wings and sequins along with zari wire. The front part has floral creepers while burfi design, recurring geometrical forms in gold wire decorate the hind part.

The contemporary style of the fashion footwear, where glass beads and stones replaced the semi-precious stones.

The Indian theatre and temple have made splendid use of zardozi work in several categories of articles such as curtains, mask, mukut, costumes, jewellery and at times even the figures of gods and goddesses. A velvet curtain from Yadgiri gutta, Andhra Pradesh, where an old temple of Narasimha (incarnation of Vishnu) exists. The temple situated on a large mound is believed to be the original hillock where Vishnu in Narasimha incarnation emerged. The red velvet curtain is drawn when the deities are resting or taking meals. The motif shows a kubhakam (vessel). This may be compared with the curtain used for background decoration during raslila performance in Mathura. Here the curtains are patterned in the architectural framework of a court and temple. The next panel shows a large peacock on full panel for the court scene. Various lines of satin fabric are embellished with gota and zari work.

Costumes in theatre are popularly worked in zari wire. A king wearing a mukut made with cardboard, paper and silver wire. Pattu (neck-band), bazuband (arm-band), kada (bracelet) etc., which were embroidered, were also used in theatre and by the dancing girls. T.N. Mukherji has also mentioned such specimens of embroidered jewellery. During the British period, these items found a popular market in Europe.

Mask is an important theatrical camouflage, which adds rhythm and rapidity to the spirit of communication. Ram Nagar in Uttar Pradesh is known for the zari masks used in theatre.

Purses and batuas used in theatre and otherwise are also embroidered with zari and beads and a few types of purses. The base fabric is generally black, red, blue or green velvet. Plate 143 shows a purse with silk thread and zari wire embroidery.

Before the advent of electricity, fans of several kinds were used by the nobility and the common people. The hand fans have lighter embroidery but sometimes with heavy frill and rope fans from the Red Fort Museum and the Crafts Museum showing zardozi work. Fans in the Bharany Collection show geometrical patterns in heavy karchobi style.

During the 18th and the 19th century, the Jain religion patronized zardozi embroidery extensively. The artisans were commissioned to embroider religious book-covers, boxes and others. A Jain miniature painting from circa 1500 A.D. shows different religious symbols occurring in Jain religion. The box for keeping religious books (Pl. 150) shows sun, moon, navgunjar, bull, elephant, kalash, swastik, fish and religious symbols embroidered in gold and silver wire and sequins on red velvet. The box is rectangular and is embroidered on sides and top. A gomukhi in red silk fabric is embroidered on both the sides with gold silver wire and sequins. The motifs show sun and moon and Krishna, the shepherd, herding cows. The gomukhi is worn on-the hand while counting the sacred beads. Stylistically the figures on these religious artefacts show expressive folk motifs which are different from conventional floral and geometric motifs.

The Muslim religion bans idol worship. But it is usual to have ornamental writing illustrating the sacred script of Kuran. These are known as tugra. They have been embroidered in metallic thread since early times. Phyllis Ackermann while discussing textiles of early Islamic and Seljung periods maintains that Khuzistan, Shustar, Sirsa and Gurdaspur were important centres of ornamental writing. Shustar was the place where the cover with ornamental writing for the Kaba was first introduced.

The earliest form of zardozi in Persia is found to have been associated with ornamental covers for Kaba, a tradition which also existed in the robe of honour made during the Sultanate period. Khalifa was generally written ornamentally on such robes. The tugre done by the zardoz are no doubt the extension of the ornamental religious writings of earlier periods. How tugra is kept in an alia (niche) in a Muslim household and tugre. Generally red, blue or black velvet base is embroidered with silver and gold thread. A fascinating gold hukka and its spread. During the early 20th century when zardozi craftspersons were searching for markets other than the courts, tie case, pin cushions, mantle-covers and many other such articles were embroidered in this style at Delhi chiefly for use of the Europeans. Some such items continue to be produced for foreign as well as the local market.

Embroidery on decorative panels, game cloth for chopad were seen. The naturalistically done peacock and architectural depiction of Taj Mahal are among the popular designs. Rakhi and Christmas hangings are also seasonally made with zardozi.

An overall glance at the objects with zardozi work from the Mughal period to contemporary times provides us a panoramic view of the craft showing gradual changes in the form of objects. What is important to notice in this context is that the motifs found in zardozi do not show any radical change. As a matter of fact several motifs of flowers, creepers and jalis are found to be percolating down the ages without any major alteration. The changes noticeable in the time frame are mere stylization of the earlier motifs with few additions or deletions with respect to the altered forms.

1.4 PROCESS OF CRAFT:

First of all the design is traced on paper by a pencil and small holes are punched on it at close intervals. The pin pricked design on the paper is placed on the piece to be embroidered and smeared with zinc powder soaked in water. The zinc solution passes through the holes making the impression on the cloth. The other powders used for tracing of designs are khadiya, neel (indigo), gum depending on the colour of the cloth to be embroidered. When the tracing is worn out after prolonged use, the copies are made by repunching the tracing on two or three papers for reuse. Traditionally during the Mughal period, nakkash, the professional artists, used to draw the design in the court karkhana™ where several crafts were carried on simultaneously. However, during the field-work, it was observed that these days zardoz draw their drawings themselves. These drawings are called khakhas generally drawn by good artists among zardoz, who provide the copies to their fellowmen. Normally the khakhas are stored for about 30 to 40 years. In commercial karkhanas, the karkhanedars keep a control on the designs.

Next process involves laying of different varieties and shapes of metallic wire and other materials like glass, beads etc. This is done by passing the needle which is threaded from underneath the fabric to the surface and then from surface to below. The needle thus moves upward from the wrong side. The zari wires cut into small pieces are laid so closely that they appear to be continuous thread even to a trained eye.

However, the tilla is not cut in small pieces. It is instead wrapped around afatila which is moved from one side to the other with the motion of needle.

A distinction of technique exists in the ari work, where instead of small pieces of pure metallic wire only kalabattu is used. Unlike the needle the ari is held in hand and passed beneath from the right side of the fabric. The gilded wire or tilla is wrapped on fatila and a portion is pulled above by keeping it in the notch of the ari.

It was asserted by zardoz during the course of interviews that ari work on karchob is comparatively a later assimilation in zardozi work and is derived from the mochi bharat of Gujarat where a similar needle is used for embroidering leather shoes with cotton thread. This technique is preponderantly employed for embroidering leather shoes in Punjab, Rajasthan also. On the fabric, however, these days it is a trend to employ zardozi and ari technique in close togetherness. Since ari work is faster, it is assimilated with zardozi stitches. It may be mentioned in this connection that ansari zardoz are very particular about not practising on technique. Many among them were found saying that bhookhe mar jayenge par ari nahin uthayenge (we may die of hunger but shall not work with needle). That is why, perhaps, tilla is also stitched with the needle in domestic karkhanas. The hath ari work was abundantly done on woollen items in the provincial courts of Punjab, Kashmir and Patiala.

Zardozi work also however has two distinct categories known as karchobi and kamdani. The embroidery done on velvet or heavy satin generally for tent coverages, furnishings etc. traditionally with badla was called karchobi. It is said to have become popular during the late Mughal period, when the Muslims came in contact with Portuguese. Presently, the shashe of the Pope in Catholic church are worked in this technique. Kamdani generally refers to the work done on muslin, silk and other fabrics. The work here is done with great deal of minute skill in delicate rhythm. This technique remained more popular on the dresses, coverlets, caps and many miscellaneous items.

An important technique, which requires to be discussed is couching. As the name implies it is the technique employed to give the embossed effect on the desired portions. Normally such effect is obtained by two processes. In the first process a cotton fabric is tied on karchob and the outline of the design is traced on its surface. Pieces of cardboard or bukram are then pasted on the portions where raised effect is desired. Next the fabric on which the work is to be done is stitched on the karchob and embroidered. The technique also known as vasli kam was more popular on furnishing materials, trappings etc. Presently it is practised on badges, insignias etc. In the second procedure of couching, the fabric which is to be embroidered is directly stretched on karchob and the area desired to be couched is filled with thick cotton yarn stitches. Sometimes a piece of foam is put underneath. Once the desired embossed effect is obtained, the area is covered with zari wire. This technique is practised on covers, costumes etc.

Minakari is another important process where the variety of silk threads along with zari wire are used for embellishment. This technique lends enamel-like view to embroidery, hence the name minakari.

It is interesting to note that despite many changes in design, form etc., the tools and technology of the craft have remained more or less unchanged. There is thus a continuity in the process, tools and equipment since the inception of the craft during Mughal period. The process of zardozi revolves around five basic designs which have larger variation. These basic designs are jali (geometric design), bharat (filler design), patti (leaf), phul (flower), pankhi (bird), janwar (animal).

Jali work is also known as tanke bandi ka kam because here the stitches are counted without a preconceived draft. Few of the jali designs are : chandi ki jali, chakle wali jali, suiyo wali jali. Bharat designs as the name indicates fill the portions by embroidery. These have mainly the geometrical patterns which are placed in the gaps in a continuous rhythm.

Popular bharat designs are: chunti ki bharat, tanke bandi ka kam, do suiyo ki bharat, khardar bharat. Other designs like patti, phul, pankhi and janwar have a wider range. Important are gende ka phul (kidney-shaped flower), ek khar, ded khar, teen khar (refer to the respective edges generally of leaves), angur (grape) etc.

Zardozi as a technique is understood to be a distinctive style of stitching as it differs from other traditions of embroidery like kantha, kasuti, phulkari etc. where the movement of the threaded needle is guided by a variety of stitches. In other embroideries silk, cotton or woollen threads are used, which are pliable enough to move freely. However, in zardozi, the thread only acts as a binding medium, whereas the body of the design is completed by laying varieties of metallic threads in several shapes and forms along with beads, stones, beetle wings etc. The whole process is more indicative of applique rather than embroidery. Thus it may be called metal applique. This is further corroborated by the fact that zardoz always get payments for amount of wire stitched on the cloth by weight. They never use the word kadai, the Hindi word for embroidery, instead refer to it as salme sitare ke kam ka takna which means laying of the salma, sitara on the body of the fabric.

MANUFACTURING PROCESSES

The multiple processes involved in zari industry are carried out in a decentralised manner at different units specialised in one or more but not all processes. The processes involved in Zari manufacturing can broadly be grouped as under depending on the final product, viz., Real or Imitation.

(1) Processes involved in the manufacture of Real Zari.

  (i) Melting of Silver (Raw).

  (ii) Preparation of Silver wire Bars.

  (iii) Hammering of Silver bars for elongation.

  (iv) Drawing of Silver Wire of different gauges, coarse, medium, fine and superfine, in Pawtha and Tania wire drawing units. (An ounce of Silver is used for making about 3000 yards of silver wire).

  (v) Flattening the wire or Lametta making in flattening machine.

  (vi) Dyeing of Cotton or Silk, or Art Silk Yarn.

  (vii) Winding of Lametta on Silk, Art Silk or Cotton on Winding machines to make Zari.

  (viii) Electroplating of silver Zari threads to make gold threads.

(2) Processes involved in the manufacture of Imitation Zari.

  (i) Making of 1/2" copper coils from copper Bars, in Rolling Milt at Udhna or Shivry.

  (ii) Copper Wire Drawing Units (PAWTHA) for drawing wire up to 30 s.w.g (drawing through dyes).

  (iii) Gilding of 30 s.w.g. copper wire by silver in cement concrete or polythene tanks.

  (iv) Further drawing of this 30 s.w.g. silver electroplated copper wire in fine gauges (TANIA UNIT).

  (v) Flattening of silver-gilded copper wire in Lametta Making flattening machine. (CHAPAD OR FLATTENING UNIT).

  (vi) Winding of Lametta on Yarn on kasab winding machines.

(vii) Gilding of Silver threads (gold or lacquer).

The usual practice is to melt the silver ingot bought from the market in furnaces and the molten mass of silver is then moulded into bars. The silver is then elongated by electric hammering and then drawn in wire-drawing units called "PAWTHA" through various tungsten dies of decreasing diameter so as to finally get the wire of 30 s.w.g. This silver wire is then further made to pass through a series of ruby dyes in another wire-drawing unit called "TANIA" so as to make the final wire of required sizes. Here the fineness up to which wire is drawn is normally between 1600 to 1800 yards per ounce. Surat zari industry has the capability to draw fine wire up to a fineness of 2500 yards per ounce, thinner then even human hair. What an achievement !

Thereafter, this fine silver wire is flattened in a flattening machine to make Silver-lametta. The Lametta (flattened and shining silver wire) is then wound round silk, art-silk or cotton thread on a machine called winding machine to make zari Thread. This "Ruperi Zari Thread" which is silvery is again then made to pass through gold solution in locally made electroplating unit (gilit-no-bankdo) to make the final "Gold Thread" for sale.

In the manufacture of Imitation Gold Thread, the imported electrolytic copper wire is first rolled into Vz rods in the rolling mill at Udhna or Amar Rolling Mill at Shivry and then further drawn to 30 s.w.g thickness/diameter in Pawtha or locally made coarse wire-drawing units. This copper wire is then electroplated with silver in tanks. The copper wire electroplated in silver is further drawn through various ruby dyes in Tania units to required gauge. The wire product is then flattened and wound round the art-silk or cotton yarn to make Imitation or Half-fine Zari threads. Imitation Zari-thread can be with actual gold gilded or gilded with lacquer without gold. If it is with some gold, it is called Half-fine Gold thread.

For the manufacture of embroidery materials, the process up to flattening is similar. The flattened wire (lametta) is then used in different equipments to make Zik, Chatak, Salmo, Kangari etc. For Stars and similar items, the flattened strip is punched in sewing machine like punching machines specially made for the purpose, with dyes of different design. For Real Zari, the basic metal used is silver, while for imitation Zari the basic metal used is copper. It will be interesting to note here that all Zari manufacturing machines right from wire-drawing to the end, are locally manufactured and this remarkable achievement in self-reliance makes this industry all the more significant and important in the National Economy. Zari making activity can be subdivided in 12 different activities which are shown in the following table :

It can be observed that all units are not necessarily involved in all activities. The industry functions in such a way that production processes of different firms are intricately and intimately coordinated. For

Table 1.4.1 Zari units in Surat 1970

Types of units	Units in 1970	Workers
Pawtha, Tania	75	400
Pawtha, Tania (I)	130	1250
Zari thread (Real / Imitaion)	800	8500
Stars & Spangles	135	1500
Embroidery & Zardosi	50	500
Gota - thappa flowers, champo	300	1500
Kinkhab - brocades unit	35	350
Laces and border unit	275	1000
TOTAL	1800	15000

Source : *Annual Report of the Surat Zari Merchant's Association, 1970*

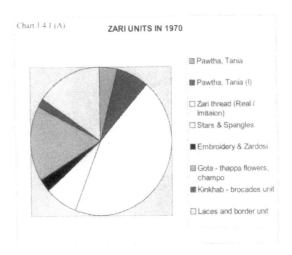

Chart 1.4.1 (A)   ZARI UNITS IN 1970

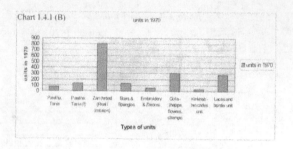

Chart 1.4.1 (B)

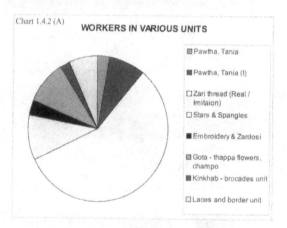

Chart 1.4.2 (A) — WORKERS IN VARIOUS UNITS

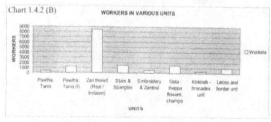

Chart 1.4.2 (B) — WORKERS IN VARIOUS UNITS

example, there are units that are engaged in only one operation/process; some are engaged in two operations/processes and some in more than two. Tania and winding operations are often found in combination. Pawtha and gilding require more capital and are often found as stand alone operations in different units. Fattening and winding operations are also found in combination in several units, probably because of the low level of investment and skills required (even women and children are often involved) and also because of winding immediately follows flattening.

Current Process involved in Zari Industry :

There are three types of Zari i.e Real, Imitation, Metallic. Each and every Zari has its own characteristics. Even the process involved in each is different.

REAL ZARI:

Zari initially got its name because originally it was made from Silver and Gold. Nowadays this type of zari is not seen in market due to high prices of Silver and Gold. The processes of this Zari are as under :

(a) Melting of Silver:

Under this process the silver is being melted in a hot Chimney, at a specific degree. Initially coal was used but nowadays to save time and cost, people are using gas and electricity to melt silver.

(b) Preparation of Silver Wire bars:

This is the second step in the preparation of Real Zari. Here the melted silver in a form of liquid is dropped in a prepared structured form, which is then moulded into makes a different sizes of Bars. Chemicals are also used to make the bars.

(c) Hammering of Silver Bars:

The prepared Bars are then further hammered to minimize the thickness. In this process only the hot silver bars are hammered.

(d) Drawing of Silver Wire:

Under this process the silver wires are drawn from various sizes of machines, which is also called "Tania". The sizes may be in Gauges i.e. 20, 40, 60, 80 etc.

(e) Flattening of Wire:

After drawing from different gauges, the wires are then stretched through the machines again which makes the wire thin like a thread. This process is popularly known as Surat Lametta.

(f) Dyeing of Cotton Or Silk Or Art Silk Yarn:

In this process readymade silk or cotton or may be art silk yarn is dyed. This process is done by various type of chemicals.

(g) Winding of Lametta on silk or Dyed silk Yarn:

The Lametta prepared is being wounded on Dyed Silk Yarn which is called winding.

(h) Electroplating of Silver Zari thread to make Gold thread:

To make Gold thread, the silver zari is electroplated on a machine.

IMITATION ZARI:

(a) Making Coils:-

Under this, the process is to make 1/2" Copper Coils from Copper wire Bars in Rolling mills at Udhana or Shivry. The imported Electrodytic Copper wire is first rolled into 1/2" rods in rolling Mill, at Udhna or AMAR rolling mill at Shivry.

(b) Drawing of Wire (PAWTHA):

This is the wire drawing unit under which various tungsten dyes are decreased in diameters so as to finally get the wire of 30 S.W.G. This process is called "Pawtha" or locally made coarse wire drawing units.

(c) Gilding:

30 s.w.g. Copper wire is gilded by silver in cement concrete tanks or polythene tanks. This copper wire is then electroplated with silver in Tanks.

(d) Tania Units:

This is the unit, under which the silver electroplated copper wire is further drawn through various ruby dyes. The dye size is prepared as per the requirement. The dyes are also called 'Hira' or "Vicer". The holes through the dyes are called "Ustad". Here the fineness upto which wire is drawn is normally between 1600 to 1800 yards per ounce. Surat can draw Fine wire upto the fineness of 2500 yards per ounce, thinner than even human hair - What an achievement!

(e) Chapad Or Flattening Unit:

This is a Lametta making unit. The wire product is flattened. The silver thread is rounded under the method of Tania. But under this method the round thread passes through the two Steel Wheels under which it becomes flat (Chapad). So it is called flattening / Chapad process. By the process of flattening, sewing becomes easy.

The flattened wire (Lametta) is used in various equipments to make Zik, Chalak, Salmo, kangari etc. For Stars etc. the flattened strip is punched in sewing machine like punching machine specially made for the purpose with different design dyes.

(f) Kasab:

Under this method the flattened wire is wound round the art silk or Cotton Yarn to make imitation or Half Fine Zari threads. The process is called Kasab.

(g) Gilit No Bakdo(gilding through chemical) :

Silvery zari thread is again made to pass through gold solution in locally made electroplating unit, which is called Gilit no Bakdo to make the final "Gold Thread' for sales in market.

METTALIC ZARI :-

Today, the precious metal gold & silver has become too costly & hence pure zari is beyond everybody's reach. Mettalic yarn zari (imitation zari) has become as an able, ideal & most suitable substitute to all types of pure zari. Due to upgradation of technology, polyester film was metallised & coated, bringing into existence the basic raw material for producing metallic yarn zari. France & Japan were the first to flood the market with zari made from polyester film in the year 1970. Since then, due to continuous research & development metallic yarn zari has gained more market compared to all other types of imitation zari (made from copper) & pure zari.

Considering the cost aspect metallic yarn zari has done a great service to the nation by saving precious metal like gold & silver & also copper. Metallic yarn zari costing Rs.350 Kg. has become an easy & affordable luxry for common man. Pure zari costing Rs.4000 per kg. has become a product beyond common man's reach.

Metallic zari industry today is an industry giving employment & self employment to more than 4000 families at other centers like Ajmer,

Maunathbhanjan, Salem, Coimbatore, Bangalore, Delhi, Malegaon, Nadiad. The process involved in making metallic zari is very simple, Metallised coated film in desired colours are available in the market.

(i) Cutting & Sizing:

This is the process which involves slitting with the help of razor blade to from pancake of small widths (normally 50 mm to 72 mm). The pancake produced is passed from the thin cutters, size of which depends upon the thickness of required zari. Generally there are 224 spindles on one machine. The capacity of this machine is to produce 3 to 3.50 Ton per month.

(ii) Winding:

The zari so produced is wound on spools with the help of winder. Here the resultant zari is produced by skilled efforts of artisans / operators.

(iii) Steaming:

After covering the zari by yarn, it is heated on given steam for 17 minutes to lend finishing to the zari.

CHART SHOWING PROCESS ON NEXT PAGE ...

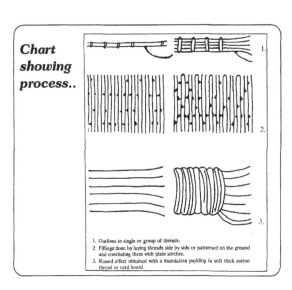

Chart showing process..

1. Outlines in single or group of threads.
2. Fillings done by laying threads side by side or patterned on the ground and conchiding them with plain stitches.
3. Raised effect obtained with a foundation padding in soft thick cotton thread or card board.

1.5 PATTERNS OF ORGANISATION

Distribution of Zari units in Surat :

Zari industry being a household industry precise information about the number of units and workers engaged was not available. Several agencies like Surat Muncipal Corporation, Zari Merchants' Association and District Industries Centre etc., with which the Zari units get registered, had some information. Information provided by these institutions was un-comprehensive, un-comparable and often contradictory. Zari Merchants' Association of Surat (with a membership of about 350) estimated 2300 units while the Municipal Corporation Office put the estimate at around 1200 units (of which information about location and employment size was available for only 759); the District Industries Centre had information about 237 units.

Table 1.5.1 below gives the spatial distribution of Surat-based zari units.

Workers	1-2	3-4	5-6	7-8	9-10	>-10	TOTAL
Gopipura	20	12	9	6	-	-	47
Navapura	121	68	18	12	1	-	220
Sagrampura	33	22	9	9	3	1	77
Wadifalia	43	52	18	18	-	-	131
Mahidharpura	8	8	2	6	2	1	27
Station-road	13	25	17	8	2	-	65
Begumpura	66	61	35	24	4	2	192
TOTAL	304	248	108	83	12	4	759

Source : SPIER Study Report.

According to 1990 economic census, there were 2553 units of Zari manufacturing -99 % of which were functioning in their own premises and only 13 % were functioning without electricity. Only 218 (9%) units employed more than 10 workers. While this number remained very close to 220 in 1980, the number of small units increased substantially from 539 to 2334.

Organisation of work in Zari Industry :

There are about 800 Merchant-manufacturers, 200 Akhadedars (job work contractors) and nearly 30,000 workers or artisans according to a report of 1970. A report of Zari Merchants' Association published in 1995 mentions the existence of 200 merchant-manufacturers, 1800 Akhadedars and 50,000 workers in the Zari industry. Machine owners and merchants employ workers. According to an estimate by Zari Merchants' Association, of the total workforce engaged in Zari Industry in Surat, nearly 1 % are merchant-manufacturers, 4 % are akhadedars or contractors and 95 % are the workers. However, as mentioned at the beginning of this chapter, the current estimates orally ascertained during the discussions put the estimates as follows:

Number of units owned by leading merchant-manufacturers :	500
Number of fragmented units engaged in one or two operations :	3000-5000
Size of workforce :	100,000

The Merchant-Manufacturers

The merchant-manufacturers supply the required capital to the

Industry. They may or may not possess or own Zari manufacturing machines or units. In addition to their own production, they may get the work of others done by the Akhadedars who are associated with them. The merchant-manufacturers, as they are called, supply the raw materials like gold/silver wire, silk, art-silk or cotton yarn etc. to Akhadedars and get, in turn, the product on payment of charges fixed by mutual negotiations, for the contracted job work done. The merchant-manufacturers deal in the goods and do the trade and business in Zari Industry.

The Akhadedars or the Job-work Contractors :

The Akhadedars or the job-work contractors act as independent contractors or manufacturers. They obtain the work orders and enter into job-contracts with merchant-manufacturers on piece-rate contract charges. They usually possess and own Zari machinery (winding or drawing or electroplating or other equipment) to do the job-work for the merchant-manufacturers. Merchant-manufacturers supply the raw materials. The Akhadedars, in turn, employ workers on piece-rate wages to work on their machines to do the job-work that they have contracted. They usually employ their family members also. These Akhadedars often also simultaneously do the job contract work as well as manufacturing and selling their own Zari products in the market.

Artisans or workers :

Workers are a class by itself. They are employed by the machine owners, namely merchant-Manufacturers or Akhadedars, to do the work on the machines and earn wages on piece-rate base wages. They are the employee class.

This, in brief, is the age old and established pattern of working in the Industry. It is an established pattern and apparently works peacefully and satisfactorily. As the industry is decentralised, there are very few composite units, possessing full equipment from wire drawing to finished product. By and large, the entire Industry has been working in this decentralised set-up from ancient days.

Distribution of family and hired workers :

During our discussion with the people connected with Zari manufacturing in Surat, it was pointed out that there is high proportion of family work in the total workforce in this industry. This could be one of the reasons for industrial peace in this industry. A 300 units survey done by SPIER puts the ratio of family workers to hired workers at 52:48 (details given in Table 1.5.2). It was also revealed that there is a change in the workforce during the last two decades. Many merchants of the past have changed their line of business and entered into textiles, while many of the akhadedars of the past have now become zari merchants. The new entrants in workforce, mainly the artisans, are from Rana community.

Table 1.5.2 Size wise distribution of family and hired workers in 300 units:

Workers in a unit	Family Workers	Hired Workers	Total Workers
1-5	151 (51)	143 (49)	294 (100)
6-10	581 (54)	491 (46)	1072 (100)
11-15	387 (52)	361 (48)	748 (100)
> - 15	339 (50)	340 (50)	679 (100)
TOTAL	1458 (52)	1335 (48)	2793 (100)

Source: SPIER Study Report.

Not much of union activity is prevelant in this industry. There are two unions viz. Zari Kamdar Mandal and Akhadedar Association and both of these unions are ineffective at present. On meeting with the past president of Zari Kamdar Mandal, it came to be known that, after independence, strike was observed twice in order to press demands for minimum wages, weekly off and compensation to the workers in the event of closing down of the factory. The union however seems to be quite passive now.

1.6 MARKETING OF ZARI

Domestic market :

In almost all the States of the Indian Union, zari threads and other zari items are marketed. The products of zari Industry are marketed not only in the country but exported abroad as well. But the marketing of zari and zari products is not systematically organised. There are no associations or rules for guidance and no standard contracts. Each producer and dealer has developed and adopted his own marketing line and the products are not sold always through organised agencies. The deals are either against definite orders or as is often the case on consignment basis. Credit is universal in the industry and extends from three to nine months and occasionally even longer. One will find marked diversity in trade practices that are followed in the industry. In short, the market is thoroughly loose and absolutely unorganised. Obviously, the first and foremost task is to have a marketing organisation not only for obtaining and distributing raw-materials for the manufacturers but also for organizing a common production programme and common marketing, that is the establishment of a service-cum-sales organization. But the established pattern will, in fact, never allow such a common marketing agency to materialize.

The marketing on the whole is bound to remain individualistic to a great extent. But looking to the established trade practices in the industry, a code of business should be evolved by the industry wherein a sale contract could be standardized, credit benefit fixed and time limit of payment can be settled. This is of paramount importance. There is a great need to make the market steady and well organized. Either the common marketing organization that may be established in future or the Associations like the Surat Zari Merchants' Association working in the Industry can take up this work. At present, goods are sold by the Zari merchants in Surat either through agents appointed by them in the marketing centres or through their own branches in such places. Goods are sold generally on credit although the traders buy the raw materials in cash. So also, the dissemination of market information, which is very important for any industry, is conspicuous by its absence. The advertisements and dissemination of product information, which is very much needed particularly for pushing sales abroad can be made by participating in exhibitions, publication of illustrated brochures, radio & TV advertisements etc. Similarly, a foreign market survey of the changing demands, tastes and fashions has to be carried out by the industry to assist planned production and ensure steady export markets.

There is also a need for the creation of new designs in the industry to develop its new markets. For this, and to attract more people towards zari products the urgent need is to establish a Design Centre exclusively for zari Industry.

The major market for the products of zari Industry is internal, though a considerable quantity of the same is marketed abroad as well.

Out of the total annual production of zari Industry, nearly 80 to 85% is consumed by the internal market while the rest i.e. about 15% is exported outside the country. The total export of zari-based products is about Rs.80 cr, mostly to USA. The potential export market is ranked in the (decreasing) order of real, plastic and imitation zari.

The principal Indian markets for Zari products are Madras, Mysore, Rajasthan, Delhi, Uttar Pradesh, Calcutta and Maharashtra. The premier centres being Bangalore, Salem, Madura, Kanjivaram, Kumbakonam etc. in the South; Jaipur, Delhi, Amritsar and Banaras in the North; Calcutta in the East; and Bombay and Nagpur in the West. Of all these, the South Indian Market consumes in bulk the well known gold and silver thread through its handloom and power-loom textile weaving units. The internal market, because of unplanned production and marketing programme, has turned a "buyer's market" and the external market is more adverse due to severe competition offered by French Zari.

While this is the situation, the advent of a rival yarn, the plastic Zari or Lurex has added fuel to the fire. Important Zari consuming centres like Benaras and Bangalore were invaded and conquered. At times, it was felt that death-knell was rung but due to serious protests and efforts of the Zari Association, Zari Federation and the Handicrafts Board and the sympathy of the Government at the Centre, the zari thread has won the battle once again and is recapturing lost markets.

Over-production and cut-throat competition has developed over time. Leaders of the industry under the auspices of the Surat Zari Merchants' Association gathered and unanimously decided to move through the Zari Development Board to invoke the assistance of the Government to come to the irrescue. The Government appointed in 1957 a Zari industry Enquiry Committee, which in consensus with the Trade also opined that the only way to save the home industry is to take urgent steps to develop the potential zari export market. The industry continues to be afflicted by these problems even now.

The Enquiry Committee also made another important recommendation and that was the 'Formation of a Committee exclusively devoted to the export promotion Job'. It is interesting to note that both these recommendations were accepted by the Central Government and were also implemented. The zari Industry was placed under the care of the All India Handicraft Board, New Delhi for its over all development including Export trade. The second important step was the announcement of Special Export Promotion Scheme in 1959 for zari exports under which 40% by way of import licence against zari exports were granted to induce zari exporters to push up sales and to give the much needed fillip.

1.7 EXPORTS OF ZARI

The zari products are in considerable demand in foreign countries and are marketed in almost all the leading marketing centres of the world. The important countries wherein zari products are marketed are Pakistan, Afghanistan, Ceylon, Burma, Indonesia, Canada and the Middle-East countries. The demand for Zari have remained in almost all these countries, but it is indeed regrettable that no organised efforts have been made as yet by the industry to explore potential foreign markets and expand the existing ones.

Export promotion schemes :

After 1959, the year in which the first ever Export Promotion Scheme was formulated for zari goods, export trade of zari began to rise till the year 1963-64. Due to malpractice by some selfish and unscrupulous self-styled zari exporters, the Government withdrew the EP Scheme and there arose a crisis. All India Zari Federation through its versatile Chairman Shri R.T. Popatwala with the representatives of the Zari Exporters' Association viz. The Surat Zari Merchants' Association, met the then Union Minister for Foreign Trade Shri Manubhai Shah. After strenuous efforts and with the sympathy of the All India Handicrafts Board they prevailed upon him to re-introduce the EP Scheme for Zari goods. Shri Manubhai Shah, convinced about the imperative need for assistance, re-introduced the zari Export Promotion Scheme in 1964 with 30% incentive that continues till today. Thanks to the sympathy of the Government and sincere efforts of the All India Handicrafts' Board, the All India Zari Federation and the premier Zari Association viz., the Surat Zari Merchants' Association, have on their rolls about 100 Zari exporters.

Under the Export Promotion Scheme in force, zari exporters are given raw material incentive licences worth 30% of the f.o.b. value of export. The items of entitlements at present allowed against zari exports are Copper, Raw Silk and Velveteen. Adequate assistance through export promotion scheme, sponsoring of a study team to undertake tour of foreign countries to explore possible markets there, studying taste and fashions in sophisticated countries like the U.S.A and latest equipment and technique, and the publicity for dissemination of useful information are the needs of the hour.

Zari has the export market from the beginning and traditionally in the Middle East countries. The major domestic market existed in southern states of India and was reached through the agents who were also in many cases relatives of the entrepreneurs. In the late sixties, zari export was affected due to the invention of plastic zari and competition from developed countries like France and Japan. The government policy was also not favourable for the export of zari as it was manufactured from gold and silver.

Zari export during 1960-61 to 1994-95 (table 2.6) included (a) gold thread (Kasaab), (b) embroidery materials like Badla (Lametta), Zik, Tiki, Chalak, Salmo, Kanagari, Sadi, Fancy Stars etc. (c) Laces, fit-boarders, trimmings, etc. (d) Zari textiles like Kinkhab, Ornis and Zari embroidered cloth purses and plaques etc. It can be seen from the table that Zari exports have been fluctuating. Zari exports that were Rs.25 lakhs in 1960-61 reached to Rs.125 lakhs in 1969-70. It reached Rs.173 lakhs in 1963-64 and fell down to Rs.32 lakhs during 1966-67. Exports in recent years have been mentioned in table 1.7.1 below: :

Table 1.7.1 Exports of Zari and Zari Goods

YEAR	VALUE IN CRORES OF RUPEES
1960-61	0.25
1961-62	0.71
1962-63	0.62
1963-64	1.73
1964-65	0.60
1966-67	0.38
1967-68	0.32
1968-69	0.80
1969-70	1.26
1985-86	6.18
1986-87	11.08
1987-88	4.97
1988-89	8.54
1989-90	6.86
1990-91	18.48
1991-92	30.60
1992-93	42.65
1993-94	48.90
1994-95	57.95

Charts are on next page...

(108)

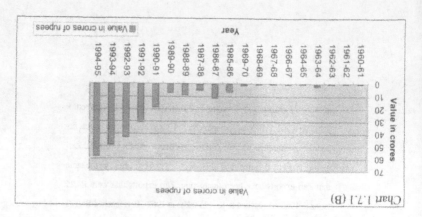

Chart 1.7.1 (B)

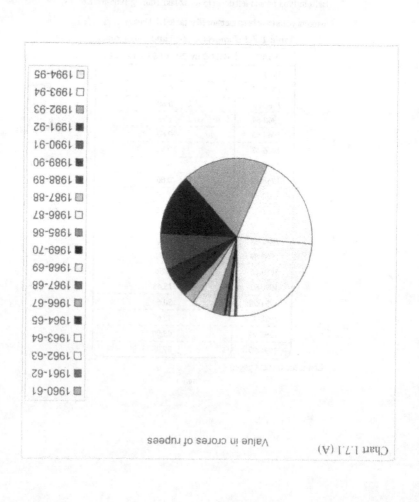

Chart 1.7.1 (A) Value in crores of rupees

The rosy picture of exports of the last decade seen in the above table is illusory. The nine-fold increase is only in terms of value; there has been only nominal increase in quantity. This is mainly due to four-fold rise in the prices of raw materials, labour and devaluation of our Indian rupee by almost 33%. While exports of handicrafts are growing at a higher rate, the growth of zari exports is lagging behind.

STATEMENT OF EXPORTS OF HANDICRAFTS ARE DEPICTED ON FURTHER PAGES ...

STATEMENT OF EXPORTS OF HANDICRAFTS
EXCLUDING HANDKNOTTED CARPET (ITEMWISE) FOR THE LAST TEN YEARS

Table 1.7.2 (RS. IN CRORES) (PROVISIONAL)

ITEMS	1991-92	1992-93	1993-94	1994-95	1995-96	1996-97	1997-98	1998-99	1999-00	2000-01
1. ARTMETALWARE	341.05	480.05	680.20	1022.25	1205.95	1370.60	1214.60	1324.16	1497.18	1778.10
2. WOODWARE	50.50	68.20	98.50	136.90	155.65	188.45	221.82	286.04	348.95	434.44
3. HANDPRINTED TEXTILE & SCARVES	149.81	196.50	354.25	475.12	580.45	595.17	838.24	1033.98	1158.05	1276.75
4. EMBROIDERED & CROCHETTED GOODS	33.20	42.70	70.45	102.20	115.30	131.10	990.75	1159.42	1584.36	1964.78
5. SHAWLS AS ARTWARE	23.18	28.15	32.95	36.90	39.75	36.43	17.08	18.18	21.50	27.20
6. ZARI & ZARI GOODS	3060	42.65	48.90	57.95	70.95	79.78	70.34	74.95	83.52	142.32
7. IMITATION JEWELLERY	14.90	19.05	28.75	36.88	40.20	44.13	98.03	104.10	113.64	121.68
8. MISC. HANDICRAFTS	421.76	534.70	656.00	767.70	812.10	1022.92	902.32	1057.57	1116.40	1210.08
TOTAL	1065.00	1412.00	1970.00	2635.90	3020.35	3568.58	4353.18	5058.40	59.23.60	69.55.35

Line Chart and different charts and graphs are depicted on further pages ...

Chart 1.7.2 EXPORTS OF HANDICRAFTS

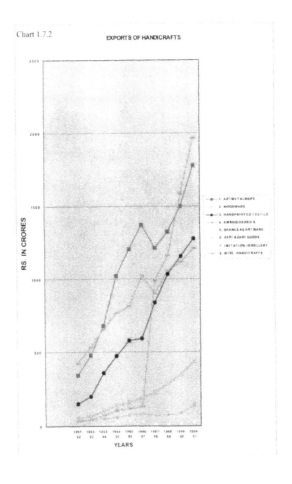

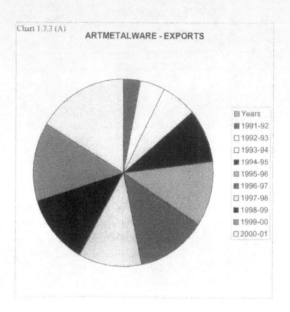

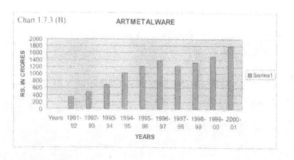

Chart 1.7.4 (A)   **WOODWARE - EXPORTS**

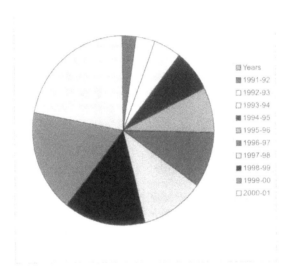

Chart 1.7.4 (B)   WOODWARE - EXPORTS

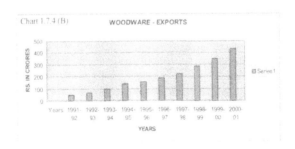

Chart 1.7.5 (A)

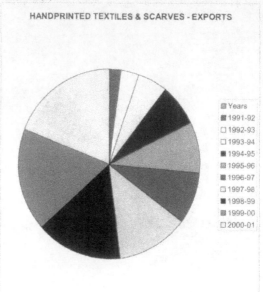

Chart 1.7.5 (B)

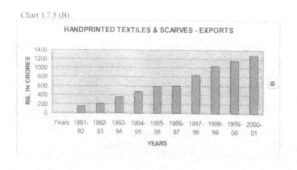

Chart 1.7.6 (A)

EMBROIDERED & CROCHETED GOODS - EXPORTS

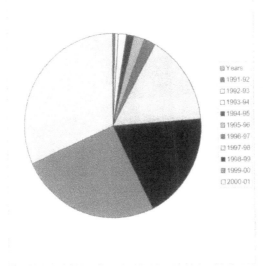

Chart 1.7.6 (B)

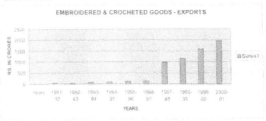

Chart 1.7.7 (A)

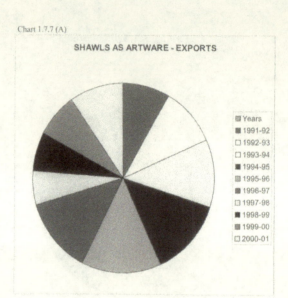

Chart 1.7.7 (B)

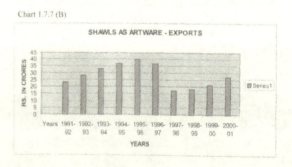

Chart 1.7.8 (A)

ZARI AND ZARI GOODS

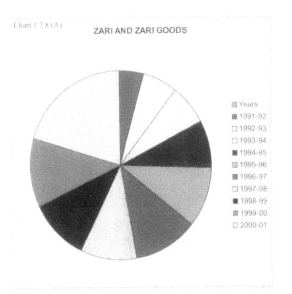

Chart 1.7.8 (B)

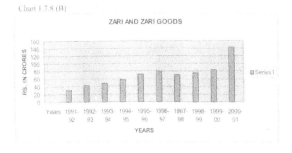

Chart 1.7.9 (A)

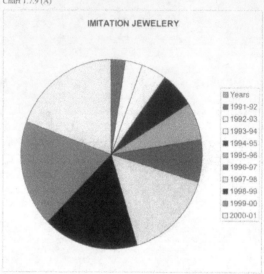

Chart 1.7.9 (B)

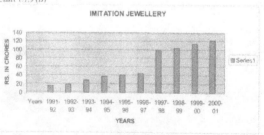

Chart 1.7.10 (A)

MISC. HANDICRAFTS

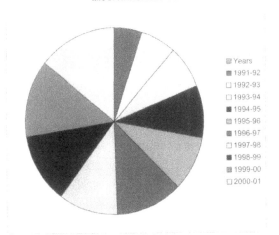

Chart 1.7.10 (B)

MISC. HANDICRAFTS

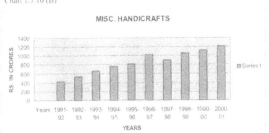

1.8 GROWTH AND DEVELOPMENT

(1947 onwards):

After 1947, industry witnessed the beginning of a troubled era. India achieved independence in 1947 and with it brought partition as well. The creation of Pakistan had its adverse effects on the home industry, as it lost the market of zari consuming centres that fell to Pakistan side. Not only this, but it also lost its real regular patrons with the abolition of Princely States bringing about yet another serious crisis for the home industry. Zari industry lost about 1/3 of its total demand. From 1947 onwards for about a decade, the industry passed through a very critical period of its existence. Renewed problems and fresh difficulties, like over-production, decline in demand, cut-throat competition, rise in raw material prices and import duty, cropped up. The immediate problem was to find out a compensatory market for the loss of Pakistan part of the consumer's demand and one due to the abolition of princely potentates. For this, the only available course was to explore possible new foreign markets and increase zari exports. Zari was in the world market from times immemorial and is still holding the fort. The industry possesses great export potential. Organised efforts to promote the export of Zari should go a long way in compensating the above loss and toning up the unhealthy condition in the industry simultaneously.

Zari industry enquiry committee (1957) and its recommendations:

The fast deteriorating conditions and the crisis prevailing in the industry created anxious moments. The efforts of the industry by itself to improve its present dismal condition were not enough. The industry therefore, naturally once again looked forward to the Government for guidance and assistance and requested it through the Surat Zari Development Board (a body constituted of the three principal organs working in the industry) to investigate into the problems of the industry and suggest remedial measures. The Government, looking to the crisis through which the industry was passing, was convinced and appointed in 1957, a Zari Industry Enquiry Committee under the chairmanship of Shri N. Mazumdar, the then Industrial Advisor (Textile production) to conduct an on-the-spot investigation. The Committee included the representatives of the industry viz., Shri Manchhubhai M. Zariwala, the then President of the Surat Zari Merchants' Association and Shri Vaikunthbhai B. Shastri & Shri R.T. Popatwala representing the employers and Shri Ishverbhai G. Desai of Zari Kamdar Mandal representing the employees. The Enquiry Committee visited all the zari centres in the country including Surat and after making all possible on-the-spot studies, submitted a report to the Government of India in the year 1958. The Zari Industry Inquiry Committee, which was the first of its kind for such a cottage and small-scale industry in our country, made very important and useful recommendations to the Government to effect an all-round improvement for the survival and organised development of the industry.

It seemed that the condition of workers was of much concern. For instance, the Zari Industry Inquiry Committee, appointed by Government of India in 1957 specifically mentioned about the worker's condition. They recommended that

(1) State Govt. should take steps to enforce such provisions of Factory Act as it relates at least to the hygienic and other amenities for workers;

(2) A few family planning centres should be established in areas where there is a concentration of Zari units and;

(3) Fixation of minimum wages for each type of work for full-time employment.

Zari Merchants Association (ZMA) contested many of these recommendations. The first very important recommendation implemented by the Government was to put the industry under the care of the All India Handicrafts Board and to take necessary steps urgently as suggested by the Committee in their report. The Handicrafts Board, as a follow-up step, constituted an All India Zari advisory Committee to find out ways and means to put the industry on a sound footing and promote zari exports. In 1959, the Government took the first concrete step in the direction of export promotion on the recommendation of the Board by announcing Zari Export Promotion Scheme. Under the scheme, zari exporters were to be given incentive licences for import of raw materials to enable them to offer zari at competitive rates in the world market. Zari exports increased slowly and helped the industry in a little way to improve its unhealthy state. But, after this major step, no noteworthy progress was made in the implementation of other recommendations either by the State or by the Central Government excepting a few.

The condition of the industry, which showed slight improvement, following the implementation of a few recommendations of the Board, continued to deteriorate due to many burning problems like the soaring market prices of the essential imported raw materials like bullion, copper, silk and art-silk and their inadequate supply, the dwindling in exports due to great price disparity of bullion in the Indian and foreign markets and cut-throat competition due to over production and glut in the market. However, in 1962, an epoch making event took place in the history of Zari Industry, viz. the formation of a Central Organisation of the Indian Zari Industry and Trade called the All India Federation of Zari Industry with its headquarters in Surat. The Federation represented all the zari centres in the country and was an all-India apex organisation of zari industry and trade. Because of its all India character the problems and issues raised, drew immediate attention of the Government. Many difficult problems like the allotment of gold under Gold Control Act and revision of the Export Promotion Scheme to make it realistic and streamlining of raw materials supply etc. were addressed with varying degrees of success.

Recent History (1980 Onwards)

Sardar Patel Institute of Economic and Social Research carried out a study on zari industry in Surat based on sample survey during 1981-

82. The study was restricted to 300 firms and 500 workers of the industry. The question arose about the number of Zari units in Surat at the time of survey. According to the officials of Zari Merchants' Association (ZMA), Surat, there were 2300 units; according to Surat Municipal Corporation (SMC) authorities, there were 1200 units and according to District Industrial Centre (DIG) there were only 237 units. Zari Merchants' Association could not provide the list of 2300 units with their location and size of employment of the unit. From the SMC's office, it was possible to get the list of 1200 units with their addresses. However, only 759 units were listed with SMC office with the correct name, address and size of employment. Thus, the preliminary observation revealed inconsistency about the number of zari manufacturing units in Surat. Based on the same study, zari production was estimated at Rs.28 crores, employment of 7000 workers and exports were estimated at Rs.7 lakhs. 52 percent of the total employment consisted of family employment and female participation was around 34 per cent. Further, it was also noted that child labour proportion was around 9 per cent in case of family employment.

TABLE 1.8.1 ON NEXT PAGE...

Table 1.8.1 ZARI INDUSTRY - 1980

	Sample	Population*
No. of Units	300	759
Output (Rs.)	11,17,20,353	28,26,52,493
Export (Rs.)	2,87,907	7,28,405
Employment (No.)	2793	7066
Family Employment (No.)	1458	3689
Hired Workers (No.)	1335	3377
Male Participation (No.)	409	1038
Total Employment	1601	4051
Female Participation (No.)	961	2431
Child Participation (No.)	231	582

Source : SPIESR Study on Zari Industry, Monograph Series, No. 17, 1992
*Estimated from the sample.

Apart from these, the study contained the following observations:

1. The extent of poverty among Zari workers was not high. Only 53 households (12.50 per cent of the sample households) or 402 persons (14.58 per cent of persons from the sampled households) were poverty-stricken.

2. Zari manufacturing consists of many activities (viz. Drawing of wire, flattening of wire, winding etc.)

3. Forty-four per cent of the units were more than 20 years old. In 89 per cent of the cases, the ownership had not changed even once, 86 per

cent of the units were found to be operating at the place of residence and 80 per cent of the entrepreneurs owned premises where firms were located. Only 13 per cent were relatively new units, which were established 5 years before the survey. The relatively older units had higher investment, higher output and higher employment.

4. Fresh additions to the machinery and equipment necessary for the manufacturing activities were quite meagre (nearly 1 per cent of the fixed assets).

5. Though testing facilities were available at nominal rates, very few units/entrepreneurs were making the use of these facilities. This indifference of the units affected the marketing activity of zari goods in the domestic market. The proportion of zari exports to total production was very low.

6. Majority of entrepreneurs and workers were from the same community i.e. Rana community. The interaction between workers and entrepreneurs was quite cordial.

7. The workers mostly inherited the craft of zari making.

8. Most of the workers received wages either equal to or more than the government recommended minimum wage rate prevailing at that time. However, no other benefits were extended to the workers.

9. Average size of the workers' family was more than 6 persons.

From then on, the zari industry picked up the speed and today zari industry is on its peak level.

1.9 PICTORIAL PRESENTATION OF ZARI AND ZARI PRODUCTS

IMPORTANT ZARDOZI CENTRES OF INDIA

Jammu & Kashmir			
Punjab	: Patiala	Madhya Pradesh	: Bhopal
Delhi			Burhanpur
Uttar Pradesh	: Agra		Ujjain
	Farrukhabad		Gwalior
	Kanpur	Maharashtra	: Bombay
	Lucknow		Aurangabad
	Banaras		Paithan
	Ramnagar	Andhra Pradesh	: Hyderabad
	Meerut	Karnataka	: Dharwar
	Bareilly		Gulbargah
Bihar	: Patna	West Bengal	: Calcutta
Rajasthan	: Jaipur	Dacca	
	Jodhpur Jaisalmer	Sind	
Gujarat	: Ahmedabad Bikaner		
	Surat Junagadh		
	Baroda Kutch		

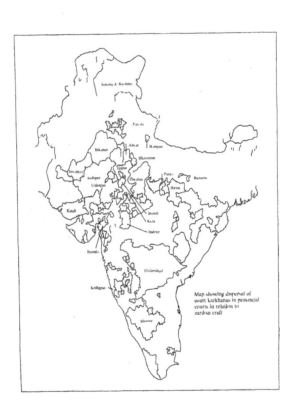

Map showing dispersal of court karkhanas in provincial courts in relation to zardozi craft

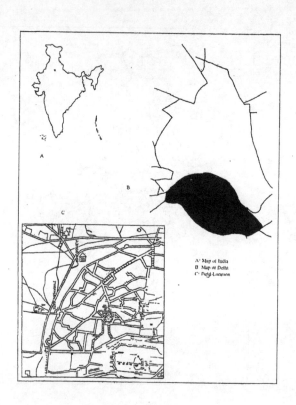

A : Map of India
B : Map of Delhi
C : Field Location

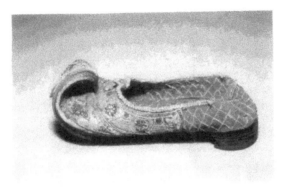

4. The footwear worn by noble ladies

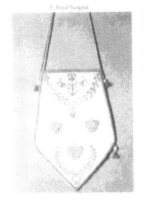

5. Royal Insignia

6. Knee-high boots

7 Miniature painting showing *Darbar of Shah Alam* end of 18th Century

8 *Takhtpush*. Complete view.

9. Detail of architectural monument of *takhtposh*.

10. Detail of tiger hunt depicted on *takhtposh*.

11. Detail of the hunter on a galloping horse.　　　　　　12. Detail of the deer running for life.

13. *Takhtposh* with floral motifs

14. Detail of the corner

15. Zaminposh, the floor spread.

16. Zaminposh, the floor cover.

17. Zaminposh, the floor cover.

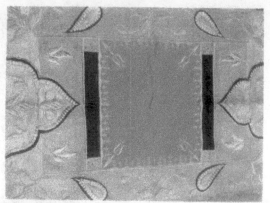

18. Khanposh, the floor spread for eating.

19. Detail of corner.

20. Miniature painting depicting raga *Hindola*.

21. Masnad Cover.

22. Cushion cover, (above)

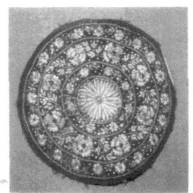

23. Thalposh with thathmana design.

24. Thalposh. Early 20the century

25. Umbrella.

26. Shia Flag.

27. Railing pillars, Sandstone, Bharhut Stupa.

28. Portrait of Sultan Hussain Mirza.

29. Darbar Hanging

30. Hanging, Puthia.

31. Hanging, Puthia.

32. Astrangir from provincial court of Rajasthan

33. Bedspread, silk, embroidered with coloured silk and gold thread.

34. Saddle cotton fabric.

35. Parasol.

36. Semi-circular holster, red velvet, depicting floral creeper design in vasli technique.

37. Camel saddle from Jodhpur showing gold and silver embroidery.

38. Mehtabgiri procession fan fixed on a tall wooden handle, brass knobs.

39. Chaubagla, man's upper garment.

40. Design detail

41. Lahenga

42. Kurtani

43. Cap of typical zardozi motifs.

44. Back view of the same.

45. Several designs and form of purses.
46. Hukka.
47. Bisat of Chopad, the spread for playing the game of chopad.
48. Elaborate process of wire drawing adopted in Punjab.
49. Panel on silk fabric with meenakari.

50. Gold wire drawers from Yeola, Uttar Pradesh

51. Gold wire drawers from Yeola, Uttar Pradesh

52. Zardoz seen working.

53. Zardoz using hath ari.

54. A zardoz woman.
55. Detail of couching technique.

56. Another hearth in the same premises.
57. A child carrying the karchob from one household to another.

58. Two girls stitching the cloth on shamsharak.

59. Karchob fitted with cloth now ready for embroidery.
60. Boys and girls working in domestic karkhana.

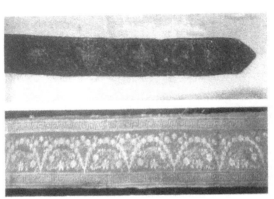

61. Patka.
62. Sword cover
63. Detail of
    sword cover (above)

64. Long shawl

65. Dupatta.   66. Neck Scarf.

67. Angarkha

68. Bugalbandi, a tight fitting ladies costume.

69. Angarkha.

70 Achkan

71. Choga.

72. Another view of choga.

73. Abho

74. Detail of design on front yoke

75. Back view

76. Jacket

77. Jacket

78. Jacket

79. Front view

80. Crown.

(159)

81. Mandel, the circular cap.

82. Topi.

83. Mandel, highly ornated cap.

84. Mandel

85. Juti.

86. Raja Bhoj, the rod puppet of prominant King.

87. Purses with meenakari work.

88. Zardoz girl posing to show the fashion accessories   89. Pankha

90. Taj with silver wire on velvet.

91. A miniature folio showing the process of gold melting. Patiala school of painting.

92. Mohd. Farid's wife working on adda.

93. Shamsharak and farad when not in use.

94. Detail of vasli ka kam.

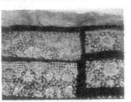
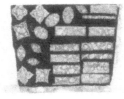

95. Position of craftsperson while working.
96. Range of buta and bel designs.
97. Range of buta and bel designs.
98. Zardoz girl learning basics of the craft.
99. Ganla batua designs.
100. Range of buta and bel designs.

101. Copper wire drawing units (PAWTHA)

102. Copper wire drawing units (PAWTHA)

103. Copper wire drawing unit

104. Flattening Unit

105. Winding of Lametta

106. Drawing through dyes

107. Kasab winding machine

108. Gilding of copper wire by silver in cement concrete or polythene tanks

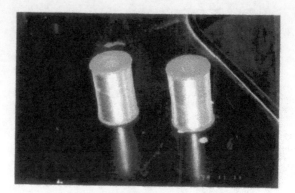

109. Zari Bobbins (Firka)

110. TANIA UNITS

111. Silver electroplated copper wire in fine gauges (Tania Units)

112. Drawing of copper wire

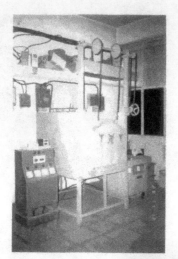

113. Melting of Silver

114. Kangri Unit

115. Hammering of Silver

116. Melting of Silver

117. INITIAL BARS OF COPPER USED IN IMITATION ZARI

118. INITIAL BARS OF COPPER USED IN IMITATION ZARI

119. BADGES

120. BADGES

121. BADGES

122. BADGES

123. BADGES

124. CUSHION COVERS

125. CUSHION AND CURTAIN COVERS

126. COVERS

127 JACKET AND COVER

128. BADGES AND PURSES

129. BOBBINS

130. BANGLES AND VARIOUS PRODUCTS

131. PURSES AND LACES

132. PURSES

133. DRESSES

134. PURSES

135. LACES

136. PURSES

137. ACCESSORIES

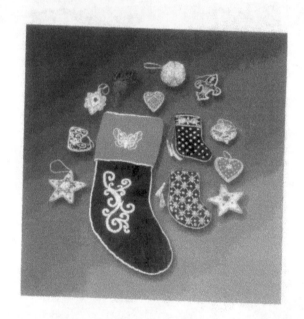

138. HAND PURSES

139. COVERS

140. BADGES AND OTHER PRODUCTS

141. LACES

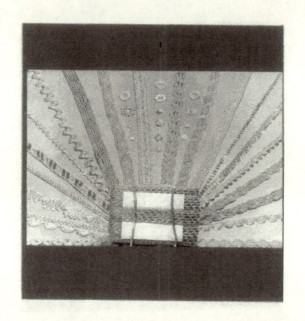

142. LACES

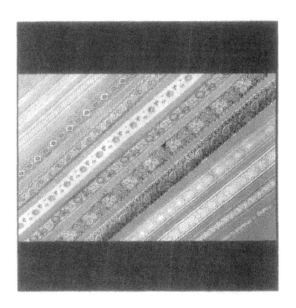

143. LACES

144. VARIOUS LACES

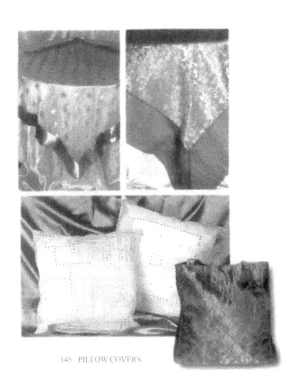

145 PILLOW COVERS

146. DRESS AND OTHERS

147. COSMETICS ACCESSORIES

148. BOBBINS AND THREADS

149. DRESSES

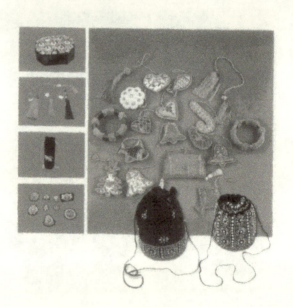

150. VARIOUS PRODUCTS

151. BLOUSES AND DRESSES

152. BUYERS AND SELLERS MEET AT BARAILEY

153. ALLOTMENT OF CERTIFICATE TO ZARIZARDOZI TRAINEE

154. INAUGURATION OF ZARI WORK TRAINING CUM DESIGN WORK SHOP

155. TRAINEES OF ZARI ZARDOZI WORK

156. PRODUCTS OF HANDICRAFTS

CHAPTER 2 :

BASIC ISSUES OF ZARI INDUSTRY

		Page No.
2.1	SWOT ANALYSIS.	213
2.2	INFRASTRUCTURE FACILITIES IN SURAT.	224
2.3	PROSPECTS AHEAD IN INDIA FOR ZARI.	226
2.4	ROLE OF PUBLIC REPRESENTATIVE i.e. MEMBER OF PARLIAMENT / MEMBER OF LEGISLATIVE ASSEMBLY.	230
2.5	ROLE OF CHAMBER OF COMMERCE.	233
2.5.1	ROLE OF GOVERNMENT IN THE DEVELOPMENT OF ZARI INDUSTRY.	234
2.5.2	ROLE OF ELECTRICITY COMPANIES IN THE DEVELOPMENT OF ZARI INDUSTRY.	235
2.5.3	ROLE OF BANKING AND TERM LENDING FINANCIAL INSTITUTION IN THE DEVELOPMENT OF ZARI INDUSTRY IN SURAT.	236
2.5.4	ROLE OF MUNICIPAL CORPORATION.	245
2.6	NEED OF MARKETING CO-OPERATIVE SOCIETY.	246
2.7	ENVIRONMENTAL ASPECTS.	247

CHAPTER 2 : BASIC ISSUES OF ZARI INDUSTRY

Zari industry is one of the oldest and antique industry. This industry is totally based on the skill and artistic pattern of labourers (artisans). It has its own reputation and goodwill in the world market. Inspite of ups and downs of the trade the industry has steadily grown. This industry earns foreign exchange also.

The survival of this industry has become difficult today because of various factors but the specific skill of the artisans and the industry still has a high reputation.

Unity of merchants in different segments of the industry is a positive indication for its survival. Particularly in Surat the unity of merchants has strengthened the industry. Specific dry weather, community, lower investment tradition are also other positive factors which have contributed immensely for the survival of this industry.

Some of the basic issues facing the zari industry are :

· Lack of administrative experiences.
· Distinctive area of marketing/decentralized marketing.
· Degradation of quality.
· Upgradation of technology.
· Lack of satisfied financial assistance.

- Higher costing of product.
- Gambling of prices.
- Non-Standardization of product.
- Lack of Research & development.
- Increasing competitors from the same industry.
- Lack of marketing network.
- Lack of publicity.
- Non-Awareness of laws and rules.
- Lack of innovation.
- Lack of strategy.
- Threat of substitutes.

2.1 SWOT ANALYSIS

#STRENGTHS:-

Zari Industry is one of the oldest and antique industry. This industry is totally based on the skill and artistic pattern of labourers (artisans). It has its own reputation and goodwill in the world market. Inspite of ups and downs of the trade, the industry has kept its stability. This industry forms a part of handicraft in National economy, which shares a major part of foreign exchange earning. The survival of this industry has become difficult today because of various factors but the specific skill of the artisans and the industry still has a high reputation.

Unity of Merchants in different segments of the industry is a positive indication for its survival. Particularly in Surat the unity of merchants has strengthened the industry. Nowadays over production is a headache for the industry and to tackle this issue, Merchants' Association observes Bandh twice a week. It is a best example of unity to curb over production.

Specific Dry Weather of Surat also is an important and favourable factor which has strengthened the industry. Entire industry's survival depends on this factor. Continuos water supply & Electricity supply are also the effective factors which has strengthened the industry at large.

The industry inspite of ups and downs has still maintained its level because it is totally community based. Specifically "RANA" community has its own identity in the zari industry. Lower investment and employment generation capacity makes the industry progress. Tradition has become a tool to strengthen the industry. Zari industry has attained the status of an art.

WEAKNESS:-

Zari industry still has not attained a satisfactory growth because of the following issues :

(1) Lack of administrative experience:

Any business/industry requires an administrative experience. However zari industry has an experience but lacks administration, It has good manufacturing units. In this business/industry people have no professional education or training. It is not properly managed. It is only on the base of thumb rule which has been traditionally achieved. The traditional approach and lack of initiativeness has led to a decline. In fact, 75% to 80% people involved in this business are illiterate.

In real practice, the location of industry and environment in which industry runs also affects the development of industry. There is lack of proper management. Management requires planning, coordination and control which this industry lacks. There is no budgetary system or cost control. In other words we can say that there is no method of cost control or knowledge of cost. People involved in the business are all from one family which leads to the concentration of functioning in the industry. There is no calculation of salary and wages also.

(2) Distinctive area of marketing:

Zari is manufactured in Surat but it is not utilised to prepare different products. The utilization of the product is made only in Varanasi, Chennai, Bareilly or other areas of southern states. Due to this, the supply & distribution of these goods is at a distinctive place. Not only this, there is even a language problem and a problem of recovery of amount from them. Merchants are required to stay for a considerably longer period of time in southern region. During this period, they suffer immense loss because they are unable to take care of their business.

(3) Degradation of Quality or Lack of Quality Product:

The industry suffers from lack of good quality. The quality is not being maintained by the merchants as well as manufacturers. Most of the traders/manufacturers stress on profit earning. They are not aware of the fact that quality makes the industry firm and strong. Manufacturers/traders are only interested in selling the product and getting back the money. There is no fixed tool for measuring the quality. The total control on quality is not there. It is based on experience and reputation of the firm in a market as well as relation developed by the forefathers. This has made the industry unsteady. People who are expert and well versed in their skill are not ready to develop their quality. There is no research and development in industry. Each one wants to earn money and also do hard work but that is laborious and unplanned. Quality has also suffered due to unavailability of laboratory. The entire quality of the product depends on the mixing of chemicals. But still there is no measurement or a fixed ratio for mixing the chemicals. Only on the tradition base and experience, industry has been able to maintain quality.

(4) Lack of Upgradation of technology:

Zari industry has its own reputation built on traditionalism and technology. Surat zari industry has its own technology of machineries which has also been traditionally developed. New technological development has not taken place. Till today the old patterns & styles of manufacturing are adopted. Compared to other countries, we are far behind technologically..

(5) Lack of satisfied financial assistance:

Financial facilities available with the industry, are insufficient. The economical situation of the merchants/traders is not good. The total finance available is also at a higher rate of interest. So even with maximum profit, earning remains low. Government has also not provided any assistance in the form of subsidies etc.

(6) Higher costing of product :

The industry suffers from a lot of over production and competitive environment. Due to that the cost of product is high. The total cost of product increases due to wastage of raw material, loss of time to start, waste of power, etc.

(7) Gambling of prices:

This is an important factor which is harmful for the industry. The whole industry collapses due to gambling of prices by the merchants or traders.

The internal competition and hazardous production amongst them, makes the traders/merchants to gamble the prices. This deteriorates the whole price structure of the industry. This is a very serious problem which the industry is facing today. For the past two months, industry is faced with a setback.

(8) Non-standardization of product:

In this industry, the product is non-standardized. No gradation is there for the product. Due to lack of quality control the industry is on the verge of collapse.

(9) Lack of Research & Development:

Any business or industry requires to be developed through Research & Development. It is the need of the hour. As we have mentioned earlier the approach of this industry is traditional and is hereditary and governed by uneducated people. Therefore, there is no research and development. We do not find any research at the level of production, administration, marketing or advertising.

(10) Increasing competitors from the same industry:

The industry faces internal competition amongst different groups. Initially those who were akhadedars have become traders and therefore the competition has increased.

On the whole, industry has become more competitive due to new entrepreneurs, lower investment and lesser risk. Initially only specific community based people were there but now other communities have also entered the industry.

(11) Lack of marketing Network:

This is an important factor which has become a permanent type of weakness. Marketing is the heart of industry. This industry suffers from lacuna in marketing. Traditionally there was direct marketing by the traders and manufacturers to utilizers in southern states which has always been a problem for the industry. This industry has not developed any marketing network.

(12) Lack of Publicity:

An important barrier for this industry is the lack of publicity.

Advertisements are not used to create awareness for the product. In order to boost sales, proper publicity is required.

(13) Non-Awareness of laws & Rules:

This is yet another flaw of the industry as there is no knowledge of rules and laws of different taxes.

(14) Lack of innovation :

Innovation is significant for any industry but this industry has not shown any innovativeness.

(15) Lack of strategy:

The industry or business requires to form strategy for further development and competitiveness. But this industry lacks strategic planning because of lack of exposure and awareness.

(16) Threat of Substitute:

This industry today suffers a big threat from the substitute product. Real and Imitation zari has replaced Mettalic zari which is very cheap and easy to produce.

OPPORTUNITIES :

Inspite of all the problems and shortcomings, Zari industry has immense chances of development, but it requires specific type of skill as well as the upgradation of technology. It requires to standardize the product. Marketing should be developed with professionalism. The domestic market should be developed. Domestic market has a lot of scope for marketing. The local market is also required to be developed. Surat is an upcoming market for readymade garments. The local manufacturers should develop their own skill by way of designing, upgrading the technical knowledge as well as research and development.

If industry follows the gradation and standardization with quality control, there is a chance to develop the market at local and national level. The home market is quite poor. Surat city has plenty of sources to develop the utilization of Zari through readymade garments. But this dearth of developing the expertise as well as specialized knowledge through artisans could be developed through adequate research in that area.

The economy of the country is developing and therefore there is a lot of chance to develop the zari industry. Globalization and Liberalization offer opportunities to increase import and export.

In the last three years, the then textile minister Kashiram Rana had even started the zari development programme by organizing training camps and arranging different fairs in different regions. He even motivated the artisans and acknowledged the importance of research. Indians have to take the benefit of that.

Fashion is a routine course of action for the new generation. Industry has to make efforts to develop different designs and special products to utilize zari.

Still there is a great scope to develop the industry as it is an antique industry.

This should be understood by the zari manufacturers. An attempt should be made to fulfill the needs of different group of customers. This industry should try and cater to the different criterial, selective, tastes of the customers.

This industry has a good future if it adopts a strategical approach by knowing the threats, weaknesses and strengths. It will have to apply aggressive strategy to create new resources to develop the industry. Strategies could be developed through different angles. There may be defensive, diversification and turn around strategies to develop the same.

Expansion of export market:

Distinctiveness.

Substitution of product.

THREATS :

(1) Industrial unrest:

The scenario of zari industry, in the last two months is quite hazy. The industry has had its good record of unity but due to the overproduction and dumping of material, there are now chances of industrial unrest.

(2) Deflationary and disguised unemployment:

Unemployment has been created due to heavy deflation. There is even disguised unemployment where there is a need of only three or four people, the whole family is employed. This factor has also adversely affected the industry.

(3) Decrease in foreign exchange:

Today the major part of foreign exchange earning is from zari industry in handicrafts. If zari industry collapses, it will reduce the foreign exchange earning. A major problem would arise in economy.

(4) Decrease in the national income:

Due to foreign exchange, there is a strengthening of national economy. If the income from foreign exchange decreases, it will also lead to a decrease in the national income.

(5) Government has to allow exemption:

Government will have to give exemption for taxes on copper, silver and gold to save the industry and also provide initiative to develop the industry to attract new investment in the industry. Special zones should be declared and exemption should be given in taxes. Special subsidized rates of interest will also have to be declared.

(6) Controlling authority on selling the product or creating the solicities for purchasing the finished goods:

There is a dearth of controlling authority to sell the goods by purchasing the total production through traders. To control the price, there is a requirement to see that the goods are purchased in one place and then it is sold by one authority to classify the grades and standards.

2.2 INFRASTRUCTURE FACILITIES IN SURAT :

Zari industry in Surat has a full fledged infrastructure facilities like transportation, electricity, raw-materials as well as other facilities like communication, banking as well as insurance.

The area in which zari industry is located gets the facility of electricity. The electricity charges are fluctuative. The total cost of production is related with the cost of electricity. Continuous supply of electricity is one of the beneficial factor for the industry. There is a continuous water supply by Municipal Corporation. Initially i.e. 10-15 years back there was the problem of availability of water, but now there is no difficulty. Due to continuous and constant flow of water the industry has flourished.

Communication today is the simple and easy. Surat is one of the major cities of Gujarat which provides enough facilities for communication. Communication takes place through telephone, postage and other courier services. Nowadays, even internet services are available.

Ten years back, people had to go to southern regions for many days, but with easy communication it is no longer required.

Transportation facilities like road transport, railway transport and other transport facilities are available which supports the industry's development. Surat is a city attached with major railway lines as well as other air lines facility and is near to Baroda & Ahmedabad. To sell the by-products and finished goods the major market is available in Surat. So the transportation facilities contributes to the industry's development.

Insurance facilities are also available for this sector. However since 80% of the people are illiterate, they are unaware of this concept. People are not taking the benefit of fire insurance as well as life insurance. Mortality rate is high and instances of fire have become more dangerous. Insurance at this stage is inevitable.

Banking facility is also easily available. The industry gets the major benefit from co-operative banks situated in their own area. The merchants have created their own credit co-op. society, which provides the raw materials like copper, silver and other materials. It also lends the money needed in different parts of the zari industry. Banks have played an important role in the development of the industry. The major role of credit co-operative society is to develop the zari industry in the region.

So, infrastructure facilities for the zari industry is the most favourable segment of Surat and adjoining regions. Infrastructure facilities inclusive of all available factors area support the industry.

2.3 PROSPECTS AHEAD IN INDIA FOR ZARI:

India is one of the major suppliers of zari handicrafts to the world market. Despite the existence of production base and a large number of craftsmen, India has not been able to cash on the opportunities. This is mainly because of the following reasons:-

a) The production and supply have continued to be inadequate.
b) The quality and finish are not upto the mark.
c) The price standard is not maintained.
d) The product development is not well conceived.

The prospects for increasing zari exports from India are considered bright provided the problems as stated above are solved and the measures as discussed and suggested in some of the following paragraphs are adopted.

Although India has a large production base for handicrafts, production of zari handicrafts is inadequate to cope with the demand. Production is erratic and is not organised on a regular or continuous basis. The craftsmen do not work full time since they have other occupations. Lack of adequate skilled craftsmen and non-availability of the raw materials are the other factors responsible for inadequate production. Inadequate and erratic production effect the overseas supplies and the delivery schedule. In order to augment production on a continuous basis for export besides ensuring organised production and adequate supplies of required quantities and quality of raw materials the strength of the artisans, particularly skilled ones, has to be increased by providing training facilities and certain production processes have to be mechanised without compromising the hand and art work involved in the same.

Besides inadequate and erratic production, the quality and finish of the zari handicrafts are not consistent. Quality of zari handicrafts has deteriorated over year. This has happened mainly because of the raw material. Quality and colour used are not consistent. Since zari handicrafts are handmade products and each piece is different from the other it may not be possible to maintain exact or accurate standard in quality while producing in bulk. Some manufactures however, in the absence of quality control measure, sometimes take undue advantage of this and spoil their own image in the overseas markets. In the interest of enhancing the image of Indian handicrafts in the overseas markets, it will be better if minimum quality standard is maintained. Apart from the use of quality raw-materials in required proportion, steps should also be taken for mechanisation of certain processes to ensure uniformity and excellent finish of the handicrafts. Workmanship could also be improved if handicrafts production (meant for export) is organised through skilled craftsmen and are strictly supervised.

Price is an important factor in the marketing of zari handicrafts. The *consumers* are price conscious. They have a liking for handicrafts but if the handicrafts are too costly in relation to the machine made product, they just do not buy it. Besides machine made substitute, Indian handicrafts face competition from handicrafts originating from other developing countries, which are cheaper. In view of this, the price of handicrafts should to the extent possible be kept within reasonable limits subject to a given quality. Prices of Indian zari handicrafts are comparatively high because of the high cost of raw material. If India has to cater to the needs of the price conscious buyers, steps should also be taken to ensure supply of raw material at reasonable price for economising export production and supplies.

Zari Handicrafts in the overseas market are liked and bought for their novelty. The novelties particularly of decorative items over years have become out of date due to changes in taste and preference. The customers as well as the importers are always on the look out for something unusual and new items of handicrafts. As a result the demand for new items of handicrafts with some unusual features is on the increase. Indian manufactures/ exporters over the years have continued to supply the same old products without taking due notice of the changing trend of demand in overseas market. The initiative taken and work done in India relating to product development and innovation in handicrafts for exports is rather insignificant despite the existence of required skill in India for innovating new products and adopting old products to suit consumer taste and preferences. The manufacturers who are mainly catering to seasonal demands in the overseas market should take necessary initatives and steps for product development and innovation in handicrafts.

2.4 ROLE OF PUBLIC REPRESENTATIVE i.e. MEMBER OF PARLIAMENT / MEMBER OF LEGISLATIVE ASSEMBLY:

Zari industry is mainly centralised in Surat. The local public representative elected from this area has also played an important role to develop the industry. Member of legislative assembly Ex. M.L.A. Gulabdas Khatri & Dhirubhai Gajera have taken keen interest to support the akhadedars manufacturers through government of Gujarat.

The Member of Parliament, the current Rural Development Minister and Ex. Textile Minister Hon'ble Kashiram Rana has played a major role to develop the industry. Actually, he started his career from the zari industry. He is also a part of zari industry. During his tenure as a Textile Minister, he tried a lot to expand the industry.

Kashiram Rana took core steps to develop the industry and laid stress on developing the zari industry by boosting export. (he earned a lot of foreign exchange for the government). His target now to revive the zari industry as he holds the portfolio of handicraft industry selection.

The steps taken by him to evolve and develop the zari industry are as follows :

ZARI PARK :

Zari is processed in different ways. Chemicalisationists, artisans, manufacturers, etc. all work with their machines in their own residential areas. A need was felt to create a ZARI PARK in Surat to provide the people with a specific area apart from their residential area to develop the zari industry.

Hon'ble Kashiram Rana got the help from Gujarat government and has launched a project of ZARI PARK at Kosad, near Surat where the project of residence as well as work-shade are underway. Gujarat government has allotted land in which 127 units would be set up.

DELEGATION OF ZARI IN FOREIGN COUNTRIES :

Hon'ble Kashiram Rana internationalized the demand for zari. He even sent a zari manufacturer's delegation to undertake research and study zari markets of different countries.

In 1998, a delegation was sent to Pakistan to see the export areas in embroidery threads, borders, termings, edges, frings, tussels, brides, etc. In 2000, another delegation was sent to France & U.K. Netherland to explore the market avenues, new technical innovations, designing, etc. in zari.

ZARI - ZARDOZHI TRAINING CAMP :

The dream of Hon'ble Kashiram Rana is to make Surat, a major centre of zari manufacturing to largest user of end product of zari. He first time in the history organised the training camp in Surat and adjoining areas. In these camps, people were trained to prepare the end product. Training was given to ladies by experts. The camps proved helpful for generating self-employment to the women in the industry. More than 300 womens underwent training and can now prepare the end product.

The women even got Rs. 500/- as stipend from the handicrafts board of textile minister. Each camp was alloted Rs. 1 lac. by the government.

ZARI - BUYER - SELLER MEET :

The full-fledged process of zari is not done in any place in the country. Surat, on the contrary, is an expert in producing all zari threads. Barelli, Varanasi, Agra, etc. are famous for the end products of zari. In order to simplify the sale and purchase of zari and zari products, to overcome the crisis between the purchaser and seller, more discussion amongst the people of zari and zari industry are held. Hon'ble Kashiram Rana initiated this buyer-seller meet and granted permission for this.

Due to this the crisis could be solved. The quality of product, price of the product, transportation problems could be solved by the government under the guidance of Hon'ble Kashiram Rana.

2.5 ROLE OF CHAMBER OF COMMERCE:

The southern chamber of commerce has played an important role in zari industry. The chamber has immensely contributed to revive the industry. A survey was conducted 5 to 6 years back by the southern chamber of commerce to study the structure of industry and it acted as an intermediary body to solve the problems. It even suggested the state government to allow more exemptions for the industry. Not only this, the chamber extended their ideas even to the central government. Chamber helped the industry to advertise the product by organizing a Fair and by giving special concessions. Chamber arranged many seminars in collaboration with the government as well as Export Promotion Council to upgrade the industry. Chamber has played a role of a friend, philosopher and guide. Chamber always was on the fore to solve the problems and provide solutions for the industry by raising the resources.

2.5.1 ROLE OF GOVERNMENT IN THE DEVELOPMENT OF ZARI INDUSTRY:

For any country's development government is an important part because it frames policies and programmes. Indeed the Indian government and government of Gujarat has tried to develop the industry accumulatively but has failed in laying specific stress on the development of zari. Specific policies have not been framed. Exemption has not been allowed. Subsidies have not been given.

Government has only linked it to handicrafts. There is a differentiation between the policies framed by state and central rulings. Political effects are more on the policies. M. P. Mr. Kashiram Rana however when became the textile minister, paid more attention and focussed on many schemes and training programmes. However still the output is not sufficient. A lot needs to be done for this neglected sector.

2.5.2 ROLE OF ELECTRICITY COMPANIES IN THE DEVELOPMENT OF ZARI INDUSTRY :

The industry runs totally on electricity so there is a vital need of power supply.

Due to power cut, the industry suffers from a severe set back. Because of it the problem of clipping and flattening the silver wires arises. The thickness is not maintained.

Sometimes the gilding is also not properly maintained due to power cuttings. The quality of product deteriorates and even the finishing suffers. Voltage fluctuation disturbs the different processes. It is harmful for real jari. Surat electricity Board has given a good continuous support to the industry by supplying continuous supply of power guarantee. If the electricity supply is not regulated it may affect the bread and butter of the people.

2.5.3 ROLE OF BANKING AND TERM LENDING FINANCIAL INSTITUTIONS IN THE DEVELOPMENT OF ZARI INDUSTRY IN SURAT:

As we know that any industrial development requires financial assistance by the financial institution, zari industry has also been developed by the financial institutions like Surat Zari Producer Co-operative Society Ltd. and other organisations. It could be said that Surat Zari Producer Co-operative Society Ltd. has actually made the survival of the industry possible. This society was established in 1944, with membership of 61 members having share capital of Rs. 14,780/- but today if we look at the membership, it is of 3004 and members share capital of Rs. 4,08,850/- and profit is of Rs. 10,23,714/-.

Society advances loans not only in cash but also provides the raw materials like silver, gold and copper. It also provides chemicals, yarn, cotton at reasonable rates to the members of zari industry. Society is not only providing the credit facilities but it is also cautious about the problems of the industry. Society solved the basic problem of excise, sale spirit, etc. It even arranged the Mega Exhibition - 98 for the development of zari with the help of government and South Gujarat Chamber of Commerce and arranged seminars and workshops training camps with the help of government. The knowledge of import/export to the members was also provided by the society and an attempt was made to cultivate a saving habit among the members and improve their socio-economic conditions.

Apart from this, the South Zari Co-operative Society, other banks like Surat Legal Commercial Bank have also played an important role in the development of zari industry. But what we observed was that the society took keen interest in providing the raw materials but it did not take any interest in the purchase of the recently made zari and neither have they helped in selling the product.

TABLE 2.5.3.1

THE SURAT ZARI GOODS PRODUCER'S CO-OP. SOC. LTD.

YEARS	MEMBER-SHIP	SHARE CAPITAL	OTHER FUNDS	RESERVE FUNDS	DIVIDEND
1944-45	251	22380	-	251	6.25%
1945-46	354	25990	-	1958	6.25%
1949-50	504	32020	-	5505	6.25%
1950-51	551	36320	-	6511	6.25%
1951-52	572	38500	-	8286	6.25%
1952-53	575	34000	-	10294	3.25%
1953-54	570	39040	-	10338	5.25%
1954-55	576	64600	-	11144	6.25%
1955-56	515	83470	-	12832	6.25%
1956-57	503	87230	7038	17132	6.25%
1957-58	503	90380	16784	26643	6.25%
1958-59	528	103140	16784	30663	6.25%
1959-60	574	137370	16031	34419	6.25%
1960-61	598	139140	13281	36417	6.25%
1961-62	616	119230	12004	39725	6.25%
1962-63	516	121590	32671	53767	8.25%
1963-64	527	124624	101277	66474	9.00%
1964-65	604	138710	142157	81707	9.00%
1965-66	602	140460	169970	93613	8.00%
1966-67	620	140590	171407	97844	-
1967-68	617	140300	171327	98002	-
1968-69	621	134680	171327	98172	-
1969-70	644	135650	170726	98412	-

Chart 2.5.3.1 (A)

MEMBERSHIP

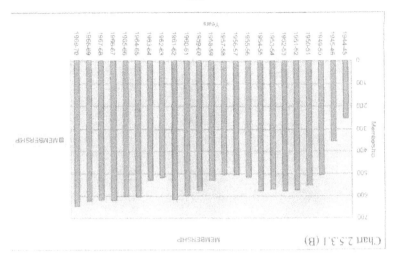

Chart 2.5.3.1 (B)

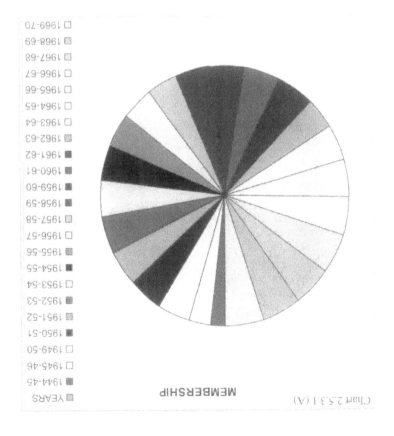

(238)

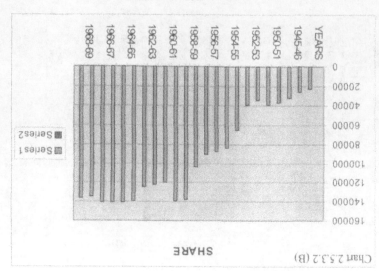

Chart 2.5.3.2 (A)

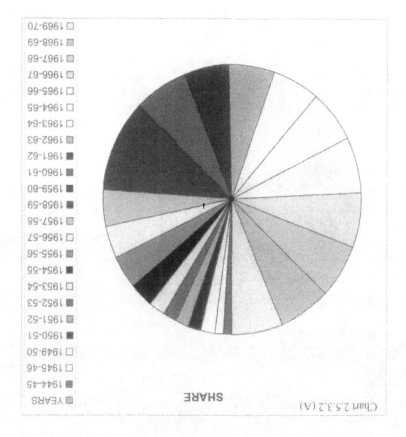

Chart 2.5.3.2 (B)

Chart 2.5.3.3 (A)

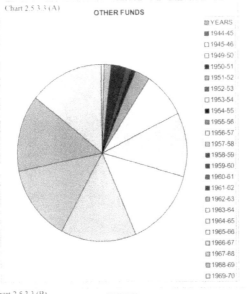

Chart 2.5.3.3 (B)

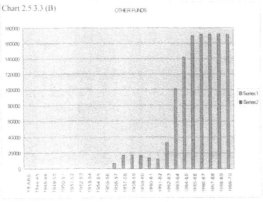

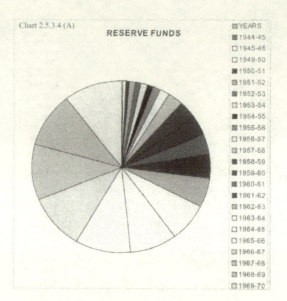

Chart 2.5.3.4 (A) RESERVE FUNDS

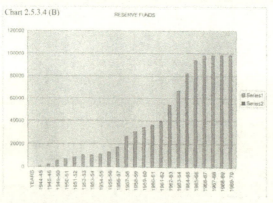

Chart 2.5.3.4 (B) RESERVE FUNDS

(241)

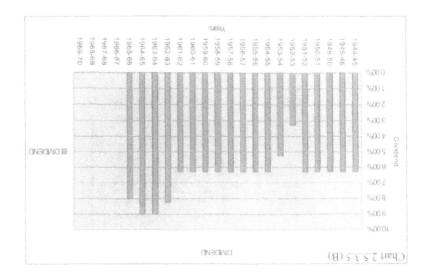

Chart 2.5.3.5 (B)

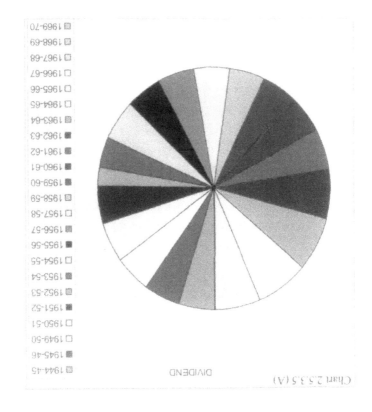

Chart 2.5.3.5 (A)

TABLE 2.5.3.2 THE SURAT ZARI GOODS PRODUCER'S CO-OP. SOC. LTD.

YEARS	PROFIT	YEARS	PROFIT
1978-79	1,08059	1991-92	7,27,457
1979-80	1,49,591	1992-93	7,97,534
1980-81	1,51,788	1993-94	9,09,492
1981-82	1,96,107	1994-95	8,40,211
1982-83	2,98,454	1995-96	8,18,639
1983-84	3,30,829	1996-97	10,31,298
1984-85	-	1997-98	10,23,714
1985-86	2,69,895	1998-99	10,45,092
1986-87	3,27,302	1999-2000	13,01,536
1987-88	3,21,116	2000-2001	-
1988-89	2,05,113	2001-2002	10,84,308
1989-90	3,81,090	2002-2003	10,99,008
1990-91	-	2003-2004	10,61,375

CHARTS SHOWING PROFIT ON NEXT PAGE :

It can be seen that Surat Zari Producers' Co-operative Society has played an important role in providing the credit facility to the manufacturers, Akhlededars / Artisans. The economical data of providing the advance shows the manner in which the Surat Zari Producers Co-operative Society has played an important role.

Still it requires to see that more advance facility is given to the specific section of the zari industry. New entrants should be helped more. Their problem is that they encourage only those who have already progressed. Special schemes and facilities should be provided to uplift the market. The institution has not laid stress on marketing. So marketing should also be a matter of concern for the society.

Chart 2.5.3.6 (A)

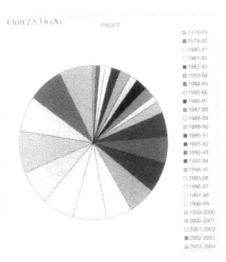

Chart 2.5.3.6 (B)

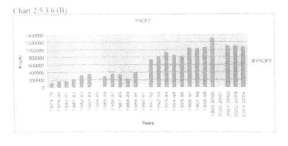

2.5.4 ROLE OF MUNICIPAL CORPORATION:

Surat Municipal Corporation has given remarkable support to the zari industry by licensing it. The simple and smooth process of licenses is extended by corporation. Corporation has also provided water facility.

2.6 NEED OF MARKETING CO-OPERATIVE SOCIETY:-

Zari Co-operative Goods' Credit Society has played an important role in providing the raw materials for the zari industry, but there is a need for monopoly marketing system through proper coding standardization and measurement tools. There should be an extension of the ZCGCS related to its original function in the sector of marketing. Otherwise, Marketing Co-operative Society separately could be formed to look after the specific functions of marketing research and development as well as distribution and sales.

2.7 ENVIRONMENTAL ASPECTS:

Environmental aspects have a profound impact on business. It is very well indicated by the fact that environmental analysis and diagnosis are among the first steps in the strategic management process. Business dynamics is in fact, a dependant factor, it depends on the environmental dynamics. Hence, the importance of environmental analysis and diagnosis.

Environmental analysis is defined as "the process by which strategists monitor the economic governmental / legal market/competitive, supplier/technological, geographic, and social settings to determine opportunities and threats to their firms."

"Environmental diagnosis consists of managerial decisions made by analysis the significance of the data (opportunities and threats) of the environmental analysis."

Environmental analysis today is an essential prerequisite for strategic management decision making. For instance, in his recent editions of Marketing Management, Philip Kotter, the world renowned professor and author, describes "Marketing Environment Audit" as the first component of marketing audit; whereas in the earlier editions of this book, the marketing audit does not have any reference to the environment.

It is now unquestionably accepted that the prospects of a business depends not only on its resources but also on the environment. Every business enterprise, thus, consists of a set of internal factors and is confronted with a set of external factors.

The internal factors are generally regarded as controllable factors because the company has control over these factors, it can alter or modify such factors as its personnel, physical facilities organization and functional means, such as the marketing mix, to suit the environment.

The external factors, on the other hand, are by and large beyond the control of a company. The external or environmental factors such as the economic factors, social-cultural factors, geo-physical factors etc. are therefore, generally regarded as uncontrollable factors.

As the environmental factors are beyond the control of a firm, its success will depend to a very large extent on its acceptability with the environment, i.e., its ability to properly design and adjust the internal factors (the controllable) variables to take advantage of the opportunities and to combat the threats in the environment.

"The micro environment consists factors in the company's immediate environment" that effect the performance of the company. This includes the suppliers, marketing immediaries, competitors, *customers and the public*. The macro environment consists of the larger societal forces that effect all the factors in the company's micro environment-namely the demographic, economic, natural, technological, political and cultural factors.

It is quite obvious that the micro environmental factors are more intimately linked with the company than the macro factors.

An important force in micro environment of zari industry is the suppliers, i.e. those who supply the inputs like raw materials and components of the firms. The importance of reliable source/sources of supply to the smooth functioning of zari business is obvious. Here it has been observed that uncertainty regarding the supply constraints often compel industry to maintain high inventories causing increase in the cost.

Zari industry faces the problem related to sensitivity of supply, high importance to vendor development, vertical integration.

Customers:-

As it is often exhorted, the major task of a business is to create and sustain customers. A business exists only because of its customers.

In zari industry what has been observed is the absence of monitoring the customer sensitivity. What is actually observed is that there is a *dependency* on a single customer which is often too risky, which has placed the industry in a poor bargaining position. Today what we find is that apart from the risk of losing business the risk of winding up of business by the customers and risk of the customers switching over to the competitors of the company is more.

Competitors:

Zari industry has competitors not only from firms which market the same or similar products but also from those who compete for the discretionary income of consumers, i.e. ready garments developed through other items of production like zari.

Marketing Intermediaries:

This is an important environmental affected factor. Because of this, industry has suffered a lot and has reached the stage of a damaged industry. It has led to a dislocation or disturbance in link between the industry and final customers and it has been observed that wrong choice of link has led the industry to collapse. The marketing intermediaries include middiment warehouses, transportation and marketing agencies. Here in this industry, there is no application of advertising agencies, marketing research firms, media firms and consulting firms.

Publicity :

An industry requires publicity which is lacking in the zari sector. Media, public citizens and local public are some of the examples. Zari *industry* has never tried to focus on the growth of consumers and therefore has failed in making the public aware of its utility.

Macro environment:

An industry operates in a larger macro environment that shapes and poses threats to the company. The macro forces are generally more uncontrollable than the micro forces.

Economic environment:

Economic conditions, economic policies and economic systems are the important external factors which constitute the economic environment of a business.

The nature of economy, the stage of development of economy, economy resources, the level of income, the distribution of income and assets found in this zari industry are important determinants. In this zari sector our observation has been that low income probably is the reason for the low demand of product. The sale of product for which the demand is income elastic naturally increases with an increase in income. The sector has been unable to increase the purchasing power of the people to generate a higher demand of its product.

Hence, it has to reduce the price of the product to increase the sales. The reductions in cost of production has to be affected to facilitate price reduction.

The *economic* policy of the government, needless to say, has a great impact on business. Government policy is neutral in respect of other industries, but government has not separately framed any policy for zari. The state government has also not promoted the industry in relation to other industries. There is a requirement of a restrictive import policy, a policy of protecting the home industries. Liberalization of the import policy has led to a difficulty for this industry.

Another important suggestion is that the industry should be kept within the priority sector, so that number of incentives and positive support could be taken from the government.

There is a need to declare it as a core sector. The monetary and fiscal policies, incentives should be framed neutrally. The state government should play a dominant role. Co-operative enterprise, joint sector enterprises and small scale units should be developed through preferential treatment by the government.

Political and governmental environment:

Political and governmental environment has a close relationship with economic system and economic policy. There are a host of statutory controls on business in India. Many countries today have laws to regulate competition in the interest of public. Elimination of unfair competition and dilution of monopoly power are important objectives of the regulations. In India the monopolistic undertakings, dominant undertakings and large industries are subject to a number of regulations which prevent the concentration of economic power to consumer determinant.

Some regulations brighten the prospects of small and new firms which are required for the zari sector. The special privileges available to the small sectors have also contributed to phenomenal success of zari.

Certain changes in government policies such as special industrial policy, fiscal policy, tariff policy etc. are required to be reframed.

Socio-Cultural environment:

Socio-cultural fabric is an important factor that should be analysed while formulating business strategies which has not been applied yet to the zari industry. Ignorance of customs, traditions, tastes and preferences of people has led to a high loss which is obviously reflected in the profit scale.

The factors like the buying and consumption habits of the people, their language, beliefs and values, customs and traditions, tastes and preferences, education are some of the important factors which have not been taken into consideration.

Zari industry requires to deal with social environment which encompasses its social responsibility and the alertness or vigilance of the consumers and society at large.

Demographic factors:

Size of population, population growth, growth rate, age composition, life expectancy, family size, spatial dispersal, occupation status, employment pattern, etc. affect the demand of zari goods. Markets with growing population and income are growth markets. In the zari industry, labour is highly heterogeneous in respect of language, caste and religion, ethnicity, etc. which makes the personnel management a more complex task. The heterogeneous population with its varied tastes, preferences, beliefs, temperaments, etc gives rise to differing demand patterns and calls for different marketing strategies.

Natural environment:

Geographical and ecological factors such as natural resource endowments, weather, climatic conditions, topographical factors, locational aspects in the global context, port facilities, etc. are all relevant to business. Due to the increase in pollution the climate of Surat has changed which is not very conducive for zari.

Physical and technological environment:

Weather and climatic conditions have affected the products of zari. Even technological factors have highly affected the zari industry but the zari industry has not been able to cope up with the changed scenario of technological changes in relation to other products.

International Market:

International market is important for the zari industry. The import export policies developed by Indian government has also affected the development of zari industry. Government of India has developed Exim policies on the basis of handicrafts. Zari is only a part of it. There is a need to frame a separate policy for zari industry.

CHAPTER 3 :

RESEARCH METHODOLOGY

	Page No.
3.1 SCOPES	256
3.2 OBJECTIVES	260
3.3 SAMPLING PLAN	263
3.4 METHOD OF DATA COLLECTION	264
3.5 LIMITATIONS	268

CHAPTER 3 : SALIENT FEATURES OF THE STUDY UNDERTAKEN

3.1 SCOPE:-

1. Extension of domestic market:-

Zari industry is today faced with recession. Because of dependency on distant market, marketing has decreased. Domestic market is required to be developed fast because it has a lot of scope. Zari as an antique product requires to be utilised maximum by producers, traders, Akhadedars, artisans themselves. In Surat there is a lot of scope for advancement because a large population wears ready-made garments, to which no attention has been given. Proper marketing of zari needs to be done throughout the country. Domestic market should become a source of supply for others. If proper attention is paid to the domestic market the problems of supply would be solved easily in the Indian market. Sometimes looking to the foreign demands one may forget local market, which has a lot of scope. Therefore, extension of domestic network requires to be developed through marketing utility of zari products.

2. Maximisation of more foreign exchange:-

As per the government records, export of handicrafts inclusive of zari and zari goods shows 2% share of zari only. It earns 142.32 crores of rupees of foreign exchange. If state and central government support and encourage separately and provide more infrastructure facilities to this industry, there is no doubt that more foreign exchange could be earned. If proper research and development is done more foreign exchange could definitely be earned.

3. Development of Byproducts:-

There is a greater scope of development of byproducts through zari/zardosi. Lack of proper attention on byproducts has ultimately led to recession. Unprofessionalised approach of zari traders, manufacturers and others is the reason for this recession. Zari is a product through which maximum byproducts can be developed by the artisans. Enough scope is there to enrich the domestic and foreign market through byproducts.

4. Generate more employment:-

Zari industry has generated maximum employment but still there is lack of education, training as well as skill development. Zari industry has its own reputation as it is an antique industry. If industry is properly developed there is no doubt that it would be able to generate maximum employment.

5. Technical Upgradation:-

The industry can cope with the downfall by going in for technical upgradation. Technically this industry lags behind in comparison to other industries. This industry has focused only on earning money but has not tried to focus on earning more foreign exchange and generating more employment, etc. It is totally based on thumb rule and has a traditional approach. Lack of modern management and non-professionalism has ultimately given a set back to the industry. If technically upgraded, the scope of expansion would widen.

6. Standardisation of costing:-

What we find in this industry is that, there is no standardisation of cost. There is a large variation in the cost of product, which varies from trader to trader and region to region. There is a gambling in costing. Cheating is also prevalent. Lack of professionalism, management application, is evident. There is a wide scope for standardisation of cost for each and every product of zari. Variation of cost is the basic reason for the decline of zari industry.

7. Pricing method:-

Prices of different products are not properly calculated, managed and standardised. Pricing method should be uniformly planned through associations, societies or any binding authorities.

8. Quality:-

Total dependency of this industry is on quality. As it requires specific skill there is need of maintaining quality as well as to develop quality measurement tools. There is no tool to measure quality. Every one tries to justify the quality on traditional approach. There is a lot of scope for gradation of products as well as standardisation. Quality thrust needs a lot of research and development. It also needs to acquire knowledge of foreign skill to develop the industry.

9. Adequate supply related to product:-

There is a gap between the two processes of each product. There is lack of proper management. Supply of adequate material should be made for every process.

3.2 OBJECTIVES :-

The aim of study has been to analyse the pattern of manufacturing, managing and distribution pattern in Zari industry in South Gujarat. This study is likely to help the small scale sector to renovate its manufacturing, managing and distribution network. Another justification behind this research could be to open the avenues of study which is likely to get attention by the industrialists and the academicians as well. The present study incorporates the activities of Pawtha, Tania, Flattening machine, winding machine, gliding machines etc. In addition to this the study also intends to include the study of existing marketing pattern of Zari in Surat, to analyse the socio economic dimensions , to assess the potential markets of Zari and evolve suitable policy recommendations, to organize zari markets for commissioning small zari enterprises with the financial and technical support of the Government of India. Since the study of universe is unmanageably large, it was decided that representative sample and study would be undertaken for the purpose of drawing inference about the universe. As secondary data becomes easily obsolete with the passage of time, more and more reliance was laid on primary data generated during the course of the study. Further due to unavoidable reasons South Gujarat region viz. Surat was selected for the purpose of present study. However Surat remained the best option as it is very popular and could be called the originator of Zari industry . The following are the basic objectives of the undertaken study :

1. To study past and present prospects of Zari product in [Surat] South Gujarat, in India and abroad.

2. To study the pattern and depth of the problem faced by Zari manufacturers / Artisans /Contractors / Akhadedars particularly in the industry.

3. To study the concurrent policy measures and related environment which has been deciding the dynamics of development of Zari manufacturers/ artisans / contractors/ akhadedars of different varities of Zari.

4. To study the degree of intermediation of [Zari traders] and the impact of such intermediation on prospects of manufacturers.

5. To study the scope for managing , reorganising , rechannelising or upgrading from the view of manufacturers/ Artisians/ Contractors/ Akhadedars.

6. To study the scope for an alternative distribution and marketing strategy from the view of Manufacturers /Artisians / Contractors/ Akhadedars.

7. To evaluate the plans and programs of the Manufacturers in terms of their future course of development and/ or expansion.

8. To study the level of satisfaction and motivation of unit holders and efforts put forth by them.

9. To evaluate the view of financial institutions towards the marketing problems faced by manufacturing units.

10. To study the quality measures and standards affecting the prospect of manufacturers.

11. To study invisible loss in manufacturing process [wastage at all stages].

3.3 SAMPLING PLAN :

The researcher has covered the entire India but practical emphasis is given to Surat district. All zari manufacturing units and processing units in the Surat district was the subject matter of study. The sample of 100 units was drawn from district that represents the total population of approximate 1200 zari units.

3.4 METHODS OF DATA COLLECTION:

3.4.1 PRIMARY DATA COLLECTION:-

Regarding the study of this sector of handicraft specifically due to lack of research, various methods of collecting the primary data were applied. The data collected is the first of its kind and is an original compilation. Different methods were used to collect primary data, particularly in surveys which are as follows:-

1. Observation:

In this method, the information was collected by observing the process at work place. The investigator himself visited different units of real zari, imitation zari as well as metallic zari processes. The responses of the manufacturers, artisans, workers, was studied and their state of minds was analyzed and the investigator even tried to eliminate bias responses.

Through this method, I mingled with the group and actively the participated in the activities of the group, for example, I visited their social functions, Annual General Meetings of Zari Producing Co-operative Societies, Varanasi Zari Association, South India Zari Merchant and Manufacturers Association, Andhra-Karnataka Zari Manufacturing Association, Varanasi Zari Mandal, Chamber of Commerce. I gained more insight into understanding the manufacturers group, Akhadedars groups, employees groups, customers groups, Socio-economic life and tried to cover up real feelings and methods of different group members.

As a member of social organization of Rana community and also as a president of Akhil Bharatiya Rana Yuva firm, I was able to get a real picture of different groups through relationships.

Under this method of observation, I felt that observation can take place in natural settings, which is uncontrolled. Things when observed naturally reflected a spontaneous picture of life and persons in the sector of zari. I also used a technique of self photography to collect data as well as analyse data successfully.

2. Interview method:-

This method of data collection was used to understand the behaviour of the people. Under this method, unstructured interview method was applied. More freedom is given to choose the form depending on the specific situation.

Under this method, I used another method for collecting information through respondents on telephone itself.

3. Questionnaire method:-

I used questionnaire for data collection which is printed and compiled to gather data from large, diverse, varied and scattered groups in zari industry. This tool proved to be objective and qualitative in *obtaining* data. I prepared structured questionnaire to collect data which is a closed form of questionnaire. The objective of questionnaire is to secure uniformity of responses as well as to get more truthful and real picture.

4. Experimentation method:

The investigator has applied this method through observation, by surveying the presence of traders, manufacturers as well as experts in the era of production market. It also studied competitors action, weather changes in co-operative dealers which are called environmental factors. This helped to know the attitudes as well as the behaviours of all the segments including the product market, etc.

5. Previewing:

The researcher quantified response in the line for the research object by structured frame work of interviewing through samples. In this method by taking interviews of groups and by asking different questions I tried to get the response from different segments like manufacturers, traders as well as artisans and also the labourers.

The interviews taken have been recorded personally through writing.

3.4.2 SECONDARY DATA COLLECTION:

In this sector, no research is available in published form either by central, state or local government, therefore the data was collected from publication of societies, other bodies like IRMA(Institute of Rural Management of Anand), Export Promotion Council for Handicrafts, RBI bulletin, Surat Zari Merchant Association, Zari Manufacturers association. Their reports helped to collect the secondary data. The reality, suitability and adequacy has been totally checked by the researcher.

3.5 LIMITATIONS:-

1. Inability to provide information:-

The questionnaire technique used was found inadequate by the researchers because of inability of respondents to provide information. This was due to lack of knowledge, laps of memory and inability to identify their notions and their inibition in asking "Why" and lack of faith in responding to the questions.

This is a traditional business industry. It has progressed from generation to generation but has failed to progress with the need of time. Some respondents even did not know the history of their forefather's business nor did they have any idea of how it evolved.

2. Human biases of respondants:

A frequently observed tendency on the part of respondents was human bias. Ego and widespread jealousy is rampant in the community. Respondents responded strangely whenever they were asked. Some respondents were not ready to talk because of others. Some respondants preferred to keep it as a secret.

3. Semantic difficulties:-

It is difficult, if not impossible to state a given question in such a way that it will mean exactly the same thing to every respondent. Similarly, two different wordings of the same question generated quite different results.

4. Non-visionary approach of respondents:-

Lack of vision to develop the business is a problem. There was no enthusiasm on part of respondents to provide information.

5. Unavailability of past data:-

The major problematic area in this research was that there is no records of data available. The total industry is unorganised. Due to unorganisation of sectors, difficulty arose in approaching and locating the people connected with this industry.

CHAPTER 4 :

ANALYSIS AND OUTCOME

		Page No.
4.1	CHARACTERISTICS OF RESPONDENTS	270
4.2	ANALYSIS	272
4.3	DATA ANALYSIS	284
4.4	SUMMARIZED FINDINGS	316

CHAPTER 4 : ANALYSIS AND OUTCOME

4.1 CHARACTERISTICS OF RESPONDENTS:-

Zari industry is an unorganized sector which lacks knowledge, technical upgradation, intellectuality, modernization, management, professionalisation. There are different groups like manufacturers, traders, akhadedars, labourers which are the respondents.

As it is an antique sector, traditionalism has flourished naturally. The respondents were found to be not knowledgable, uneducated as well as biased. Some respondents had no interest in answering the questions as their only aim was to get their wages. Some respondents did not understand the objective of research and illiteracy on their part proved to be an obstacle for us. Since the zari sector has an interrelated process, the respondents are also biased. Some respondent did not wanted to know or interact with others. Some respondents feared that the information would be used against him/her or would become an invasion of their privacy. These types of respondents omitted sensitive questions. Some respondents answered in a very normative way i.e. the way he/she thinks.

It was also observed that respondents were even afraid that his/her responses would reveal their lack of education and that he/she would appear stupid. Some respondents behaved as if their time was too valuable to waste on study which was not applicable to him/her. Their argument was that there is no need for such a study..

A common observation amongst respondents was that they lack vision, understanding, capability to understand others, social awareness, etc. It was also observed that the disappointment due to continuous fall of business which had made a psychological effect on them.

4.2 ANALYSIS

Zari manufacturing is a traditional craft of Surat. Entrepreneurs and workers, predominantly of Rana community, had helped in the smooth functioning of Zari industry. In the changing industrial scene of Surat, the existence of Zari industry needs to be protected both in terms of historical importance and the size of employment. The database of industry needs to be strengthened. With the change in economic policy, the export of Zari needs to be encouraged. The prices of raw materials not only need to be monitored but also their regular supply to the manufacturers should be ensured for the survival and growth of the industry.

Although the development of small-scale enterprises has received increasing attention as an element of industrial policy in many developing countries, India is unique in both the extent and duration of its efforts to promote and protect small-scale firms. The rhetoric of industrial policy toward small-scale firms in India, as in other countries, tends to stress their role in the de-concentration of economic power as well as creation of employment. The history of and the present state of affairs in the industrial countries may provide a glimpse of what is in store for developing countries. In manufacturing, the very small enterprises (fewer than ten employees) are destined to near extinction unless they become a protected species. In this aspect, India is trying to swim against the tide of history. In many other developing countries, relative or even absolute decline is in evidence. In services, very small enterprises also suffer relative decline but are nevertheless likely to survive in large numbers.

An interesting typology of business-persons has been proposed by Smith (1967). He distinguishes two polar types, craft-entrepreneurs and opportunist-entrepreneurs. The craft-entrepreneurs have a narrow, mainly technical, education and little social awareness and involvement. They are not very good at delegation, hire on a personal basis, and have limited horizons in the realm of finance and marketing. They have no long-range plans that might involve a change in the character of the business. Opportunist-entrepreneurs are of course just the reverses. They build more adaptable firms, and success stories mostly concern such entrepreneurs and their firms. Artisans in zari industry are craft entrepreneurs rather than opportunist-entrepreneurs. On the other hand, zari trader-manufacturers are opportunist-entrepreneurs capable of making investments if favourable policy environment is created. As of now, they are not making these investments because of inadequate policy support and discouraging trends in fiscal and labour policies. One must clearly distinguish the nature of small firm economies in the zari industry and should not subject them to general industrial, labour and fiscal policies without exercising discretion. Supply constraint in the zari industry is not low productivity of small units but the difficulties encountered by many small production units in acquiring the necessary intermediate inputs and raw materials of right quality. The over all productivity of small production units is a function of the following: adopted production technique, labour productivity, adopted organisation of production and managerial skills. As far as zari industry is concerned, the adopted production technique is alright, even though there is scope for improvement. Labour productivity seems to be low in comparison with other countries but the capital intensity is also low. Production organisation in the form of merchants-job contractors-artisans is far too advantageous to the merchants and very disadvantageous to others; and lastly, the industry does not seem to suffer from lack of managerial skills, even though there are very few trained professionals working.

Contrary to popular notion, these small manufacturing firms can not succeed if they are highly dispersed. On the other hand, they require what are referred to as economies of agglomeration to supply themselves with components and services or even attract potential customers including exporters. The fact that not only Zari production but its subsequent use in other industries like textiles is also confined to certain demand centres makes it all the more clear that there are economies of agglomeration in this industry. We will gain by strengthening this process by evolving a suitable policy framework. A new approach was out lined by Hubert Schmitz (1995) that distinguishes between:

- **Geographically and sectorally dispersed producers. Most rural small industry falls into this category. The village blacksmith and carpenter are the archetypal examples. Their growth prospects essentially depend on demand from local**

agriculture. The scope for division of labour and hence for economies of scale is small.
- **Clusters of small enterprises.** Clustering is meant here to embrace both geographical and sectoral concentration. In contrast to the previous case, there is wide scope for division of labour between enterprises and hence for specialisation and innovation, essential for competing beyond local markets.

Clustering opens up efficiency gains which individual producers can rarely attain. A group of producers making the same or similar things in close vicinity to each other constitute a cluster, but such geographical and sectoral concentration in itself brings few benefits. It is, however, a major facilitating factor, if not a necessary condition. A number of subsequent developments are possible (some of which may or may not occur). These developments are as follows:

- division of labour and specialisation amongst small producers;
- the provision of their specialised products at short notice and at great speed;
- the emergence of suppliers who provide raw materials or components, new and second-hand machinery, and spare parts;
- the emergence of agents who sell to distant national and international markets; the emergence of specialised services in technical, financial, and accounting matters; the emergence of a pool of wage workers with sector specific skills;

- the formation of consortia for specific tasks and of associations providing services and lobbying for its members.

Most of these are present in Surat giving scope for realising collective efficiency. Even where a collective capacity to compete, adapt and innovate has emerged, it is important not to expect an island of unity and solidarity. Collective efficiency is the outcome of an internal process in which some enterprises grow and others decline. In order to understand this process, it is useful to distinguish between vertical and horizontal inter-firm relations. As regards the former, firms buy products and services either through the market or subcontracting arrangements.

In Surat, it is largely done through subcontracting arrangements. The nature of the relationship can range from exploitation to strategic collaboration. The scope for conflict is greatest at the horizontal level, because producers often compete for orders. However, competition does not exclude joint action for solving specific problems, particularly in pre-competitive areas such as the provision of services, infrastructure, or training. Thus, the notion of collective efficiency neither denies conflict nor competition amongst enterprises in the cluster. On the contrary, clustering makes the market more transparent and induces local rivalry. Equally important, it facilitates collective action to tackle common problems, either directly through self-help institutions or indirectly through local government.

Single small manufacturers can cater for local demand in non-trading goods, but when it comes to competing for distant markets they can rarely do so without being part of a local network in which firms specialise and complement each other. As stressed by Sengenberger and Pyke (1991), the problem of many small manufacturers is not their size but being isolated. Indeed, it could be argued that clustering raises the capacity to respond to crisis and opportunity since the capabilities of specialised clustering firms can be combined in many different ways; and the mastery of one process or product can lay the basis for shifting into new lines of production.

Clustering also has a **dampening effect on wages** because of abundance of labour. This large labour surplus induces competition based on low wages rather than innovation and quality improvements. This is what happened and is currently happening in Surat's Zari industry.

The idea that there are gains in clustering is an old concept in industrial economics. It can be traced back to Alfred Marshall's analysis of industrial districts in Britain. In his Principles of Economics (1st edition, 1890), Marshall stressed the economies which "can often be secured by the concentration of many small businesses of a similar character in particular localities' (8th edition, 1920:221). He refers to such gains as 'external economies' and sees them as particularly relevant to small firms. This section draws together briefly what we can learn from

Marshall for our enquiry and why his concepts are insufficient to explain the competitive advantage that some industrial districts have demonstrated in recent history. One of Marshall's most lasting contributions to economic science is the distinction between internal and external economies. The former 'are dependent on the resources of the individual houses or businesses engaged in it, on their organisation and the efficiency of their management'; the latter 'are dependent on the general development of the industry' [1920:221]. While only providing this loose definition, Marshall leaves it sufficiently clear that the concept of external economies is not tied to geographical proximity. There are external economies that can be reaped in far-away places. This is also reflected in the way contemporary economics defines external economies or diseconomies: they occur where market-priced transactions do not fully incorporate the costs and benefits to economic agents.

However, external economies are particularly significant when specialised industries concentrate in particular localities. Indeed, the concept of external economies is introduced by Marshall in order to draw out (a) why and how the location of industry matters and (b) why and how small firms can be efficient and competitive. In his own words, 'we now proceed to examine those very important external economies which can often be secured by the concentration of many small businesses of a similar character in particular localities' [1920:221]. He refers to such *localities* as 'localised industry' or 'industrial districts'. He does not provide a definition for either, but his examples make it clear that he meant a cluster with a deep inter-firm division of labour like what is obtained in Surat.

To make the point more forcefully, the notion of external economies has come to be associated with gains (or losses) arising from the operations of firms which are connected through an anonymous market and whose behaviour is determined merely by price and cost signals. This tends to conceal essential traits of firms in a well developed cluster: namely the boundaries between firms are often flexible, the relationship between them is characterised by both competition and co-operation, and trust and reciprocity are important to understand the density of transactions and the incidence of joint action in the cluster [Becattini, 1990; Harrison, 1992].

The first questions addressed were where industrial clusters can be found and how common they are in developing countries. Statistics are not available for this purpose, but an overview was pieced together on the basis of examples found in the recent literature. The main conclusion was that clustering seems common in a wide range of countries and sectors. Some clusters in Latin America and Asia have acquired great depth in terms of the concentration of specialised suppliers and support bodies. Among these are the metalworking and textile industries of Ludhiana in the Indian Punjab [Tewari, 1990; 1992]; *the cotton*-knitwear industry of Tiruppur in Tamil Nadu [Cawthorne,

1990; 1995]; the diamond industry of Surat in Gujarat [Kashyap, 1992]; the engineering and electronics cluster of Bangalore in Karnataka [Holmstrom, 1994]; the footwear clusters of Agra in Uttar Pradesh [Knorringa, 1994], Trujilio in Peru [Tavara, 1993; San Martin Baldwin et al., 1994], and Leon and Guadalajara in Mexico [Rabellotti, 1993]; the Korean textile cluster in Daegu [Cho, 1994]; sports goods and surgical equipment in Sialkot and cutlery in Wazirabad in Pakistan [Nadvi, 1992a]. In African clusters, the inter-firm division of labour and institutional support tend to be less developed, as observed in the metalworking, furniture making and other clusters in Kenya, Zimbabwe and Tanzania [Rasmussen, 1991; Sverrisson, 1993].

While primarily an urban phenomenon, clustering can also be a feature of rural industrialisation, as in Indonesia where one can find the specialisation of entire villages [Weijland, 1994], for example, the manufacture of roof tiles [Sandee, 1994] or rattan furniture in Java [Smyth, 1992]. Within the urban arena, clusters located in intermediate towns seem to have been particularly successful, as indicated by their growth records and ability to compete in export markets. In contrast to clusters in small and medium-sized towns, those in major cities tend to be less well-rooted and have sometimes emerged from informal self-employment coping strategies of the poor. Despite that, many such clusters display a growth potential that goes beyond informal survival strategies and indicates localised competitiveness based on increasing *specialisation* amongst small firms; examples are the metal and repair workshops in the Takora district of Lima. Peru [Villaran, 1993], and Suame, the industrial shanty suburb of Kumasi, Ghana [Dawson, 1992]. These are just some examples which suggest that clustering is of significance to the industrial organisation of small-scale manufacturing in developing countries [For details and further references see Nadvi and Schmitz, 1994].

The way clusters are organised varies a great deal. Vertical relationships range from large firms orchestrating the division of labour amongst small firms to ever-changing permutations of small firms complementing each other; and from casual exchanges of information and tools to close inter-firm collaboration. Horizontal relationships are marked by intense rivalry but evidence of inter-firm co-operation is more varied. Socio-cultural ties - where they were studied -seem to heighten economic performance, but there are exceptions. These inter-firm relationships are hard to summarise and some aspects deserve elaboration.

The sharing of knowledge of new products or processes, labour availability, reliability of suppliers and traders, featured in most surveyed studies; lending each other tools and machinery was also common. Closer forms of inter-firm co-operation were found where extensive vertical production chains had developed, both in arrangements between large and small enterprises and amongst process-*specialised* small units. Such co-operation often resulted in improvements in technological standards and skill levels, but rarely produced major innovations. Improvements in processes and products were typically of an incremental kind. Inter-firm co-operation in Surat seems to be very low. Horizontal co-operation through sectoral associations existed in a number of clusters although with varying degrees of strength and effectiveness. Not all associations served the collective interest of the cluster, some were the preserve of more powerful elements within the cluster. A few, however, stood out either for their role in providing, what Brusco [1990] terms as 'real services', or as a lobbying body articulating the cluster's collective interests. Zari merchants' Association in Surat leaves us with mixed feelings.

Clusters in developing countries tend to be associated with some form of common socio-cultural identity. Shared identity often plays an active part in providing the basis for trust and reciprocity, and for providing social sanctions that limit the boundaries of unaccepted competitive behaviour. This is true in case of Surat as well. Our understanding of how social networks actually function and influence economic relations within clusters continues to remain rather inadequate. There are indications that where over-arching social networks are weak, inter-firm co-operation is limited. There are also signs, however, that social identities can have a negative influence on inter-firm relations - as with the caste divisions in the Agra shoe cluster [Knorringa, 1994].

The case studies from developing countries suggest that clustering has not been the outcome of a planned intervention by the state but has emerged from within. Zari industry in Surat is a case like this. This lends credence to the view that, as in the European industrial districts, collective efficiency based on the economic and social activities of a community is difficult to create from above, and develops best as an endogenous process. Nevertheless, the state, particularly at the regional level, can play an important facilitative role for small firm clusters, as shown by the example of the state administration of the Indian Punjab [Tewari, 1992; Kashyap, 1992]. Another example comes from the Brazilian Northeast where the state government of Ceara, through its procurement policy, transformed a dormant cluster into a growing one [Amorim, 1994; Tendier, forthcoming].

4.2 DATA ANALYSIS :

Table 4.2.1. TYPES OF FIRMS :

No.	Types of Firms	No. of Units	%
1	Sole Proprietorship	10	12.80
2	Partnership	46	59.00
3	Private Ltd.	21	27.00

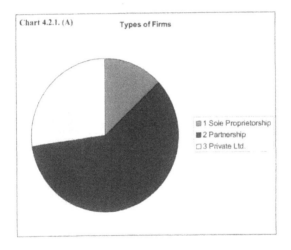

Chart 4.2.1. (A) Types of Firms

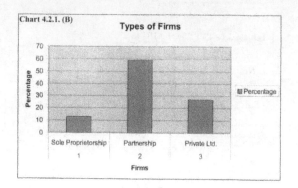

Chart 4.2.1. (B) Types of Firms

ANALYSIS:

It appears from the above table that more than half of the units belong to Partnership firm and only 10% belongs to Sole-proprietorship. Less than 25% belongs to Private Ltd. Co.

CONCLUSION:

We can conclude from the above analysis that people prefer to do their business in partnership only, because it is a business inherited from their forefathers.. They divide the profit only for the purpose of tax burden. They do not expect any benefits accept profit division amongst the family members.

Table 4.2.2. TYPES OF ZARI PRODUCT :

No.	Types of Product	No. of Units	%
1	Real	32	33.3
2	Imitation	50	52.8
3	Metallic	14	14.58

Chart 4.2.2. (A)

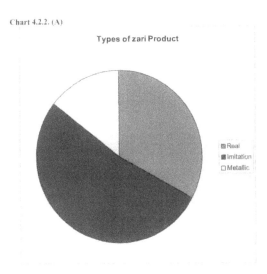

Types of zari Product

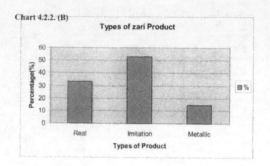

Chart 4.2.2. (B)

ANALYSIS:

There are mainly three types of products in zari, i.e: Real, Imitation and Metallic. It appears from the above table that half of the units belongs to imitation zari. 30% of the units belong to real zari. But it is also seen that metallic zari trend has started and 14% of units have entered in the latest zari.

CONCLUSION:

We can conclude from the above analysis that people prefer to enter in the area which is current or upcoming in the market. It is also observed that the production of real zari has decreased. Imitation zari still is being produced. But metallic zari is in the developing stage, which has a lot of scope due to less weight and cost. Some of the manufacturers today produce all types of zari. Some of them have stopped producing real jari, due to high cost of gold and silver. Imitation zari requires copper which has also becomes highly costly these days because of which the manufacturers find it difficult to survive.

Table 4.2.3. TENURE OF PRODUCTION:

No.	Tenure of Production (Years)	No. of Units	%
1	0-5	3	3.8
2	5-10	9	11.4
3	10-15	3	3.8
4	15-20	20	25.3
5	20-30	10	12.6
6	30-40	12	15.2
7	40-50	14	17.7
8	50-60	6	7.6
9	60-70	2	2.5

Chart 4.2.3. (A) Tenure of Production

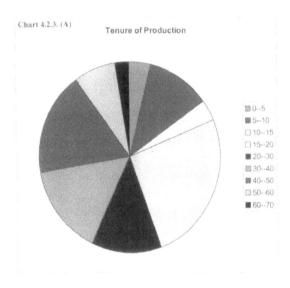

Chart 4.2.3. (B)

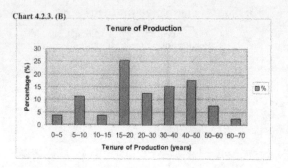

ANALYSIS:

It appears from the above table that 25% of the units started producing 20 years back, 27% of the units started producing 50 years back and only 3 to 4% units have started functioning in less than 5 years. Maximum units had setup their own business 10 years back.

CONCLUSION:

We can conclude from the above analysis that the zari industry has its own reputation and that too from long time. It is a hereditary profession. Many people have specified that their choice of joining the industry was compulsory and there is a desire hesitation on the part of their parents to keep this business alive. It is the oldest profession continuing from five decades. This shows that Rana community has its own hereditary business. It is an old and a traditional business.

Table 4.2.4. INVESTMENT :

No.	Capital Invested	No. of Units	%
1	0 - 10,000	1	1.3
2	10,000 - 50,000	10	13.2
3	50,000 - 1,00,000	23	30.2
4	1,00,000 - 2,00,000	6	7.8
5	2,00,000 - 3,00,000	2	2.6
6	3,00,000 - 4,00,000	2	2.6
7	4,00,000 - 5,00,000	6	7.8
8	5,00,000 - 10,00,000	5	6.5
9	10,00,000 - 20,00,000	18	23.7
10	20,00,000 - 50,00,000	1	1.3
11	50,00,000 - 1,00,00,000	2	2.6

Chart 4.2.4. (A)

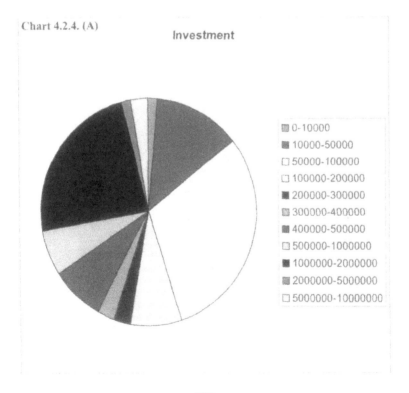

Investment

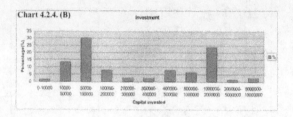

Chart 4.2.4. (B)

ANALYSIS:

It appears from the above table that 25% of the units have invested in more than 10 lacs of rupees. 30% of units have invested between 5 lacs to 10 lacs of rupees. 25% of the units have invested 1 lac to 5 lacs of rupees. 3% of the units have invested upto 1 crore rupees. The ratio of investment is not very high.

CONCLUSION:

We can conclude from the above analysis that investment done by manufacturers/traders is for a long period of time. It is an old industry but the investment is not much in proportion to the development. Development always shows more investment but whatever is shown is not on a wider scale. Size and nature of business is always related to the investment, but in this industry expansion is not visible.

Table 4.2.5. HOW MANY MACHINES UTILISED IN PRODUCTION :

No.	No. of machines	No. of Units	%
1	0-5	44	57.14
2	5-10	12	15.58
3	10-15	3	3.9
4	15-20	15	19.5
5	20-25	3	3.9

Chart 4.2.5. (A)

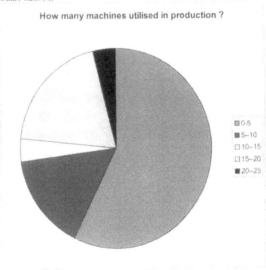

How many machines utilised in production ?

Chart 4.2.5. (B)

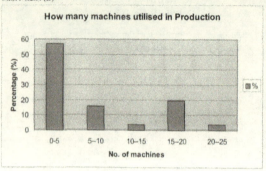

ANALYSIS:

It appears from the above table that according to the nature of business, the number of machines utilized by the manufacturers and others have not properly increased. The quantum of machines always speaks about the size of business. Only 18% manufacturers have more than 15 machines. Half of the manufacturers/traders have less than five machines. This shows that the number of machines have not increased in relation with the development of industry.

Table 4.2.6. ANY TECHNICAL CHANGE HAS BEEN DONE OR NOT :

No.	Types of Product	No. of Units	%
1	Yes	28	35.89
2	No	37	47.43
3	Not answered	13	16.66

Chart 4.2.6. (A)

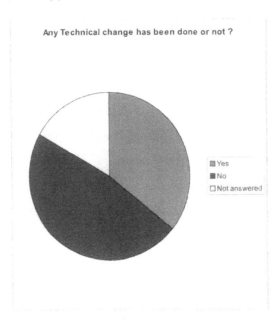

Any Technical change has been done or not ?

Chart 4.2.6. (B)

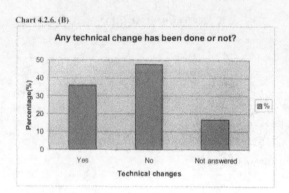

ANALYSIS:

From the above analytical table, it can be seen that people are not interested for a change in technical matters. 37% respondants were found to be disinterested in a change in the technical field. 13% respondants were even interested in the questions posed. They were not even aware of technical change. Whenever the question on technical change was asked, the respondants asked in detail about it and were not able to answer properly. 37% respondants did respond properly. What they quoted as change could be called a minor change. The technical change has been less. Whatever change has come has come in only six to seven years.

CONCLUSION:

As the analytical table shows, the technical change has not been properly understood by the manufacturers/traders. Even what has been reported as a change, that too is quite minor. Minimum changes in the

Table 4.2.7. SUPPLY OF FINISHED GOODS :

No.	Market	No. of Units	% of Units
1	Local (Domestic)	41	35.04
2	Outside within country	68	58.11
3	Not decided	3	2.56
4	Outside country	4	3.41

Chart 4.2.7. (A)

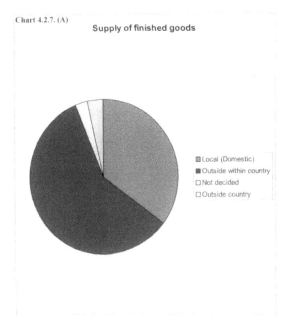

Supply of finished goods

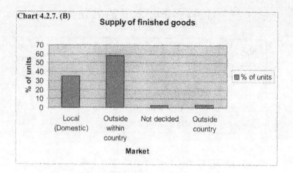

Chart 4.2.7. (B) Supply of finished goods

ANALYSIS:

From the above analytical table, it can be seen that market i.e. supply of finished goods at local level is 35%, whereas, outside and within India, it is 58.11%. The trend of local market shows that it is an interrelated process. Outside the country, it is only 3.45% which shows that no more export is there. Even 2.56% people don't want to take any decision.

CONCLUSION:

It can be observed through the analysis that market is very much expected. Maximum part of the zari has local market and maximum part of the process related to zari is interdependent. Processed zari does not have a full market at domestic level. The last product of zari has an outside market only. Maximum part of that market is at a distant. The domestic market of ready made goods prepared through the use of zari has not yet been developed. The market for end product has been developed only in southern part of India.

Table 4.2.8. AVAILABILITY OF RAW MATERIAL :

No.	Market	No. of Units	%
1	Local	75	94.9
2	Outside	4	5.06

Chart 4.2.8. (A)

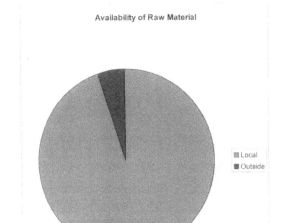

Chart 4.2.8. (B)

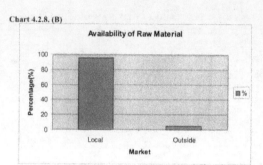

ANALYSIS:

Analytical table shows that 95% people of zari industry get the raw material the local market. This shows that the material is not being bargained with different types of suppliers from other areas. Only local level suppliers transact. There is no commercial aspect in purchasing raw material.

CONCLUSION:

From the above analysis, it can be seen that maximum people purchase the raw material from local area. Only 5% people purchase it from other than local. This shows that there is lack of professionalism. It shows that material management which is an important part of manufacturing concern is not there. There is no inventory control or supervision for material. Due to this the quality of product is not maintained. Deterioration of material is found at each and every process. Planning of purchasing-unnecessary investment-short supply.

Table 4.2.9. TRAINING RECEIVED OR NOT :

No.	Training	No. of Units	%
1	Training taken	35	22.58
2	Not taken	43	27.74
3	Needed to take training	35	22.58
4	No need to take training	42	27.09

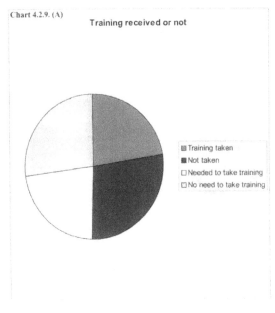

Chart 4.2.9. (A) Training received or not

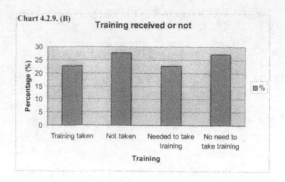

Chart 4.2.9. (B) Training received or not

ANALYSIS:

It can be observed from the table that 27% people have not taken any type of training and 27% people do not agree to undertake training or require training. Only 22% people have undergone training but that also is not proper. Only minor training has been taken by them in some process of zari. 27% people are in favour of training.

This shows that training aspect has not been properly attended by the owners, manufacturers and labourers.

CONCLUSION:

It is observed from the analysis that no formal training has been taken by any employee, manufacturer, artisan or any other segment of zari industry. There is no desired requirement felt by the industry. The analysis and observation also focus on the matter that people are not aware of this aspect which is required for developing the industry.

Table 4.2.10. FINANCE FOR BUSINESS :

No.	Types of Finance	No. of Units	%
1	Family	45	51.13
2	Society	0	0
3	Govt. Loan	10	11.36
4	Supplier advance	0	0
5	Private finance	19	21.59
6	Govt. grant	0	0
7	Banks	3	3.4
8	No response	11	12.5

Chart 4.2.10. (A)

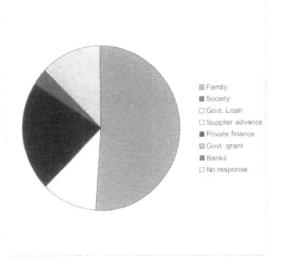

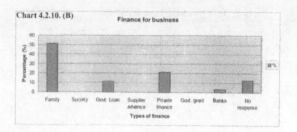

Chart 4.2.10. (B)

ANALYSIS:

The financial source of this industry is from family background. Only 20% of the total units borrowed money from govt. agencies, private sources. The table shows that 45% of the total units employ the fund from their hereditary family backgrounds. Not much finance has been acquired from outside.

CONCLUSION:

The above analysis shows that maximum fund is not from outside. Family is the source for finance. Only 20% money is borrowed from private organisations and others. This finance is not sufficient for the industry to survive. Financial management is not there in the industry. Good knowledge is required to manage the finance.

RECOMMENDATIONS:

Financial management required to be develop:

In zari industry, there is no management regarding the collection of the finance. There is an urgent need to develop financial

Table 4.2.11. MANAGEMENT APPLIED IN BUSINESS :

No.	Education	No. of Units	%
1	X	4	5.12
2	XII	14	17.94
3	Graduation	27	34.01
4	Post graduate	2	2.56
5	Uneducated	31	39.74

Chart 4.2.11. (A)

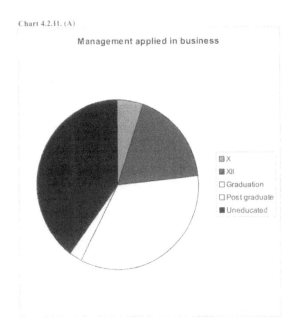

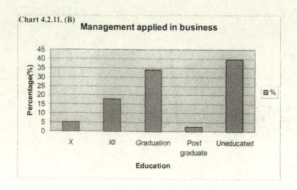

Chart 4.2.11. (B) Management applied in business

ANALYSIS:

The table shows analytical approach. Specific management is lacking and there is non-professionalism of business. Specific person is not appointed for the management purpose. Education ratio also shows that 35% people related with business are graduates, only 25% are post graduates where as 23% are only H.S.C. pass and 30% people engaged are uneducated.

CONCLUSION:

Zari industry seems to be totally unmanaged. There is no management concept amongst the manufacturers, traders and akhadedars. Simple business is going on. No professional education is there in the industry. Industry lacks knowledge of management. In each and every concept management should be implemented. Management of labour, finance, personnel, market, distribution system, etc.

Table 4.2.12. ANY REASONABLE RESEARCH HAS BEEN DONE FOR THE BUSINESS :

No.	Researchable or not	No. of Units	%
1	Research has been done	47	60.25
2	Research has not been done	31	39.74

Table 4.2.13. OFFERING STUDY OR NOT :

No.	Offering for study or not	No. of Units	%
1	Offering	7	8.97
2	Not offer	71	91.025

Chart 4.2.12. (A)

12. Research done or not

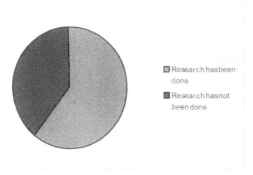

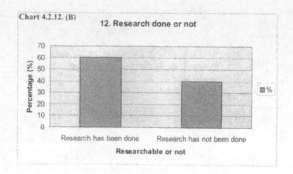

Chart 4.2.12. (B) 12. Research done or not

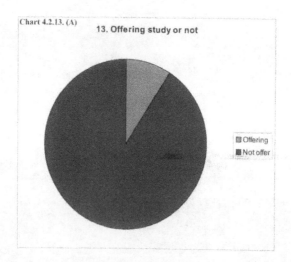

Chart 4.2.13. (A) 13. Offering study or not

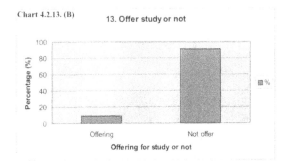

Chart 4.2.13. (B) 13. Offer study or not

12. and 13. (combined)

ANALYSIS:

The analysis table consists of two concepts i.e. research has to be done or not? and whether the respondent offers to study or not?

60% people favoured the research, whereas 31% people did not respond to the study. This shows that the people those who are interested in the concept, even they have not offered for study in any organization/profession, which can be seen from the table that 2. 91% people have never offered for study. Only 8% got the chance but that was also not proper.

CONCLUSION:

This analysis shows that the industry only at the time of crisis strives for research. This also implies that people do not have any knowledge of research. People only favour the wind of short term gains. They are not

4.4 SUMMARIZED FINDINGS / OUTCOMES OF STUDY:

 # MANAGEMENT:

In zari industry, there seems a lack of management. There is no management in market, human resource management, production, finance and accounting, information technology, material planning and production control, purchasing function, advertising and sales promotion function, social function, which enables an industry to fulfill its social responsibility.

No financial management is there in the zari industry. There is no planning for ratio-analysis. Ratio analysis helps to understand the requirement of resources. Rationing of resources means optimum utilization of different funds available for industry. Cost of capital is not calculated. Manufacturers/traders are only using capital, but they do not have any calculation of the cost of capital. They don't have a knowledge of liquidity constraint, like whatever the surplus money or profit that is invested in fixed assets like big houses or property.

It has also been noted by observation & by talking with the people that the industry has not been able to maintain the required liquidity level for ensuring the requirement of the working capital. So industry is bound to suffer from operational problems which in the long run affects profitability.

Apart from this, the non-availability of working capital in time, and holding of excess liquidity again affects the company's profitability. So there is no assurance of the minimum & optimum holding of the liquid assets of the company.

As we know that in any organization, profitability largely depends on the efficient handling of financial resources but what we find in zari industry is lack of management of assets and financial market analysis.

A major portion of working capital in this industry is invested in the purchase of raw materials and inventories alone, business houses unnecessarily hold capital in excess of requirement, and thereby strain their profitability. A major problem according to me is the problem of excess storage cost for finished product. When there is more production without taking cognizance of the market potentialities, the industry faces the problem of storing finished products which occupies maximum space and involves a lot of cost. Not only this at a lower cost the traders are compelled to sell the product.

In this industry, the major problem of lack of management of funds, assets as well as lack of analyzing the financial market. There is dearth of planning of borrowing long term, short term, and medium term loans. The industry has some traditional ways of borrowings, borrowings from societies, banks, private financers. There is no method of issuing shares/debentures. There is a need of choosing the alternative which should be analyzed and kept most effective to ensure maximum profitability.

Similarly financial management, production management is vitally important for the same industry especially because it is engaged in manufacturing operation. Goods or products should manufactured in time. If it is not done the industry can lose its market stake or the market share. What I found in the industry is that there is no assurance about manufacturing of goods and products in the right quantity and to make it available in the market for the ultimate users. There is no effort made for cost minimization, work simplification, inventory control, product design, process improvement, quality control, etc.

The need of the industry is to use the suitable capital budgeting and to make the machines and equipments right in time and even replaced the machines with the modern available technology.

Product development and product design is also equally important as far as the management is concerned. The changing demand of the consumers heavily influences the product design and product innovation.

Nowadays the industry is suffering because they have not produced the right quantity or right product for the consumers as per their changing requirement. Free market or free competition today to a great extent exerts pressure on the industry. So industry should keep in mind that unless a product is developed suitably, based on consumer requirements, the production in the long run is bound to suffer. Similarly, product development and product innovation with work simplification and performance improving approaches ensure cost minimization also.

Industry has never seen cost efficiency, work simplification, work measurement with the help of industrial engineering, which can enable the industry to find out the exact work unit required for doing a job which in long run can help to decide wage rate more scientifically. In this industry today the major absorption of laborers/workers is there, and so whatever the efficiency industry acquires, it looses.

The major problem today is due to inventory control because unless inventory is controlled rightly or the optimum utilization of inventory resource is ensured, the production operation will definitely suffer in the long run and ultimately it will affect the company's profitability.

In this industry, there is a big lapse of market survey. There is no survey for any product market or the product value. Actually the preference of consumer has not been taken into account. "Packaging" is based on traditional system. The market potentiality has not been created by this industry. Economic and sales forecast has not been there. The Marketing research has not been done by the industry.

Nowadays the things created in the industry are produced in a static quantity, keeping in view the market stake that they having for this much quantity. Today the industry finds itself out of place because of competitors who may gradually grab the increased market potentiality for the product or products.

Suitable expansion programmes have not been undertaken from the cost point of view. No manufacturer has achieved production efficiency. Cost efficiency is only possible when a company enjoys the benefit of producing an economically run quantity and developing by products.

So in this industry, there is lack of proper development of byproducts because there is no suitable marketing research. An important part of this industry is distribution channel. In this industry, manufacturers or traders have not developed the distribution channels properly. This situation has arisen due to the improper distribution of channels. Products may not reach the ultimate consumers and users for reasons of inefficient channels of distribution. This industry needs to ensure that its products reach the ultimate users in time. It requires or needs to ensure development of further marketing potential.

Apart from this, advertising as well as sales promotion is important in marketing. The Zari industry is today facing a serious and sensitive problem and there is a fear of closure due to lacking of proper distribution channels. This industry has not tried to promote the sales.

CHAPTER 5 :
RECOMMENDATIONS AND SUGGESSTIONS

	Page No.
5.1. CHALLENGES IN TIMES TO COME	322
5.2 RECOMMENDATIONS	325
5.3 FURTHER RESEARCH AVENUES	333

5.1 CHALLENGES IN TIME TO COME

(1) With the growing competition, product differentiation and positioning will become more important. Due to globalization, liberalization and the changing scenario of competititiveness and product differentiation, zari indstry is faced with a bigger challenge ahead. Zari industry requires to produce different products. Nowadays, France is competing with Indian zari market. The product differentiation as well as positioning is also required to be undertaken.

(2) Class marketing/niche marketing will grow in importance and there will be a decline in the relative importance of mass marketing, barring certain exceptions. This is a challenge to be faced by the zari industry. Due to the absence of class marketing such a situation has arisen. Mass marketing today is a problem in the zari sector.

(3) The growing competition will also increase very considerably the importance of augmented product. Levitz's comment that " the new competition is not between what companies produce in their factories but between what they add to their factory output in the form of packaging, service, advertising, customer advice, financing, delivery arrangements, warehousing and other things that people value" will become very relevant in India.

(4) Zari industry will be required to pay more attention to quality and price to survive in this competitive market.

(5) The variety of products and product forms available in the market will significantly and substantially increase the consumer choice. The zari industry requires to think and work keeping in mind the above considerations.

(6) Yet another challenge is posed by the factors which have become more popular viz. licensing, franchising and multi-level marketing.

(7) The social marketing concept will gain more acceptance.

(8) Direct marketing will gain more importance in future than today.

(9) People with technical expertise and enterprise will have enormous opportunities. It is pointed out that in future "Industries would be neither capital intensive but skill or enthusiasm intensive."

(10) Abundant entrepreneurial chances will be provided by the fast growing service sector.

(11) Personal rewards, particularly at the managerial level, will be linked to the results, much more than today. Even the tenure of employ will tend to be so linked in many companies.

(12) Companies will tend to adopt a lean structure and cut the extra flap.

(13) **Global economic boom:**

Naisbitt and Aburdence point out that in the decade of the 1990's the world is entering a period of economic prosperity. There is no single factor behind the economic boom, but instead an extraordinary confluence of factors the economic forces of the world are surging across national borders, resulting in more democracy, more freedom, more trade, more opportunity and greater prosperity. The growing population, the rising income and new conducive policy environment will attract more investment into the developing countries. This also will pose a challenge for the zari industry.

(14) **Global strategy:**

As Porter argues that a company must move towards a global strategy as soon as its resources and competitive position allow. If it is competing in global industry. A high domestic cost of capital, high domestic factors and strong currency are no excuse in global competition. Yet competing internationally is not a substitute for improvement and innovation at home. This also is a challenge for zari industry.

5.2 RECOMMENDATIONS :

1. Inputs to be declined through assessment :

Recommendations about supply of raw materials through Producers' Co-operative Society and about giving concessions, subsidies to be limited to raw materials but to abolish multiple point purchase tax on raw materials should be adopted.

The zari industry suffers from fluctuation in prices and availability of quality raw materials like gold, silver, copper, silk yarn, film and other chemicals. I also recommend to abolish multiple point purchase tax on raw materials.

2. Labour laws required to be restructured or amended:

Advantages of small firms are there in higher productivity and absentism from strikes, child labour should be stopped. The enforcement of Minimum Wages Act for the employment in zari industry should be strictly followed.

Government of Gujarat enforces "Minimum Wages Act" for the employment in zari industry. This is necessary in my opinion, to counter the dampening effect on wages due to the phenomenon of clustering, but its extension making it applicable to job contractors (Akhadedars) who are running their job work units supposedly registered under Shops and Establishment Act and who work for more than one principle is not warranted. I recommend to think on it.

3. To uplift the end product producer:

There is a necessity to uplift the end product producers, as it consumes the intermediate product totally.

4. To overcome the unorganized groups of different products:

Since there is over production, it is important to make formal groups of zari manufacturers, akhadedars and others. Z.M.A. should organise common services to those in membership and as self-help organisation, to set up the institution and service the business community requires. The separate and independent promotion of zari goods producers' co-operative society in my opinion has divided the leadership and led to unnecessary antagonistic and competitive posters they can think of sorting out problems by providing half of the positions in their respective boards for the representative of others. This way, they may be able to work with cohesion and synergy. They should not function in isolation, as they tend to do today. I recommend ZMA should not only undertake organising tours at regular intervals but should study different changes in technology, distribution and sales, advertising and also professionalism. ZMA should organise annual exhibitions and promote export market pro-actively. ZMA must be the body to expertise to undertake studies forward for organising market services including exports. ZMA must be grievance ventilating body by conducting regular meetings.

5. To upgrade the technology and research and development management :

There is a requirement for upgradation in technology as well as there should be a centre of research and development in the field of zari. For this there is need for developing 'Zari Park' in surat and adjoining areas.

The main competition comes from import. In terms of quality and price, imported zari seems to be genuinely competitive. One must raise the competitiveness of industry. It is necessary to formulate an overall development plan for zari industry. Direct assistance in form of supplying credit, raw materials, equipments, dissemination of technology information research and market development. Enumerating the characteristics of this zari industry can better do this.

An important distinguishing feature is that the units covered utilised low level traditional technologies that are characterised by manual operations most of the time employ less than 10% and do not keep any systematic record. Most of these operate either as individual units or firm part of household. Enumeration of these units causes the problem of identifying units which operates mostly inside the home or in other scheduled areas of the house hold. Out of traditional technologies may combine the largest amount of labour with unit of capital and yeild the highest value of output per unit of capital, it may not necessarily mean that these technologies optimize on the use of available resources. Technologies that are neither most labour intensive nor most capital intensive have to be thought over to avoid drudgery and / or possible exposure to hazardous condition. The role of woman in small enterprises in zari industry constitutes another difficulty on the basis of available evidents, it would seem that women make an important contribution in this industry. I do not visualise improvements in technology been feasible until zari industry moves from the status of cottage industry. Craft enterpreneurs neither have capital to invest nor have the vision and abilities to manage the zari industry at above current level of technology. The industry will continue to stagnant and may disappear under the onslaught of better and cheaper zari imports.

I recommend that government should insist on bringing zari producing firms under small scale industry category and not under category of cottage industry. Production process involving power and chemicals should not be allowed to continue in dwelling houses. Government should bring suitable legislation to shift these production activities to a carefully plant Zari Industrial Estate in consultation with The Chamber Of Commerce and Industry , Zari Merchants' Association, persons involved in zari production and Surat Municipal Corporation.

6. Substantial Reinvestment :

It is very difficult to isolate the savings and reinvestment rates for these enterprises that are components of a more complex household. Reinvestment capacity of these small entrepreneurs in the zari industry *either out* of profits or institutional credit is not very substantial.

The ability of small production units to save out their profits and reinvest such saving in their activities is essential for their growth. In many cases, their current dwelling is quite unsuitable and far too small to do these and it may not be desirable to let these units expand in the residential areas where they are currently located. Available evidence shows that very small entrepreneurs do not have access to institutional credit facilities provided by banks and other agencies. Thus, the reinvestment capacity of many of these small entrepreneurs in zari industry either out of profits or by raising institutional credit is not very substantial. In these units, the majority of which are family owned enterprises, the profits from the enterprises are often mixed with saving and expenditures from other household activities. Thus, it becomes to isolate the savings and reinvestment rates for this enterprises that are a component of more complex household.

I recommend working out long term institutional credit arrangement with S. I. D. B. I. and our commercial banks for mobilising necessary investment and working capital for transforming cottage based zari industry into a well organised small scale industry with an exclusively established zari industrial estate in Surat.

7. Suitable structure of employees/intermediary persons :

In this industry, there is no guarantee for steady employment. So there should be a proper structure of employment. Schemes like subsistence allowance, unemployment insurance can also be thought of.

As many of job work units, the availabilities of raw material is an important factor for their survival and development. In this regard, the way the production and marketing of zari goods in Surat is organised in such a manner that the entire risk are shifted on to these units. If the market is flourishing, they are flooded with orders or otherwise, they are forced to eke-out some living at the mercy of Akhadedars or Merchant Manufacturers the raw materials are very costly and long operational cycle of production and marketing in distant markets on credit leaves very little hope for these units to take up this task independently. Inspite of tax like minimum wages, child labour, etc. there is no guarantee for steady employment opportunities and stable income. When the market is not in boom, the Merchant Manufacturers minimise or completely stop their activities. Many a times, the wage rate (job work rates) are squeezed to cut short losses or avoid reduction in profit. Due to nature and structure of these job contractors in the best of times, these units survive providing subsistence and in the worst of times, they force the persons dependent on them to seek out other avenues of livelihood. In short, in the best of the times the merchants makes the best of profits and in the worst times the merchants suffers the minimum, as he has no obligations to workers. In order to minimise the losses, he withdraws from the business for a while or shifts the burden of losses, partially if not fully, to workers by making them accept to work for less rewards. This gives the merchant an opportunity to corner most of the benefit in the *best of times* and suffer the least either withdrawing or shifting most of losses to workers by resorting to wage cuts in the worst of times.

8. To create monopoly market is an urgent need :

Bulk of output in zari industry gets saturated and is dumped same. If there is a marketing facility, it can develop new products based on marketing intelligence.

9. To fix the standards of quality :

Globalisation entails the enforcement of stringent standards of zari products of small units. Enforcement of stringent standards for zari products of small units may also have both positive and negative impacts. While such measures could contribute to high quality and therefore render them competitive, as well as safe guard public health and safety they could be inconsistent with both types of technologies used within industry and skill availability. Ultimately these policies may constitute a cause of attention for units already operating for barriers to entry of new ones.

10. To develop the infrastructure :

The provision of infrastructure, primarily in the form of industrial estates, marketing services including export marketing and other industrial services including technology development, extension and training is required.

In addition to the financial incentives offered, both central and state governments offer a broad range of services. In broad terms, these consist of the provision of infrastructure, primarily in the from of industrial estates, marketing services including export mak\rketing and other industrial services including technology development, extension and training. Co-ordination is lacking between the promotional agencies and financial intermediaries entrusted with the administration of small enterprise lending schemes. In many instances, small firms are expected to come to the organisations that provide technical and financial assistance rather than other way organisation seeking them out.

11. Promoting zari industrial estate :

The zari industry requires to have a separate industrial estate with the help of government of states and centre.

12. A separate policy should be framed :

No specific policy is there regarding zari but it is a part of handicraft. It should be advisable that proper policy may be framed for the development and upliftment of industry.

5.3 FURTHER RESEARCH AVENUES :

Research, unless it is understood in its right spirit, cannot be undertaken with success. What is important for researchers is to take research more as a passion than for career progress.

There are so many areas in zari industry for further research. Marketing of zari is one of the area where zari industry could be explored. We have different areas of research like marketing policy which involves pricing, advertising service, channels of distribution, product research, etc. Marketing research, as we all know is primarily interested in finding out the market potentiality.

A prospective researcher on management will get immense scope to investigate into these three core functional areas of management i.e. finance, production and marketing.

Research competency development is another important aspect. It focusses on integration of business plan of the company by selecting the right individual for the job. Competence is defined as the smallest unit of on-the job behaviour that is observable, measurable and changes overtime. Innovation and creativity, supply chain management knowledge, management issues, customer relationship, management (CRM), etc. are areas of researcher's interest.

One such area of interest is the financial management research. Research on financial managemnt includes different operations like: Financial Analysis, Capital Structure, Ratio Analysis, etc. Capital structure and ratio analysis enable a company to ration the requirement of resources. Rationing of resources means optimum utilization of different funds available for a company. Unless the resources available in a company are utilized we may need to find out various sources of funds and costs of capital, liquidity constraint, for a more clear understanding. Unless a company is able to maintain the required liquidity level for ensuring the requirements of the working capital, the company is bound to suffer from operational problems which in the long run may affect profitability.

Apart from such an affect, the non-availability of working capital in time, and holding of excess liquidity again affects the company's profitability. So what is needed is to ensure the minimum or the optimum holding of the liquid assets of the company. Other areas of financial management research may be the management of different funds, management of assets and financial market analysis, etc. Now we all know that in any company, profitability largely depends on the efficient handling of financial resources. Financial management research enables us to compare the operation of different companies with the help of financial analysis. If a major portion of the working capital is invested for purchase of raw materials and inventories alone, companies will unnecessarily hold capital in excess of requirements and thereby strain their profitability.

Apart from holding of raw materials and inventories which need to be controlled, companies may have the problem of excess storage costs for finished products. When we produce more without taking in to cognizance the market potentialities, we face the problem of storing finished products, which occupy maximum godown space and involve a lot of costs.

Although rationing of resources is primarily a concern for the cost management function, with the help of financial management research, using different cost indicators or using different ratios, we may find out what exactly is the optimum resource holding and in what way a company is able to hold that optimum level of the resources. Management of funds and assets and analyzing the financial market are also equally important for the financial management research.

Management of funds require an efficient planning of borrowing long term, short term and medium term loans as per the requirements. When to borrow, how to borrow and from whom to borrow is important for the company to understand in the context of different data of the company itself. The company may have some traditional ways of borrowing, like, borrowing from banks, borrowing from other financial agencies like different development banks or they may borrow by *issuing debentures* in the market or they may raise their capital by issuing shares, etc. All these alternatives need to be compared and anlaysed and the most cost effective one needs to be chosen to ensure maximum profitability.

Similarly, production research is vitally important for a company which is engaged in the manufacturing opertion. Unless goods or products are manufactured right in time or made available in time in the market, the company may loose the market stake or the market share.

Thus, what is primarily important for a production department is to ensure manufacturing of the right goods and products in the right quantity and to make it available in the market for the ultimate users. Thus there is a need for the development of different cost minimization alternatives, work simplification, inventory control, product design, process improvement, quality control, etc. With the help of suitable capital budgeting unless the required machines and equipments are made available right in time or unless the available machines are replaced with the modern available technology right in time, the production process will itself suffer.

Product development and product design research is also equally important. A good number of companies gradually find themselves out of market simply because they are not able to produce the right quantity or the right product for the consumers as per their changing requirements. Free market or free competition to a great extent exerts pressure on the company. Thus unless a product is developed suitably, based on consumer requirements the production in the long run is bound to suffer. Similarly, product development and product innovation with work simplification and performance improving approaches ensure cost minimization also. With the help of industrial engineering, development of the product with simultaneous reduction of the total costs is possible. Cost efficiency, work simplification, work measurement with the help of industrial engineering, development of the product with the value engineering approach, among other things, enable us to find out the excess work unit required for doing a job which in the long run helps us to decide wage rate scientifically. Unless inventory is controlled rightly or the optimum utilization of inventory resources is ensured, the production operation will definitely suffer in the long run and ultimately affect the company's profitability.

While surveying the market we found different areas of research like marketing policy which involves pricing, advertising service, channels of distribution product research, etc. Product research helps us to find out the changing consumers' requirements by carrying out survey. Improvement and use value of the present product may be carried out, as also in packaging based on consumers' preferences.

Marketing research as we all know is primarily initiated to find out the market potentiality of a particular company. With the help of economic analysis and forecasts with the help of survey of consumers or the potential consumers of the society, a company can take suitable decisions on expansion or design or outline their product process exactly coping with the requirements.

Unless a company is undertaking suitable marketing research it will definitely suffer in the long run. As we all know, no company can afford to remain in a static product or system indefinitely. To clarify this point further, company remains in producing a static quantity of some products keeping in view the market stake that they are having for this much quantity alone, in future the company may find themselves out of place because of their competitors who may gradually grab the increased market potentiality for that particular product or products.

Moreover unless suitable expansion programmes are undertaken, from costing point of view, no company can achieve production efficiency. Cost efficiency is only possible when a company enjoys the benefit of producing an economically run quantity and developing by-products. So, undertaking suitable marketing research is of utmost importance for a company.

Apart from all these things, there are other areas of research on marketing like, research on channels of distribution, etc. A company sends its products to the ultimate consumers through different channels of distributions. Products may not reach the ultimate consumer and users for reasons of inefficient channels of distribution. Thus, a company needs to ensure that its products reach the ultimate users on time. Efficient channels of distribution also ensure development of further marketing potential.

Apart from the channels of distribution, advertising as well as sales promotion research are important areas of marketing.

Thus, a prospective researcher on management gets immense scope to investigate into these three core functional areas of management, i.e., finance, production and marketing.

II : BIBLIOGRAPHY

BIBLIOGRAPHY

1. **Abdul Haqa Dehlavi** — Akhbarul Akhiar, Delhi, 1889.
2. **Abraham T. M.** — Handicrafts in India, New Delhi, 1964.
3. **Abul Fazl Allami:** — The Ain-i-Akbari, Translated by H. Blochmann, 2nd Edition, New Imperial Book Depot, New Delhi, 1965.
4. **Academy of Fine Arts:** — Old Textiles of India, Academy of fine Arts, New Delhi
5. **"Acharanga Sutra"** — Tr. By H. Jacobi, Sacred Books of the East, Vol. XXII, Oxford, 1884.
6. **Ackermann, Phyllis:** — "Indian Embroidery", Embroidery, Vol. 3 No. 1, London, 1934, 4-10. "Textiles of the Islamic Periods – A History", in A Survey of Persian Arts, A. V. Pope (ed.), Vol. 3, Oxford University press, London, 1939, pp. 1995-2162.
7. **Alif, Shams Siraj** — Tarikh-i-Firoz shahi, Calcutta, 1890.
8. **Agrawal S. N.** — "Textile". Craft Horizon, Vol. XIX, No. 4, July-August 1959.
9. **Agrawal V. S.** — Harsha Charita-Ek Samskritika Adhyayana, 1953. "Reference to Textiles in Bana's Harshacharita", J. I. T. H., No. IV, 1959, pp. 65-68, India as known to panini, Varanasi, 1963.

10	**Ahmad, I**	"Economic and Social changes", in Jafar Imam (ed.), Muslims in India, Orient Longman, New Delhi, 1975.
11	**Ahmed, Ali**	Twilight in Delhi, Champak Library, New Delhi
12	**"Aiteraya Brahmana"**	Ed. By Th. Aufrechi, Bonn, 1879. Ed. By K. S. Agashe, Poona, 1896. tr. By Keith, HOS, Vol. XXV, Cambridge, Mass., 1920.
13	**Aiyangar, R. K. V.**	Some aspects of the Hindu view of Life according to Dharmashstra, Baroda, 1952.
14	**Al-Beruni**	Al-Beruni's India, Ed. With notes and Indices by E. C. Sachau, S. Chand, Delhi, 1964.
15	**Al-Umari**	Masalik al absar, 1838.
16	**Ali, A. Yusuf**	"A monograph on silk fabrics produced in the North Western Provinces and Oudh", Allahabad, 1900, Calico Museum of Textiles, Reprint 1974.
17	**Ali, Athar**	The Mughal Nobility under Aurangzeb, Asia Publishing House, 1966.
18	**Alkazi, Roshan**	Ancient Indian Costumes, Art Heritage Boks, 1983.
19	**Anonymous**	Travels of Sebastian Manrique, Vol. 1 and Vol. 2, New Delhi.

20	**Anonymous**	"Embroideries", The imperial gazetteer of India, Oxford, Vol. IV, 1908, pp. 218-222.
21	**Anonymous**	"Embroidered Vestments", Census of India, Vol VII, vii(a),, Census of India, Vol. VIII. vii(a) I, 1961.
22	**Anonymous**	"Catalogue of embroidered and Woven Indian Shawls and Historic Textiles from the Victoria and Albert Museum, Exhibited in the Department of Textile Industries", University of Leeds, 1st-15th May, 1970.
23	**Anonymous**	"The Zari Industry of Surat", I.E.T.J. (Handicrafts Supplement), Sept.-Oct. 1970. p. 10.
24	**Anonymous**	"Embroidery", J.I.A., Vol. II, No. 18, 1880.
25	**Ansari G.**	Muslim Castes in Uttar Pradesh, Lucknow, E.F.C.S., 1960.
26	**Archer, M.**	"Lockwood Kipling: Champions of Indian Arts and Crafts", in Dimensions of Indian Arts and Crafts: Pupul Jayakar Seventy, L. Chandra and J. Jain (Ed.), Agam Kala Prakashan, 1986, pp. 7-12.
27	**Ashraf, K. M.**	Life and conditions of People of Hindustan 1200-1550, Delhi, 1970.

28	**Ashton, Leigh**	"The Art of India and Pakistan: A Commemorative Catalogue of exhibition held at the Royal Academy of Arts", London, Faber and Faber Ltd., London, 1947-1948.
29	**Atkinson, J.**	Customs and Manners of the Women of Persia and their domestic Superstitions, London, 1832.
30	**Auboyer, Jeannine**	Daily Life in Ancient India (200 B.C. 700 A.D.), France, 1965.
31	**Aziz, Abdul**	The Imperial Treasury of the Indian Mughals, Lahore, 1942.
32	**Baden Powell, B. H.**	Handbook of the Manufacturers and Arts of the Punjab, 8 Vols. Lahore, 1872.
33	**Bahadur, K. D.**	A history of Indian Civilisaton, Ess Ess Publications, 1980.
34	**Baihaqi Abdul Fazal**	"Tarikh-i-Baihaqi", Ed. W. H. Morley, Calcutta, 1862.
35	**Banabhatta**	"Harshacharita", Ed. By K. P. Parab, Bombay, 1925. English Trans. By E. B. Cowell and F. W. Thomas, London, 1897.
36	**Bandopadhyaya, N. C.**	"Economic Life and Progress in Ancient India, Calcutta, 1945.

37	**Barani, Ziyauddin**	"Tarikh Firuzshahi", Calcutta, 1862, ed. Saiyid Ahmed Khan, 1888-91.
38	**Barth, Frederick**	Indus and Swat Kohistan: an Ethnographic survey, Oslo, 1956.
39	**Barua, B. M.**	Barhut, Parts I, II and III, Indian Research Institute, Calcutta, 1934, Reprint 1979.
40	**Barve, V. R.**	Complete Textile Encyclopaedia, D. B. Taraporevala Sons & Co., Bombay, 1967.
41	**Basham, A. L.**	The wonder that was India, London, 1954.
42	**Basham, R.**	Urban Anthropology, The Cross Cultural Study of Complex Societies, 1978.
43	**Batuta, Ibn**	"Travels in Asia and Africa", 1325-1354, Trans. By H. A. R. Gibb, Inst. Ed. London, 1929.
44	**Behrua, N. K.**	Peasant Potters of Orissa: A Sociological Study, Sterling Publishers Pvt. Ltd., New Delhi, 1978.
45	**Belshaw, C. S.**	Traditional Exchange and Modern Marets, Prentice Hall, Eaglewood Cliffs, 1965.
46	**Belshaw, M.**	A Village economy: Land and People of Huecoria, Columbia University, New York, 1967.
47	**Beni Prasad**	History of Jahangir, Indian Press, Allahabad, 1930

48	**Bernier, Francois**	Travels in the Mughal Empire (1656-1668 A.D.), Ed. By A. Constable, 1891, Reprint S. Chand and Co., New Delhi, 1972.
49	**Bhatnagar, I. K.**	Brocaded Textiles and their conservation, C.C.P.I. Part I and Part II, Vol. VIII, Vol. IX, 1975, pp. 41-45. 73-75.
50	**Bhatt, G. S.**	"Trends and measures of status mobility among the chamars of Dehradun", in Tribe, Caste and Peasantry, K. S. Mathur and B. C. Agrawal (Ed.), E.F.C.S., 1974
51	**Bhushan, Jamila Brij**	The Costumes and Textiles of India", D. B. Taraporevala Sons and Co. Ltd., Bombay, 1959.
52	**Bhushan Kavi**	Bhushan Granthavali, Hindi Bhavan of allahabad, Allahabad.
53	**Birdwood George**	Industrial Arts of India, Chapman and Hall, London, 1880
54	**Birrell, Verla**	The Textile Arts, New York, 1959.
55	**Blat, Solvyns**	Costume of Hindustan, 1807
56	**Blau, Peter**	On the nature of organization, John Wiley and Sons, New York, 1974.
57	**Blunt, E. A. H.**	The Caste system of Northern India, S. Chand and Company, 1969.

58	Bopegamage, A.	Delhi: A study of Urban Sociology, University of Bombay, Bombay, 1957.
59	Bott, Elizabeth	"Family and Social Network roles, Norms and External relationships in Ordinary Urban Families", Tavistock, London, 1971.
60	Braun-Ronsdorf, M.	"Gold and Textiles, Gold and Silver Fabrics from Medieval to Modern Times", CIBA review, Vol. 3, 1961, pp. 2-16.
61	Breese, Gerald	Urbanization in Newly Developing Countries, Prentice Hall Inc., Delhi, 1966.
62	Budauni, Abdul Malik	"Muntakhabut-twarikh", English trans. By Ranking, Lowe and Haig, 3 Vols., Calcutta, 1889-1925.
63	Bunt, Cyril G. E.	"An Indo-Portuguese Embroidery in the Bargello", B. M., London, 1942.
64	Burdon, E.	"Monograph on the wire and Tinsel Industry in the Punjab", Authority Civil and Military Gazette Press, Lahore, 1909.
65	Burgess, Robert G.	In the Field: An introduction to Field Research, George, Allen and Unwin, London, 1984.
66	Cable, V., Weston, A. and Jain, L. C.	"The commerce of culture: experience of Indian Handicrafts", Lancer International, 1985.

67	Caine, W. S.	Picturesque India: A handbook for European travelers, George Routledge and Sons Ltd., 1891.
68	Carori, John Francis Gemelli	"A voyage round the world", 6 Parts, Part III dealing with India, 1704.
69	Cecil, B.	India, Thacker and Co. Ltd., Bombay, New Delhi.
70	Chakledar, H. C.	Social life in ancient India, Calcutta, 1929.
71	Chandra L. and J. Jain	Dimensions of Indian Art, Pupul Jayakar Seventy, 2 Vols. Agam Kala Prakashan, 1986.
72	Channa, Subhadra	Tradition and Rationality in Economic behaviour, Cosmo Publications, New Delhi, 1985.
73	Channa, V. C	Caste: Identity and Continuity, B. R. Publishing Corp., Delhi, 1979.
74	Chatterjee, A. C.	"Notes on the industries of the United Provinces", Supdt. Govt. Press, Allahabad, 1908.
75	Chatterjee, C. K.	"Bibliography of Small Scale and cottage Industries and Handicrafts", Vol. I, Part XI (i) Census of India, 1961.
76	**Chattopadhyaya, Kamla Devi**	Indian Embroidery, Wiley Eastern Limited, New Delhi, 1977.

77	**Claemer, John(Ed.)**	The new economic Anthropology, The McMillan Press Ltd., 1978.
78	**Clark, G. S.**	Indo-Dutch Embroideries of the 17th Century, Vol. I, London, 1914.
79	**Cole, A.S**	"Ornament in European Silks", Encyclopaedia Britannica, London, 1899.
80	**Collman, Jeff**	Handbook of Social and Cultural Anthropology, 1973.
81	**Cowell, E. B**	The Jatakas or stories of Buddha's former Births, Tr. By Francis H. T., Vols. I to VII, 1973.
82	**Creswell, K. A.**	A bibliography of the Architecture, Arts and Crafts of Islam to 1st January 1960, The American University at Cairo Press, 1961.
83	**Crill, Rosemary**	"Hats from India", Victoria and Albert Museum, London, 1985.
84	**Dalton, George**	"Economic Theory and primitive society", A. A., Vol. 63, 1961, pp. 1-25.
85	**Dar, S. N.**	Costumes of India and Pakistan, Taraporevala Sons and Co., Bombay, 1969.
86	**Das, S. K.**	Economic history of ancient India, Calcutta, 1925.

87	**Das, Sukla**	Socio-economic life in Northern India (A.D. 550 to A. D. 650), Abhinav Publications, New Delhi, 1980.
88	**Dayal, M.**	"Rediscovering Delhi", Hindustan Times, Sunday, World, 7th January, 1973.
89	**De, B. N.**	"A monograph on the wire and tinsel industry in the central provinces", Govt. Press, Nagpur, 1910.
90	**Desai, V. N.**	Life at court: art for Inida's rulers, 16th – 19th century, museum of fine arts, Boston, 1985.
91	**Dey, N. L.**	The geographical dictionary of ancient and medieval India, London, 1927.
92	**Dhamija, J.**	The survey of embroidery traditions, Marg. Vol. XVII, No. 2, Embroidery, Bombay, March, 1964.
93	**Dimand, M. S.**	A handbook of Muham-madan art, 2nd edn., New York Metropolitan museum of art.
94	**Dixit, P. K**	"Zari embroidery and Batwa making of Bhopal, Madhya Pradesh", Handicrafts survey monographs, Vol. VIII, Part VII-A, 1965, No. 1, Census of India, 1961, New Delhi, 1965.

95	Doctor, B.C	"Contemporary costumes and ornaments as reflected in bharut sculpture, J.M.S.U.B, 1997, pp. 143-151.
96	Doshi, Harish	Traditional neighbourhood in a modern city, Abhinav publications, New Delhi, 1974.
97	Dozy, R.P.A	Dictionnarie detaille des norms des vetemensts chezles arabs, Amsterdam, 1845.
98	Dutt, M.N.	"The Mahabharata: Adi parva", English prose translation (Ed.), 1895.
99	Edel, Mathew	Economic analysis in an anthropological setting: Some methodological considerations, A.A., 71, pp. 421-433.
100	Elliot, H.M and Dowson J.	The history of India as told b its own historians (the muhammadan period), vol. I, New Delhi.
101	Elphinstone	History of India, 2nd edition, P. 599.
102	Emery, Irene	The primary structures of fabrics, Washington, D.C. 1966.
103	Estrade, C.	Broideries Hindories, Paris, 1926.
104	Etizioni, Amitai	Modern Organization, Prentice Hall of India, New Delhi, 1965.

105	**Fabri, C.L**	Ballet costumes in Akbar's times, Marg. Bombay, Vol. VII, No. 1, 1953.
106	**Fakhruddin, M.**	"Tarikh-i-Fakhruddin Mubarakshah", Ed. E. D. Ross, London, 1927.
107	**Fanshawe, H.C**	Delhi past and present, johm murray, London, 1902.
108	**Fergusson**	Tree and Serpent Worship, Pt. LXXXVI, p. 206, 1971.
109	**Firth, Raymond**	Elements of Social Organisatin, Tavistock Publications, London, 1969.
110	**Fisher, B.A**	Small group decision making, McGraw-Hill, New York, 1974.
111	**Flangan, J.F**	The earliest dated Islamic textiles, B.M., L.X, 1932, pp. 313-314.
112	**Flemming, E.**	An encyclopaedia of textiles, New York, 1927.
113	**Folcker, E.G**	A silk and gold carpet in the national museum, Stockholm, B.M., XXX, New Delhi.
114	**Foster, William (Ed.)**	Early travels in India, 1583-1619, London, 1921.
115	**Fryer, John**	A new account of east India and Persia, London, 1898.

116	**Garner, Julian**	Indian embroideries of the Mughal period, International studies, June, 1927.
117	**Ghurye, G. S**	Indian costumes (Bharatiya Vesabhusa), Popular Book Depot, Bombay, 1951.
118	**Goetz, H**	Indian costumes of the 18th and early 19th century in the Indian Museum,, London, N.S., II, No. 6, 1927, pp. 140-147.
119	**Golombek, L. and V. Gervers**	Tiraz fabrics in the royal Ontario museum, in studies in textile history, V. Gervers (Ed.), royal ontario museum, Toronto, 1977, pp. 82-125.
120	**Goswamy, B. N**	A jainesque sultanate shahnamah and the content of the pre-mughal painting in India, Zurich, 1988.
121	**Gould, H.A**	Lucknow rickshawallah, the social organization of an occupational category, I.J.C.S, pp. 24-24, 1965.
122	**Green, L.B**	Gold and Silver lace thread industry, Census of India, Vol. XIV, Madras, Part I report, 1932, Appendix II, P. 249.
123	**Gupta, B.A**	Embroidery, J.I.A.I, Vol. II, No. 18, London, 1888, pp. 9-16.
124	**Gupta, Charu S.**	The gilded thread, India magazine, Anniversary issue on gold, December 1991.

125	**Gupta, Raghuraj**	Caste ranking and intercaste relations among the muslims of a village in North-western U.P., in Tribe, Caste and Peasantry, K.S. Mathur and B.C. Agrawal (Ed.), E.F.C.S., 1974.
126	**Habibullah, A.B.M**	The foundation of muslim rule in India, central book depot, Allahabad, 1961.
127	**Hadaway, W.S**	Monograph on tinsel and wire in the madras presidency, Supdt. Govt. Press, Madras, 1909.
128	**Hall, Richard H.**	Occupations and the social structure, Prentice Hall Inc., New Jersey, 1975.
129	**Hammel E. and Lasbett, P**	Comparing household structure over time and between cultures, Comparative studies in society and history, Vol. 18, 1974, pp. 73-109.
130	**Hammersley, Martyn and Atkinson, Paul**	Ethnography principles in practice, Tavistock publications, London, 1983.
131	**Havell, E.B**	The industries of madras(Embroidery), J.I.A.I., Vol. III, 1890, p. 114.
132	**Hendley, T. H**	Embroidery, J.I.A.I., Vol. IV, 1891, p. 5
133	**Herringham,**	Ajanta Frescoes, London, O.U.P., 1915.

134	**Herskovits, M.J**	Economic anthropology, Knopf, New York, 1952.
135	**Hopkins, E. W**	India, Old and New, New York, 1902.
136	**Howell-Smith, A.P**	Indian embroidery, J.E.G., Vol. 3. No. 3, 1935.
137	**Hughes, Thomas**	Dictionary of Islam (Reprint)
138	**Hunter, George Leland**	Decorative textiles, Lippincott, Philadelphia and London, 1918.
139	**Hunter, W.W**	The Indian Mussalman, 3rd Ed., London, 1858.
140	**Irwin, J.C**	Embroidery, Asia, Encyclopaedia Britannica, William Benton, Vol. 8, 1965, p. 316.
141	**Irwin J. and Hall Margaret**	Indian embroideries, Vol. II, historic textiles of India at the Calico Museum, Calico museum of textiles, Ahmedabad, 1973.
142	**Irwin, John**	Indian embroider, His majesty's stationary office, London, a publication of the Victoria and Albert museum, No. 7, 1951.
143	**Iyengar, H.K. Rama**	Gold Lace, Census of India, Vol. XXV, Mysore, Part I, report, Appendix IV, 1931, pp. 343-344.
144	**Jaffar, S.M**	Education in Muslim India, 1936
145	**Jagmohan**	Rebuilding Shahjahanabad, the walled city of Delhi, Vikas, 1975.

146	**Jahangir**	Tuzuk-i-Jahangir (Trans. By A. Rogers and H. Beveridge), Delhi, 1968.
147	**Jacobi, H**	Jain Sutras, tr. From Prakrit, Motilal Banarasidas, 1964.
148	**Jain, J.C**	Life in ancient India as depicted in the jain canon and commentaries: 6th century B.C. to 17th century A.D., Munshiram Manoharlal, 1984.
149	**Jeannine, Auboyer**	Daily life in ancient India (from 200 B.C. to 700 A.D.), translated from the French by Simon Watson Taylor, 1965.
150	**Jinavijaya(Ed.)**	Puratana Prabandha Sangraha, Calcutta, 1936, p. 39.
151	**Johnson, Allen W.**	Research methods in social anthropology, 1978.
152	**Johnson A.W. and George, C. B**	Kinship, friendship and exchange in two communities: A comparative analysis of norms and behaviour, J.A.R., 30, 1974, pp. 55-68.
153	**Joy, Leonard**	One economist's view of the relationship between economics and anthropology, Raymond Firth (Ed.), Tavistock, London, 1967.
154	**Kaegi, Adolf**	Life in ancient India, Calcutta, 1950.

155	**Kalhana**	Rajataranginin, Ed. And Trans. By M.A.Stein, London, 1900, 2 Vols.
156	**Karsten, D.**	The economics of handicrafts in traditional societies (an investigation in Sidamo and Gemu Goffa province of southern Ethiopia), Weltforven Verlag: Munchen, 1972.
157	**Keay, f.E and Karve, D.D**	A history of education in India and Pakistan, Calcutta, 1964.
158	**Keith A.B and Macdonell, A.**	A vedic index, 2 Vols., London, 1912.
159	**Kendrick, A.F and Cole, A.S**	Embroidery, in encyclopaedia Britannica, 11th ed., 1911.
160	**Kipling, J.J**	Industries of the Punjab gold and silver embroidery, J.I.A.I., Vol. II, Nos. 20, 23, 24, Oct 1988, pp. 30-32.
161	**Kluckhon, Clyde**	Culture and behaviour, the free press of Glencoe, 1962.
162	**Knight, F. H**	The economic organisaton, Harper Torch Books, New York, 1965, originally published, 1931.
163	**Krishna A. and Krishna V.**	Banaras brocades, edited by Ajit Mukherjee, Crafts museum, New Delhi, 1966.
164	**Kulshreshtha, S.S**	The development of trade and industry under the mughals (1526-1707 A.D), 1964.

165	**Kuznets, S.**	Economic change, Sprengler, J.J. (Ed.), New York, 1953.
166	**Lancaster, C.S**	The econmics of social organization in an ethnic border zone: the gold (Northern Shena) of the Zobegi valley, Ethnology, 10, pp. 445, 1971.
167	**Lane, Poole**	Medieval India under Mohammadan rule, 1917.
168	**Laslett, P. and Wall, R.**	Household and family in past time, Cambridge Univ. Press, Cambridge, 1972.
169	**Latifi, A.**	The industrial Punjab, 8 Vols., Longmans, London, 1911.
170	**Leach, E.R (Ed.)**	Aspects of Caste in south Inida, Ceylon and North-West Pakistan Cambridge papers in social anthropology, No. 2, Cambridge, Cambridge University press, 1960.
171	**Leclair, E.E(Jr.)**	Economic theory and economic anthropology, A.A., 64, pp. 1179-1203, 1962.
172	**Levine, G. Harold**	Scientists and culture heroes in ethnographic method, in reviews in anthropology, Vol. 12, No. 4, 1985, pp. 338-345.
173	**Maity, S.K**	The economic life of Northern India (300-500 A.D), Calcutta, 1957.

174	**Majumdar, R.C**	Classical accounts of India, the greek and roman accounts of ancient India, Firma K.L.M. Pvt. Ltd., 1989.
175	**Majumdar, R.C (Ed.)**	The Delhi sultanate, Vol. VI, Bombay, 1967.
176	**Manucci, Niccolao**	Storia de moguls, Trans. with introduction and notes by William Irvine, 3 vols., Calcutta, 1965-66.
177	**Markrish, Lilo**	The myth of the improving Westerner, in civilization on loan by Hernz Edgar Kroine, Oxford, 1973
178	**Marshall, Shalins**	Stone age economics, Tavistock, 1974.
179	**Martin, F. R**	The miniature painting and painters of Persia, India and Turkey, 2 vols., 8th to 18th century, reprint, B.R. Pub., 1985.
180	**Mathur, N.L**	Red fort and Mughal life, New Delhi, Pub. by the Author, 1964.
181	**Maurice, T**	History of Hindustan: Its arts and its sciences, Navrang, New Delhi, Vols, I and II, 1974.
182	**Mehta, R.J**	The handicrafts and industrial arts of India, Bombay, 1960.
183	**Mehta, R.N**	The historical evidence for two Jaina Velvets, J.I.T.H., No. 2, 1956, pp. 53-55.
184	**Merutunga**	Prabandha Cintamani, 14th century, 1932.

185	**Mirza, M.W**	Life and works of amir khusro, Punjab university, 1935.
186	**Mishra, J.S**	Ancient Inidan Textile designs, Part one, Prithvi prakashan, 1981.
187	**Mitchell, G**	Social networks in urban situation, 1975.
188	**Mitra, R.L**	Lalita Vistara, Calcutta, 1877.
189	**Mohanty, B.C**	Brocaded fabrics of India, Alfred Buhler (Ed.), 2 Vols., Calico museum of textiles, Ahmedabad, 1984.
190	**Monier-Williams**	A Sanskrit English dictionary, Oxford, 1956. Modern India and Indians, Kegan Paul, London, 1891.
191	**Monserrate, Antonia**	The commentary of father Monserrate, S.J. on his journey to the court of Akbar, Tr. By J.S.Hoylard, London, 1922.
192	**Moorcroft W. and Trebeck, G.**	Travels in the Himalayan provinces of Hindustan and the Punjab: in ladakh and Kashmir, 1819-25, patiala, 1970.
193	**Mukherjee, R.K**	The economic history of India (1600-1800), J.U.P.H.S., Vol. XV, pt. I, p. 91.
194	**Mukherjee, T.N**	Art manufactures of India, 8 Vols. Supdt. Govt. printing press, Calcutta, 1888.
195	**Nainar, M.H**	Arab geographer's knowledge of south India, Madras, 1942.

196	**Nissim, Ezekiel**	Calico museum of textiles, Ahmedabad, J.I.T.H., nos. 2.3.4.5 and 6, 1956,1957,1959,1960 and 1961.
197	**Nissim J. A**	Portfolio of Indian Art, London, 1881-1886.
198	**Oaten, Edward Farley**	Travel and Travellers in India (1400-1700 A.D.), London, 1909.
199	**Opler, M.E and R.D.Singh**	Economic, Political and social change in a village of central India, Human organization, 2, 1952.
200	**Oppert, G**	On the ancient commerce of India, Madras, 1879.
201	**Ovington, J**	A voyage to surat in the year 1689, London, Oxford Univ. press, 1929.
202	**Panikkar, K.M**	A survey of Indian history, Bombay, 1956.
203	**Paul Stephens C**	Persian-English-Urdu dictionary, deep pubication, 1989, pp. 309,271.
204	**Prithviraj**	Prithi Chandra Charita, prachin Gujarat kavya samagama, baroda, 1920
205	**Pope, A.U. (Ed.)**	A survey of Persian art, Vol. 3, Oxford Univ. Press, London and New York, 1939.
206	**Pope, A.U and P. Ackermann (Ed.)**	A survey of persian art, Oxford Univ. press, London and New York, Vol. XIV, 1967.
207	**Quluqshandi**	Al-Subhul Asha, Darul Kutub kadiviah, cairo, Vols. 83 and 84, 1913.

208	Rao, V.L.S. Prakasa and K. V. Sundaram	Delhi, encyclopaedia Britannica, revised edition, 1974.
209	Ray, Mallinath	A monograph on the wire and tinsel industry in Bengal, Bengal secretariat book depot, Calcutta, 1910.
210	Riefstani, R. M	Persian and Indian textiles from the 16th to the early 19th century, New York, 1923.
211	Rizvi, S.M.A	Some aspects of industry and social change among the muslim karkhanedars, Doctor of Philosophy, University of Delhi, 1981.
212	Robert, Layton	The anthropology of art, New York, Columbia university press, 1981.
213	Rose, A.	Glossary of the tribes and castes of the Punjab and N.W.F.P., Vol. 1, p. 489, 1911.
214	Rose, H.A	Rites and ceremonies of hindus and muslims (reprint), Amar prakashan, New Delhi, 1983.
215	Roy, Shibani	Status of muslim women in North India, B.R. Pubishing, Delhi, 1979.
216	Salar Jung	Munaga-i-Delhi, 1739.
217	Saletore, R.N	Life in the Gupta age, Bombay, 1943.
218	Saraf, D.N	Indian Crafts: Development and potential, Vikas Publishers, New Delhi, 1982.
219	Saraswati, S.K	Indian textiles, the publication division, 1961.

220	**Sarkar, Jadunath**	The India of Aurangzeb, Calcutta, 1901.
221	**Sarkar, S.C**	Some aspects of the earliest social history of India, p. 63, (fn. 120, New Delhi.
222	**Saxena, B.P**	History of Shahjahan of Delhi, Allahabad, 1932.
223	**Schneider, H.K**	Economic development and economic change: The caste of East African cattle, C.A., 15, pp. 259-277, 1974.
224	**Schoff, W.H.(Ed.)**	The periplus of the erythream sea, London, 1912.
225	**Sen, Geeti**	Paintings from the Akbarnama, Rupa and Co., 1984.
226	**Serjeant, R.B.**	Islamic textiles, material for a history of Islamic textiles upto the Mongol conquest, Ars Islamica, Vols. XI-XII, Ann arbor, University of Michigan press, 1946, pp. 98-145.
227	**Sewell, Robert**	A forgotten empire, London, 1924.
228	**Shanti Swarup**	The arts and crafts of India and Pakistan, Bombay, 1957.
229	**Singh, C.**	Textiles and Costumes from the Maharaja Savai Maan Singh II Museum, MSMS II Trust, City Palace, Jaipur, 1979.

230	**Singh C. and Ahiuasi, P.**	Woollen textiles and costumes from Bharat Kala Bhavan, Banaras Hindu University, 1981.
231	**Sinha, Bipin K.**	The beauties of Indian embroideries, American Magazine of Art, XVII, 1926, pp. 586-587.
232	**Smith, M.G**	The economy of the Hausa communities of Zaria, London, H. M. Stationery office, 1955.
233	**Smith, V.A**	The treasure of Akbar, J.R.A.S., 1915, pp. 231-242.
234	**Spear, P.**	The twilight of the Moghuls, Cambridge University press, p. 140.
235	**Spies, O.**	An Arab account of India in the 14th century, translated from Persian and Arabic, the Muslim University jounal, 1935, pp. 69-70.
236	**Strong, Roy**	The Indian heritage, Court life and arts under Mughal rule, V. and A. museum and the Herbert press, 65, Belsize law, 1982.
237	**Stuers Vreeda de**	Purdah among muslim women, 1971.
238	**Sykes, Sire Percy**	A history of Persia, 2nd edition, 2 Vols., London, 1921.
239	**Tann, E. H.**	Notes on eastern embroideries, Art worker's quarterly, III, pp. 147-150., with 1 coloured plate, 5 examples and 4 figures.

240	**Tansukhram (Ed.)**	Kuttanimatam, Bombay, 1923.
241	**Tavernier, Jean Baptiste,**	Travels in India, translated from the original French edititon of 1676 by V. Ball, 2 Vols., 1889.
242	**Terry, Edward**	A voyage to East India, London, 1777.
243	**Tilke, Max**	Oriental costumes-their designs and colours, translated by C. Hamilton (German).
244	**Vasu, S.C**	Astadhyayi of Panini, 1962.
245	**Veblen, T.**	Theory of leisure class: An economic study of institutions, Unwin books, London, 1912.
246	**Vyas, S. N**	Ramayan Kalin Sanskriti, Satsahitya prakashan, Delhi, 1958.
247	**Warmingtin, E.H**	Commerce between the roman empire and India, Cambridge, 1928.
248	**Watson, John Forbes**	Indian costumes and textile fabrics, Edinburgh review, Vol. 126, 1867.
249	**Watt, George**	J.I.A.I., Vol. II, Nos. 17-24, Oct 1858.
250	**Weber, M.**	The theory of social and economic organizations, New York, translated by A.M. Henderson and Talcott Parsons(Ed.), The Free press of Glencoe, 1947.
251	**Wehr, Hans**	A dictionary of modern written Arabic, ed. By J. Milton Cornon, Wiesbaden, 1979.

252	Weibel. A.E	Two thousand years of textiles, New York, 1952.
253	Welch, S.C	Indian art and culture 1300-1900, Mapin publishing, 1986.
254	Wheeler, J.T	India, Vedic and Post vedic, Calcutta, 1952.
255	Williamson, Thos	The costumes and customs of modern India, London, 1813.
256	Wilson, H.H.	The Persian Gulf, Oxford, 1928.
257	Wingate, B. Isabel	Textile fabrics and their selection, Prentice Hall Inc., Eaglewood Cliffs, New jersey, 1976.
258	Yasin, Mohammad	A social history of Islamic India, Munshiram Manoharlal Publishers Pvt. Ltd., New Delhi, 1971.
259	Yates, J.	Textrinum Antiquorum, London, 1843, Bk. III, Ch. II.
260	Yule, H. (Ed.)	The book of sir Marco Polo, third edition revised by H. Cordier, 2 Vols., p.304, London, 1903.
261	Zahida, Amjad Ali	Embroidery in Pakistan, Pakistan quarterly, VI, No. 1, 1956, pp. 51-56.
262	Zahiruddin, Faruki	Aurangzeb and his times. Zari the golden thread of India, A.I.H.B., New Delhi.

III : APPENDIX

MANAGING ZARI INDUSTRY IN SOUTH GUJARAT
QUESTIONNAIRE

(1) Name of Manufacturer : ....
....

(2) Address : ....
....

(3) Which type of firm? :   [   ]
    (a) Sole Proprietorship
    (b) Partnership
    (c) Private Limited

(4) Which type of Zari product? : (Fill as per 'Annexure')   [   ]
    (a) REAL
    (b) IMITATION
    (c) METALLIC

(5) Since how long producing?
....
....
....

(6) How much capital invested?
....
....
....

(7) How many machines utilized in production?
....
....
....

(8) Which process adopted in production?
....
....
....

(9) Do you have applied any technical idea ?   Yes/No   [   ]
    Or whether try to change technicality ?   Yes/No   [   ]
    In which year ?..
    Which change you have done ?..

(10) To whom you are supplying/selling your finished product ?
    ....
    ....
    ....

(11) Source of raw materials:
    ....
    ....
    ....

(12) What is labour hour rate for your process ?
    ....
    ....
    ....

(13) How much hours machine is operated ?
    ....
    ....
    ....

(14) Have you got any training ?   Yes/No   [   ]
(15) Is there any need of training ?
    ....
    ....
    ....

(16) In which type we keep this industry ?
    (1) Tiny   (2) Cottage   (3) Small   (4) Medium   (5) Large

(17) At present which concessions/incentives offered by Government ?

(1)	Sale Tax benefit	Yes / No	[	]
(2)	Income Tax benefit	Yes / No	[	]
(3)	Electricity benefit	Yes / No	[	]
(4)	Municipal Corp.	Yes / No	[	]
(5)	GIDC benefit	Yes / No	[	]
	* Shade	Yes / No	[	]
	* Rehabilitation	Yes / No	[	]
	* SSI	Yes / No	[	]
	* Others			

(18) Which expectations you have from Government ?

....
....
....
....
....

(19) Which are the sources of finance for business ?

(1) Relative ☐   (2) Private finance ☐

(3) Societies ☐   (4) Govt. grants ☐

(5) Govt. Loans ☐   (6) Bank ☐

(7) Supplier's Advance ☐   (8) Others. ☐

(20) Any management applied in your business ?   Yes / No   [   ]

Who looks after management ?

Name : ....

Relation : ....

Education :........................ Professional .... Academic ....

Salary :..

Experience :..

(21) Any research has been done for this business?   Yes / No   [   ]
    # Which type of research? ....
    ....
    ....

(22) Are you offering any type of work done
    for study purpose to anyone?   Yes / No   [   ]
    # Any recommendations?   [   ]
    # Which?   [   ]

(23) Are you doing any Export?   Yes / No   [   ]
    # Since how many years? ....
    # Where you are sending your material? ....
    # How much you are sending? ....
    # How much turnover? (annual) ....
    # Are you expecting to increase your exports? ....
    # Any difficulty found in Export? ....
    # Which type? ....

(24) Is quality of product required in business?   Yes / No   [   ]
    # Do you agree? ....
    # Which type of quality you expect? ....

(25) Do you have any competition in your business?   Yes / No   [   ]
    # Which type?   [   ]

(26) Are you getting satisfied price for your product?   Yes / No   [   ]
    # Price according to cost ....
    # Ratio of profit ....
    # If not, Why? ....
    ....
    ....
    ....

(27) Any pollution in your business for your product? Yes / No [ ]
 If yes, which type of pollution? [ ]
 Air / Water / Sound
(28) Any risk do you find in your business? ....
 Fire / Accident / Physical / Investment / Rejection / Others
(29) Is a business organized? Yes / No [ ]
 If No, Why? ....
 ....
(30) Is there any wastage in your business? Yes / No [ ]
 How much? ....
 Which type? ....
(31) Are you utilizing chemicals in your business? Yes / No [ ]
 * If yes, which chemicals you are utilizing in your business? ....
 * Are you using laboratory? ....
(32) Which other factories are affecting your business? ....
 * Seasonal change
 * Fashion
 * Over production
(33) Which type of license needed in your business?
 * Spirit [ ]
 * Others [ ]
(34) Any effect of Globalisation for the business? ....
 ....
 ....
(35) Any labour law applied for the business? ....
 Which difficulty do you find? ....
 ....
 ....

ANNNEXURE - 1

Imitation Zari Process

Sr. No.	Process	No. of Units	No. of Persons	Family Others	Electricity Consumption
I	Melting of Silver				
II	Preparation of Silver Wire Bars				
III	Hamering of Silver Bars				
IV	Drawing of Silver Wire of different Gauges. 20, 40, 60, 80				
V	Flattening of Wire Lametta (Thining)				
VI	Dyeing of Cotton or Silk or Art Silk Yarn				
VII	Winding of Lametta on Silk Art Silk or Cotton				
VIII	Electroplating of Silver Zari threads to make Gold thread.				

ANNNEXURE - 2

Real Zari Process

Sr. No.	Process	No. of Units	No. of Persons	Family Others	Electricity Supply (HP)
I	Making of 1/2 copper coils from copper bars in Rolling Mill				
II	Copper Wire Drawing Units (Pawtha) for Drawing wire upto 30 SWG (drawing through Dies)				
III	Gilding of 30 SWG Copper wire by Silver in Cement Concrete Tanks Or Polythene tanks				
IV	Further Drawing of this 30 SWG Silver Electroplated Copper Wire in fine gauges. (Tania Units)				
V	Flatting of Silver glited copper wire (Lametta making) flatting machine. (Chapad or Flattering Unit)				
VI	Wounding of Lametta on yarn on Kasab winding machines.				
VII	Gilding of Silver threads (Gold or Lacquer) (Kasab) (A) Powder Gilding (B) Fast Gilding				

ANNNEXURE - 3

Metallic Zari Process

Sr. No.	Process	No. of Units	No. of Persons	Family Others	Electricity Supply (HP)
I	Coating of Sheet (Film)				
II	Cutting of Sheet				
III	Twisting				
IV	Steaming				
V	Winding				
VI	Packing				

ANNEXURE-4

(Rs. crore at 2001-02 prices)

BUDGET SUPPORT, IEBR AND OUTLAY FOR CENTRAL MINISTRIES / DEPARTMENT : NINTH PLAN REALIZATION AND TENTH PLAN PROJECTIONS

	MINISTRY / DEPARTMENT	BUDGETARY SUPPORT			IEBR			TOTAL OUTLAY		
		Ninth Plan Realization	Tenth Plan Projections	% Increase	Ninth Plan Realization	Tenth Plan Projections	% Increase	Ninth Plan Realization	Tenth Plan Projections	% Increase
1.	Agriculture and Co-operation	8308	13200	58.9	-	-	-	8303	13200	58.9
2.	Agriculture Research & Education	2673	5368	100.8	-	-	-	2673	5368	100.8
3.	Animal Husbandry & Dairying	1027	2500	143.4	-	-	-	1027	2500	143.4
4.	Agro & Rural Industries	2675	2950	10.3	-	-	-	2675	2950	10.3
5.	Atomic Energy	6771	21550	218.3	1671	10820	547.5	8442	32370	283.4
6.	Chemicals & Petro-Chemicals	191	300	57.1	5516	2744	-50.3	5707	3044	-46.7
7.	Fertilizers	1013	1050	3.7	4474	4850	8.4	5487	5900	7.5
8.	Civil Aviation	204	400	96.1	9228	12528	35.8	9432	12928	37.1
9.	Coal	2233	1050	-53.0	14823	30541	106.0	17056	31591	85.2
10.	Mines	950	1271	33.8	4873	8187	68.0	5823	9458	62.4
11.	Commerce	1876	4547	142.4	169	15	-91.1	2045	4562	123.1
12.	Industrial Policy and Promotion	2113	2000	-5.3	-	-	-	2113	2000	-5.3
13.	Information Technology	1236	2714	119.6	619	2778	348.8	1855	5492	196.1
14.	Post	443	1350	204.7	-	-	-	443	1350	204.7
15.	Telecommunications	915	1500	63.9	86435	85484	-1.1	87350	86984	-0.4
16.	Food and Public Distribution	236	250	5.9	620	485	-21.8	856	735	-14.1
17.	Consumer Affairs	52	55	5.8	-	-	-	52	55	5.8
18.	Disinvestment	-	-	-	-	-	-	-	-	-

MINISTRY / DEPARTMENT	BUDGETARY SUPPORT			IEBR			TOTAL OUTLAY		
	Ninth Plan Realization	Tenth Plan Projections	% Increase	Ninth Plan Realization	Tenth Plan Projections	% Increase	Ninth Plan Realization	Tenth Plan Projections	% Increase
19. Development of North-Eastern region	-	150	-	-	-	-	-	150	-
20. Environment and Forests	3186	5770	81.1	-	-	-	3186	5770	81.1
21. External Affairs	1803	2811	55.9	-	-	-	1803	2811	55.9
22. Economic affairs	2931	300	-89.8	-	-	-	2931	300	-89.8
23. Expenditure	15	2	-86.7	-	-	-	15	2	-86.7
24. Revenue	3	1	-66.7	-	-	-	3	1	-66.7
25. Food Processing Industries	216	650	200.9	-	-	-	216	650	200.9
26. Health	5314	9253	74.1	-	-	-	5314	9253	74.1
27. Family Welfare	15088	27125	79.8	-	-	-	15088	27125	79.8
28. Indian systems of Medicine and Homeopathy	322	775	140.7	-	-	-	322	775	140.7
29. Heavy industries	958	700	-26.9	1649	1363	-17.3	2607	2063	-20.9
30. Public Enterprises	-	50	-	-	-	-	-	50	-
31. Home affairs	707	2000	182.9	-	-	-	707	2000	182.9
32. Elimentary education and literacy	23792	30000	26.1	-	-	-	23792	30000	26.1
33. Secondary education and Higher education	-	13825	-	-	-	-	-	13825	-
34. Women and child development	6729	13780	104.8	-	-	-	6729	13780	104.8
35. Information and Broadcasting	965	2380	146.6	2209	2750	24.5	3174	5130	61.6
36. Labour	510	1500	194.1	-	-	-	510	1500	194.1
37. Company affairs	1	50	4900.0	-	-	-	1	50	4900.0
38. Justice	397	700	76.3	-	-	-	397	700	76.3

MINISTRY / DEPARTMENT		BUDGETARY SUPPORT			IEBR			TOTAL OUTLAY		
		Ninth Plan Realization	Tenth Plan Projections	% Increase	Ninth Plan Realization	Tenth Plan Projections	% Increase	Ninth Plan Realization	Tenth Plan Projections	% Increase
39.	Non-conventional energy sources	1721	4000	132.4	2140	3167	48.0	3861	7167	85.6
40.	Ocean development	498	1125	125.9	-	-	-	498	1125	125.9
41.	Personnel, Public grievance and Pensions	78	250	220.5	-	-	-	78	250	220.5
42.	Petroleum and Natural gas	-	-	-	70338	103656	47.4	70338	103656	47.4
43.	Planning Commission	614	340	-44.6	-	-	-	614	340	-44.6
44.	Power	14907	25000	67.7	29785	118399	297.5	44692	143399	220.9
45.	Railways	16491	27600	67.4	34120	33000	-3.3	50611	60600	19.7
46.	Road transport and Highways	19393	35000	80.5	18279	24700	35.1	37672	59700	58.5
47.	Drinking water supply	8052	14200	76.4	-	-	-	8052	14200	76.4
48.	Land resources	2404	6526	171.5	-	-	-	2404	6526	171.5
49.	Rural development	43273	56748	31.1	-	-	-	43273	56748	31.1
50.	Biotechnology	669	1450	116.7	-	-	-	669	1450	116.7
51.	Science and technology	1635	3400	108.0	11	-	-	1646	3400	106.6
52.	Scientific and Industrial research	1478	2575	74.2	-	-	-	1478	2575	74.2
53.	Shipping	696	2350	237.6	-	11870	-	696	14220	1943.1
54.	Small Scale Industries	-	2200	-	666	384	-42.3	666	2584	288.0
55.	Social justice and empowerment	5404	8530	57.8	-	-	-	5404	8530	57.8
56.	Space	7097	13250	86.7	-	-	-	7097	13250	86.7
57.	Statistics and Programme implementation	215	900	318.6	-	-	-	215	900	318.6
58.	Steel	85	65	-23.5	8882	10978	23.6	8967	11043	23.2

	MINISTRY / DEPARTMENT	BUDGETARY SUPPORT			IEBR			TOTAL OUTLAY		
		Ninth Plan Realization	Tenth Plan Projections	% Increase	Ninth Plan Realization	Tenth Plan Projections	% Increase	Ninth Plan Realization	Tenth Plan Projections	% Increase
59.	Textiles	1836	3500	90.6	42	80	90.5	1878	3580	90.6
60.	Tourism	640	2900	353.1	171	-	-	811	2900	257.6
61.	Culture	740	1720	132.4	-	-	-	740	1720	132.4
62.	Tribal affairs	654	1754	168.2	-	-	-	654	1754	168.2
63.	Urban development	4754	7000	47.2	2571	5168	101.0	7325	12168	66.1
64.	Urban employment and poverty alleviation	1150	4050	252.2	8644	13501	56.2	9794	17551	79.2
65.	Water resources	1955	3600	84.1	-	-	-	1955	3600	84.1
66.	Youth affairs and sports	980	1825	86.2	-	-	-	980	1825	86.2
	TOTAL	233272	405735	73.9	307935	487448	58.3	541207	893183	65.0

NOTE : Zari is a part of Handicraft which becomes the budgetary part of Textile Ministry.
Ninth and Tenth Plan of Government related to Textile.

MANAGING ZARI INDUSTRY IN SOUTH GUJARAT

A STUDY

THESIS
Submitted for the Degree of

DOCTOR OF PHILOSOPHY IN COMMERCE

By

GIRISHKUMAR NAVNITLAL RANA
M. COM.

Under Supervision of

DR. V. B. PATEL

Professor
Department of Business and Industrial Management

**VEER NARMAD SOUTH GUJARAT UNIVERSITY,
SURAT - 395 007.
FEBRUARY - 2005**

CERTIFICATE

This is to certify that **Girishkumar Navnitlal Rana** has made a study on **"MANAGING ZARI INDUSTRY IN SOUTH GUJARAT" a study** under my supervision. The study is based on his own work and analysis. I recommend this report to be sent for evaluation in partial fulfillment of the requirement for the degree of Ph. D.

Patel

Dr. V. B. Patel
Project Guide

Dr. (Prof.) S. Kumar
Head of the Department & Dean
D. B. I. M.

(Department of Business and Industrial Management)
VEER NARMAD SOUTH GUJARAT UNIVERSITY
SURAT.

GIRISHKUMAR N. RANA
                M. COM.
Research Student
Department of Commerce,
Veer Narmad South Gujarat University
SURAT

DECLARATION

      I hereby declare that the thesis titled "MANAGING ZARI INDUSTRY IN SOUTH GUJARAT" A STUDY submitted for the award of Doctor of Philosophy in Commerce of VEER NARMAD SOUTH GUJARAT UNIVERSITY, Surat is a record of research work done by me under the supervision and guidance of Dr. Vinod B. Patel, Professor, Department of D.B.I.M., South Gujarat University, Surat-395 007. and no part of the thesis has been submitted for any other degree or diploma prior to this date.

Date :

Place : **SURAT.**   (GIRISHKUMAR N.RANA)

PREFACE

Zari is a historic product of surat. The glitter of zari attracted British, French and Dutch people to Surat. The golden/silver thread is produced from solid pure gold and silver metal. The skilled craftsmen produce hair thin zari thread, which is a state of the art product. The zari thread has been an attraction for everybody. Today the precious metal gold and silver has become too costly and hence pure zari is beyond everybody's reach. Metallic Yarn Zari (imitation zari) has come as an able, ideal and most suitable substitute to all types of pure zari.

The zari industry in Surat is marked by division of processes between enterprises. Theoretically speaking, this gives scope for specialization, efficiency and innovation, essential for competing beyond local markets. Surat based zari has not been able to build on these advantages of clustering, due to mutual suspicion, distrust and lack of unity, coupled with agreed and exploitative labour practices, prevalent among the manufacuters.

The industry caters to the end product made in different parts of the country by supplying three distinct classes of products viz. real zari, imitation zari and plastic zari. It is unfortunate that despite surat being a major synthetic textiles production centre, the zari produced in surat cannot be interwoven with synthetic textiles due to technical inadequacies having their roots in lack of innovation in products and processes. Our study has brought out this as a major constraint as well as a major opportunity if the challenges is overcome. In the absence of local demand and due to severe and unhealthy competition in catering to the limited and stagnant distant markets of zari products, the industry has wounded up with adverse terms of trade. Our recommendations based on view of historical experiences of small manufacturing units and our understanding of the current scenario of the surat zari industry, naturally follow similar lines.

An attempt has been made in the present study about 'managing zari industry in South Gujarat'. The primary objective of the study was to revive the sagging zari industry so as to improve the employment potential of the industry. Due to peculiar nature of traditional industry working with a stagnant market in a very competitive atmosphere, it became necessary to give up formalise empirical research method. The study had to be based on informal interviews, and discussions at various levels and field visits to a few units in several parts of surat.

The present study is divided into five chapters. Chapter one, which is introductory in nature, inclusive of historical background. It also reflects the products of zari industry, the process of different zari's, the types of patterns of organization, marketing, export, the growth and the developmental situation of the industry.

Second chapter focuses on the issues of zari industry. It also includes SWOT analysis. The infrastructure facilities, prospectus ahead, role of co-operative societies, role of government as well as environmental aspects have been analysed in the second chapter.

The third chapter reflects the research methodology, scopes and objectives and limitation of the study.

Chapter four shows the characteristics of respondents, analysis of the data as well as summarized findings.

The fifth chapter enlightens the challenges in time to come, recommendations and further research avenues.

ACKNOWLEDGEMENT

The present study has been made possible through the co-operation, assistance and encouragement of many individuals to whom I wish to express my gratitude. I sincerely express my gratitude to my guide Dr. Vinod B. Patel, Professor, Department of Business and Industrial Management, Veer Narmad South Gujarat University, Surat, for his invaluable guidance. His constant encouragement and tireless assistance helped me to complete my study so successfully.

I owe lot to Dr. Satyendra Kumar - Professor and Head, Department of Business and Industrial Management for his precious guidance and assistance. I fall short of words to express my deep sense of gratefulness to Shri J. B. Shah, Principal, Arts & Commerce college, Amroli, for his constant motivation and direction throughout my study. I wish to express my thanks to Shri Champakbhai Gandhi, Shri Ranjitbhai Gilitwala, Shri Shantilal Jariwala, Shri Ramanbhai Jariwala and all other office bearers as well as members of Zari Goods Producers' Co-operative Credit Society, South India Zari Merchant and Manufacturer's Association, Andhra-Karnatak Zari Manufacturing Association, Varanasi Zari Mandal to provide me all the necessary information. I also wish to express my thanks to Chamber of Commerce, Surat for providing me the details.

I would like to express my sincere gratitude to all my colleagues who besides encouraging me to go deeper into the subject helped me in more than one way. Yet specific mention must be made of Prof. Ritu Agarwal, Professor in English, who carefully reviewed the manuscript and gave helpful comments. I express my deep gratitude to my dearest friends Shri Navin Chapadia, Ex-member of Handicraft and Handloom Board, Government of India, New Delhi (Surat), Shri Kapil Puri (Guru), Prof. B. N. Patel who have provided me constant inspiration and helped me a lot in the successful completion of my study. I am grateful to Hon'ble Kashiram Rana, the then Textile Minister, Government of India and his staff of ministry who have provided me the required information and also extend needed co-operation.

During my research work, The computerised and printing work was handled by my student, Kasim M. Varsi, and thereby I express my heart felt thanks to him.

Last but not the least, specific mention must be made to my parents, and above all my wife, Aruna, daughter Heta as well as Ashuthosh, my son, whose inspiration and assistance at various stages not only goaded me on but boosted my self confidence while relieving me of my odd domestic chores. Lastly, I thank one and all, who inspired and helped me directly or otherwise, in providing the necessary form of the study.

SURAT   **(GIRISH N. RANA)**

MANAGING ZARI INDUSTRY IN SOUTH GUJARAT - A STUDY

● CONTENTS ●

CHAPTER NO.	TITLE	PAGE NO.
1	**INTRODUCTION AND HISTORY**	
	1.1 INTRODUCTION	1
	1.2 HISTORY	7
	1.3 PRODUCTION OF ZARI INDUSTRY	37
	1.4 PROCESS OF CRAFT	79
	1.5 PATTERNS OF ORGANISATION	96
	1.6 MARKETING OF ZARI	101
	1.7 EXPORTS OF ZARI	105
	1.8 GROWTH AND DEVELOPMENT	120
	1.9 PICTORIAL PRESENTATION OF ZARI AND ZARI PRODUCTS.	128
2	**BASIC ISSUES OF ZARI INDUSTRY**	
	2.1 SWOT ANALYSIS.	213
	2.2 INFRASTRUCTURE FACILITIES IN SURAT.	224
	2.3 PROSPECTS AHEAD IN INDIA FOR ZARI.	226
	2.4 ROLE OF PUBLIC REPRESENTATIVE i.e. MEMBER OF PARLIAMENT / MEMBER OF LEGISLATIVE ASSEMBLY.	230
	2.5 ROLE OF CHAMBER OF COMMERCE.	233
	CONT...	

CHAPTER NO.	TITLE	PAGE NO.
	2.5.1 ROLE OF GOVERNMENT IN THE DEVELOPMENT OF ZARI INDUSTRY.	234
	2.5.2 ROLE OF ELECTRICITY COMPANIES IN THE DEVELOPMENT OF ZARI INDUSTRY.	235
	2.5.3 ROLE OF BANKING AND TERM LENDING FINANCIAL INSTITUTION IN THE DEVELOPMENT OF ZARI INDUSTRY IN SURAT.	236
	2.5.4 ROLE OF MUNICIPAL CORPORATION.	245
	2.6 NEED OF MARKETING CO-OPERATIVE SOCIETY.	246
	2.7 ENVIRONMENTAL ASPECTS.	247
3	**RESEARCH METHODOLOGY**	
	3.1 SCOPES	256
	3.2 OBJECTIVES	260
	3.3 SAMPLING PLAN	263
	3.4 METHOD OF DATA COLLECTION	264
	3.4 LIMITATIONS	268
4	**ANALYSIS AND OUTCOME**	
	4.1 CHARACTERISTICS OF RESPONDENTS	270
	4.2 ANALYSIS	272
	4.3 DATA ANALYSIS	284
	4.4 SUMMARIZED FINDINGS	316
	CONT...	

CHAPTER NO.	TITLE	PAGE NO.
5	**RECOMMENDATIONS AND SUGGESSTIONS**	
	5.1. CHALLENGES IN TIMES TO COME	322
	5.2 RECOMMENDATIONS	325
	5.3 FURTHER RESEARCH AVENUES	333
I	**REFERENCES**	340
II	**BIBLIOGRAPHY**	343
III	**APPENDIX**	369

LIST OF TABLES

TABLE NO.	TITLE	PAGE NO.
1.4.1	Zari Units In Surat - 1970.	87
1.5.1	Spatial Distribution Of Surat Based Zari Units.	96
1.5.2	Distribution of Family and Hired Workers in Units.	100
1.7.1	Exports of Zari and Zari Goods.	107
1.7.2	Statement of Exports of Handicrafts.	110
1.8.1	Zari Industry - 1980.	125
2.5.3.1	Statement of Surat Zari Goods Producers Co-op.Soc.	237
2.5.3.2	Profit - Surat Zari Goods Producers Co-op.Soc.	243
4.3.1	Types of Firms.	284
4.3.2	Types of Zari Products.	286
4.3.3	Tenure of Production.	288
4.3.4	Investment.	290
4.3.5	How many Machines Utilized in Production.	292
4.3.6	Any Technical changes done or not.	294
4.3.7	Supply of Finished Goods.	297
4.3.8	Availability of Raw-Material.	300
4.3.9	Training received or not.	303
4.3.10	Finance for Business.	306
4.3.11	Management Applied in Business.	309
4.3.12	Any reasonable Research done for Business.	312
4.3.13	Offering Study or not.	312

LIST OF CHARTS

CHART NO.	TITLE	PAGE NO.
1.4.1 (A)	Zari Units In Surat - 1970.	87
1.4.1 (B)	Zari Units In Surat - 1970.	88
1.4.2 (A)	Workers in Various Units.	88
1.4.2 (B)	Workers in Various Units.	88
1.7.1 (A)	Exports Value in Crores of Rupees.	108
1.7.1 (B)	Exports Value in Crores of Rupees.	108
1.7.2	Exports of Handicrafts.	111
1.7.2 (A)	Artmetalware - Exports.	112
1.7.2 (B)	Artmetalware - Exports.	112
1.7.3 (A)	Woodware - Exports.	113
1.7.3 (B)	Woodware - Exports.	113
1.7.4 (A)	Handprinted Textiles and Scarves - Exports.	114
1.7.4 (B)	Handprinted Textiles and Scarves - Exports.	114
1.7.5 (A)	Embroidered & Crocheted Goods - Exports.	115
1.7.5 (B)	Embroidered & Crocheted Goods - Exports.	115
1.7.6 (A)	Shawls as Artware - Exports.	116
1.7.6 (B)	Shawls as Artware - Exports.	116
1.7.7 (A)	Zari and Zari Goods - Exports.	117
1.7.7 (B)	Zari and Zari Goods - Exports.	117
1.7.8 (A)	Imitaion Jewellery - Exports.	118
1.7.8 (B)	Imitaion Jewellery - Exports.	118
1.7.9 (A)	Miscellaneous Handicrafts - Exports.	119
1.7.9 (B)	Miscellaneous Handicrafts - Exports.	119

CHART NO.	TITLE	PAGE NO.
2.5.3.1(A)	Membership.	238
2.5.3.1(B)	Membership.	238
2.5.3.2(A)	Share.	239
2.5.3.2(B)	Share.	239
2.5.3.3(A)	Other Funds.	240
2.5.3.3(B)	Other Funds.	240
2.5.3.4(A)	Reserve Funds.	241
2.5.3.4(B)	Reserve Funds.	241
2.5.3.5(A)	Dividend.	242
2.5.3.5(B)	Dividend.	242
2.5.3.6(A)	Profit.	244
2.5.3.6(B)	Profit.	244
4.3.1 (A)	Types of Firms.	284
4.3.1 (B)	Types of Firms.	285
4.3.2 (A)	Types of Zari Products.	286
4.3.2 (B)	Types of Zari Products.	287
4.3.3 (A)	Tenure of Production.	288
4.3.3 (B)	Tenure of Production.	289
4.3.4 (A)	Investment.	290
4.3.4 (B)	Investment.	291
4.3.5 (A)	How many Machines Utilized in Production.	292
4.3.5 (B)	How many Machines Utilized in Production.	293
4.3.5 (A)	Any Technical changes done or not.	294
4.3.5 (B)	Any Technical changes done or not.	295

CHART NO.	TITLE	PAGE NO.
4.3.7 (A)	Supply of Finished Goods.	297
4.3.7 (B)	Supply of Finished Goods.	298
4.3.8 (A)	Availability of Raw-Material.	300
4.3.8 (B)	Availability of Raw-Material.	301
4.3.9 (A)	Training received or not.	303
4.3.9 (A)	Training received or not.	304
4.3.10(A)	Finance for Business.	306
4.3.10(B)	Finance for Business.	307
4.3.11(A)	Management Applied in Business.	309
4.3.11(B)	Management Applied in Business.	310
4.3.12(A)	Any reasonable Research done for Business.	312
4.3.12(B)	Any reasonable Research done for Business.	313
4.3.13(A)	Offering Study or not.	313
4.3.13(B)	Offering Study or not.	314

ABBREVIATIONS

SGCCI	:	Southern Gujarat Chamber of Commerce and Industry.
ZMA	:	Zari Merchants' Association.
ZGPCOS	:	Zari Goods Producers Co-operative Societies.
IRMA	:	Institute of Rural Marketing Association.
SMC	:	Surat Municipal Corporation.
DIC	:	District Industrial Centre.
AIHB	:	All India Handicrafts Board.
C.A.	:	Current Anthropology
G.O.I	:	Government of India.
IETJ	:	Indian Export Trade Journal
EFCS	:	Ethnographic and Folk Culture Society.
JIAI	:	Journal of Indian Art and Industry.
TTPR	:	The Town Planning Reveiw
Z.I.IC.	:	Zari Industry Inquiry Centre.
A.I.Z.F.	:	All India Zari Federation

CHAPTER 1 :

INTRODUCTION AND HISTORY

		Page No.
1.1	INTRODUCTION	1
1.2	HISTORY	7
1.3	PRODUCTION OF ZARI INDUSTRY	37
1.4	PROCESS OF CRAFT	79
1.5	PATTERNS OF ORGANISATION	96
1.6	MARKETING OF ZARI	101
1.7	EXPORTS OF ZARI	105
1.8	GROWTH AND DEVELOPMENT	120
1.9	PICTORIAL PRESENTATION OF ZARI AND ZARI PRODUCTS.	128

CHAPTER 1 : INTRODUCTION AND HISTORY

1.1 INTRODUCTION:

From Rigvedic times, we have been hearing of several varieties of textiles, among which cloth of gold-hiranya , figures as a distinguished type. Gods in their grandeur wear it, as they ride in their stately chariots. Hiranya cloth has usually been considered the earliest equivalent of present-day zari work of kimkhwabs (brocades).

India has long been known for its golden thread, for Zari. Well-known products of the Indian Zari industry, besides gold and silver thread (Zari kasab) are the embroidery materials like stars and spangles, chalak, champo, kinari, salma and badla. The zari craft includes making zari thread and other materials, as well as thread. The latter covers zari embroidered saris, evening-bags, foot-wear and belts, zari textiles and the world-famous brocades.

Surat is the biggest zari thread-making centre in the country, followed by Varanasi. Both imitation and real zari threads, zari embroidery material and zari lace and borders are manufactured in Surat. Varanasi, on the other hand, is a big centre for the manufacture of superior quality real zan thread (kalabattu) zari textiles and zari brocades. Other centers of production are Jaipur and Ajmer which specialise in zari gota and zari thappa work.

The other centres of zari embroidery products are Agra, Bareilly, Varanasi. The items of zari are handbags, belts, shoe uppers, etc. Other popular items of export are zari badges all produced manually by skilled craftsmen in Bareilly and Varanasi. Zari threads are used extensively in handloom (and powerloom) saris which are manufactured all over India, especially in Varanasi, Bangalore, Dharmavaram, Kanchipuram and Paithan.

Zari is a historic product of Surat. The glitter of zari attracted British, French & Dutch people to Surat. The golden/silver thread is produced from solid pure gold & silver metal. The skilled craftsmen produce hair thin zari thread, which is a state of the art product. This zari thread has been a center of attraction for everybody. Today, the precious metal gold & silver has become too costly & hence pure zan is beyond everybody's reach.

Metallic yarn zari (imitation zari) has come as an able, ideal & most suitable substitute to all types of pure zari. Due to upgradation of technology, polyester film was metallised & coated, bringing into to existence the basic raw material for producing metallic yarn zari. France & Japan were the first to flood the market with zari made from polyester film in the year 1970. Since then, due to continous research & development metallic yarn zari has gained more market compared to all other types of imitation zari (made from copper) and pure zari.

Considering the cost aspect metallic yarn zari has done a great service to the nation by saving precious metal like gold & silver & also copper. Metallic yarn zari costing Rs.350/kg has become an easy & affordable luxury for common man. Pure zari costing Rs.4000 per kg has become a product beyond common man's reach.

Metallic zari industry today is an industry giving employment & self employment to more then 4000 families in Surat & to families at other centres like Ajmer, Maunathbhanjan. Salem, Coimbatore, Bangalore, Delhi, Malegaon, Nadiad. The process involved in making zari is very simple. Metallised coated film in desired colours are available in the market. This metallised coated film is first slitted with the help of a razor blade to pancake of small widths(normally 50 mm to 72 mm). The pancake produced are passed from the thin cutters, size of which depends upon the thickness of required zari. The zari so produced is wound on spools with the help of winder.

Major centers using metallic yarn zari are Surat, (used in

making various products viz kasab tilla, champo, gotta, zalar, etc.), Ahmedabad. (used in making borders for various gift applicatious), Bombay (used in ornamentation of fabrics meant for exports & used in decoration items), Bhivandi (used in fabrics & tapestry), Bangalore (used in handlooms), Salem, Coimbatore (handloom), Madras, Banaras, Maunathbhanajan (making sarees traditionally worn in marriage).

The questionnaire planned to be administrated to the zari workers broadly related to collection of information on:

(a) socio-economic conditions

(b) working environment

(c) employment and income distribution

(d) technology and extension services, and

(e) marketing pattern

This was done as the zari industry is predominantly owned by the zari merchants without whose active cooperation and willingness, access to information from the workers and fellow merchants would not have been possible.

Right from the beginning, zari merchants were extremely reluctant to part with any information relating to the zari industry. The stock answer provided by them was that since the industry was operating from the houses of the workers and merchants, and there existed no mechanism for collection and analysis of data on the industry, they would not be in a position to provide any information.

Further, on account of a possible suspicion on the part of the zari merchants about possible misuse of any information against their own interests, they systematically discouraged direct interaction with the workers and with fellow-merchants. In view of the impossibility of administering the questionnaires prepared by me, it became necessary to abandon the collection of primary data through structured interviews/questionnaires. It was considered advisable to elicit information through a process of unstructured dialogue, provided the zari merchants saw some purpose which would benefit them from the study.

After a lot of persuasion with the past and present office bearers of the Surat Zari Merchants' Association, a few meetings and visits could be organised. The meetings and visits, conducted in an informal and unstructured way, brought to fore many issues surrounding the zari industry of Surat. The report discusses these issues with reference to the structure of the zari industry in Surat and makes certain recommendations on the basis of the field observations. While it may be argued that strict research methodology by administration of questionnaires and collection and analysis of data could have provided statistically significant results, the study had to assume the course it had taken owing to the structure of the industry and the results had to be arrived at on the basis of unstructured interviews and informal observations. Further, visits of several zari units engaged in different processes and magnitudes of operation brought out the commonality of the pattern of issues in all units.

1.2 HISTORY:

1.2.1 ZARDOZI AS A CRAFT

Fabrics ornated with gold suggest regal opulence evoking historic splendour. In any artefact and culture, the use of gold tends to symbolise wealth and power, the fabrics with zardozi are no exception. The oldest documentary evidence to what might have been the earliest artefacts embroidered in precious metal is to be found in the Vedic age. However, zardoz[1] as a class of artisans along with other artisans followed the footsteps of the sultanate conquerors in the twelfth century down the mountain passes of the Khyber on to the plains of Indian sub-continent. A popular myth is found among the zardoz of Delhi, relating to the origin of this craft. This runs as follows:

Once a mosquito found entrance to a king's head. The fluttering of this mosquito caused the king severe headache. Every kind of treatment had failed. Finally Paigamber himself advised the head hakim in his dream that the king would be cured of his headache if he is hit by a shoe in the area of pain. The hakim narrated his dream to his associates. They executed a plan. A shoe decorated with pure gold and silver threads was ordered to be made for the purpose. The king was hit with the shoe. This killed the mosquito, curing the king of his ailment. He appreciated the artistic outlay on the shoe and desired to patronise the work. Other emperors and nobles followed him.

Retracing the history we come across the mention of hiranyan atkan which emphasises that the garments in the Vedic age were often embroidered with gold. Marut is often described as wearing mantles adorned with gold. Usha is described as wearing shining clothes, which were resplendent with gold. Apart from the unsewn garments which were general in those days, the Rigveda also refers to some words atka,[5] drapi, pesas indicating sewn garments. The term atka means a garment embroidered with gold thread. Another word hiranyair vyutarn signifies dresses worked with gold, reflecting like the sun. Rigvedic texts make innumerable allusions to such dresses which were worn by both men and women of high social ranking. References indicate this continuity in the epic period as well. Swarnatantu nirmita, the word occurring in Valmiki Ramayana, means adorned by gold wire.

Adiparva and Sabhaparva of the Mahabharata give interesting accounts of costly clothes embroidered with gold. Maharhavasthambra is a variety of costly robe mentioned at the time of marriage of the five Pandavas with Draupadi. The king of Kamboja is said to have presented Yudhishtara with many kinds of animal skins and woollen blankets all inlaid with threads of gold during the rajasuya sacrifice ceremony (jiftarupa-parishkitari), During this ceremony the kings of Chola and Pandya countries also presented fine clothing studded with shining precious stones. Even the gifts from Sinhal Desh were studded with precious stones. All these accounts are indicative of the fact that royal courts were making frequent presentations of fabrics with gold and precious stone work.

Valmiki's Ramayana speaks about maharajatvasas, the clothes embroidered with gold and silver. Rama and Sita were attired in yellow clothes (ratnambar) embroidered with gold thread and jewels when they went into exile. Dress of Ravana is described as maharhvastra sambaddh and mahamjatvasas indicating that the kingly costumes were expensive. Maharshaum sanvit is another reference in the same text implying the embroidery of fine expensive clothes. All these references indicate beyond doubt that embroidered costumes worked in gold, silver and precious stones were part of opulent tradition during the epic period. Vyasa also makes this observation in his accounts. This tradition seems to have extended to greater India.

No textual reference is available in support of the existence of this craft during the lull after the epic period. Panini, however, refers to a kind of silken cloth named koseyya signifying possibly the fabric adorned with gold. Buddhist literature provides very little evidence of embroidered clothes. It is possible that in the new stage of economy, when urbanism was in the process of emergence, and people were trading in exchange of gold bullion, there was less demand for gold decoration on fabric. But that the skill was present in some form could be known from the Jatakas where the stories refer to golden turbans used by kings and golden trappings used for state elephants. Sona-Nanda Jataka gives an elaborate description of the use of a heavily embroidered turban in gold in connection with king Manoja's entering the hermitage of Bodhisattva who in this blaze of glory comes, with turban cloth of gold", Such evidences would clearly indicate that the lavish use of gold and silver threads on turbans was in fashion among the nobility.

Jain literature provides interesting information about the silver or gold work on clothes, the text categorically banned the acceptance of such precious clothes by the monks and nuns, when they were begging for clothes. The sacred text says, 'no monk or nun should accept golden plaids, glittering like gold, embroidered with gold'. This description in Acharanga Sutra clearly spells out the evidence of the use of such clothings either by the royal courts or moneyed people. Kanakakhachiya was a kind of cloth embroidered with golden thread.

Several references, however, have been found in the accounts of Greek travellers throwing light on the existence of the gold embroidery tradition of the 4th century B.C. onwards. Describing the Indian ways of living as seen by Megasthenes, Strabo writes, "Contrary to their simplicity in general, they like to adorn themselves with apparels embroidered with gold." Strabo on another occasion says, 'the variegated garments spangled with gold' were in fashion. Curtius Rufus Quintus says that a king rides in a golden palanquin, garnished with pearls which dangle all round it and he is robed in fine muslin embroidered with purple and gold. Ptolemy speaks about the manufacture of muslin adorned with small pearls. These references distinctly reflect that gold and precious stone embroidery on various fabrics including muslin was much in vogue amongst the nobility. It is difficult to find out a corroboration of the texts with the contemporary life pattern of the Indians. But one may make a good attempt at it, if one tries to analyse the contemporary art pieces which depict men and women wearing draperies and jewellery.

Starting with Bharhut which in the true sense illustrates human figures in all poses and postures for the first time, we find a tradition of textiles which is usually plain without much decorations, except for a narrow decorative band made to hang between the legs attached to the kamarband. Unlike the other parts of dress, which are plain and simple, one would notice that this strip was beautifully decorated and perhaps also embroidered. This is found in Sanchi as well.

There is reason to believe that this piece of cloth attached to drapery later on came to be known as patka. Barua observed that kamarband, the belt around the waist, was also embroidered. The painting from Ajanta shows three women attendants wearing kamarband heavily embroidered in gold colour. One may perhaps speculate that the use of gold and silver thread was in currency during the period.

With the Kushanas, the socio-cultural and economic life of India seems to have taken a new turn. During this period India witnessed two cultural forces, one from central Asia and the other through the coast because of Indo-Roman trade. Indian economy not only reached a stable stage, but a new socio-historical phenomenon called urbanism swept practically the whole of India. The contemporary texts such as Divyavadana and Lalitavistara refer to a word hiryani or hirivastra indicating a cloth of gold. For the first time in a historical text we find reference to a cloth embroidered or woven with gold. It is not known whether hiryani was changed into kinkhab of later time. But on the testimony of Divyavadana, we may say that the shawls richly embroidered and brocaded with precious stones and gold became popular during this period. This is inferred from the mention of the term ratna-swarna-pravaraka. Here pravamka possibly means a dupatta, the head veil and ratna-swarna refers to precious stones and gold, hence meaning a dupatta adorned with gold and precious stones.

Much like the earlier sculptures, the Mathura sculptures of the Kushana period also show embroideries of various kinds. The seated image of Surya as illustrated by Vogel is shown wearing a short sleeved tight tunic fitting closely to the body and the arms. The tunic, having a semi-circular neck, has embroidered borders made of a scale pattern running down the middle of the chest. The cap which he is found to have worn is also heavily embroidered.

Another figure which by its beard and frizzled hair seems to be Persian or Saka, is shown wearing what appears to be a heavily embroidered tunic. The patterns seem to be embroidered in arched panels with simple beading and rope-like designs on both sides. The hem of the hemispherical cap is embroidered and decorated with the figures of sun and moon on the left. The decorative designs found on these sculptures may be claimed to be in gold and silver thread, as these are very similar to objects found on the grave goods of the Scythian burials. But one is also not very sure whether these designs developed later into what we understand as the zardozi embroidery of a later period.

The second phase of Ajanta painting, which is contemporary to the Guptas, provides a better picture in this regard. It is interesting to notice that the costumes of the local kings, their guards etc. represented in the Ajanta paintings are very plain and do not show any ostentatious decorations on their garments. But while representing foreigners, the painters are very particular about emphasising designed costumes. In Cave No. XVII, where a number of foreigners, apparently of Iranian descent, are depicted, they are shown wearing dresses heavily embroidered in gold colour, indicating gold thread. On top of the left side of the painting, an Iranian is shown riding on an elephant wearing a tunic with sleeves, the cuffs and the front portion of which are beautifully embroidered. Another fat attendant apparently of foreign origin, with a humorous face wears an embroidered dress with design consisting of bands decorated with solid triangles and circles. The tunic is tied around the waist with folds of a kamarband.

The women in Ajanta are also represented wearing embroidered clothes showing profusion of gold colour. In Cave XVII, a woman (otherwise without much clothing) wears an embroidered scarf covering her hair. In Cave II a woman is represented wearing a striped and embroidered cap. The colour and intricate design shown in the painting suggest embroidery done by gold thread. The Champiya Jataka represented in Cave No. I illustrates small stars worked in silk and gold or silver thread on a dull yellowish texture over the cushions and backrests. The black spaces visible underneath indicate the embroidered portion. Plate (b) shows the cushion for an arm rest embroidered with golden stripe in the centre, on the blue base. One may apprehend perhaps that the stuff of the cloth was possibly tash, embroidered with gold and silver wire. The patterns shown in the plate are so well marked that one may consider these as specimens of zardozi workmanship. There are a number of other paintings in Ajanta, where similar evidence is available. But the texts of the contemporary time are not very explicit about embroideries done in metal thread. An interesting evidence is however noteworthy in Harshacharita though late in date, referring to a dazzling muslin robe embroidered with hundreds of diverse flowers and birds gently rippledby the motion of the breeze, bahuvidha kusuma sakunisata sabhisatta.

Indeed, the descriptions found in Harshacharita and Kadambari, the popular works of Banabhatta, speaking eloquently about embroidery work in metal, leave no room for doubt that silk clothings of different colours (indrayudhajala-varnamsuka) were embroidered with gold and jewels, muktamsuka, meaning studded with fine pearls. The expression tara mukta phalopachiyamanas referred to the couches whose gay coverlets cast the hamsa tribes into shade as the bodies were overlaid with star-like pearls. Verse 243 of Harshacharita however mentions kararange meaning leather buckles having charming borders adorned with bright gold leaf work. We are not sure whether this gold work on leather followed the zardoz technique, but in view of the myth found among the zardoz living in Delhi, it is highly probable that gold work on leather might have been in practice during that time. We may however recall in this context that leather objects found in the Scythian burials have designs embroidered in gold and contemporary designs of leather upper and leather shoes.

A text called Kuttanimatam belonging to a later period gives an important information about the craft. Damodar Gupta, the minister of Jaypida, categorically speaks about this work, when he refers to the shoes worn by Bhattasuta Chintamani, a person of affluent position. His shoes were embroidered with gold thread and decorated with a floral meander (kusumadana). His lower garment also shows work done in gold thread (uchanda-kanaka-garbhita).

On surveying the contemporary lexicons, Sanskrit and Prakrit texts, we come across the word khalikachitavastram as some kind of embroidered clothes. Incidentally during the voyage of Marcopolo through India in the early 13th century, he found that gold working was at an opulent stage both in leather and textile. While describing the robes received by the twelve thousand barons from the emperor on the great festivals of India, he commented that "these robes are garnished with gems and pearls and other precious things in a very rich and costly manner. A fine golden girdle of great richness and value and likewise a pair of boots of camut, i.e., of Borgal" curiously wrought with silver thread.

At another place, while mentioning the prices of the commodities found in the coast of Gujarat, he observed that the Indians living in this part of country decorated cushions with gold embroidery. He writes, "they also work here beautiful mats in red and blue leather, exquisitely inlaid with figures of birds and beasts and skilfully embroidered with gold and silver wire. They also embroidered cushions in gold thread, so fine that they are worth six marks of silver apiece." In the explanatory note, Marcopolo observes that in places like Gujarat, Kathiawar and Rajasthan inlaid gold and stone working on leather for making bed covers and palanquin mats were in great fashion during this time. The accounts are very important, as these tell us how silver embroideries were practised on objects like dress materials, furnishing and other items of use particularly of leather.

The historical references cited above from Vedic times to thirteenth century enumerate several references pointing to ornamentation with gold and silver along with precious stones on a variety of fabrics including wool and leather.

Although repeated mention of gold embroidery in variegated forms occurs at several places in early history, absence of material indicating elaborate production of such embroidery leads us to believe that the craft had marginal existence in relation to the main cultural stream in terms of manufacture or production. However, definite evidences are found for large scale manufacture of zardozi textiles after the advent of Sultanate rule in India. It is difficult to accept that zardozi work found in this period was really a continuation of the earlier tradition. Instead one would find that the craft reached new heights at this stage. One may remember in this context that the Persian vocabulary uses a term zarkas during this period, which means zari embroidery. The practice of offering a robe of honour embroidered with gold and silver thread to the noble guest was in vogue during the period. Accounts are also available regarding the master craftspersons coming from Persia for teaching skills to local craftspersons in the production centres which were known as tiraz factory. It may be mentioned here that such references of manufacture are found during Tughlak dynasty, which seems to be the earliest evidence in so far as India is concerned.

Quluqshandi, a writer of the contemporary times, provides a detailed account of state-owned factories under the rule of the Tughlaks. He writes, " therein, of these who are master craftsmen are...makers of embroidery (zarakisa). The Sultan of Delhi has a tiraz factory (dar-al-tiraz) in which there are four thousand manufacturers of silk making all kinds of textiles for robes of honour (khilla), robes (kasawa) and presents (itlakat)." Al-Umari while speaking about the dress of the nobles of Delhi during the reign of Sultan Muhammad Tughlak writes, "No Indian but the Sultan and those whom he permits could use saddles with gold embroideries. The rest according to him could use only silver embroideries." Regarding the costumes of the Indians, he wrote, "most of their tartar (tartari) robes are embroidered with gold (muzarkasa-bi-dhahab). Some wear garments with both sleeves having a tiraz border of gold embroidery (zarkas). Giving an account of Sultan Muhammad (1320-51 A.D.), Barani writes that "Sultan Muhammad decided to recognise the Abbasid caliphate." He paid allegiance to the representatives of the family, who were in Egypt in the year (1343-44 A.D.) and in return he received a robe of honour (khilla) (dar tiraz-i-djamsha-yi-zarbaft-u-kimati) meaning that on the tiraz inscription of gold embroidered robes of value, they should inscribe the name of Caliph and nothing else. These are said to have been the specific orders given by Muhammad Tughlak.

Making an overview of the accounts left by Quluqshandi, Umari and Barani, there is no doubt that the Sultanate period was the time when there was a preponderance of gold/silver embroidery on dresses and on saddles and other leather works. The precious embroideries were affixed either on the arms or on the shoulders or in front or even at the skirt edges of garments. The use of such decoration by the Muslim aristocrats came into fashion at this time. One interesting custom noticed during this time was embroidering of the writings from holy scriptures with metal thread, indicating perhaps that this work was well absorbed in the mainstream of culture by that time. Gold embroideries in India seem to have reached a new phase in history. This could be known from frequent references to costumes of different kinds embroidered with gold and silver by several workers. But what is important to note in this context is that initially the tiraz inscription in the name of Caliph started to be made in zarkas. The makers of such embroideries were called zarkisa.

The other sources of information of this period are translations of the works of Ibn Batuta, who travelled through India during the Sultanate period (1287-1290). He has given interesting details of gold embroidery. Giving an account of a robe of honour which probably came from the Delhi tiraz factory, Ibn Batuta writes, "after the maghrib prayer they brought to Amir Ghadda a silk robe of blue colour embroidered with gold and studded with precious stones with a cap to match. The precious stones were so many in number that even the colour of the cloth was hidden from view." Describing the same robe R.B. Serjeant opines that it was presented to him by the king of India Muhammad Shah.

Ibn Batuta goes on to say: In the year 743 H (1342 A.D.) the king of China sent to the Sultan of India at Delhi a present containing, among other things, five garments studded with jewels and five gold embroidered quivers (tarakis muzarkasa). These beautiful exquisite zari works were found not only on the dresses and draperies, but Batuta has left a picturesque description about the majestic pavilion, with five parasols, where Sultan Kaiqubad celebrated Navroz festival. During the festival time, the white parasol was embedded with gold; the curtains were made of velvet and silk and these were of different colours. The most popular colours were violet, purple and blue. These were all decorated with embroideries in gold. According to the description, the king used to wear a long coat and belt interwoven with high workmanship of gold. It seems that when the Sultans after the initial invasions settled down in Delhi, they adapted this embroidery from the Tartar and Khotan. Thus by the time Muhammad Tughlak ascended the throne, zardozi became the dress of the court and courtly nobles.

Amir Khusro, the Persian poet who came during the time of Iltutmish, has also left a narration of this. He has given a list of foreign stuffs which seems to have had gold embroidery.

Among these one was nasiz translated as a kind of silken stuff with gold embroidery. According to him Sultan Kaiqubad sent an embroidered cloth to Bughra Khan's camp.

During the Sultanate time saddles were elaborately embroidered. Ibn Batuta tells us that these were decorated with gold embroideries. The text narrates that during the Id morning, the elephants were adorned with saddles embroidered with silk and gold threads and these were kept reserved for the Sultan's use only. Each elephant was decorated with a silk parasol studded with jewels and pure gold. On the back of each elephant was placed a seat, which was again studded with most precious jewels. The narration tells us how in front of the royal elephant marched the servants and slaves, each wearing a gold cap and a gold belt, which were studded in some cases with jewels. Ibn Batuta further describes that during the Id festival, the entire palace was decorated with jewels and gold: A throne was placed for the Sultan, over which there was a parasol studded with jewels.[71] The banners and standards which were used by the footmen in the processions were said to have been embroidered in gold.

The narration also tells us how the number of tents in the city of Cambay were made not only of expensive pieces of cloth, but these were embroidered with gold and bedecked with jewels. A confirmation of this statement is found from the travel accounts of Marcopolo, who himself had seen some of these gold embroideries.

Ibn Batuta tells us that Khudawandzada Ziya-ud-din, who was appointed as lord of justice (amir-i-dad), was offered a robe of silk, embroidered with gold called surat-i-sher (i.e. image of lion) by the Sultan. The robe which included the lion motif was done with intricate stitches in gold thread. Ibn Batuta further writes that when he attended the court of Ala-ud-din Tarmashirin of Transoxiana which was situated between China, India, Iraq and Uzbek, he found that the king who was sitting inside the tent was draped in a silk dress decorated with embroidery in gold. This information is very interesting, as it suggests that zardozi work was popular as a form of royal dress even as far as this region, which might have been the result of direct or indirect trade contacts between India and Trans-Asia. The travel account of Ibn Batuta clearly reveals that embroidery in gold on both silk and velvet was very popular among the nobility and royalty.

The next literary source which is of immense importance in regard to this craft is the Futuhat-i-Firozshahi, the autobiography of Firozshah Tughlak, where for the first time the word zardozi appeared. This gives an elaborate description of the dresses of the Sultans which were made with this form of embroidery.

According to this account, the Sultan is said to have worn kulah (turban) on his head, which was studded with precious stones. In public meetings the Sultan used to wear barani (either of wool or of silk) with its shoulders beautifully embroidered. The textiles which were presented to people from the courts were always embroidered with gold. Delhi being the centre of the Sultanate power became an important centre of zardozi work as well. Simultaneously several new centres came up in places like Gujarat, Rajasthan and Bengal. Needless to say, these centres grew up because of the patronage extended by the provincial Sultans and the Hindu kings of the respective regions.

The Futuhat-i-Firozshahi gives us elaborate information about this craft. We are told that Firozshah Tughlak classified this exotic embroidery into various types. According to clause 13, the objects prepared for giving as presents by the kings or royal nobles should be the best ones; in other words these should be beautifully embroidered. But at the same time a restriction was imposed on figurative motifs on the robes. Firoz ordered that only those symbols could be used for decoration which were allowed in the Shariyat. In clause 14, Firoz writes prior to this, clothes of the rich people were made of silk, embroidered with gold or zaridar. But from this time these have been banned as there was prohibition for such clothes in the Shariyat. Firoz says, "I have been empowered that only such garments should be worn as have been approved by the Prophet as lawful."

Thus all embroidered costumes were banned allowing only small-sized embroidered banners and caps. In clause 51, he reminds his readers once again about the prohibition of the use of embroidered clothes.

Apart from imposing general restrictions on gold embroidery, he restricted designs also. It is clear from his account that a Sultan can easily be distinguished by his dress, which was lavishly embroidered by gold, from other persons of noble birth. This is also evident in some of the paintings of the period.

Thus we see that during Firozshah's time, either for Firoz's own bigotry or for some other reason, the craft faced a setback. With him thus ended the climax of the zardozi work of the Sultanate period.

Ziya-ul-din Barani has left an interesting account of the

regulations imposed by Ala-ud-din for control of prices of such luxury goods. By regulation, the Sultan controlled the prices of five stuffs i.e. tasbin, tabrizi, zamaizarbaft wazarnigar (embroideredbrocades) and khaz-hia Delhi (Delhi alike). According to the court instructions, these objects could not be sold at Sarai Adl (main business centre of the city) without the order of the superintendent.

There is thus no doubt that the turning period of zardozi craft may be observed during the time of Firozshah Tughlak, who in his official capacity imposed restrictions and curtailed the production of the craft. This left a deep impact on the gold embroidery craft in general.

We may also recall here Marcopolo's mentioning of a kind of stuff which was among the articles sent from Baghdad to Okkodai Khan. The material is called dardas (a stuff embroidered with gold). Motichandra correctly observed that these terms were indications of their origin, which were definitely not of indigenous nature.

Spies in his translation of Subh-ul-asa mentions an authority namely Ash-Shauf Nasir-al Din al-Husayuial-Adami, who writes that during the 14th century the nobility used to wear gold embroidered tartaric gowns, having embroidered sleeves and an embroidered cloth between the shoulders.

Here we may compare the Sanskrit literature of the 14th and the

15th century, which throws light on the existence of gold and silver embroidery. As narrated in the Prabandhachintamani, the king of Kolhapur received sandals inlaid with jewels. Two words svarnopadan and svarna valaksagumphita refer to shoes embroidered with gold and inlaid with jewels. These words occur in the Purntana-prabandha-sangmha. The Varnamtnakara, a 14th century work written by Jyotirisvara Thakura, cites two words: sonapalika manikanti. Jyotirisvara has written his work in Maithili and the area he talks about is North Bihar or present-day Mithila. It mentions Sonasuchika karao ekadevagiria pachitta eka phanda badhane, implying a gold embroidered dhoti on deogiri stuff. His list of stuffs includes varieties of silks manufactured in the country either indigenously or imported from outside. Suchisona as implied by the name indicates that the silk was embroidered with gold. Similarly kanakpatra probably refers to gold leaf on silk.

Dr. B.J. Sandesara has compiled a list of textile stuffs (varnakas) which refers to traditional stuffs and imported items prevalent in Gujarat during the 14th and the 15th century. The compilation called varnakasamuchaya mentions terms Tikejarabapha referring to Persian zarbaft; karmadana the sanskritised form of the Persian word kamdanitiie gold embroidered stuff; pataniya sachopa, where sachopa implies gold embroidery and pataniya indicates the centre of manufacture of such stuff, which is Patan, probably in Gujarat. The Prithvichandracharita written in 1421 also gives reflections of textiles with work in gold and precious stones. Phudadiya indicates a rich silk stuff with jewel setting. The Jain miniature paintings of Kalpasutra also show use of gold.

The Kanhadade Prabandha of Padmanabha refers to the word sonapana which may be the same as kanakapatra. All these imply a rich silk stuff decorated with gold leaf. Such textiles were worn by the merchants of Kalavagudra, Anagundi which were located in present-day Bidar and Telengana. It means that the zardozi had already started penetrating the South. Phaudadi was some kind of rich stuff in which gold and gems were used. The study of several texts from Gujarat, Bihar and Andhra-Telengana mentioning textile stocks, clearly reveals that in spite of all the restrictions and temporary setbacks imposed by Firozshah Tughlak at the main seat of Sultanate power i.e. Delhi, the zardozi with its intricaties was fully imbibed in the Hindu mainstream. The rich and the aristocrats both Hindus and Muslims had been using them as a special form of distinction. The cultural absorption of the zari embroidery was so deep that the original Persian names were suitably adopted in the local dialects of Gujarat, Bihar and Andhra. We may mention here that silk handkerchiefs and caps embroidered with gold were reported to be manufactured in Bengal also. But this seems to have been connected with the emergence of the Muslim nobility in Bengal.

During the 16th century, the zardozi craft seems to have reached a flourishing stage in Vijayanagar under the Hindu rule of Krishnadev Rai

(1509-1530). Robert Sewell mentions the visit of a Portuguese traveller named Christana de Figueiredo to the court of Krishnadev Rai, where he found the king wearing expensive dresses made with gold and jewels.

The king was clothed in certain white clothes embroidered with many roses in gold and to each Portuguese he gave such embroidered cloth designed with many pretty figures as tokens of friendship and love. This account is important, as it throws an interesting light on the design of the gold embroidery work, which was in practice in Vijayanagar during the 16th century. This seems to have been also a popular commodity of export craftwork in Europe. The influence of gold embroidery in the Vijayanagar empire continued during the time of Achyuta Rai (1530-1542). Fernao Nunex, another Portuguese traveller, mentions that king Achyuta Rai's clothes were all made of precious silk stuff worked with gold.

The above two narrations indicate very clearly that gold embroidery was very much a part of the court culture in the Deccan during the 16th century and the Portuguese naturally became attracted to this prestigious craft. It was probably at this stage that the Portuguese influence started making an impression on the craft.

A new revival is noticed in this craft during the Mughal period. The court costumes of the Mughal emperors were all made in zardozi work. Consequently, there grew up important centres of this craft, as the centre of court karkhana shifted with the change in capital by different Mughal emperors. Akbar's court was at Agra, which was shifted to Delhi by Shahjahan, the epicentres of the Mughal culture. But court-run workshops were organised in several other places to cater to the requirement of the court, small or big. The craftsmen grew in number and came over to these places from all parts of the country. But their centre of attraction was the Mughal court where they could take advantage of the court-run workshops and could sell their objects at high prices. In a separate section we have dealt with in detail how these karkhanas provided economic stability to the artisans by offering theoretical and practical knowledge to the craftspersons on the one hand, and negotiating market facilities on the other. The Mughal paintings from the time of Akbar provided an illuminating picture of zardozi work prevalent during this time. Not only were the royalty and nobility represented richly attired in gold and jewels; the horses, camels, the elephants are all depicted with richly embroidered saddles. Thus while appearing in public a king not only tied pearl-strings around his neck but used to wear dresses like achkan embroidered with pearls. Such gold embroidered pieces became popular with the Mughal kings as gift items as well. The gifting of such items to the non-Muslim nobles, rulers etc. extended this craft to the non-Muslim courts, particularly in Rajasthan and Gujarat, where the opulent traditions already existed. Slowly the Hindu elite also started using gold embroidered dresses as a form of aristocracy in contemporary India.

The Ain-i-Akbari gives a rich account of zardozi work in various items, particularly the shawls. The text elaborately speaks about the production of the embroideries under the karkhana system. It further refers to people generally wearing tus shawls without altering its natural colour. His majesty had them dyed. The emperor paid much attention to craftsmanship and the genuineness of the materials. He took care that pure gold and silver was used. All embedded textured fabrics used to give the finished product a subtle aura.

Besides garments, the Mughals adopted this craft in various other items. One of the most important objects which seems to have been decorated with zardozi work was the tent materials. In describing the camp furnishing of the tents Abul Fazl commented about various types of tent structures viz. chubin, rawati, do-ashiyana manzil, zarhindoz, ajaibi, mandal shamiyana, all having inner linings of velvet brocade. It is to be noted that he did not specifically mention gold embroidery, but he referred to zardozi tent in some places in connection with the servants. It is thus clear that the temporary structures for the emperors also had works in gold embroidery on the inner side. Looking at the rich assemblage of zardozi material, and on the basis of the information giving Akbar's patronage, there is no doubt that the zardozi craft reached its highest peak during this time.

Monserrate also corroborates this view. It is said that the emperor used to wear garments of silk, beautifully embroidered in gold with pearls and gold jewellery. The list of the official records presenting the state of things at the death of Akbar was included in De Laet and Manrique's Itinerario Itenerten ts. These were published in 1531 and 1640. Abdul Aziz reproducing these facts states that there were 5,000,000 items with gold and silver decorations, which included tents, kanats etc. decorated with gold and silver; covering clothes for horses and elephants, cloak of every kind etc. Also various kinds of coats and equestrian ornaments, worked and embroidered with gold, silver and precious stones, including the arms borne and insignia carried before the imperial persons and those of the royal house.

The zardozi embroidery which was firmly established by then in the large production system, continued to maintain its excellence during the regime of Jahangir. His memoir Tuzuk-i-Jahangiri mentions at several places such expensive, gorgeous robes of honour. At one place he mentions, "on Tuesday, the 17 zi-gada, he (Shahjahan, his son) was free to go, I presented him with a special gold embroidered robe of honour. Describing the Nauroz festival, Jahangir has mentioned a tent erected at divan-i-am having canopies of the richest and most finely embroidered velvet, silk and cloth of gold. These were inlaid with pearls, jewels and diamonds."

The glory of zardozi as a craft in Mughal period was noticed by Tavernier in his Indian Travels. He says that "The great Mughal has seven thrones, some set all over with diamonds, others with rubies, emeralds and pearls. But the longest throne is erected in the hall of first court of palace. The underpart of the canopy is embedded with pearls entirely, fringe of pearls round the edge, upon the top of the canopy which is made like an arch with four panes, stands a peacock with its tail spread consisting entirely of sapphires and other precious coloured stones. At the distance of 4 feet upon each side of throne are placed two umbrellas, the handles of which are about 5 feet high covered with the diamonds, the umbrellas themselves, being of crimson velvet, embroidered and fringed with pearls. This is the famous throne which Timur began and Shahjahan finished and is really reported to have costed a hundred and sixty millions and five hundred thousand and time of our money."

The author of the Khulasat-ut-tawarikh while giving an account of craft and industries of different provinces writes, "Agra was famous for its gold and silver embroidery on turbans and Gujarat for stuffs of gold embroidered velvet."

Shahjahan's period may be called the golden period in regard to sophistication of this craft. With the shifting of his political seat from Agra to Delhi, the court-based karkhanas spread up in and around Delhi; the karkhanas then worked in full swing, and the craftsmen got patronage from all sections of rich people. As the seat of Mughal rule was shifted to Delhi, a large number of craftsmen moved to Delhi from Agra as well as other parts of the country.

But the period of Aurangzeb shows a turning point in zardozi work. Due to incessant warfare, royal resources became scarce. Besides, Aurangzeb was in favour of austere living. The court no longer patronized this art and as a result many craftsmen left the Mughal metropolis and took shelter around provincial courts. Many craftsmen were then recruited by the Rajput rajas, who by this time had not only become conversant with Mughal luxuries, but in their respective ways had become quite powerful independently. Quite naturally they wished to emulate Mughal sophistication in their own courts. In the south, at Srirangapatam and Hyderabad the zardozi craft got a fresh swing under Tipu Sultan's and the Nizam's rule respectively. The comparative study of the items manufactured in these places reveals that zardozi craft of these places was influenced by the contemporary Mughal tradition. In spite of the overwhelming influence of the Mughal style, the period saw the emergence of several regional centres with their distinctive quality. The craftsmen who dispersed to the provincial courts, got a new boost by the introduction of riyasati karkhanas which replaced the earlier court karkhanas. The system of karkhanas which was introduced during the Mughal period was a vital economic system and after a lapse of time this became rejuvenated in the provincial courts under the riyasati karkhana system. The zardozi craftsmen working at Delhi and Agra at this stage shifted to the provincial centres. Thus, while the traditional karkhana system was losing its roots in Delhi, it was gaining in strength in the provincial areas.

This new socio-economic and political factor provided some impetus for the continuation of this craft. The artisan group during this time got some opportunities from the newly created urban elite class, who by that time inherited some of the tastes and preferences of their rulers. Though the work was not on an opulent scale, there was more or less a steady market, as there was an increase in demand for smaller work. Most of the objects were small domestic articles but the court tradition was not lost totally.

Meanwhile the discovery of the Cape route at the end of the 15th century provided a major change in the structure of Euro-Asian trade. The Portuguese participated in intra-Asian trade. They naturally became interested in this luxurious product for export to European markets.

It is, therefore, clear that before the East India Company, Europe had become a market for the zardozi craft. Lotika Vardarajan has rightly observed that "there was an opulent tradition of couch work based on the usage of metallic thread, and interspersed on occasions with precious stones." The Portuguese were great patrons of this craft, and as a result, the European market to which the Portuguese were attached was flooded with this prestigious handicraft.

The popularity of zardozi craft in Europe in the 16th century gave a boost to the craft, when the East India Company set its foot on the

Indian soil. Also this opened channels for marketing of the zardozi craft in later periods.

Having survived the vicissitudes of time and fortune, Delhi in the latter half of the 19th century came to acquire again a new look under the British rule. The new political power provided a fresh impetus for the revival of the city culture. On January 1,1877, Delhi celebrated the great occasion of the assumption of the title Kaisar-i-Hind or Empress of India by Queen Victoria. The activities were arranged in grand Mughal fashion. Durbar was once again organised, first by Lord Lytton and then 26 years later on January 1,1903 by the Viceroy Lord Curzon to coincide with the proclamation ceremony of Edward VII as the King Emperor. This durbar was planned on the model of the King Durbar of 1877 but it was on a vastly larger and more gorgeous scale. Lord Curzon took great pains to plan the whole show himself. During this time, the special durbar issue, India Durbar, London reported of this unique situation. The main streets of Shahjahanabad again witnessed an imposing spectacle of splendid processions in the finest tradition of Mughal rule. The third durbar was held on 12th December, 1911 in the presence of Emperor George V, who on that occasion announced the transfer of the capital of India from Calcutta to Delhi. The insignia worn by the emperor is exhibited. This was borne out by the tremendous increase in the population of Delhi. Ghurye observes, "Delhi's great growth began after it became capital of the country registering an increase of population of 30.7% in 1921."

With the gradual inception of British rule, the zardozi craft underwent changes at two levels. Firstly, as there was no longer royal patronage, both the karkhana and riyasati karkhana systems completely crumbled down. Secondly, the craftspersons felt the need of finding a market to sell the finished products. The expensive nature of the craft restricted its use. But fortunately a new group of patrons emerged as there was a substantial section of the administration, rich traders among the European population who seemed to have shown their appreciation for the skills of the zardozi craftspersons. New types of articles were manufactured to cater to the needs of this new group of elite. This was the time when the craftspersons started doing new items like uniforms, table covers, etc. Naturally a remarkable change in the sizes and hence in the forms of the objects could be noticed at this time. We propose to take up this aspect in detail in the chapter on design and forms. But one important socio-economic phenomenon arose during this time. Formerly this work had been restricted to Muslim artisans, but now with the change in fashions and requirements the skill was found to have penetrated into the cultural stream of the Hindu society as well.

The brief historical background indicates that this noble craft adapted itself suitably to every political change. The craft spread to the European market and later sought American, Middle East and Japanese outlets. Overseas patronisation provided a backbone to the crumbling market outlets for the craft. These economic networks had direct influence on the design, form, social and production pattern. The material about its history is indeed most inadequate. We are not yet sure about the origins of the craft, but there is enough evidence to indicate that the craft was in existence in the pre-Islamic period. During the Sultanate and Mughal periods due to the patronage extended by the rulers, the craft seems to have established firm roots in India. But the fall of the Mughal empire resulted in complete dislocation of the craft tradition, forcing it to shift its activities from Delhi and Agra to several provincial courts. During this period new centres like Hyderabad, Jaipur, Patiala, Rampur, Bhopal and Banaras emerged as active centres of this craft. The next stage of development was the result of patronage offered by the Portuguese and other European traders. Lately, it is being patronised by several eastern countries, America, Japan and European nations.

1.3 PRODUCTION OF ZARI INDUSTRY :

From Rigvedic times, we hear of several varieties of textiles, among which cloth of gold "hiranya" figures as a distinguished type. Gods in their grandeur wear it, as they ride in their stately chariots. Hiranya cloth has usually been considered the earliest equivalent of present day zari work of kimkhabs (brocades).

India has long been known for its golden thread, for Zari. Well known products of the Indian Zari industry, besides gold and silver thread (Zari Kasab) are the embroidery materials like stars and Spangles, Chalak, Champo Kinari, Salma and badla. The Zari craft includes making Zari thread and other materials as well as thread. The latter covers Zari embroidered saris, evening bags, foot wear and belts. Zari textiles and world famous brocades.

Surat is the biggest Zari thread making center in the country, followed by Varanasi in both imitation and real Zari threads. Zari embroidery material and Zari lace and borders are manufactured in Surat. Varansi on the other hand is a big center for the manufacture of superior quality real Zari thread (kalabattu), Zari textiles and Zari brocades. Other centers of production are Jaipur and Ajmer which specialize in Zari gota and Zari thappa work.

The other centers of Zari products are Agra, Bareilly, Varansi. The items of zari are handbags, belts, shoe uppers etc. Other popular items of export are zari badges all produced manually by skilled craftsmen in Barreily and varansi. Zari threads are used extensively in handloom (and powerloom) saris which are manufactured all over India, especially in Varansi, bangalore, Dharmavaram, Kanchipuram and Paithan.

The principal products of the Zari Industry in Surat are the gold and Silver threads alias Zari Kasab and Zari embroidery materials like Badla alias Lametta etc. but the Industry has produced with amazing skill and techniques other allied zari products in response to the demand of the loving people of our great country related to fashion, dress, costumes and tradition.

PRINCIPAL PRODUCTS:

(i) Real and Imitation zari threads or kasab or gold and silver threads.

(ii) Real and Imitation Badia or Lametta.

ANCILLIARY PRODUCTS:

(i) Real and Imitation Zari Embroidery materials like stars, Spangles, Ring katori, Sadi, Salma, Zik, Tiki, and Kangri etc.

(ii) Laces, Fifth-kinari and Borders.

(iii) Gota Thappa, Ful, Champo, Chatai etc.

(iv) Zari embroidered sarees and Ornis, Evening Bags, Money Purses, Latest hand Bags, Table Clothes, Foot Wears and Shoe Uppers,

Zari belts Spectacle cases, Picture plaques, Photo designs, caps and such artistic zari embroideries.

(v) Zari textiles like the welknown kinkab or Gold cloth, Brocades, Lungies, Tissue, and Banarsi Sarees.

Of the above mentioned products of zari industry, Gold Thread(Zari) and Badla are mainly used in the manufacture of the welknown Kinkab, Tissue and Banarsi sarees, Scarfes, Laces and Borders. Badla which is also generally used for embroidery purposes also forms raw materials like chalak.

The allied products like stars, Spangles, Zik, Tiki, Salmo, kangri, Ring Katori etc. are used as embroidery work on Sarees, Evening Bags, Money Purses and such works of handicraft like zina caps.

All these different zari products have different markets in India and in foreign countries. For example Zari threads find its principal market in South Indian States particularly in the states of Chennai and Mysore, Banaras in U.P. Embroidery materials like salmo, Zik, Tiki, Ring, Katori etc. are consumed in the states of Gujarat and Maharashtra while Gota thappa and full champo in the states of Rajasthan, U.P and Delhi. All these products have also captured markets in all the principal cities of the world though the west Asian Countries, Indonesia, Malasiya, Pakistan and ceylone are leading consumers of Gold Thread and other zari items. Enchanting and artistic zari textiles and emboroidered zari goods like purses, bags etc. are sold mostly in the shophisticated markets like the U.K and U.S.A.

The industry produces all these items in its two principal sectors viz. The real and the Imitation It is indeed a noteworthy feature that looking to the needs and aspirations of the "Janta Class" the wonderful zari artisans have succesfully manufactured imitation zari or say "Jantajari Cheap zari" for the lower strata of its customers. The difference is only in the basic raw material which is silver for Real Zari and Copper (Silver Electroplated Wire) for imitation or Janta zari.

Furnishing Items and Accessories :

Tent hangings, kanats, covers, spreads, trappings, umbrellas, parasols, etc. form an important part of the furnishing itineraries. The cultural scene which was oriented to the floor required a variety of carpets, pillows of assorted types and sizes as home furnishings and court furnishings. The large bolsters generally known as masnads were used for back support. As my discussions have basically developed from the literary and illustrative sources, time and again I have referred to the illustrations in the miniature paintings as the source of reference. Very few examples of pre-Mughal work have come down to us. The illustrative examples have been taken from various museums and private collections. During the Sultanate period, the enclosures or tents were called seracheh. These were made with separate pieces of fabric, suitably embroidered with gold. Sivan is the pandal proportionate to the court furnishings. Ibn Batuta is full of such accounts. Sayabans, the ceiling covers of gold embroidery, are referred to in Ain-i-Akbari. The beautiful wall-hangings decorating the walls also recall at once the typical courtly Mughal form of style.

Hangings and Kanats :

The earliest examples of gold work represented in furnishings are seen in the folios from Kalpasutra dating back to circa 1475-1500 A.D. Calico Museum and Victoria and Albert Museum, London have in their collections a number of tent-covers or hangings which have been published elsewhere. An interesting hanging illustrates a group of human figures in a garden scenario. A noble woman is shown holding a branch of the tree. A lady musician is playing on veena near her with another lady accompanying her on tanpum. Two other lady attendants are shown standing on sides. The noble woman by her features and costume appears to be a Mughal lady. She is followed by a female attendant holding a tray. A variety of Indian birds are chirping on the tree. Two bucks with their young ones are seen in the foreground. Everybody is enchanted by the musical notes, which is clearly depicted by the postures of gazelles and deer in the scenery. The conventional flowering tree is covered by a semi-circular arch. The outer border is filled with continuous floral stems interspersed with birds. Thematically this embroidered panel is more in the fashion of a miniature painting. The design shows metal wire couched in basket pattern on the background. The figures are embroidered with silk thread in satin stitch. A two-dimensional effect has been given to the human figures, as is usually found in miniature paintings. But in rendering the stags, the vision and execution of the roundity is presented in almost a sculpturesque manner. The movement of the stags contributes to the dynamism of otherwise static composition. The intrusion of the Iranian element is clearly visible, in the manner of using the semi-circular arch, at times encircled by creeper blossoms. There is no doubt that the zardozi work through the compositional scheme is reminiscent of Mughal court painting.

It is known that zardozi embroidery became popular in Gujarat during the late Mughal period with arrival of Dara Shikoh and his court. A new class of patrons grew up during this time, who by their profession were traders and Jains in their religious affiliation. A wall-hanging embroidered with silver gilt thread on velvet. By and large, the designs and motifs and even the workmanship of embroidery referred to above are courtly in character. The hangings behind the Jain abbot were in reality the enlargement of the puthias which were meant to be hung for religious purposes. Interestingly, here too one finds an illustration of a throne in the centre, over which is placed a decorated canopy. It may be mentioned here that the cushion on the throne exhibits lavish decoration in couching technique, a tradition which was very popular during the Mughal period. Two creepers with leaves, buds and flowers are found placed on opposite sides of the throne.

The highly stylized art found in this embroidery is a characteristic hieratic type of the Jain miniature. This is shown in the facial and physiognomical features in the dresses and headgears of the two chauri-bearers standing opposite to each other across the throne and in high boots. Indeed the type seems to have been imitated from such paintings which were presumably available in the Jain manuscript painting and in the courts of Muslim nobles. This may be compared with the Jain miniature paintings of the Kalpasutra. It is also well-recognized that the trees and plants which are represented in these paintings are more symbolical than elements of natural life. It is noteworthy about the embroidery on these hangings that the general direction of the decorative devices is on the vertical plane rather than a horizontal spread.

A kanat on red velvet again rendering a vertical design shows star patterns encircled in medallions. Two roaring lions are seen holding hoisted flag each with the front paws above a lotus motif encircled in a pan-shaped device. This composite design is the insignia of the princely court to which the kanat belongs. This kanat is from Rajasthan, probably late 19th century. The style of execution is mainly karchobi.

Carpets and Covers :

The next group of furnishings discussed are the carpets or floor spreads, ceiling covers, bed covers, etc. All these items have more emphasis on spread-out patterns. The span of designs varies from all over spread to concentration in centre and four corners.

Carpet was more or less a generic name for a variety of floor spreads. In the Mughal court each covering had a distinctive term based on its individual usage or function. Zaminposh, the cover for the floor; takhtposh, the cover for the takht or raised rectangular, square or circular wooden platform with supporting legs; palangposh, the bed spread; dastarkhan, the spread used for dining purposes; janamaz, the prayer mat; khanposh, the cover for food trays; saazposh, the spread for the musical instruments and so on. The design orientation in each variety was specifically related to its usage. Janamaz, the prayer mat, would depict a mehrab, an arch with pillars signifying the mosque or a rectangular niche in a wall with the tree of life. Inscriptions from the Kuran were often embroidered. The central area in all coverings was deliberately left plain to suit the purpose of sitting while offering prayers. Dastarkhan would again be devoid of any embroidery in the areas meant for sitting and keeping food. Saazposh often in the form of the particular instrument had embroidery only along the borders. Similarly zaminposh which is used for general or occasional purpose of sitting would have embroidery restricted to the borders.

Covers like the takhtposh and khanposh, however, infrequently used the entire surface of the fabric for decoration. Patterns with gold and silver composed the motif defining and giving the textured surface a uniform tone. Such covers gave the embroiderer ample opportunity to demonstrate his skills. Such orientation of the spread of design in accordance with its usage is typical of zardozi artefacts.

The folios of the miniature painting in Persian style describing the story of Sheikh Sanah and Christian maiden dated circa 1595 A.D. show resplendent use of gold decorations in hangings and carpets. Similarly, a painting describing darbar of Shah Alam at the end of 18th century depicts usage of furnishings with decorations in zardozi style. Bernier in his travel accounts has mentioned fine coverings with delicate silk embroidery interspersed with gold and silver. The folios from Ragini Kangra circa 1785-90 A.D. show geometrical pattern in gold on the rolled curtain, whereas the borders of the carpet show gold embroidery, the all over spread design of creepers in the centre may be in silver wire and silk thread. The actual specimens studied include a takhtposh, which is presently in the Indian Section at the Victoria and Albert Museum, London bearing Ace. No. 0762. The base fabric of this takhtposh is red and green velvet and white satin. The picturesque embroidery here is comparable to any painted narrative. The name of the zardoz as evident from the signage was Sherendazka, a Muslim embroiderer.

This splendid takhtposh has an outer border of repetitive floral motifs depicting alternately ath dane ki nargis and khairu ke dam ka chaugula. Nargis and khairu are two Indian flowers often repeated in metal embroidery. The space between the floral motifs is filled by chakle walijali and sitare ki bharat. Sequins are liberally used to bring lustre to the design. The impenetrable undersurface is visible. The border is edged with a gold and silver braid, ending in tassels.

The body of this takhtposh is divided into three panels. The undersurface is mainly red velvet. The two panels on either side have an octagonal wheel with eight spokes as the central motif. Half replicas of the wheel are repeated at the corners. The wheels are embroidered with gold and silver kalabatoon in ari bharat. The spaces between the spokes depict foliage. Repetitive motifs of pairs of peacocks, four pairs in all, each holding a beaded necklace in its beak, are excellent examples of the meenakari effect in embroidery. The body of each peacock is embellished with alternate rows of blue silk and silver thread. The creeping foliage surrounding the peacocks renders traditionally prevalent motifs of zardozi embroidery, for example, karan ka phul, karan ki kali and the patti design.

The central panel is the main scene of the narration. The portion is divided into two sections by a canal or river. Over the water, linking the two banks, is a bridge embroidered in gold and silver wire. The canal is highlighted by appliquing a white stripe in the satin fabric, thus matching the colour and ripple of flowing water. This water intersection seems to be an important channel linking the two banks for trade and communication. Navigational activity is illustrated by varieties of small boats, nine in number, floating in the canal. These are palinav, decorated boats, mayur pankhi (a boat with a peacock head) and a steamer. Apart from these, four fish and a large number of floating ducks represent marine life. The surface of the land, marked by the red velvet background, illustrates the city and the forest on the same plain, without confusing periphery demarcations. A city in the vicinity of the forest is marked by several buildings in Hindu and Muslim architectural styles. Most of the fortifications run along the outer border away from the water source except for one structure, which is centrally placed close to the river. This is perhaps a Hindu temple. A large tree with a thick growth on one side suggests a forest in the background. Stylistically the citadel is more prominent but it is devoid of any rhythm or movement indicating the presence of life. The area portraying the forest is adorned with creeping foliage with repetitive motifs of karan ka phul, lot ka phul and patti. Life here is represented by a tiger hunting a deer on one side. Details of the animals' bodies have been traced in the ent ki jail and nakhuni jali motifs. The blood-stained mouth of the tiger is represented by stitches in red silk, while the eyes, nose, ears and tail have a black silk filling. A leaping deer in the farthest corner suggests a large forest area. A palm tree has been embroidered against the backdrop of the building on this side. On the other side of the river, forest life is represented by a deer hunt.

A hunter, holding a large bow, is seen sitting on a galloping horse on the other side of the temple-like structure. Apparently, the hunter is chasing the two deer who are running for their life. The outlines of all the figurative and architectural forms as well as the leaves, branches and stem of the tree and other floral motifs are indicated by silver wire of the kora variety. The wire is laid according to the conventional method of zari embroidery whereby it is attached to the surface of the fabric with the help of silk and cotton thread. The body of the horse has an embossed pattern which appears to be khardar bharat. The hoofs, eyes, ears, tail are all filled with black silk thread. The finer details on the body of the horse, like the hair on the neck, saddle and rein are again depicted with kora wire. The embroidery here is important in the context that each anatomical and subject detail has been exemplified by using varieties of gold and silver wire, kalabatoon and silk thread in variegated thickness. This elevates the rhythm and movement of the figurative forms as well as the structural specifications of the architecture. The door, windows, dome, flag and so on are all individually and specifically highlighted. Another interesting representation is of a two-wheeled locomotive placed amidst the floral foliage near the river bank. The depiction of this mode of road transport highlights as to how industrialisation has influenced the embroiderer. The locomotive, which appears to be more like a cycle, has a short front wheel and a large back wheel.

The central panel is more like a painted canvas where life, in water and on land, has been manifested. The delicacy of each motif, which is rather difficult to achieve in non-pliable metallic wire, is clearly visible. The takhtposh distinctly reveals that gold embroidery styles had strong links with the tradition of floor coverings commonly called carpet in the courts of upper India.

A takhtposh from Bharany's collection in Delhi in red velvet shows repetitive floral motifs, dense in the border and much apart in the centre.

Another zaminposh from the Victoria and Albert Museum collection in red velvet has resplendent embroidery, gold and silver gilt wire, spangles and sequins only on the borders with repetitive flower and geometric patterns. Four turanj i.e. corner motifs inside the border are in kairi shape.

These can be compared with the private collections of Bharany in India, where the border and the body are in two colours i.e. green and red velvet. The joint of the two fabrics has been skilfully hidden with continuous couching stitch in metal wire. Here the base colour of the fabric, particularly in the border, forms part of the repetitive patti wall buti design. The outer border has continuous teele wall jali along with guldaudi floral motif. Here the under-surface is totally invisible. The turanj depicts champa, ded khar ki patti buta.

Another zaminposh also has similar execution of design. In both these coverings couching technique has been employed. However, this double colour scheme is not seen in another cover from the same collection.

Khanposh, the cover for food, has very elaborate embroidery on the four borders, which is extending to almost half the width of the total fabric. This again reflects the decoration of the parts more visible to the eyes. The cover when put on the large food tray hangs down, when the bearer carries the tray. The cover is rectangular but the central part is squarish. Black and red velvet form the border and the centre. The border has splendid bharat work with only deliberate spaces of the outlines of the buta and patti motifs. Silver wire has also been used to depict champa ki buti. Thus the whole design is composed in gold, interspersed with silver and black hues. The central part has a running border in gold gilt wire with turanj in kairi motif. Such massive embroideries were done on long rectangular strips which were joined later. The style is karchobi. The finer embroidery is however rendered on bed spreads.

A saazposh is the spread for keeping the string instruments like sitar. The shape of the spread eloquently speaks of the purpose for which it is used. The blue velvet is the circular form to which a tapering rectangular fabric is joined. The silver and gold wire embroidery in repetitive guldaudi buti adorns the continuous border of the spread. The centre of each buti has red silk embroidery, border designs are used to fill the inter-spaces. Two buta designs again in floral pattern adorn the inner borders of the extended arm. The central part both in head and the arm is devoid of any embroidery.

Asmangir or the canopy is another furnishing accessory which was abundantly used inside the palace, courtyards, terraces, gardens and other outside locations. The famous peacock throne of Shahjahan, which was installed in the diwan-i-khas (hall of private audience) of the Red Fort, Delhi, has been described as the major symbol of Mughal wealth.

A painting from National Museum showing Raja Prithvi Singh of Datia with his sons dating circa 1736-1752 A.D. depicts a beautiful canopy in green colour having resplendent gold work which may be embroidery. A specimen of asmangir is said to have belonged to the time of the last Mughal Emperor Bahadur Shah Zafar. This asmangir of silk fabric shows an element of decorative device during the decline of Mughal art. Earlier very often the richly illuminated border decorations composed of conventional trees, stylised flowers, galloping stags, running lions, revealed clearly a very skilful manipulation of a number of central Asian/Iranian decorative designs. The trends in conception and execution were more towards large and heavy proportion, which was presumably the requirement of the objects.

The red asmangir, however, has a border design of conventional repetitive floral motifs in gold gilt thread, which appears to be ath dane ki nargis along with neem ki patti and ded khar ki patti. The span of design is on the running borders, the corners and the central spaces.

The outer covering of this asmangir is of thick cotton. The piece is important since it shows the technique called vasli, where a thick cardboard is put beneath the motifs; to give the desired raised effect, gold gilded wire is used. Also such work was generally done on velvet for kanats etc. but since asmangir hangs below the ceiling or acts as a sky cover, the light weight fabric was preferred, since silk cannot carry very heavy embroidery.

Another asmangir of early 20th century from Rajasthan. The base fabric is maroon velvet and gold gilded wire is used for couching. The embroidery depicts a jungle scene where a lion is hunting the deer. Similar depiction was found in the carpet of Victoria and Albert Museum of 18th century. However, here the jungle scene includes variety of flowers, birds and insects. Such designs became popular in the provincial courts after the decline of Mughal court and many of the zardoz from Delhi remember such designs.

We may say that after the decline of the Mughal rule, there was a perceptible decrease in the gorgeousness of zan-workon tents, kanats, etc. With the slow decline in patronage from the Mughal courts, the zardoz faced a major setback. At this juncture the artisans sought patronage from the provincial courts and carried the design prevalent in Mughal courts to the provincial courts. A lady at bath under the canopy, a miniature from National Museum, highlighting the transitional influence in provincial courts. Another miniature painting from the same collection portrays Maharaja Anup Singh of Jodhpur seated under an asmangir which has resplendent gold work.

Other furnishing accessories include various types of cushion covers, pillow covers (takiya cover) of different sizes and shapes. A painting of circa 1759-1806 A.D. shows Shah Alam seated on the throne with an elaborately gold-embroidered masnad (bolster) cover on the back in red fabric. This painting is from National Museum collection.

Another painting describing raga Hindola from the same collection Uniara circa 1770-80 A.D. also shows delicate gold embroidery on masnad cover. During the examination of the actual specimens, it was uniformly observed that the kalabatoon wire was used instead of pure metallic wire for embroidering the bolster covers. The soft and supple kalabatoon wire was not injurious to the body on touch. The pillows were in all sizes and shapes, square, semi-circular, circular. The designs on the covers of these supports matched the design of the floor spread.

Plate 46 shows a rectangular masnad in green velvet. This is from the Red Fort Museum in Delhi and belongs to the court of the last Mughal Emperor Bahadur Shah Zafar. The worn-out condition of the velvet is indicative of the regular use of this masnad. Here the design is kamal ki bel (lotus creeper) repeated all along the patti i.e. the strip joining the two sides of the masnad. Four turanj motifs are embroidered on the four corners. The central space is left bare.

A cushion cover in semi-circular shape from Salarjung Museum, of late 19th century. Here the central motif, a floral pattern, radiates in butis and pattis. Such are the conventional buta designs which were very popular during the 18th-19th century. Later on such designs were embroidered on purses etc. These cushion covers are further decorated with sequin.

The oval masnad cover in green and red velvet from Bharany

collection is similar in design depiction to the jaminposh described earlier; the design of the gold embroidery is confined to the ends of the red velvet, the green velvet has silver sequins placed graphically. The masnad covers were tightened by fastening the string; for this purpose a red cotton tape is stitched on the end.

India has a long tradition of offering presentations to the nobilities. The presentation or exchange of items was done in the thai which was normally circular in shape. The goods were arranged in containers or otherwise in the thai and were covered with a fabric cover. Zardozi embroidery was extensively used on these covers. Generally the ends of these covers had gold or silver-braided tassels. Although no illustrative example is shown here, but the palanquins were also covered with such gorgeously embroidered cover. Tray covers or thai posh were eloquently adapted by the Britishers in their day-to-day utilitarian items.

Two thai posh from Victoria and Albert Museum collection bearing Acc. Nos. 4756/3667 and 4757/3487. The red and black base is embroidered with gold silver wire.

It is customary for the royal entourage to have a large number of accessories known as insignias. Flags, qur, alam, parasols, umbrellas, trappings are included in these items. There are descriptive accounts in the Rehla of Batuta. He speaks of horses bearing the insignias of khilafat, which according to his description were girdles of silk, woven with gold.

There were others which were ornamented with white silk embroidered with gold. Batuta has specifically mentioned that these decorated horses were not used by anyone but the Sultan himself. Batuta has made here a very clear distinction between gold weaving and gold embroidery. It is apparent that the Sultan had this insignia beautifully embroidered for his personal use on his horses, the other senior members of the royalty could use the horses with woven girths. At another place Batuta mentions, "out of these sixteen elephants the Sultan rides one, in front of which the saddle-cover studded with the most precious jewels is carried." Here although the specific symbolisation in the form of the design is not mentioned, it is clearly stated that the elephant used by the Sultan could be easily distinguished from others. Describing a royal procession Batuta narrates, "and before him was carried the ghasia which is a saddle-cover studded with gold and precious stones."

Ghasia is a term which is not found to be used elsewhere, but Mehdi Hussain, the commentator of Ibn Batuta, says, "Ghasia was carried before the king being the equerry as a sign of majesty among the Egyptian members." Here ghasia is referred to as an insignia of the royalty and not the trapping. In spite of these elaborate descriptions and specifications of items in the text, we have no extant example of the objects belonging to the Sultanate period. But information regarding trappings, insignias etc. during the Mughal period seems to be more complete due to the availability of textual and pictorial materials. Shahjahan Nama of Inayat Khan has referred to the presentation of horses and elephants received and given to the honoured guest. "On the 16th of Shawwal 1061 (2 October, 1651) Muhyi-al-din, the ambassador, presented to His Majesty a saddle cloth sewn with pearls."

The miniature paintings of different schools show various kinds of animal trappings. It was customary to adorn the horse, camel, donkey or an elephant. A folio of the miniature painting of Persian tradition narrating the story of Sheikh Sanah and Christian Maiden, circa 1595 A.D., shows the Sheikh visiting the maiden. He is seen riding on what looks like a donkey. Although the gait of the animal is horse-like but long ears and elongated face place it closer to a donkey. The borders of the red trapping are adorned with gold embroidery. Another painting from Mughal school belonging to Jahangir period (1605-1629) depicting a scene of camel fight interestingly shows both the camels wearing black girdles with gold embroidery in geometric pattern. These are from National Museum collection.

The saddle cloth was also known as zinposh. John Irwin has illustrated two of them, which are said to be in the collection of the toshkhana of the Nizam of Hyderabad, Deccan, belonging to the 17th century. While describing this zinposh, Irwin writes, "The foundation is a double thickness of loosely woven cotton fabric, upon which is an applique pattern in pieces of red, green and yellow velvet and a ground embroidered in twisted silver gilt thread." This saddle cloth is in line with the design of the zardozi style prevalent during the 17th century, where the ground is extensively embroidered in metal embroidery and the patterns are done with silk thread; here, however, the patterns are in velvet which is appliqued. Stylistically there is a difference between zinposh and jhool. The former as described above remains tightly fitted on the body of the animal whereas jhool elaborately hangs down the sides.

A ragini painting from Malwa School of circa 1680-90 A.D. shows zinposh on horse and jhool on elephant. The painting describing raga Nata depicts a battle-scene. The gold work on the body of the jhool and zinposh is elaborate. Another painting of Ragmala series circa A.D. 1785-90 shows an elephant jhool with orange body and green border. The design here is more specific on the borders and the corners while the depiction of Nat Ragini of circa 1680 A.D. shows the horse trapping covering the body of the horse upto the neck.

An actual specimen of a camel trapping depicts the buti pattern in gold gilded wire on the maroon velvet body. The design is repetitive. The zinposh has a hole in the centre which suitably fits the hood of the camel. A Sikh style miniature painting showing Krishna hurling the wheel is a scene from the Mahabharata. Two horses in the forefront show the trappings with gold work.

A camel saddle in accoutrement from Jodhpur also shows gold embroidery. Later references to the trappings are available in the

Imperial Gazetteers, where brief accounts of various animal trappings with metal embroidery testify to the continuity of the tradition till the abolition of princely states. Delhi, Patna, Murshidabad, Agra, Banaras, Lucknow, Gulbarga and Aurangabad were some of the important centres of metal embroidery where animal trappings were adorned with gold embroidery. We come to know from the contemporary records that Deccan was an important centre where animal trappings with heavy karchobi on velvet were manufactured. These massive forms of animal decorations were adapted by provincial courts. Later the same opulence was seen to impress the British emperor. So on their visit to Delhi when the Delhi Durbars were held in 1903 and 1911, the British Highness rode on the elephant, the jhool for which was worked upon by the zardoz of Delhi. The memories of the two Delhi durbars were recounted by the senior members of few zardoz families in Delhi who had worked frivolously for these durbars. They emphasized that apart from royal processions, it was customary in Delhi even for the religious processions and marriage processions to adorn the animals with tastefully embroidered covers. These massive forms of decorations were mostly composed of floral and geometric devices often accompanied with elaborately embroidered insignias of the state court. This important item of metal embroidery has totally disappeared from the scene.

Parasol :

The umbrellas and parasols (aftabgir), which formed essential part of the noble regalia, right from the Sultanate period, were also profusely embroidered in metal; unlike the trappings, these were often studded with precious and semi-precious stones. Although such parasols might have formed an important part of noble processions, they have not been well preserved. The main reason perhaps being the possible looting of the precious stones used in the embroidery.

The earliest references to parasols are again found in 'Rehla of Batuta', where he has described sixteen elephant seats reserved for the use of the Sultan, having over each of them a silk parasol.[16] The elephants in front of the Sultan were adorned, the standards and sixteen parasols being attached to them. The latter were hoisted, some of these were embroidered with gold and some bejewelled. One of the parasols was raised over the Sultan's head.

We find a brief account of parasols which were also termed as chatars in Ain-i-Akbari where a number of jewels were affixed to adorn a chatar.

Tavernier, while describing the famous peacock throne, also spoke about two umbrellas. These umbrellas were placed at a distance of about four feet on each side of the throne, and were of crimson velvet, embroidered and fringed with pearls. A late example is from Bharany's collection showing karchobi work on an umbrella.

Birdwood has left a detailed description about gorgeous gold embroideries on the velvet cloth of the umbrellas, which were made in

Lucknow, Gulbarga, Aurangabad and Hyderabad. Hunter also referred to embroidered umbrellas. All these clearly indicate that the contemporary provincial courts continued to display the same adornment on umbrellas, which were popularly known as chatar. After the abolition of these courts, umbrellas were found to have been used in religious processions alone. But by that time the adornment had lost much of its gorgeousness.

The embroidery on parasols was done for the temples. These were placed above the idols. The religious proceedings also earmarked the use of metal embroidered parasols. Crafts Museum has such examples in its collection [Ace. No. 84/6740 shows figures of Krishna and his cow, child Krishna amidst dense foliage]. In the late fifties craftsmen of Delhi were commissioned to embroider such parasols in bulk for various religious institutions. Although the use of velvet umbrellas for deities is still popular, the fashion of embroidering with metal thread has now declined altogether.

Badges, Banners, Uniforms etc.:

The articles falling under this category mainly refer to decorations, presentations and identifications related to social and religious institutions. The items embroidered generally have well-defined designs which may be affixed on any dress, material or may be carried independently.

Their history goes back to as early as the Sultanate period. Ibn Batuta mentions, "He conferred on him a silk robe embroidered with gold called surat-i-sher i.e. the image of a lion which it bears on its front and back." Batuta has also mentioned another robe which he has classified as mahairibi robe. Mahairibi is derived from the Persian word mihrab meaning an arch. Thus the robe has on its front and back the embroidered design of an arch. Batuta has also written about the standards made of silk embroidered with gold.

The Futuhat-i-Firozshahi [clause 48] says that Allaudin Khilzi gifted to Allaul-Mulk a golden zardozi robe which had a figure of lion. In the same text [clause 14] he mentions embroidering of banners with golden thread which are not more than four fingers. Here the imposition is in terms of the design restricting it to a minimum width of four fingers. Accounts regarding the motifs given by Batuta and Firozshah refer to zari embroidered robe with lion, which was perhaps the insignia during the Sultanate period. During the Mughal period a specific terminology was used for items falling under royal insignias. These devices were called qur. The Ain-i-Akbari has described qur as a collection of flags, arms and other insignias which follow the king wherever he goes. It is therefore clear that these insignias embroidered with metal thread were very significant during this period. The forms of insignias at times were different, but the symbolic meaning of depicting insignia was universally accepted. The lion shown in also depicts insignia of provincial courts.

Coming to the next period, we find that the tradition of symbolic designs in various forms continued even in the provincial courts. Salarjung Museum, Hyderabad, has a good collection of mehtabgiri procession fans or standards which accompanied the Nawabs of Hyderabad. These standards were also embroidered with metal embroidery.

It is understandable that adornment of military dress with metallic embroidery was a tradition from the earlier period. But lack of evidence both pictorial or written restrains us from corroborating it. However, such adornments are continuing even today. A flag staff in the -miniature painting showing Raga hindola. Ace. No. 567A/1952 from Victoria and Albert Museum, London, depicts the insignia of the English Crown. This is said to have been worn around the neck so that the insignia hangs in front. This is simple embroidery on white satin. It was used by royal personages visiting the Delhi durbar as mentioned earlier. The Imperial Gazetteer also mentions uniforms with metal embroidery. T. N. Mukherji while describing the Glasgow exhibition writes, "Gold and silver embroidered banners were made both at Lucknow and Banaras." Many articles for use in the church were also embroidered with gold and silver. These were exported to Europe from various parts of India. The Shia flag from Victoria and Albert Museum collection is another religious flag taken out during the Moharram procession.

After independence, when the provincial courts were abolished, the symbolic meaning of the insignia was lost, and thus there was very little demand for these objects. The zardozi community then faced a massive setback. But a new channel was opened. A large number of zardozi craftsmen from the walled city of Delhi took up assignments of embroidering small badges, insignias etc. mainly for foreign market, particularly for Europe and America. As described in the socio-economic section, a major part of the zardozi community now produces such articles in their domestic karkhanas. There are large varieties of designs pertaining to this category. The designs show no specification for floral, faunal or geometrical devices, instead the new motifs are a blend of all the three. The articles, whether small or large, are worked with fine karchikan work.

Costumes and Related Accessories :

The rich costume tradition of India has been exemplarily decorated with gold embroidery. A variety of unstitched lengths of fabrics worn in different ways were gorgeously worked with zardozi. The discussion in this section starts from the unstitched fabric used as costume or accessories like the belt, patka, kamarband, shawl, misir, chunri, dupatta, sari. The variety of unstitched lengths have different purposes. Sometimes used for covering the upper body like shawl or else used as head veil (chunri, dupatta, scarf), a dress like sari or just a belt used for tightening the costume.

Raja Dhirajpal of Raghogarh (Madhya Pradesh) of circa 17th century highlights the costume details. The magnanimous size of the patka with beautiful gold design is seen to be held around the waist of the king as well as his attendant. Several words like prota, pota mean an embroidered or patterned cloth. Another word futa which was found to occur in the travel accounts of Ibn Batuta represents a belt for tightening the dress. If we accept/Ufa as a piece of cloth to be tied around waist, it is then similar to patka. But the latter has sometimes dual function of serving as a waist-band as well as a turban. With the emergence of the Sultanate power in India during the 12th and 13th century A.D., when the zardozi craft occupied a very important position, this embroidered cloth used for tying around the waist or sometimes head locally called as patka became very popular.

Another miniature painting, where Raja Bhav Singh is visiting the court of Bahadur Shah I, depicts the waist-girdle also known as kamarband with elaborate gold work. Examples from Crafts Museum collection depict that thinner fabric like muslin, tash, brocade cloth is generally used as the base material. A variety of floral motifs are done with silk, silver gilt wire, flat wire (badla) using simultaneously sequin, sitaras and beetle wings. Lucknow Museum has a patka embroidered in gold gilded silver kalabatoon wire on red velvet. This patka is dated around 18th century. The design here seems to have affiliation with the zardozi objects found in the Red Fort Museum collection. The nobles from the Mughal court in the later period started favouring belt which could be used as the arms borne for keeping their swords. An example is reported from the Red Fort Museum. It shows a bel and patti motif on red silk fabric in gold gilded wire. These belts were adapted commercially with modified designs and forms in European and American market and continued to be commercial success.

Shawl is the particular article of dress, which could well signify a scarf, a mantle or at times a turban and which could be square, rectangular, triangular or even circular. Generally the style of wearing a shawl guided the flow of design. We get graphic descriptions of shawls with zardozi work in the Ain-i-Akbari.

There are references, as cited by Manrique in 1630, to borders ornamented with fringes of gold, silver and silk thread, indicating that shawls were embellished with gold and silver thread in the early Mughal period. However, there are no extant examples illustrating presence of such shawls prior to the late 18th century. Khwaja Yusuf, while promoting embroidery on woven shawls, encouraged use of zari wire for decoration. The main industry was located in Punjab and Delhi. A shawl from Victoria and Albert Museum collection. This is a black woollen rectangular fabric left plain in the centre. The tanzir or the side border has narrow stripe of repetitive floral motif in gold gilded wire. The pallu on both ends has two bands of red wool fabric interspersed with black bands. Each of these has dense embroidery in gold colour. The joints are skilfully concealed with the embroidery.

Another example from Bharany collection shows dense

embroidery in silk, wool and kalabatoon wire on the whole body of the fabric, making the base invisible. The pallu has repetitive paisley motifs. Red wool fabric with gold gilded wire embroidery. Here again the concentration is to decorate the sides and borders. Plate 81 depicts a shawl bel which is stitched on another fabric. A doshala, again a woollen shawl in which multicolour stripes are joined together with gold kalabatoon embroidery infused with floral designs. The stripes are already worked with zardozi motifs.

Satbanteli, odhani, chunri, dupatta are other varieties of unstitched garment adorned with gold embroidery. A satbanteli depicts elaborate medallion design in gold, silver zari wire and spangles on the centre of the side border in the area which covers the head when this is worn. The side borders have the running design. Satbanteli is worn by the proud mother of a first-born baby among the Rabari community of Kutch, Gujarat.

In other parts of the country chunri, much like patka, is made of a thinner fabric, generally transparent. There are several representations of chunri in the miniature paintings, showing exemplary use of the beetle wings, precious stones and gold wire in ornating this piece of garment. Plate 84 depicts a chunri worn by the bride. Here the blue-coloured centre is followed by the red yellow and red stripes of continuous border, which are joined to each other with fine embroidery stitches. The body design is in ari bel, while border has repetitive floral motifs and bharat design.

Sari, one of the most important untailored dresses, has been replenished with metal embroidery for a long time. The pallus and border of the sari continue to be decorated with zari embroidery representing floral and creeper designs. Among the Parsi community it is customary to have velvet border embroidered with zardozi design stitched on the sari border. Plate 85 shows a fine tissue sari from Victoria and Albert Museum having embroidery with gold tinsel sitara and goldgizai wire. The design is floral depicting karan ka phul motif. Red silk thread is used to embroider the centre of the phul which appears like vermilion mark on fair body. Resplendent embroidery with beetle wings and metal wire on red fabric.

A purple neck scarf which is in the collection of Victoria and Albert Museum. This is an illustrative example of the small unstitched costume accessory embroidered in zardozi technique. Here the span of the design is the same as in the Kashmir shawls but in smaller dimension.

The evidence of earliest embroidered clothes for the upper and lower garments of men and women of high social status is found in historical texts. During Maurya and Sunga periods antariya and pattika are seen to have been embroidered with floral motifs. Though this is conjectural, these embroideries were possible in gold and precious stones. Gold embroidered fillets are mentioned to be used by richer classes of women during the Satavahana period. Antariya, the upper garment worn by men, is reported to have gold embroidery. The Gupta period also makes mention of few costumes embroidered in gold and silver.

The custom of embroidering clothes by profuse use of gold and silver became very popular. Batuta in his writings has mentioned that Sultan Muhammad Shah granted Nasir-ud-din a gilded robe of black abfasi colour embedded with precious stones together with a turban to match the robe. At another place, he has described among the presentations to amir Ghadda a silk robe of blue colour embroidered with gold which was studded with precious stones, together with a cap to match. Batuta has also described presentation of linen embroidered in gold by the Sultan to newcomers on the 4th of Shawwal (8th June, 1334). Miniature paintings of the Sultanate period also show Sultans dressed up in robes decorated ostentatiously.

During the Mughal period, dresses with gold and silver embroidery were much in fashion with the royalty and the nobility. The treasure of Akbar included a vide range of stitched garments which were embellished with metal embroidery. Bernier while describing Shahjahan's appearance in the court in his accounts wrote, "The king appeared seated upon his throne at the end of the great hall in the most magnificent attire, which was of white and delicately flowered satin with a silk and gold embroidery of fine texture." He also mentioned other stuffs striped with gold and silver and also turbans embroidered with gold.

A folio from the story of Sheikh Sanah and Christian maiden depicts the Sheikh sitting with the holy men. The Sheikh is seen wearing a choga with gold ornamentation. The canopy on the top also has a gold fringe. This miniature painting is from the National Museum collection and stylistic costumes of Mughal and provincial courts.

Various texts of the 19th century mention different types of dresses embroidered with zardozi work. As regards the nature of embroidery on dresses and costumes, the work is reported to have been of fine variety of karchikan for female costumes, whereas the karchobi for male costumes. The distinction in the fineness of embroidery for women and men perhaps characterises the delicacy and roughness of the two sexes.

Various museums in India and abroad are credited with having a good collection of costumes with zari embroidery from the late 18th, 19th and 20th centuries. Several kinds of male robes like choga, achkan, angarkha, jama, bugal-bandi, coat have various spans of ornamental embroidery. A variety of majestic robes in woollen fabric have dense or sparse embroidery. In bugalbandi and the coat the embroidery travels along the tailored cut on the front, the edges of the sleeves, the slits and the hem. In achkans and chogas, the front and the back yoke, the shoulder, the cuff, the border and the edges of the front opening are heavily embroidered. The rest of the body is either left plain as in Pl. 91 where the base fabric is kani style woven material or the design moves along the boundaries of the flowered pattern on the fabric. At times the body is covered with repetitive pattern of lobes or designs along trailing stems.

Sometimes the design on the body is in ari bel (slanting creepers) at intervals. Generally kalabatoon wire is employed by a hath ari, the hand-operated awl, which became very popular in the late 19th century. The bugalbandi has kamdaniwork. Here the embroidery in gold wire and precious stones was done on the satin fabric. This was stitched on the desired parts along the seams and edges. Flowering scrolls and paisley motifs are repeated. Among the desert clans of western India, the zardozi skills are amply found to occur on white cotton robes. The abhor have thick minakari work in silk and zari wire with repetitive medallion design.

Under the British influence, the Indian nobility slowly started abandoning their traditional attires and adopted the British costumes. Among the men's robe, coat was one of the important upper garments which was adopted all over the country. However, since it was a prerogative with the nobility to have their garments embroidered in zari wire, the coats were also tastefully embroidered. The back of the coat tastefully embroidered much in the same span as the choga.

Coming next to the women's costume, it is observed that there was more emphasis on adorning the lower garments such as lahenga, sharara, ghaghra, garara. These garments provided vast span for the embroiderers to show their skills. The work profusely remained in the kamdani style. Plate 108 depicting ragini Vinod shows the nayika wearing a lahenga probably with gold work. A sharara i.e. a lower garment with two legs but having a very broad circumference at the lower end; the waist end remaining generally near the waist size. The width in the lower part is achieved by adding tapering strips of cloth. Sometimes it requires about 9 to 12 metres of fabric to make a sharara. This is a popular Muslim dress and is worn even today by elite on auspicious occasions. The sharara described here is from the Crafts Museum collection mainly in green crepe satin. The lower portion or the gher has alternate stripes of green, blue, pink and mauve crepe satin fabric. There is continuous band of zardozi embroidery along with gota kinari to conceal the joint. The body of the garment is embroidered in jali pattern with buti motifs in each jali on the upper part. This pattern is intercepted by the vertical bands at intervals. There is repetitive creeper (bel) design on the gher.

The lahenga is green satin fabric restricting embroidery to the gher. The embroidery is the floral pattern mainly in the gold gilded wire intercepted at places with silver cups placed in shapes of a flower. A ghaghra from Gujarat in plain dark maroon silk fabric shows small kairi butis placed in squares in gold gilded wire. The lower end has a gold braid. Another lahenga worn by the bride.

Kurti, kurtani, kameej, choli, jumper, angiya are the upper garments for women. These have different lengths and are worn with salwar, sharara, ghaghra or lahenga. Kurtani is worn together with lahenga and kurti. A choli in orange silk fabric with bands of green silk on the sleeves and the waist. This exquisitely embroidered choli is worn with white muslin lahenga. Ornately embroidered kanchali in red silk fabric has ari bel design on the back and the front part shows creepers. The borders on the sleeves, the waist and the back have repetitive floral patterns.

A stylishly cut jacket in the European tradition - a combination of green and red velvet. This jacket with full sleeves shows stripes running with neck line, shoulder seam, arm joint where the green and red fabric are joined at sleeve ends. This tight-fitting jacket was perhaps worn with a skirt. Another jacket from the Victoria and Albert Museum collection having profuse gold work on front and back yoke.

Vaskets worn both by men and women are customarily worked with zardozi. Several museums including the National Museum in New Delhi have vaskets in their collections. A mauve-coloured vasket with polyester fabric as the base. This is worked with hath ari. The base cloth is removed from the area with dense jali work in the front and back portion. These parts reflect the colour of the garment over which the jacket is worn. There is running floral pattern on the waist, arm, front opening and neck border and certain portion of the back, which appears as appliqued work.

Having discussed the costumes we come next to the related accessories. Headgears, shoes, purses, belts are the important accessories, which have zardozi work. A variety of turbans and caps from several Indian provincial courts reflect usage of zardozi work.

The tradition of gold embroidered accessories was in vogue during the Sultanate and Mughal period. Though there are no exact references in the texts but the miniature paintings give vivid references. Shiraj painting from the folios of Sheikh Sanah and Christian Maiden shows the nobleman and his visitor wearing turbans with gold work. This painting is of circa 1595 A.D. There are ample evidences of a variety of headgears and footwear in the Mughal miniature paintings and paintings from the provincial courts. A portrait of Shah Shuja, son of Shahjahan, circa 1680 A.D. The stylish turban and jutis show zardozi work.

A crown-like cap in red velvet cardboard bands, gold, silver wire and sequins. A six-petalled blooming bud is shown emerging from the tight-fitting circular band. This type of cap which was similar to the European crown became popular in Oudh court.

From the 18th century to the middle of the 20th century, caps with zardozi embroidery were used by both Muslims and Hindus belonging to all social strata. The base fabric was mainly velvet or satin. These were made in vasli technique i.e. a cardboard was always used between two layers of fabric. Circular caps were worn by upper caste Hindus, particularly Brahmins, Baniyas and Jain community. The caps used by the Nawab of Hyderabad were conical in shape. The embroidery on the cap is done by laying a lining on the under-surface. A cardboard piece is placed between the two fabric layers for stiffening.

Such caps were functional and elaborate. These were worn with the formal dress. This cap seems to have emerged from dopalri where two circular halves are stitched together. Elaborate use of beetle wings along with sequins lends indigenous charm to this cap.

The traditional footwear such as jutis continued to be embroidered with gold silver wire. During the Mughal period the paintings show the royalty in elegant footwear with zardozi work. The upper part of juti known as uparla is worked on a velvet pasted on cardboard. These uppers are then stitched with the sole or tala.

A variety of uparla worked in zardozi karkhana and the collection of the Indian Museum. This kind of juti has a burzi or curved extension of uparla, which depicts the high status of the wearer. Such jutis were worn in Bengal. A knee high shoe from the Victoria and Albert Museum shows stylistic adaptation of Indian skill on European design. The blue and red velvet is covered with couched floral patterns in badla wire along with sequins.

Ladies juti has more delicate form. Here the uparla has red and gold base, worked with semi-precious stones, beetle wings and sequins along with zari wire. The front part has floral creepers while burfi design, recurring geometrical forms in gold wire decorate the hind part.

The contemporary style of the fashion footwear, where glass beads and stones replaced the semi-precious stones.

The Indian theatre and temple have made splendid use of zardozi work in several categories of articles such as curtains, mask, mukut, costumes, jewellery and at times even the figures of gods and goddesses. A velvet curtain from Yadgiri gutta, Andhra Pradesh, where an old temple of Narasimha (incarnation of Vishnu) exists. The temple situated on a large mound is believed to be the original hillock where Vishnu in Narasimha incarnation emerged. The red velvet curtain is drawn when the deities are resting or taking meals. The motif shows a kubhakam (vessel). This may be compared with the curtain used for background decoration during raslila performance in Mathura. Here the curtains are patterned in the architectural framework of a court and temple. The next panel shows a large peacock on full panel for the court scene. Various lines of satin fabric are embellished with gota and zari work.

Costumes in theatre are popularly worked in zari wire. A king wearing a mukut made with cardboard, paper and silver wire. Pattu (neck-band), bazuband (arm-band), kada (bracelet) etc., which were embroidered, were also used in theatre and by the dancing girls. T.N. Mukherji has also mentioned such specimens of embroidered jewellery. During the British period, these items found a popular market in Europe.

Mask is an important theatrical camouflage, which adds rhythm and rapidity to the spirit of communication. Ram Nagar in Uttar Pradesh is known for the zari masks used in theatre.

Purses and batuas used in theatre and otherwise are also embroidered with zari and beads and a few types of purses. The base fabric is generally black, red, blue or green velvet. Plate 143 shows a purse with silk thread and zari wire embroidery.

Before the advent of electricity, fans of several kinds were used by the nobility and the common people. The hand fans have lighter embroidery but sometimes with heavy frill and rope fans from the Red Fort Museum and the Crafts Museum showing zardozi work. Fans in the Bharany Collection show geometrical patterns in heavy karchobi style.

During the 18th and the 19th century, the Jain religion patronized zardozi embroidery extensively. The artisans were commissioned to embroider religious book-covers, boxes and others. A Jain miniature painting from circa 1500 A.D. shows different religious symbols occurring in Jain religion. The box for keeping religious books (PL 150) shows sun, moon, navgunjar, bull, elephant, kalash, swastik, fish and religious symbols embroidered in gold and silver wire and sequins on red velvet. The box is rectangular and is embroidered on sides and top. A gomukhi in red silk fabric is embroidered on both the sides with gold silver wire and sequins. The motifs show sun and moon and Krishna, the shepherd, herding cows. The gomukhi is worn on-the hand while counting the sacred beads. Stylistically the figures on these religious artefacts show expressive folk motifs which are different from conventional floral and geometric motifs.

The Muslim religion bans idol worship. But it is usual to have ornamental writing illustrating the sacred script of Kuran. These are known as tugra. They have been embroidered in metallic thread since early times. Phyllis Ackermann while discussing textiles of early Islamic and Seljung periods maintains that Khuzistan, Shustar, Sirsa and Gurdaspur were important centres of ornamental writing. Shustar was the place where the cover with ornamental writing for the Kaba was first introduced.

The earliest form of zardozi in Persia is found to have been associated with ornamental covers for Kaba, a tradition which also existed in the robe of honour made during the Sultanate period. Khalifa was generally written ornamentally on such robes. The tugre done by the zardoz are no doubt the extension of the ornamental religious writings of earlier periods. How tugra is kept in an alia (niche) in a Muslim household and tugre. Generally red, blue or black velvet base is embroidered with silver and gold thread. A fascinating gold hukka and its spread. During the early 20th century when zardozi craftspersons were searching for markets other than the courts, tie case, pin cushions, mantle-covers and many other such articles were embroidered in this style at Delhi chiefly for use of the Europeans. Some such items continue to be produced for foreign as well as the local market.

Embroidery on decorative panels, game cloth for chopad were seen. The naturalistically done peacock and architectural depiction of Taj Mahal are among the popular designs. Rakhi and Christmas hangings are also seasonally made with zardozi.

An overall glance at the objects with zardozi work from the Mughal period to contemporary times provides us a panoramic view of the craft showing gradual changes in the form of objects. What is important to notice in this context is that the motifs found in zardozi do not show any radical change. As a matter of fact several motifs of flowers, creepers and jalis are found to be percolating down the ages without any major alteration. The changes noticeable in the time frame are mere stylization of the earlier motifs with few additions or deletions with respect to the altered forms.

1.4 PROCESS OF CRAFT :

First of all the design is traced on paper by a pencil and small holes are punched on it at close intervals. The pin pricked design on the paper is placed on the piece to be embroidered and smeared with zinc powder soaked in water. The zinc solution passes through the holes making the impression on the cloth. The other powders used for tracing of designs are khadiya, neel (indigo), gum depending on the colour of the cloth to be embroidered. When the tracing is worn out after prolonged use, the copies are made by repunching the tracing on two or three papers for reuse. Traditionally during the Mughal period, nakkash, the professional artists, used to draw the design in the court karkhana™ where several crafts were carried on simultaneously. However, during the field-work, it was observed that these days zardoz draw their drawings themselves. These drawings are called khakhas generally drawn by good artists among zardoz, who provide the copies to their fellowmen. Normally the khakhas are stored for about 30 to 40 years. In commercial karkhanas, the karkhanedars keep a control on the designs.

Next process involves laying of different varieties and shapes of metallic wire and other materials like glass, beads etc. This is done by passing the needle which is threaded from underneath the fabric to the surface and then from surface to below. The needle thus moves upward from the wrong side. The zari wires cut into small pieces are laid so closely that they appear to be continuous thread even to a trained eye.

However, the tilla is not cut in small pieces. It is instead wrapped around a fatila which is moved from one side to the other with the motion of needle.

A distinction of technique exists in the ari work, where instead of small pieces of pure metallic wire only kalabattu is used. Unlike the needle the ari is held in hand and passed beneath from the right side of the fabric. The gilded wire or tilla is wrapped on fatila and a portion is pulled above by keeping it in the notch of the ari.

It was asserted by zardoz during the course of interviews that ari work on karchob is comparatively a later assimilation in zardozi work and is derived from the mochi bharat of Gujarat where a similar needle is used for embroidering leather shoes with cotton thread. This technique is preponderantly employed for embroidering leather shoes in Punjab, Rajasthan also. On the fabric, however, these days it is a trend to employ zardozi and ari technique in close togetherness. Since ari work is faster, it is assimilated with zardozi stitches. It may be mentioned in this connection that ansari zardoz are very particular about not practising on technique. Many among them were found saying that bhookhe mar jayenge par ari nahin uthayenge (we may die of hunger but shall not work with needle). That is why, perhaps, tilla is also stitched with the needle in domestic karkhanas. The hath ari work was abundantly done on woollen items in the provincial courts of Punjab, Kashmir and Patiala.

Zardozi work also however has two distinct categories known as karchobi and kamdani. The embroidery done on velvet or heavy satin generally for tent coverages, furnishings etc. traditionally with badla was called karchobi. It is said to have become popular during the late Mughal period, when the Muslims came in contact with Portuguese. Presently, the shashe of the Pope in Catholic church are worked in this technique. Kamdani generally refers to the work done on muslin, silk and other fabrics. The work here is done with great deal of minute skill in delicate rhythm. This technique remained more popular on the dresses, coverlets, caps and many miscellaneous items.

An important technique, which requires to be discussed is couching. As the name implies it is the technique employed to give the embossed effect on the desired portions. Normally such effect is obtained by two processes. In the first process a cotton fabric is tied on karchob and the outline of the design is traced on its surface. Pieces of cardboard or bukram are then pasted on the portions where raised effect is desired. Next the fabric on which the work is to be done is stitched on the karchob and embroidered. The technique also known as vasli kam was more popular on furnishing materials, trappings etc. Presently it is practised on badges, insignias etc. In the second procedure of couching, the fabric which is to be embroidered is directly stretched on karchob and the area desired to be couched is filled with thick cotton yarn stitches. Sometimes a piece of foam is put underneath. Once the desired embossed effect is obtained, the area is covered with zari wire. This technique is practised on covers, costumes etc.

Minakari is another important process where the variety of silk threads along with zari wire are used for embellishment. This technique lends enamel-like view to embroidery, hence the name minakari.

It is interesting to note that despite many changes in design, form etc., the tools and technology of the craft have remained more or less unchanged. There is thus a continuity in the process, tools and equipment since the inception of the craft during Mughal period. The process of zardozi revolves around five basic designs which have larger variation. These basic designs are jali (geometric design), bharat (filler design), patti (leaf), phul (flower), pankhi (bird), janwar (animal).

Jali work is also known as tanke bandi ka kam because here the stitches are counted without a preconceived draft. Few of the jali designs are : chandi ki jali, chakle wali jali, suiyo wali jali. Bharat designs as the name indicates fill the portions by embroidery. These have mainly the geometrical patterns which are placed in the gaps in a continuous rhythm.

Popular bharat designs are: chunti ki bharat, tanke bandi ka kam, do suiyo ki bharat, khardar bharat. Other designs like patti, phul, pankhi and janwar have a wider range. Important are gende ka phul (kidney-shaped flower), ek khar, ded khar, teen khar (refer to the respective edges generally of leaves), angur (grape) etc.

Zardozi as a technique is understood to be a distinctive style of stitching as it differs from other traditions of embroidery like kantha, kasuti, phulkari etc. where the movement of the threaded needle is guided by a variety of stitches. In other embroideries silk, cotton or woollen threads are used, which are pliable enough to move freely. However, in zardozi, the thread only acts as a binding medium, whereas the body of the design is completed by laying varieties of metallic threads in several shapes and forms along with beads, stones, beetle wings etc. The whole process is more indicative of applique rather than embroidery. Thus it may be called metal applique. This is further corroborated by the fact that zardoz always get payments for amount of wire stitched on the cloth by weight. They never use the word kadai, the Hindi word for embroidery, instead refer to it as salme sitare ke kam ka takna which means laying of the salma, sitara on the body of the fabric.

MANUFACTURING PROCESSES

The multiple processes involved in zari industry are carried out in a decentralised manner at different units specialised in one or more but not all processes. The processes involved in Zari manufacturing can broadly be grouped as under depending on the final product, viz., Real or Imitation.

(1) Processes involved in the manufacture of Real Zari.

    (i) Melting of Silver (Raw).

    (ii) Preparation of Silver wire Bars.

    (iii) Hammering of Silver bars for elongation.

    (iv) Drawing of Silver Wire of different gauges, coarse, medium, fine and superfine, in Pawtha and Tania wire drawing units. (An ounce of Silver is used for making about 3000 yards of silver wire).

    (v) Flattening the wire or Lametta making in flattening machine.

(vi) Dyeing of Cotton or Silk, or Art Silk Yarn.

    (vii) Winding of Lametta on Silk, Art Silk or Cotton on Winding machines to make Zari.

    (viii) Electroplating of silver Zari threads to make gold threads.

(2) Processes involved in the manufacture of Imitation Zari.

    (i) Making of 1/2" copper coils from copper Bars, in Rolling Milt at Udhna or Shivry.

    (ii) Copper Wire Drawing Units (PAWTHA) for drawing wire up to 30 s.w.g (drawing through dyes).

    (iii) Gilding of 30 s.w.g. copper wire by silver in cement concrete or polythene tanks.

    (iv) Further drawing of this 30 s.w.g. silver electroplated copper wire in fine gauges (TANIA UNIT).

    (v) Flattening of silver-gilded copper wire in Lametta Making flattening machine. (CHAPAD OR FLATTENING UNIT).

    (vi) Winding of Lametta on Yarn on kasab winding machines.

(vii) Gilding of Silver threads (gold or lacquer).

The usual practice is to melt the silver ingot bought from the market in furnaces and the molten mass of silver is then moulded into bars. The silver is then elongated by electric hammering and then drawn in wire-drawing units called "PAWTHA" through various tungsten dies of decreasing diameter so as to finally get the wire of 30 s.w.g. This silver wire is then further made to pass through a series of ruby dyes in another wire-drawing unit called "TANIA" so as to make the final wire of required sizes. Here the fineness up to which wire is drawn is normally between 1600 to 1800 yards per ounce. Surat zari industry has the capability to draw fine wire up to a fineness of 2500 yards per ounce, thinner then even human hair. What an achievement !

Thereafter, this fine silver wire is flattened in a flattening machine to make Silver-lametta. The Lametta (flattened and shining silver wire) is then wound round silk, art-silk or cotton thread on a machine called winding machine to make zari Thread. This "Ruperi Zari Thread" which is silvery is again then made to pass through gold solution in locally made electroplating unit (gilit-no-bankdo) to make the final "Gold Thread" for sale.

In the manufacture of Imitation Gold Thread, the imported electrolytic copper wire is first rolled into Vz rods in the rolling mill at Udhna or Amar Rolling Mill at Shivry and then further drawn to 30 s.w.g thickness/diameter in Pawtha or locally made coarse wire-drawing units. This copper wire is then electroplated with silver in tanks. The copper wire electroplated in silver is further drawn through various ruby dyes in Tania units to required gauge. The wire product is then flattened and wound round the art-silk or cotton yarn to make Imitation or Half-fine Zari threads. Imitation Zari-thread can be with actual gold gilded or gilded with lacquer without gold. If it is with some gold, it is called Half-fine Gold thread.

For the manufacture of embroidery materials, the process up to flattening is similar. The flattened wire (lametta) is then used in different equipments to make Zik, Chatak, Salmo, Kangari etc. For Stars and similar items, the flattened strip is punched in sewing machine like punching machines specially made for the purpose, with dyes of different design. For Real Zari, the basic metal used is silver, while for imitation Zari the basic metal used is copper. It will be interesting to note here that all Zari manufacturing machines right from wire-drawing to the end, are locally manufactured and this remarkable achievement in self-reliance makes this industry all the more significant and important in the National Economy. Zari making activity can be subdivided in 12 different activities which are shown in the following table :

It can be observed that all units are not necessarily involved in all activities. The industry functions in such a way that production processes of different firms are intricately and intimately coordinated. For

Table 1.4.1 Zari units in Surat 1970

Types of units	Units in 1970	Workers
Pawtha, Tania	75	400
Pawtha, Tania (I)	130	1250
Zari thread (Real / Imitaion)	800	8500
Stars & Spangles	135	1500
Embroidery & Zardosi	50	500
Gota - thappa flowers, champo	300	1500
Kinkhab - brocades unit	35	350
Laces and border unit	275	1000
TOTAL	**1800**	**15000**

Source : *Annual Report of the Surat Zari Merchant's Association, 1970*

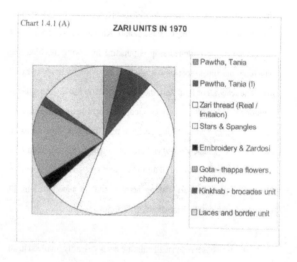

Chart 1.4.1 (A) ZARI UNITS IN 1970

Chart 1.4.1 (B)

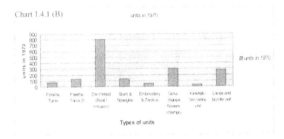

Chart 1.4.2 (A) **WORKERS IN VARIOUS UNITS**

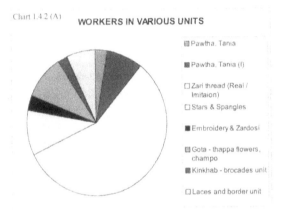

Chart 1.4.2 (B) WORKERS IN VARIOUS UNITS

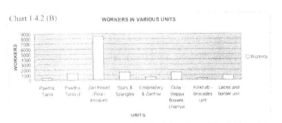

example, there are units that are engaged in only one operation/process; some are engaged in two operations/processes and some in more than two. Tania and winding operations are often found in combination. Pawtha and gilding require more capital and are often found as stand alone operations in different units. Fattening and winding operations are also found in combination in several units, probably because of the low level of investment and skills required (even women and children are often involved) and also because of winding immediately follows flattening.

Current Process involved in Zari Industry :

There are three types of Zari i.e Real, Imitation, Metallic. Each and every Zari has its own characteristics. Even the process involved in each is different.

REAL ZARI:

Zari initially got its name because originally it was made from Silver and Gold. Nowadays this type of zari is not seen in market due to high prices of Silver and Gold. The processes of this Zari are as under :

(a) Melting of Silver:

Under this process the silver is being melted in a hot Chimney, at a specific degree. Initially coal was used but nowadays to save time and cost, people are using gas and electricity to melt silver.

(b) Preparation of Silver Wire bars:

This is the second step in the preparation of Real Zari. Here the melted silver in a form of liquid is dropped in a prepared structured form, which is then moulded into makes a different sizes of Bars. Chemicals are also used to make the bars.

(c) Hammering of Silver Bars:

The prepared Bars are then further hammered to minimize the thickness. In this process only the hot silver bars are hammered.

(d) Drawing of Silver Wire:

Under this process the silver wires are drawn from various sizes of machines, which is also called "Tania". The sizes may be in Gauges i.e. 20, 40, 60, 80 etc.

(e) Flattening of Wire:

After drawing from different gauges, the wires are then stretched through the machines again which makes the wire thin like a thread. This process is popularly known as Surat Lametta.

(f) Dyeing of Cotton <u>Or</u> Silk <u>Or</u> Art Silk Yarn:

In this process readymade silk or cotton or may be art silk yarn is dyed. This process is done by various type of chemicals.

(g) Winding of Lametta on silk or Dyed silk Yarn:

The Lametta prepared is being wounded on Dyed Silk Yarn which is called winding.

(h) Electroplating of Silver Zari thread to make Gold thread:

To make Gold thread, the silver zari is electroplated on a machine.

IMITATION ZARI:

(a) Making Coils:-

Under this, the process is to make 1/2" Copper Coils from Copper wire Bars in Rolling mills at Udhana or Shivry. The imported Electrodytic Copper wire is first rolled into 1/2" rods in rolling Mill, at Udhna or AMAR rolling mill at Shivry.

(b) Drawing of Wire (PAWTHA):

This is the wire drawing unit under which various tungsten dyes are decreased in diameters so as to finally get the wire of 30 S.W.G. This process is called "Pawtha" or locally made coarse wire drawing units.

(c) Gilding:

30 s.w.g. Copper wire is gilded by silver in cement concrete tanks or polythene tanks. This copper wire is then electroplated with silver in Tanks.

(d) Tania Units:

This is the unit, under which the silver electroplated copper wire is further drawn through various ruby dyes. The dye size is prepared as per the requirement. The dyes are also called 'Hira' or "Vicer". The holes through the dyes are called "Ustad". Here the fineness upto which wire is drawn is normally between 1600 to 1800 yards per ounce. Surat can draw Fine wire upto the fineness of 2500 yards per ounce, thinner than even human hair - What an achievement!

(e) Chapad Or Flattening Unit:

This is a Lametta making unit. The wire product is flattened. The silver thread is rounded under the method of Tania. But under this method the round thread passes through the two Steel Wheels under which it becomes flat (Chapad). So it is called flattening / Chapad process. By the process of flattening, sewing becomes easy.

The flattened wire (Lametta) is used in various equipments to make Zik, Chalak, Salmo, kangari etc. For Stars etc. the flattened strip is punched in sewing machine like punching machine specially made for the purpose with different design dyes.

(f) Kasab:

Under this method the flattened wire is wound round the art silk or Cotton Yarn to make imitation or Half Fine Zari threads. The process is called Kasab.

(g) Gilit No Bakdo(gilding through chemical) :

Silvery zari thread is again made to pass through gold solution in locally made electroplating unit, which is called Gilit no Bakdo to make the final "Gold Thread' for sales in market.

METTALIC ZARI :-

Today, the precious metal gold & silver has become too costly & hence pure zari is beyond everybody's reach. Mettalic yarn zari (imitation zari) has become as an able, ideal & most suitable substitute to all types of pure zari. Due to upgradation of technology, polyester film was metallised & coated, bringing into existence the basic raw material for producing metallic yarn zari. France & Japan were the first to flood the market with zari made from polyester film in the year 1970. Since then, due to continuous research & development metallic yarn zari has gained more market compared to all other types of imitation zari (made from copper) & pure zari.

Considering the cost aspect metallic yarn zari has done a great service to the nation by saving precious metal like gold & silver & also copper. Metallic yarn zari costing Rs.350 Kg. has become an easy & affordable luxry for common man. Pure zari costing Rs.4000 per kg. has become a product beyond common man's reach.

Metallic zari industry today is an industry giving employment & *self employment* to more than 4000 families at other centers like Ajmer,

Maunathbhanjan, Salem, Coimbatore, Bangalore, Delhi, Malegaon, Nadiad. The process involved in making metallic zari is very simple, Metallised coated film in desired colours are available in the market.

(i) Cutting & Sizing:

This is the process which involves slitting with the help of razor blade to from pancake of small widths (normally 50 mm to 72 mm). The pancake produced is passed from the thin cutters, size of which depends upon the thickness of required zari. Generally there are 224 spindles on one machine. The capacity of this machine is to produce 3 to 3.50 Ton per month.

(ii) Winding:

The zari so produced is wound on spools with the help of winder. Here the resultant zari is produced by skilled efforts of artisans / operators.

(iii) Steaming:

After covering the zari by yarn, it is heated on given steam for 17 minutes to lend finishing to the zari.

CHART SHOWING PROCESS ON NEXT PAGE ...

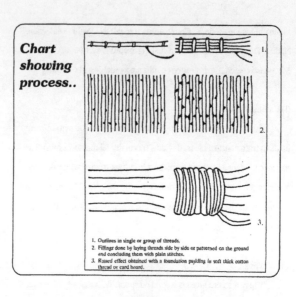

Chart showing process..

1. Outlines in single or group of threads.
2. Fillings done by laying threads side by side or patterned on the ground and concluding them with plain stitches.
3. Raised effect obtained with a foundation padding in soft thick cotton thread or card board.

1.5 PATTERNS OF ORGANISATION

Distribution of Zari units in Surat:

Zari industry being a household industry precise information about the number of units and workers engaged was not available. Several agencies like Surat Muncipal Corporation, Zari Merchants' Association and District Industries Centre etc., with which the Zari units get registered, had some information. Information provided by these institutions was un-comprehensive, un-comparable and often contradictory. Zari Merchants' Association of Surat (with a membership of about 350) estimated 2300 units while the Municipal Corporation Office put the estimate at around 1200 units (of which information about location and employment size was available for only 759); the District Industries Centre had information about 237 units.

Table 1.5.1 below gives the spatial distribution of Surat-based zari units.

Workers	1-2	3-4	5-6	7-8	9-10	>-10	TOTAL
Gopipura	20	12	9	6	-	-	47
Navapura	121	68	18	12	1	-	220
Sagrampura	33	22	9	9	3	1	77
Wadifalia	43	52	18	18	-	-	131
Mahidharpura	8	8	2	6	2	1	27
Station-road	13	25	17	8	2	-	65
Begumpura	66	61	35	24	4	2	192
TOTAL	304	248	108	83	12	4	759

Source: SPIER Study Report.

According to 1990 economic census, there were 2553 units of Zari manufacturing -99 % of which were functioning in their own premises and only 13 % were functioning without electricity. Only 218 (9%) units employed more than 10 workers. While this number remained very close to 220 in 1980, the number of small units increased substantially from 539 to 2334.

Organisation of work in Zari Industry :

There are about 800 Merchant-manufacturers, 200 Akhadedars (job work contractors) and nearly 30,000 workers or artisans according to a report of 1970. A report of Zari Merchants' Association published in 1995 mentions the existence of 200 merchant-manufacturers, 1800 Akhadedars and 50,000 workers in the Zari industry. Machine owners and merchants employ workers. According to an estimate by Zari Merchants' Association, of the total workforce engaged in Zari Industry in Surat, nearly 1% are merchant-manufacturers, 4% are akhadedars or contractors and 95% are the workers. However, as mentioned at the beginning of this chapter, the current estimates orally ascertained during the discussions put the estimates as follows:

Number of units owned by leading merchant-manufacturers :	500
Number of fragmented units engaged in one or two operations :	3000-5000
Size of workforce :	100,000

The Merchant-Manufacturers

The merchant-manufacturers supply the required capital to the

Industry. They may or may not possess or own Zari manufacturing machines or units. In addition to their own production, they may get the work of others done by the Akhadedars who are associated with them. The merchant-manufacturers, as they are called, supply the raw materials like gold/silver wire, silk, art-silk or cotton yarn etc. to Akhadedars and get, in turn, the product on payment of charges fixed by mutual negotiations, for the contracted job work done. The merchant-manufacturers deal in the goods and do the trade and business in Zari Industry.

The Akhadedars or the Job-work Contractors:

The Akhadedars or the job-work contractors act as independent contractors or manufacturers. They obtain the work orders and enter into job-contracts with merchant-manufacturers on piece-rate contract charges. They usually possess and own Zari machinery (winding or drawing or electroplating or other equipment) to do the job-work for the merchant-manufacturers. Merchant-manufacturers supply the raw materials. The Akhadedars, in turn, employ workers on piece-rate wages to work on their machines to do the job-work that they have contracted. They usually employ their family members also. These Akhadedars often also simultaneously do the job contract work as well as manufacturing and selling their own Zari products in the market.

Artisans or workers:

Workers are a class by itself. They are employed by the machine owners, namely merchant-Manufacturers or Akhadedars, to do the work on the machines and earn wages on piece-rate base wages. They are the employee class.

This, in brief, is the age old and established pattern of working in the Industry. It is an established pattern and apparently works peacefully and satisfactorily. As the industry is decentralised, there are very few composite units, possessing full equipment from wire drawing to finished product. By and large, the entire Industry has been working in this decentralised set-up from ancient days.

Distribution of family and hired workers :

During our discussion with the people connected with Zari manufacturing in Surat, it was pointed out that there is high proportion of family work in the total workforce in this industry. This could be one of the reasons for industrial peace in this industry. A 300 units survey done by SPIER puts the ratio of family workers to hired workers at 52:48 (details given in Table 1.5.2). It was also revealed that there is a change in the workforce during the last two decades. Many merchants of the past have changed their line of business and entered into textiles, while many of the akhadedars of the past have now become zari merchants. The new entrants in workforce, mainly the artisans, are from Rana community.

Table 1.5.2 Size wise distribution of family and hired workers in 300 units :

Workers in a unit	Family Workers	Hired Workers	Total Workers
1-5	151 (51)	143 (49)	294 (100)
6-10	581 (54)	491 (46)	1072 (100)
11-15	387 (52)	361 (48)	748 (100)
> - 15	339 (50)	340 (50)	679 (100)
TOTAL	1458 (52)	1335 (48)	2793 (100)

Source: SPIER Study Report.

Not much of union activity is prevelant in this industry. There are two unions viz. Zari Kamdar Mandal and Akhadedar Association and both of these unions are ineffective at present. On meeting with the past president of Zari Kamdar Mandal, it came to be known that, after independence, strike was observed twice in order to press demands for minimum wages, weekly off and compensation to the workers in the event of closing down of the factory. The union however seems to be quite passive now.

1.6 MARKETING OF ZARI

Domestic market :

In almost all the States of the Indian Union, zari threads and other zari items are marketed. The products of zari Industry are marketed not only in the country but exported abroad as well. But the marketing of zari and zari products is not systematically organised. There are no associations or rules for guidance and no standard contracts. Each producer and dealer has developed and adopted his own marketing line and the products are not sold always through organised agencies. The deals are either against definite orders or as is often the case on consignment basis. Credit is universal in the industry and extends from three to nine months and occasionally even longer. One will find marked diversity in trade practices that are followed in the industry. In short, the market is thoroughly loose and absolutely unorganised. Obviously, the first and foremost task is to have a marketing organisation not only for obtaining and distributing raw-materials for the manufacturers but also for organizing a common production programme and common marketing, that is the establishment of a service-cum-sales organization. But the established pattern will, in fact, never allow such a common marketing agency to materialize.

The marketing on the whole is bound to remain individualistic to a great extent. But looking to the established trade practices in the industry, a code of business should be evolved by the industry wherein a sale contract could be standardized, credit benefit fixed and time limit of payment can be settled. This is of paramount importance. There is a great need to make the market steady and well organized. Either the common marketing organization that may be established in future or the Associations like the Surat Zari Merchants' Association working in the Industry can take up this work. At present, goods are sold by the Zari merchants in Surat either through agents appointed by them in the marketing centres or through their own branches in such places. Goods are sold generally on credit although the traders buy the raw materials in cash. So also, the dissemination of market information, which is very important for any industry, is conspicuous by its absence. The advertisements and dissemination of product information, which is very much needed particularly for pushing sales abroad can be made by participating in exhibitions, publication of illustrated brochures, radio & TV advertisements etc. Similarly, a foreign market survey of the changing demands, tastes and fashions has to be carried out by the industry to assist planned production and ensure steady export markets.

There is also a need for the creation of new designs in the industry to develop its new markets. For this, and to attract more people towards zari products the urgent need is to establish a Design Centre exclusively for zari Industry.

The major market for the products of zari Industry is internal, though a considerable quantity of the same is marketed abroad as well.

Out of the total annual production of zari Industry, nearly 80 to 85% is consumed by the internal market while the rest i.e. about 15% is exported outside the country. The total export of zari-based products is about Rs.80 cr, mostly to USA. The potential export market is ranked in the (decreasing) order of real, plastic and imitation zari.

The principal Indian markets for Zari products are Madras, Mysore, Rajasthan, Delhi, Uttar Pradesh, Calcutta and Maharashtra. The premier centres being Bangalore, Salem, Madura, Kanjivaram, Kumbakonam etc. in the South; Jaipur, Delhi, Amritsar and Banaras in the North; Calcutta in the East; and Bombay and Nagpur in the West. Of all these, the South Indian Market consumes in bulk the well known gold and silver thread through its handloom and power-loom textile weaving units. The internal market, because of unplanned production and marketing programme, has turned a "buyer's market" and the external market is more adverse due to severe competition offered by French Zari.

While this is the situation, the advent of a rival yarn, the plastic Zari or Lurex has added fuel to the fire. Important Zari consuming centres like Benaras and Bangalore were invaded and conquered. At times, it was felt that death-knell was rung but due to serious protests and efforts of the Zari Association, Zari Federation and the Handicrafts Board and the sympathy of the Government at the Centre, the zari thread has won the battle once again and is recapturing lost markets.

Over-production and cut-throat competition has developed over time. Leaders of the industry under the auspices of the Surat Zari Merchants' Association gathered and unanimously decided to move through the Zari Development Board to invoke the assistance of the Government to come to the irrescue. The Government appointed in 1957 a Zari industry Enquiry Committee, which in consensus with the Trade also opined that the only way to save the home industry is to take urgent steps to develop the potential zari export market. The industry continues to be afflicted by these problems even now.

The Enquiry Committee also made another important recommendation and that was the 'Formation of a Committee exclusively devoted to the export promotion Job'. It is interesting to note that both these recommendations were accepted by the Central Government and were also implemented. The zari Industry was placed under the care of the All India Handicraft Board, New Delhi for its over all development including Export trade. The second important step was the announcement of Special Export Promotion Scheme in 1959 for zari exports under which 40% by way of import licence against zari exports were granted to induce zari exporters to push up sales and to give the much needed fillip.

1.7 EXPORTS OF ZARI

The zari products are in considerable demand in foreign countries and are marketed in almost all the leading marketing centres of the world. The important countries wherein zari products are marketed are Pakistan, Afghanistan, Ceylon, Burma, Indonesia, Canada and the Middle-East countries. The demand for Zari have remained in almost all these countries, but it is indeed regrettable that no organised efforts have been made as yet by the industry to explore potential foreign markets and expand the existing ones.

Export promotion schemes :

After 1959, the year in which the first ever Export Promotion Scheme was formulated for zari goods, export trade of zari began to rise till the year 1963-64. Due to malpractice by some selfish and unscrupulous self-styled zari exporters, the Government withdrew the EP Scheme and there arose a crisis. All India Zari Federation through its versatile Chairman Shri R.T. Popatwala with the representatives of the Zari Exporters' Association viz. The Surat Zari Merchants' Association, met the then Union Minister for Foreign Trade Shri Manubhai Shah. After strenuous efforts and with the sympathy of the All India Handicrafts Board they prevailed upon him to re-introduce the EP Scheme for Zari goods. Shri Manubhai Shah, convinced about the imperative need for assistance, re-introduced the zari Export Promotion Scheme in 1964 with 30% incentive that continues till today. Thanks to the sympathy of the Government and sincere efforts of the All India Handicrafts' Board, the All India Zari Federation and the premier Zari Association viz., the Surat Zari Merchants' Association, have on their rolls about 100 Zari exporters.

Under the Export Promotion Scheme in force, zari exporters are given raw material incentive licences worth 30% of the f.o.b. value of export. The items of entitlements at present allowed against zari exports are Copper, Raw Silk and Velveteen. Adequate assistance through export promotion scheme, sponsoring of a study team to undertake tour of foreign countries to explore possible markets there, studying taste and fashions in sophisticated countries like the U.S.A and latest equipment and technique, and the publicity for dissemination of useful information are the needs of the hour.

Zari has the export market from the beginning and traditionally in the Middle East countries. The major domestic market existed in southern states of India and was reached through the agents who were also in many cases relatives of the entrepreneurs. In the late sixties, zari export was affected due to the invention of plastic zari and competition from developed countries like France and Japan. The government policy was also not favourable for the export of zari as it was manufactured from gold and silver.

Zari export during 1960-61 to 1994-95 (table 2.6) included (a) gold thread (Kasaab), (b) embroidery materials like Badla (Lametta), Zik, Tiki, Chalak, Salmo, Kanagari, Sadi, Fancy Stars etc. (c) Laces, fit-boarders, trimmings, etc. (d) Zari textiles like Kinkhab, Ornis and Zari embroidered cloth purses and plaques etc. It can be seen from the table that Zari exports have been fluctuating. Zari exports that were Rs.25 lakhs in 1960-61 reached to Rs.125 lakhs in 1969-70. It reached Rs.173 lakhs in 1963-64 and fell down to Rs.32 lakhs during 1966-67. Exports in recent years have been mentioned in table 1.7.1 below::

Table 1.7.1 Exports of Zari and Zari Goods

YEAR	VALUE IN CRORES OF RUPEES
1960-61	0.25
1961-62	0.71
1962-63	0.62
1963-64	1.73
1964-65	0.60
1966-67	0.38
1967-68	0.32
1968-69	0.80
1969-70	1.26
1985-86	6.18
1986-87	11.08
1987-88	4.97
1988-89	8.54
1989-90	6.86
1990-91	18.48
1991-92	30.60
1992-93	42.65
1993-94	48.90
1994-95	57.95

Charts are on next page...

(108)

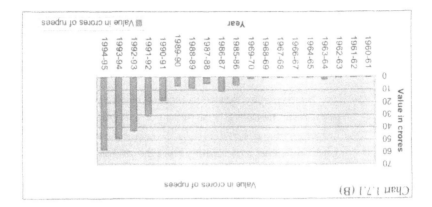

Chart 1.7.1 (B)

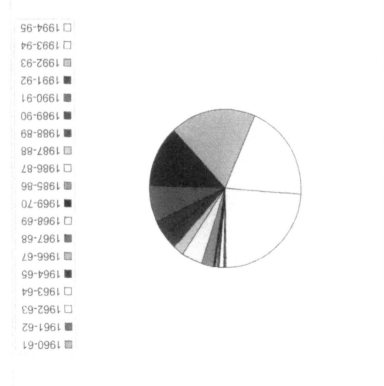

Value in crores of rupees

Chart 1.7.1 (A)

The rosy picture of exports of the last decade seen in the above table is illusory. The nine-fold increase is only in terms of value; there has been only nominal increase in quantity. This is mainly due to four-fold rise in the prices of raw materials, labour and devaluation of our Indian rupee by almost 33%. While exports of handicrafts are growing at a higher rate, the growth of zari exports is lagging behind.

STATEMENT OF EXPORTS OF HANDICRAFTS ARE DEPICTED ON FURTHER PAGES ...

STATEMENT OF EXPORTS OF HANDICRAFTS
EXCLUDING HANDKNOTTED CARPET (ITEMWISE) FOR THE LAST TEN YEARS

Table 1.7.2   (RS. IN CRORES)   (PROVISIONAL)

ITEMS	1991-92	1992-93	1993-94	1994-95	1995-96	1996-97	1997-98	1998-99	1999-00	2000-01
1. ARTMETALWARE	341.05	480.05	680.20	1022.25	1205.95	1370.60	1214.60	1324.16	1497.18	1778.10
2. WOODWARE	50.50	68.20	98.50	136.90	155.65	188.45	221.82	286.04	348.95	434.44
3. HANDPRINTED TEXTILE & SCARVES	149.81	196.50	354.25	475.12	580.45	595.17	838.24	1033.98	1158.05	1276.75
4. EMBROIDERED & CROCHETTED GOODS	33.20	42.70	70.45	102.20	115.30	131.10	990.75	1159.42	1584.36	1964.78
5. SHAWLS AS ARTWARE	23.18	28.15	32.95	36.90	39.75	36.43	17.08	18.18	21.50	27.20
6. ZARI & ZARI GOODS	3060	42.65	48.90	57.95	70.95	79.78	70.34	74.95	83.52	142.32
7. IMITATION JEWELLERY	14.90	19.05	28.75	36.88	40.20	44.13	98.03	104.10	113.64	121.68
8. MISC. HANDICRAFTS	421.76	534.70	656.00	767.70	812.10	1022.92	902.32	1057.57	1116.40	1210.08
TOTAL	1065.00	1412.00	1970.00	2635.90	3020.35	3568.58	4353.18	5058.40	59.23.60	69.55.35

Line Chart and different charts and graphs are depicted on further pages ...

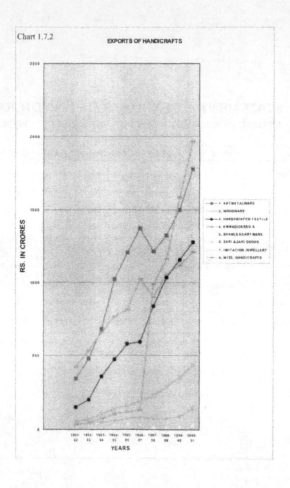

Chart 1.7.2 EXPORTS OF HANDICRAFTS

Chart 1.7.3 (A)   ARTMETALWARE - EXPORTS

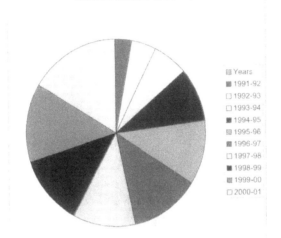

Chart 1.7.3 (B)   ARTMETALWARE

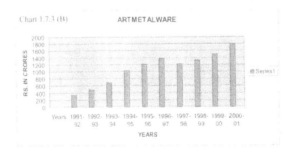

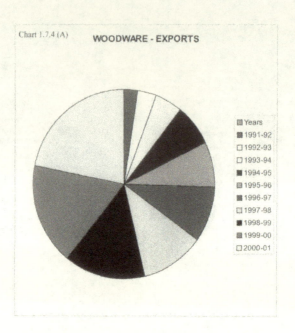

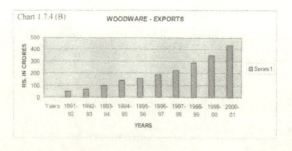

Chart 1.7.5 (A)

HANDPRINTED TEXTILES & SCARVES - EXPORTS

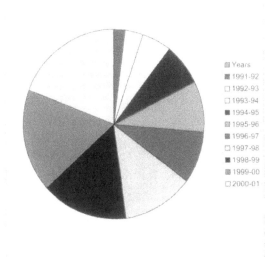

Chart 1.7.5 (B)

HANDPRINTED TEXTILES & SCARVES - EXPORTS

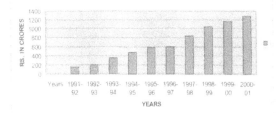

Chart 1.7.6 (A)

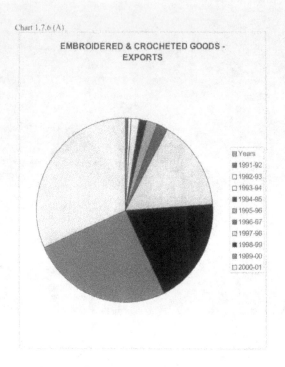

Chart 1.7.6 (B)

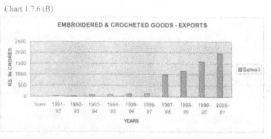

Chart 1.7.7 (A)

SHAWLS AS ARTWARE - EXPORTS

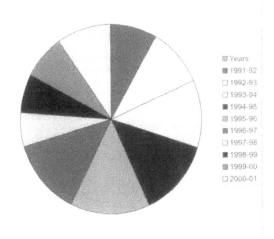

Chart 1.7.7 (B)

Chart 1.7.8 (A)

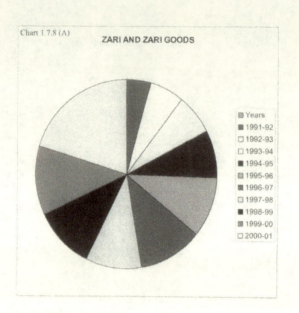

Chart 1.7.8 (B)

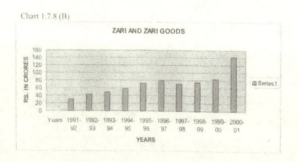

Chart 1.7.9 (A)

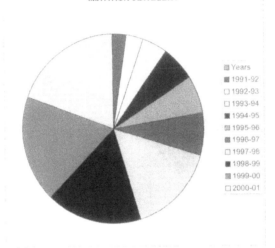

IMITATION JEWELERY

Chart 1.7.9 (B)

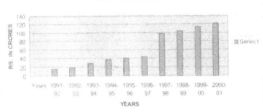

IMITATION JEWELLERY

Chart 1.7.10 (A)

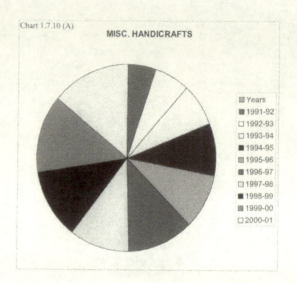

Chart 1.7.10 (B)

1.8 GROWTH AND DEVELOPMENT

(1947 onwards):

After 1947, industry witnessed the beginning of a troubled era. India achieved independence in 1947 and with it brought partition as well. The creation of Pakistan had its adverse effects on the home industry, as it lost the market of zari consuming centres that fell to Pakistan side. Not only this, but it also lost its real regular patrons with the abolition of Princely States bringing about yet another serious crisis for the home industry. Zari industry lost about 1/3 of its total demand. From 1947 onwards for about a decade, the industry passed through a very critical period of its existence. Renewed problems and fresh difficulties, like over-production, decline in demand, cut-throat competition, rise in raw material prices and import duty, cropped up. The immediate problem was to find out a compensatory market for the loss of Pakistan part of the consumer's demand and one due to the abolition of princely potentates. For this, the only available course was to explore possible new foreign markets and increase zari exports. Zari was in the world market from times immemorial and is still holding the fort. The industry possesses great export potential. Organised efforts to promote the export of Zari should go a long way in compensating the above loss and toning up the unhealthy condition in the industry simultaneously.

Zari industry enquiry committee (1957) and its recommendations:

The fast deteriorating conditions and the crisis prevailing in the industry created anxious moments. The efforts of the industry by itself to improve its present dismal condition were not enough. The industry therefore, naturally once again looked forward to the Government for guidance and assistance and requested it through the Surat Zari Development Board (a body constituted of the three principal organs working in the industry) to investigate into the problems of the industry and suggest remedial measures. The Government, looking to the crisis through which the industry was passing, was convinced and appointed in 1957, a Zari Industry Enquiry Committee under the chairmanship of Shri N. Mazumdar, the then Industrial Advisor (Textile production) to conduct an on-the-spot investigation. The Committee included the representatives of the industry viz., Shri Manchhubhai M. Zariwala, the then President of the Surat Zari Merchants' Association and Shri Vaikunthbhai B. Shastri & Shri R.T. Popatwala representing the employers and Shri Ishverbhai G. Desai of Zari Kamdar Mandal representing the employees. The Enquiry Committee visited all the zari centres in the country including Surat and after making all possible on-the-spot studies, submitted a report to the Government of India in the year 1958. The Zari Industry Inquiry Committee, which was the first of its kind for such a cottage and small-scale industry in our country, made very important and useful recommendations to the Government to effect an all-round improvement for the survival and organised development of the industry.

It seemed that the condition of workers was of much concern. For instance, the Zari Industry Inquiry Committee, appointed by Government of India in 1957 specifically mentioned about the worker's condition. They recommended that

(1) State Govt. should take steps to enforce such provisions of Factory Act as it relates at least to the hygienic and other amenities for workers;

(2) A few family planning centres should be established in areas where there is a concentration of Zari units and;

(3) Fixation of minimum wages for each type of work for full-time employment.

Zari Merchants Association (ZMA) contested many of these recommendations. The first very important recommendation implemented by the Government was to put the industry under the care of the All India Handicrafts Board and to take necessary steps urgently as suggested by the Committee in their report. The Handicrafts Board, as a follow-up step, constituted an All India Zari advisory Committee to find out ways and means to put the industry on a sound footing and promote zari exports. In 1959, the Government took the first concrete step in the direction of export promotion on the recommendation of the Board by announcing Zari Export Promotion Scheme. Under the scheme, zari exporters were to be given incentive licences for import of raw materials to enable them to offer zari at competitive rates in the world market. Zari exports increased slowly and helped the industry in a little way to improve its unhealthy state. But, after this major step, no noteworthy progress was made in the implementation of other recommendations either by the State or by the Central Government excepting a few.

The condition of the industry, which showed slight improvement, following the implementation of a few recommendations of the Board, continued to deteriorate due to many burning problems like the soaring market prices of the essential imported raw materials like bullion, copper, silk and art-silk and their inadequate supply, the dwindling in exports due to great price disparity of bullion in the Indian and foreign markets and cut-throat competition due to over production and glut in the market. However, in 1962, an epoch making event took place in the history of Zari Industry, viz. the formation of a Central Organisation of the Indian Zari Industry and Trade called the All India Federation of Zari Industry with its headquarters in Surat. The Federation represented all the zari centres in the country and was an all-India apex organisation of zari industry and trade. Because of its all India character the problems and issues raised, drew immediate attention of the Government. Many difficult problems like the allotment of gold under Gold Control Act and revision of the Export Promotion Scheme to make it realistic and streamlining of raw materials supply etc. were addressed with varying degrees of success.

Recent History (1980 Onwards)

Sardar Patel Institute of Economic and Social Research carried out a study on zari industry in Surat based on sample survey during 1981-

82. The study was restricted to 300 firms and 500 workers of the industry. The question arose about the number of Zari units in Surat at the time of survey. According to the officials of Zari Merchants' Association (ZMA), Surat, there were 2300 units; according to Surat Municipal Corporation (SMC) authorities, there were 1200 units and according to District Industrial Centre (DIG) there were only 237 units. Zari Merchants' Association could not provide the list of 2300 units with their location and size of employment of the unit. From the SMC's office, it was possible to get the list of 1200 units with their addresses. However, only 759 units were listed with SMC office with the correct name, address and size of employment. Thus, the preliminary observation revealed inconsistency about the number of zari manufacturing units in Surat. Based on the same study, zari production was estimated at Rs.28 crores, employment of 7000 workers and exports were estimated at Rs.7 lakhs. 52 percent of the total employment consisted of family employment and female participation was around 34 per cent. Further, it was also noted that child labour proportion was around 9 per cent in case of family employment.

TABLE 1.8.1 ON NEXT PAGE...

Table 1.8.1 ZARI INDUSTRY - 1980

	Sample	Population*
No. of Units	300	759
Output (Rs.)	11,17,20,353	28,26,52,493
Export (Rs.)	2,87,907	7,28,405
Employment (No.)	2793	7066
Family Employment (No.)	1458	3689
Hired Workers (No.)	1335	3377
Male Participation (No.)	409	1038
Total Employment	1601	4051
Female Participation (No.)	961	2431
Child Participation (No.)	231	582

Source : SPIESR Study on Zari Industry, Monograph Series, No. 17, 1992
*Estimated from the sample.

Apart from these, the study contained the following observations:

1. The extent of poverty among Zari workers was not high. Only 53 households (12.50 per cent of the sample households) or 402 persons (14.58 per cent of persons from the sampled households) were poverty-stricken.

2. Zari manufacturing consists of many activities (viz. Drawing of wire, flattening of wire, winding etc.)

3. Forty-four per cent of the units were more than 20 years old. In 89 per cent of the cases, the ownership had not changed even once, 86 per

cent of the units were found to be operating at the place of residence and 80 per cent of the entrepreneurs owned premises where firms were located. Only 13 per cent were relatively new units, which were established 5 years before the survey. The relatively older units had higher investment, higher output and higher employment.

4. Fresh additions to the machinery and equipment necessary for the manufacturing activities were quite meagre (nearly 1 per cent of the fixed assets).

5. Though testing facilities were available at nominal rates, very few units/entrepreneurs were making the use of these facilities. This indifference of the units affected the marketing activity of zari goods in the domestic market. The proportion of zari exports to total production was very low.

6. Majority of entrepreneurs and workers were from the same community i.e. Rana community. The interaction between workers and entrepreneurs was quite cordial.

7. The workers mostly inherited the craft of zari making.

8. Most of the workers received wages either equal to or more than the government recommended minimum wage rate prevailing at *that time*. However, no other benefits were extended to the workers.

9. Average size of the workers' family was more than 6 persons.

From then on, the zari industry picked up the speed and today zari industry is on its peak level.

1.9 PICTORIAL PRESENTATION OF ZARI AND ZARI PRODUCTS

IMPORTANT ZARDOZI CENTRES OF INDIA

Jammu & Kashmir			
Punjab	: Patiala	Madhya Pradesh	: Bhopal
Delhi			Burhanpur
Uttar Pradesh	: Agra		Ujjain
	Farrukhabad		Gwalior
	Kanpur	Maharashtra	: Bombay
	Lucknow		Aurangabad
	Banaras		Paithan
	Ramnagar	Andhra Pradesh	: Hyderabad
	Meerut	Karnataka	: Dharwar
	Bareilly		Gulbargah
Bihar	: Patna	West Bengal	: Calcutta
Rajasthan	: Jaipur	Dacca	
	Jodhpur Jaisalmer	Sind	
Gujarat	: Ahmedabad Bikaner		
	Surat Junagadh		
	Baroda Kutch		

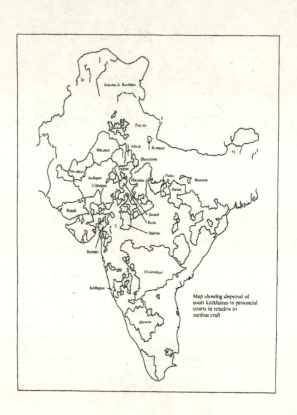

Map showing dispersal of court karkhanas in provincial courts in relation to zardozi craft

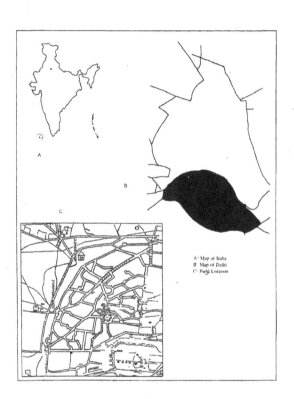

A: Map of India
B: Map of Delhi
C: Field Location

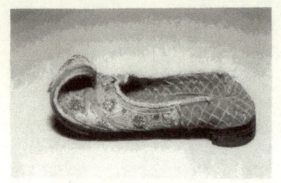

4. The footwear worn by noble ladies.

5. Royal Insignia.

6. Knee-high boots.

7. Miniature painting showing *Durbar of Shah Alam* end of 18th Century

8. *Takthposh*, Complete view.

9. Detail of architectural monument of *takhtpush*.

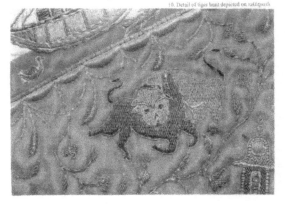
10. Detail of tiger hunt depicted on *takhtpush*.

11. Detail of the hunter on a galloping horse.

12. Detail of the deer running for life.

13. *Takhoposh* with floral motifs.

14. Detail of the corner

15. Zamīnposh, the floor spread.

16. Zamīnposh, the floor cover.

17. Zamīnposh, the floor cover.

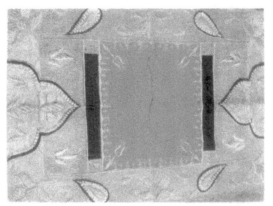
18. Khanposh, the floor spread for eating.

19. Detail of corner

20. Miniature painting depicting raga *Hindola*.

21. Masnad Cover.

22. Cushion cover. (above)

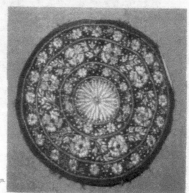

23. Thalposh with thalinuma design.

24. Thalposh. Early 20the century.

25. Umbrella

26. Shri Flag

27. Railing pillars, Sandstone, Bharhut Stupa.

28. Portrait of Sultan Hussain Mirza.

29. Darbar Hanging.

30. Hanging, Puthia.

31. Hanging, Puthia.

32. Aurangir from provincial court of Rajasthan.

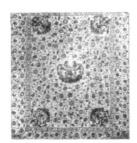

33. Bedspread, silk, embroidered with coloured silk and gold thread.

34. Saddle cotton fabric.

35. Parasol.

36. Semi-circular bolster, red velvet, depicting floral creeper design in vasli technique.

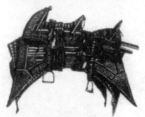

37. Camel saddle from Jodhpur showing gold and silver embroidery.

38. Mehtagiri procession fan fixed on a tall wooden handle, brass knobs.

39. Chaubagla, man's upper garment.

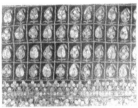

40. Design detail.

41. Lahenga.

42. Kurtani.

43. Cap of typical zardozi motifs.

44. Back view of the same.

45. Several designs and form of purses.
46. Hukka.
47. Bisat of Chopad, the spread for playing the game of chopad.
48. Elaborate process of wire drawing adopted in Punjab.
49. Panel on silk fabric with meenakari.

50. Gold wire drawers from Yeola, Uttar Pradesh

51. Gold wire drawers from Yeola, Uttar Pradesh

52. Zardoz seen working.

53. Zardoz using hath ari.

54. A zardoz woman.

55. Detail of couching technique.

56. Another hearth in the same premises.

57. A child carrying the karchob from one household to another.

58. Two girls stitching the cloth on shamsharak.

59. Karchob fitted with cloth now ready for embroidery.

60. Boys and girls working in domestic karkhana.

61. Patka.
62. Sword cover
63. Detail of sword cover.(above)

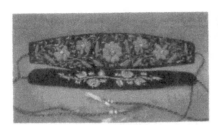

64. Long shawl

65. Dupatta.   66. Neck Scarf.

67. Angarkha

68. Bugalbandi, a tight fitting ladies costume

69. Angarkha.

70. Achkan

71. Choga.

72. Another view of choga.   73. Abho

74. Detail of design on front yoke

75. Back view

76. Jacket

77. Jacket

78. Jacket

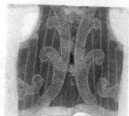

79. Front view

80. Crown.

81. Mandel, the circular cap.   82. Topi

83. Mandel, highly ornated cap.   84. Mandel

85. Juti

86. Raja Bhoj, the rod puppet of prominent King.

87. Purses with meenakari work.

88. Zardoz girl posing to show the fashion accessories   89. Pankha

90. Taj with silver wire on velvet.

91. A miniature folio showing the process of gold melting. Patiala school of painting.

92. Mohd. Farat's wife working on adda.

93. Shamsharak and rarad when not in use.

94. Detail of vasli ka kam.

95. Position of craftsperson while working.
96. Range of buta and bel designs.
97. Range of buta and bel designs.
98. Zardoz girl learning basics of the craft.
99. Gamla batua designs.
100. Range of buta and bel designs.

101. Copper wire drawing units (PAWTHA)

102. Copper wire drawing units (PAWTHA)

103. Copper wire drawing unit

104. Flattening Unit

105. Winding of Lametta

106. Drawing through dyes

107. Kasab winding machine

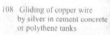

108. Gliding of copper wire by silver in cement concrete or polythene tanks

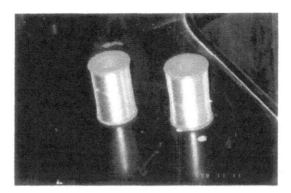

109. Zari Bobbins (Firka)

110. TANIA UNITS

111. Silver electroplated copper wire in fine gauges (Tania Units)

112. Drawing of copper wire

113. Melting of Silver

114. Kangri Unit

115. Hammering of Silver

116. Melting of Silver

(173)

117. INITIAL BARS OF COPPER USED IN IMITATION ZARI

118. INITIAL BARS OF COPPER USED IN IMITATION ZARI

119. BADGES

120. BADGES

121. BADGES

122. BADGES

123. BADGES

124. CUSHION COVERS

125. CUSHION AND CURTAIN COVERS

126. COVERS

127. JACKET AND COVER

128. BADGES AND PURSES

129. BOBBINS

130. BANGLES AND VARIOUS PRODUCTS

131. PURSES AND LACES

132. PURSES

133. DRESSES

134. PURSES

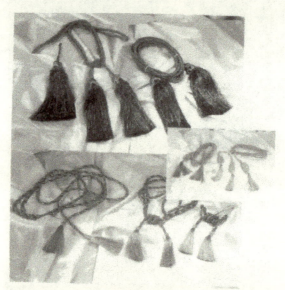
135. LACES

136. PURSES

137. ACCESSORIES

138. HAND PURSES

139. COVERS

140. BADGES AND OTHER PRODUCTS

141. LACES

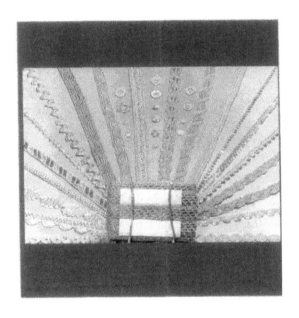

142. LACES

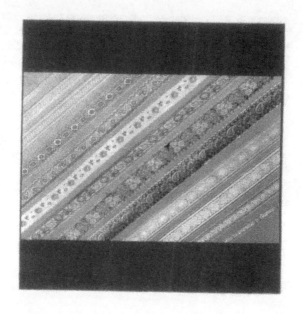

143. LACES

144. VARIOUS LACES

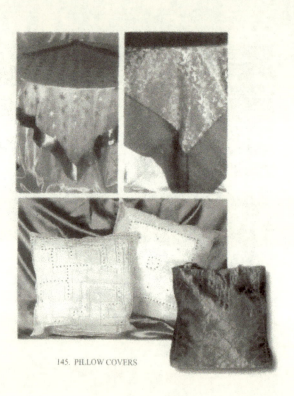
145. PILLOW COVERS

146. DRESS AND OTHERS

147. COSMETICS ACCESSORIES

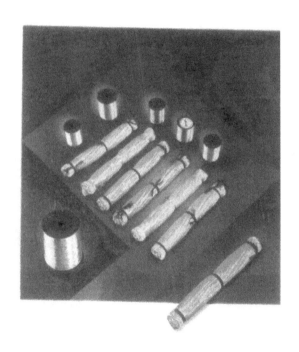

148 BOBBINS AND THREADS

149. DRESSES

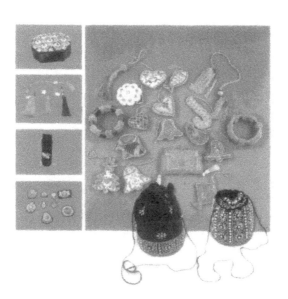

150. VARIOUS PRODUCTS

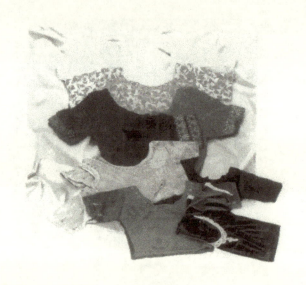

151. BLOUSES AND DRESSES

152. BUYERS AND SELLERS MEET AT BARAILEY

153. ALLOTMENT OF CERTIFICATE TO ZARIZARDOZI TRAINEE

154. INAUGURATION OF ZARI WORK TRAINING CUM DESIGN WORK SHOP

155. TRAINEES OF ZARI ZARDOZI WORK

156. PRODUCTS OF HANDICRAFTS

CHAPTER 2 :

BASIC ISSUES OF ZARI INDUSTRY

		Page No.
2.1	SWOT ANALYSIS.	213
2.2	INFRASTRUCTURE FACILITIES IN SURAT.	224
2.3	PROSPECTS AHEAD IN INDIA FOR ZARI.	226
2.4	ROLE OF PUBLIC REPRESENTATIVE i.e. MEMBER OF PARLIAMENT / MEMBER OF LEGISLATIVE ASSEMBLY.	230
2.5	ROLE OF CHAMBER OF COMMERCE.	233
2.5.1	ROLE OF GOVERNMENT IN THE DEVELOPMENT OF ZARI INDUSTRY.	234
2.5.2	ROLE OF ELECTRICITY COMPANIES IN THE DEVELOPMENT OF ZARI INDUSTRY.	235
2.5.3	ROLE OF BANKING AND TERM LENDING FINANCIAL INSTITUTION IN THE DEVELOPMENT OF ZARI INDUSTRY IN SURAT.	236
2.5.4	ROLE OF MUNICIPAL CORPORATION.	245
2.6	NEED OF MARKETING CO-OPERATIVE SOCIETY.	246
2.7	ENVIRONMENTAL ASPECTS.	247

CHAPTER 2 : BASIC ISSUES OF ZARI INDUSTRY

Zari industry is one of the oldest and antique industry. This industry is totally based on the skill and artistic pattern of labourers (artisans). It has its own reputation and goodwill in the world market. Inspite of ups and downs of the trade the industry has steadily grown. This industry earns foreign exchange also.

The survival of this industry has become difficult today because of various factors but the specific skill of the artisans and the industry still has a high reputation.

Unity of merchants in different segments of the industry is a positive indication for its survival. Particularly in Surat the unity of merchants has strengthened the industry. Specific dry weather, community, lower investment tradition are also other positive factors which have contributed immensely for the survival of this industry.

Some of the basic issues facing the zari industry are :

- Lack of administrative experiences.
- Distinctive area of marketing/decentralized marketing.
- Degradation of quality.
- Upgradation of technology.
- Lack of satisfied financial assistance.

- Higher costing of product.
- Gambling of prices.
- Non-Standardization of product.
- Lack of Research & development.
- Increasing competitors from the same industry.
- Lack of marketing network.
- Lack of publicity.
- Non-Awareness of laws and rules.
- Lack of innovation.
- Lack of strategy.
- Threat of substitutes.

2.1 SWOT ANALYSIS

STRENGTHS:-

Zari Industry is one of the oldest and antique industry. This industry is totally based on the skill and artistic pattern of labourers (artisans). It has its own reputation and goodwill in the world market. Inspite of ups and downs of the trade, the industry has kept its stability. This industry forms a part of handicraft in National economy, which shares a major part of foreign exchange earning. The survival of this industry has become difficult today because of various factors but the specific skill of the artisans and the industry still has a high reputation.

Unity of Merchants in different segments of the industry is a positive indication for its survival. Particularly in Surat the unity of merchants has strengthened the industry. Nowadays over production is a headache for the industry and to tackle this issue, Merchants' Association observes Bandh twice a week. It is a best example of unity to curb over production.

Specific Dry Weather of Surat also is an important and favourable factor which has strengthened the industry. Entire industry's survival depends on this factor. Continuos water supply & Electricity supply are also the effective factors which has strengthened the industry at large.

The industry inspite of ups and downs has still maintained its level because it is totally community based. Specifically "RANA" community has its own identity in the zari industry. Lower investment and employment generation capacity makes the industry progress. Tradition has become a tool to strengthen the industry. Zari industry has attained the status of an art.

WEAKNESS:-

Zari industry still has not attained a satisfactory growth because of the following issues :

(1) Lack of administrative experience:

Any business/industry requires an administrative experience. However zari industry has an experience but lacks administration, It has good manufacturing units. In this business/industry people have no professional education or training. It is not properly managed. It is only on the base of thumb rule which has been traditionally achieved. The traditional approach and lack of initiativeness has led to a decline. In fact, 75% to 80% people involved in this business are illiterate.

In real practice, the location of industry and environment in which industry runs also affects the development of industry. There is lack of proper management. Management requires planning, coordination and control which this industry lacks. There is no budgetary system or cost control. In other words we can say that there is no method of cost control or knowledge of cost. People involved in the business are all from one family which leads to the concentration of functioning in the industry. There is no calculation of salary and wages also.

(2) Distinctive area of marketing:

Zari is manufactured in Surat but it is not utilised to prepare different products. The utilization of the product is made only in Varanasi, Chennai, Bareilly or other areas of southern states. Due to this, the supply & distribution of these goods is at a distinctive place. Not only this, there is even a language problem and a problem of recovery of amount from them. Merchants are required to stay for a considerably longer period of time in southern region. During this period, they suffer immense loss because they are unable to take care of their business.

(3) Degradation of Quality or Lack of Quality Product:

The industry suffers from lack of good quality. The quality is not being maintained by the merchants as well as manufacturers. Most of the traders/manufacturers stress on profit earning. They are not aware of the fact that quality makes the industry firm and strong. Manufacturers/traders are only interested in selling the product and getting back the money. There is no fixed tool for measuring the quality. The total control on quality is not there. It is based on experience and reputation of the firm in a market as well as relation developed by the forefathers. This has made the industry unsteady. People who are expert and well versed in their skill are not ready to develop their quality. There is no research and development in industry. Each one wants to earn money and also do hard work but that is laborious and unplanned. Quality has also suffered due to unavailability of laboratory. The entire quality of the product depends on the mixing of chemicals. But still there is no measurement or a fixed ratio for mixing the chemicals. Only on the tradition base and experience, industry has been able to maintain quality.

(4) Lack of Upgradation of technology:

Zari industry has its own reputation built on traditionalism and technology. Surat zari industry has its own technology of machineries which has also been traditionally developed. New technological development has not taken place. Till today the old patterns & styles of manufacturing are adopted. Compared to other countries, we are far behind technologically..

(5) Lack of satisfied financial assistance:

Financial facilities available with the industry, are insufficient. The economical situation of the merchants/traders is not good. The total finance available is also at a higher rate of interest. So even with maximum profit, earning remains low. Government has also not provided any assistance in the form of subsidies etc.

(6) Higher costing of product :

The industry suffers from a lot of over production and competitive environment. Due to that the cost of product is high. The total cost of product increases due to wastage of raw material, loss of time to start, waste of power, etc.

(7) Gambling of prices:

This is an important factor which is harmful for the industry. The whole industry collapses due to gambling of prices by the merchants or traders.

The internal competition and hazardous production amongst them, makes the traders/merchants to gamble the prices. This deteriorates the whole price structure of the industry. This is a very serious problem which the industry is facing today. For the past two months, industry is faced with a setback.

(8) Non-standardization of product:

In this industry, the product is non-standardized. No gradation is there for the product. Due to lack of quality control the industry is on the verge of collapse.

(9) Lack of Research & Development:

Any business or industry requires to be developed through Research & Development. It is the need of the hour. As we have mentioned earlier the approach of this industry is traditional and is hereditary and governed by uneducated people. Therefore, there is no research and development. We do not find any research at the level of production, administration, marketing or advertising.

(10) Increasing competitors from the same industry:

The industry faces internal competition amongst different groups. Initially those who were akhadedars have become traders and therefore the competition has increased.

On the whole, industry has become more competitive due to new entrepreneurs, lower investment and lesser risk. Initially only specific community based people were there but now other communities have also entered the industry.

(11) Lack of marketing Network:

This is an important factor which has become a permanent type of weakness. Marketing is the heart of industry. This industry suffers from lacuna in marketing. Traditionally there was direct marketing by the traders and manufacturers to utilizers in southern states which has always been a problem for the industry. This industry has not developed any marketing network.

(12) Lack of Publicity:

An important barrier for this industry is the lack of publicity.

Advertisements are not used to create awareness for the product. In order to boost sales, proper publicity is required.

(13) Non-Awareness of laws & Rules:

This is yet another flaw of the industry as there is no knowledge of rules and laws of different taxes.

(14) Lack of innovation :

Innovation is significant for any industry but this industry has not shown any innovativeness.

(15) Lack of strategy:

The industry or business requires to form strategy for further development and competitiveness. But this industry lacks strategic planning because of lack of exposure and awareness.

(16) Threat of Substitute:

This industry today suffers a big threat from the substitute product. Real and Imitation zari has replaced Mettalic zari which is very cheap and easy to produce.

OPPORTUNITIES :

Inspite of all the problems and shortcomings, Zari industry has immense chances of development, but it requires specific type of skill as well as the upgradation of technology. It requires to standardize the product. Marketing should be developed with professionalism. The domestic market should be developed. Domestic market has a lot of scope for marketing. The local market is also required to be developed. Surat is an upcoming market for readymade garments. The local manufacturers should develop their own skill by way of designing, upgrading the technical knowledge as well as research and development.

If industry follows the gradation and standardization with quality control, there is a chance to develop the market at local and national level. The home market is quite poor. Surat city has plenty of sources to develop the utilization of Zari through readymade garments. But this dearth of developing the expertise as well as specialized knowledge through artisans could be developed through adequate research in that area.

The economy of the country is developing and therefore there is a lot of chance to develop the zari industry. Globalization and Liberalization offer opportunities to increase import and export.

In the last three years, the then textile minister Kashiram Rana had even started the zari development programme by organizing training camps and arranging different fairs in different regions. He even motivated the artisans and acknowledged the importance of research. Indians have to take the benefit of that.

Fashion is a routine course of action for the new generation. Industry has to make efforts to develop different designs and special products to utilize zari.

Still there is a great scope to develop the industry as it is an antique industry.

This should be understood by the zari manufacturers. An attempt should be made to fulfill the needs of different group of customers. This industry should try and cater to the different criterial, selective, tastes of the customers.

This industry has a good future if it adopts a strategical approach by knowing the threats, weaknesses and strengths. It will have to apply aggressive strategy to create new resources to develop the industry. Strategies could be developed through different angles. There may be defensive, diversification and turn around strategies to develop the same.

Expansion of export market:

Distinctiveness.

Substitution of product.

THREATS :

(1) Industrial unrest:

The scenario of zari industry, in the last two months is quite hazy. The industry has had its good record of unity but due to the overproduction and dumping of material, there are now chances of industrial unrest.

(2) Deflationary and disguised unemployment:

Unemployment has been created due to heavy deflation. There is even disguised unemployment where there is a need of only three or four people, the whole family is employed. This factor has also adversely affected the industry.

(3) Decrease in foreign exchange:

Today the major part of foreign exchange earning is from zari industry in handicrafts. If zari industry collapses, it will reduce the foreign exchange earning. A major problem would arise in economy.

(4) Decrease in the national income:

Due to foreign exchange, there is a strengthening of national economy. If the income from foreign exchange decreases, it will also lead to a decrease in the national income.

(5) Government has to allow exemption:

Government will have to give exemption for taxes on copper, silver and gold to save the industry and also provide initiative to develop the industry to attract new investment in the industry. Special zones should be declared and exemption should be given in taxes. Special subsidized rates of interest will also have to be declared.

(6) Controlling authority on selling the product or creating the solicities for purchasing the finished goods:

There is a dearth of controlling authority to sell the goods by purchasing the total production through traders. To control the price, there is a requirement to see that the goods are purchased in one place and then it is sold by one authority to classify the grades and standards.

2.2 INFRASTRUCTURE FACILITIES IN SURAT:

Zari industry in Surat has a full fledged infrastructure facilities like transportation, electricity, raw-materials as well as other facilities like communication, banking as well as insurance.

The area in which zari industry is located gets the facility of electricity. The electricity charges are fluctuative. The total cost of production is related with the cost of electricity. Continuous supply of electricity is one of the beneficial factor for the industry. There is a continuous water supply by Municipal Corporation. Initially i.e. 10-15 years back there was the problem of availability of water, but now there is no difficulty. Due to continuous and constant flow of water the industry has flourished.

Communication today is the simple and easy. Surat is one of the major cities of Gujarat which provides enough facilities for communication. Communication takes place through telephone, postage and other courier services. Nowadays, even internet services are available.

Ten years back, people had to go to southern regions for many days, but with easy communication it is no longer required.

Transportation facilities like road transport, railway transport and other transport facilities are available which supports the industry's development. Surat is a city attached with major railway lines as well as other air lines facility and is near to Baroda & Ahmedabad. To sell the by-products and finished goods the major market is available in Surat. So the transportation facilities contributes to the industry's development.

Insurance facilities are also available for this sector. However since 80% of the people are illiterate, they are unaware of this concept. People are not taking the benefit of fire insurance as well as life insurance. Mortality rate is high and instances of fire have become more dangerous. Insurance at this stage is inevitable.

Banking facility is also easily available. The industry gets the major benefit from co-operative banks situated in their own area. The merchants have created their own credit co-op. society, which provides the raw materials like copper, silver and other materials. It also lends the money needed in different parts of the zari industry. Banks have played an important role in the development of the industry. The major role of credit co-operative society is to develop the zari industry in the region.

So, infrastructure facilities for the zari industry is the most favourable segment of Surat and adjoining regions. Infrastructure facilities inclusive of all available factors area support the industry.

2.3 PROSPECTS AHEAD IN INDIA FOR ZARI :

India is one of the major suppliers of zari handicrafts to the world market. Despite the existence of production base and a large number of craftsmen, India has not been able to cash on the opportunities. This is mainly because of the following reasons:-

a) The production and supply have continued to be inadequate.
b) The quality and finish are not upto the mark.
c) The price standard is not maintained.
d) The product development is not well conceived.

The prospects for increasing zari exports from India are considered bright provided the problems as stated above are solved and the measures as discussed and suggested in some of the following paragraphs are adopted.

Although India has a large production base for handicrafts, production of zari handicrafts is inadequate to cope with the demand. Production is erratic and is not organised on a regular or continuous basis. The craftsmen do not work full time since they have other occupations. Lack of adequate skilled craftsmen and non-availability of the raw materials are the other factors responsible for inadequate production. Inadequate and erratic production effect the overseas supplies and the delivery schedule. In order to augment production on a *continuous* basis for export besides ensuring organised production and adequate supplies of required quantities and quality of raw materials the strength of the artisans, particularly skilled ones, has to be increased by providing training facilities and certain production processes have to be mechanised without compromising the hand and art work involved in the same.

Besides inadequate and erratic production, the quality and finish of the zari handicrafts are not consistent. Quality of zari handicrafts has deteriorated over year. This has happened mainly because of the raw material. Quality and colour used are not consistent. Since zari handicrafts are handmade products and each piece is different from the other it may not be possible to maintain exact or accurate standard in quality while producing in bulk. Some manufactures however, in the absence of quality control measure, sometimes take undue advantage of this and spoil their own image in the overseas markets. In the interest of enhancing the image of Indian handicrafts in the overseas markets, it will be better if minimum quality standard is maintained. Apart from the use of quality raw-materials in required proportion, steps should also be taken for mechanisation of certain processes to ensure uniformity and excellent finish of the handicrafts. Workmanship could also be improved if handicrafts production (meant for export) is organised through skilled craftsmen and are strictly supervised.

Price is an important factor in the marketing of zari handicrafts. The consumers are price conscious. They have a liking for handicrafts but if the handicrafts are too costly in relation to the machine made product, they just do not buy it. Besides machine made substitute, Indian handicrafts face competition from handicrafts originating from other developing countries, which are cheaper. In view of this, the price of handicrafts should to the extent possible be kept within reasonable limits subject to a given quality. Prices of Indian zari handicrafts are comparatively high because of the high cost of raw material. If India has to cater to the needs of the price conscious buyers, steps should also be taken to ensure supply of raw material at reasonable price for economising export production and supplies.

Zari Handicrafts in the overseas market are liked and bought for their novelty. The novelties particularly of decorative items over years have become out of date due to changes in taste and preference. The customers as well as the importers are always on the look out for something unusual and new items of handicrafts. As a result the demand for new items of handicrafts with some unusual features is on the increase. Indian manufactures/ exporters over the years have continued to supply the same old products without taking due notice of the changing trend of demand in overseas market. The initiative taken and work done in India relating to product development and innovation in handicrafts for exports is rather insignificant despite the existence of required skill in India for innovating new products and adopting old products to suit consumer taste and preferences. The manufacturers who are mainly catering to seasonal demands in the overseas market should take necessary initatives and steps for product development and innovation in handicrafts.

2.4 ROLE OF PUBLIC REPRESENTATIVE i.e. MEMBER OF PARLIAMENT / MEMBER OF LEGISLATIVE ASSEMBLY :

Zari industry is mainly centralised in Surat. The local public representative elected from this area has also played an important role to develop the industry. Member of legislative assembly Ex. M.L.A. Gulabdas Khatri & Dhirubhai Gajera have taken keen interest to support the akhadedars manufacturers through government of Gujarat.

The Member of Parliament, the current Rural Development Minister and Ex. Textile Minister Hon'ble Kashiram Rana has played a major role to develop the industry. Actually, he started his career from the zari industry. He is also a part of zari industry. During his tenure as a Textile Minister, he tried a lot to expand the industry.

Kashiram Rana took core steps to develop the industry and laid stress on developing the zari industry by boosting export. (he earned a lot of foreign exchange for the government). His target now to revive the zari industry as he holds the portfolio of handicraft industry selection.

The steps taken by him to evolve and develop the zari industry are as follows :

ZARI PARK:

Zari is processed in different ways. Chemicalisationists, artisans, manufacturers, etc. all work with their machines in their own residential areas. A need was felt to create a ZARI PARK in Surat to provide the people with a specific area apart from their residential area to develop the zari industry.

Hon'ble Kashiram Rana got the help from Gujarat government and has launched a project of ZARI PARK at Kosad, near Surat where the project of residence as well as work-shade are underway. Gujarat government has allotted land in which 127 units would be set up.

DELEGATION OF ZARI IN FOREIGN COUNTRIES:

Hon'ble Kashiram Rana internationalized the demand for zari. He even sent a zari manufacturer's delegation to undertake research and study zari markets of different countries.

In 1998, a delegation was sent to Pakistan to see the export areas in embroidery threads, borders, termings, edges, frings, tussels, brides, etc. In 2000, another delegation was sent to France & U.K. Netherland to explore the market avenues, new technical innovations, designing, etc. in zari.

ZARI - ZARDOZHI TRAINING CAMP:

The dream of Hon'ble Kashiram Rana is to make Surat, a major centre of zari manufacturing to largest user of end product of zari. He first time in the history organised the training camp in Surat and adjoining areas. In these camps, people were trained to prepare the end product. Training was given to ladies by experts. The camps proved helpful for generating self-employment to the women in the industry. More than 300 womens underwent training and can now prepare the end product.

The women even got Rs. 500/- as stipend from the handicrafts board of textile minister. Each camp was alloted Rs. 1 lac. by the government.

ZARI - BUYER - SELLER MEET :

The full-fledged process of zari is not done in any place in the country. Surat, on the contrary, is an expert in producing all zari threads. Barelli, Varanasi, Agra, etc. are famous for the end products of zari. In order to simplify the sale and purchase of zari and zari products, to overcome the crisis between the purchaser and seller, more discussion amongst the people of zari and zari industry are held. Hon'ble Kashiram Rana initiated this buyer-seller meet and granted permission for this.

Due to this the crisis could be solved. The quality of product, price of the product, transportation problems could be solved by the government under the guidance of Hon'ble Kashiram Rana.

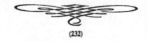

2.5 ROLE OF CHAMBER OF COMMERCE:

The southern chamber of commerce has played an important role in zari industry. The chamber has immensely contributed to revive the industry. A survey was conducted 5 to 6 years back by the southern chamber of commerce to study the structure of industry and it acted as an intermediary body to solve the problems. It even suggested the state government to allow more exemptions for the industry. Not only this, the chamber extended their ideas even to the central government. Chamber helped the industry to advertise the product by organizing a Fair and by giving special concessions. Chamber arranged many seminars in collaboration with the government as well as Export Promotion Council to upgrade the industry. Chamber has played a role of a friend, philosopher and guide. Chamber always was on the fore to solve the problems and provide solutions for the industry by raising the resources.

2.5.1 ROLE OF GOVERNMENT IN THE DEVELOPMENT OF ZARI INDUSTRY:

For any country's development government is an important part because it frames policies and programmes. Indeed the Indian government and government of Gujarat has tried to develop the industry accumulatively but has failed in laying specific stress on the development of zari. Specific policies have not been framed. Exemption has not been allowed. Subsidies have not been given.

Government has only linked it to handicrafts. There is a differentiation between the policies framed by state and central rulings. Political effects are more on the policies. M. P. Mr. Kashiram Rana however when became the textile minister, paid more attention and focussed on many schemes and training programmes. However still the output is not sufficient. A lot needs to be done for this neglected sector.

2.5.2 ROLE OF ELECTRICITY COMPANIES IN THE DEVELOPMENT OF ZARI INDUSTRY :

The industry runs totally on electricity so there is a vital need of power supply.

Due to power cut, the industry suffers from a severe set back. Because of it the problem of clipping and flattening the silver wires arises. The thickness is not maintained.

Sometimes the gilding is also not properly maintained due to power cuttings. The quality of product deteriorates and even the finishing suffers. Voltage fluctuation disturbs the different processes. It is harmful for real jari. Surat electricity Board has given a good continuous support to the industry by supplying continuous supply of power guarantee. If the electricity supply is not regulated it may affect the bread and butter of the people.

2.5.3 ROLE OF BANKING AND TERM LENDING FINANCIAL INSTITUTIONS IN THE DEVELOPMENT OF ZARI INDUSTRY IN SURAT :

As we know that any industrial development requires financial assistance by the financial institution, zari industry has also been developed by the financial institutions like Surat Zari Producer Co-operative Society Ltd. and other organisations. It could be said that Surat Zari Producer Co-operative Society Ltd. has actually made the survival of the industry possible. This society was established in 1944, with membership of 61 members having share capital of Rs. 14,780/- but today if we look at the membership, it is of 3004 and members share capital of Rs. 4,08,850/- and profit is of Rs. 10,23,714/-.

Society advances loans not only in cash but also provides the raw materials like silver, gold and copper. It also provides chemicals, yarn, cotton at reasonable rates to the members of zari industry. Society is not only providing the credit facilities but it is also cautious about the problems of the industry. Society solved the basic problem of excise, sale spirit, etc. It even arranged the Mega Exhibition - 98 for the development of zari with the help of government and South Gujarat Chamber of Commerce and arranged seminars and workshops training camps with the help of government. The knowledge of import/export to the members was also provided by the society and an attempt was made to cultivate a saving habit among the members and improve their socio-economic conditions.

Apart from this, the South Zari Co-operative Society, other banks like Surat Legal Commercial Bank have also played an important role in the development of zari industry. But what we observed was that the society took keen interest in providing the raw materials but it did not take any interest in the purchase of the recently made zari and neither have they helped in selling the product.

TABLE 2.5.3.1

THE SURAT ZARI GOODS PRODUCER'S CO-OP. SOC. LTD.

YEARS	MEMBER-SHIP	SHARE CAPITAL	OTHER FUNDS	RESERVE FUNDS	DIVIDEND
1944-45	251	22380	-	251	6.25%
1945-46	354	25990	-	1958	6.25%
1949-50	504	32020	-	5505	6.25%
1950-51	551	36320	-	6511	6.25%
1951-52	572	38500	-	8286	6.25%
1952-53	575	34000	-	10294	3.25%
1953-54	570	39040	-	10338	5.25%
1954-55	576	64600	-	11144	6.25%
1955-56	515	83470	-	12832	6.25%
1956-57	503	87230	7038	17132	6.25%
1957-58	503	90380	16784	26643	6.25%
1958-59	528	103140	16784	30663	6.25%
1959-60	574	137370	16031	34419	6.25%
1960-61	598	139140	13281	36417	6.25%
1961-62	616	119230	12004	39725	6.25%
1962-63	516	121590	32671	53767	8.25%
1963-64	527	124624	101277	66474	9.00%
1964-65	604	138710	142157	81707	9.00%
1965-66	602	140460	169970	93613	8.00%
1966-67	620	140590	171407	97844	-
1967-68	617	140300	171327	98002	-
1968-69	621	134680	171327	98172	-
1969-70	644	135650	170726	98412	-

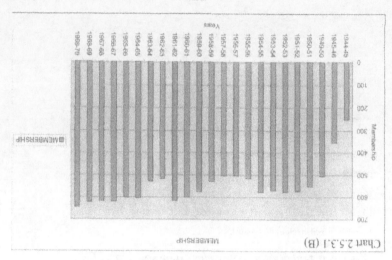

Chart 2.5.3.1 (A)

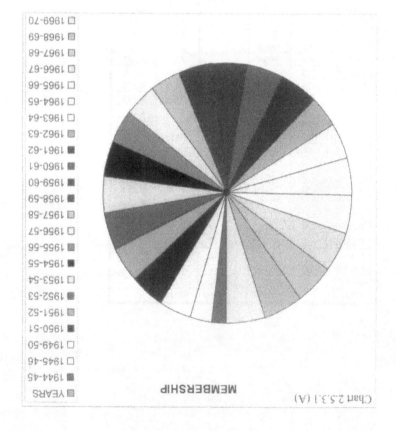

Chart 2.5.3.1 (B)

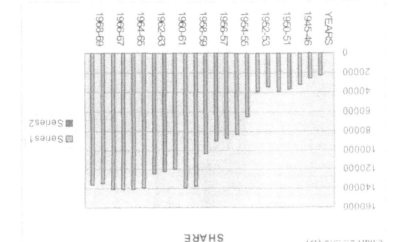

Chart 2.5.3.2 (B)

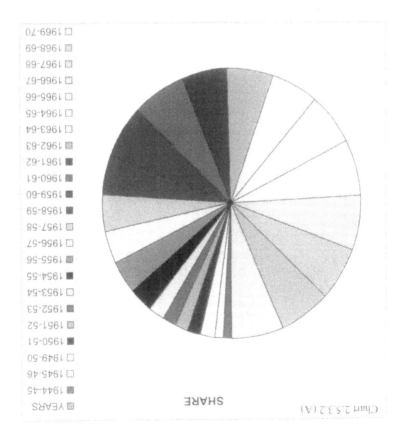

Chart 2.5.3.2 (A)

(239)

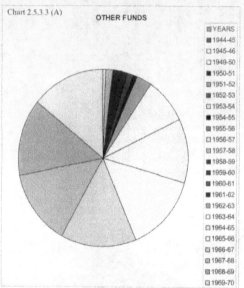

Chart 2.5.3.3 (A) OTHER FUNDS

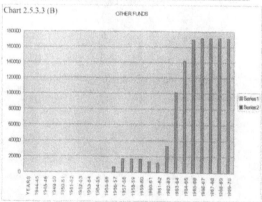

Chart 2.5.3.3 (B) OTHER FUNDS

(240)

Chart 2.5.3.4 (A)

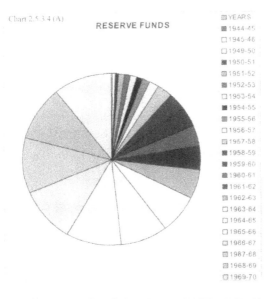

Chart 2.5.3.4 (B)

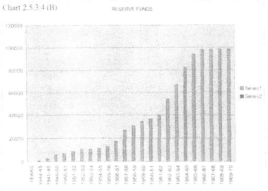

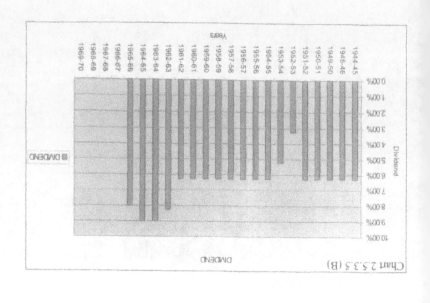

Chart 2.5.3.5 (B)

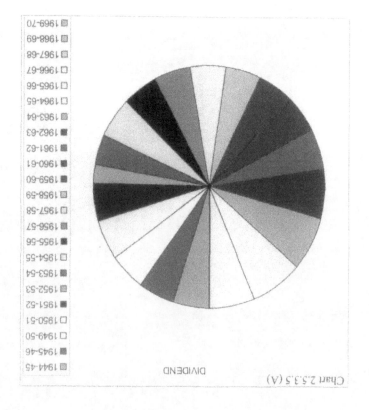

Chart 2.5.3.5 (A)

TABLE 2.5.3.2 THE SURAT ZARI GOODS PRODUCER'S CO-OP. SOC. LTD.

YEARS	PROFIT	YEARS	PROFIT
1978-79	1,08059	1991-92	7,27,457
1979-80	1,49,591	1992-93	7,97,534
1980-81	1,51,788	1993-94	9,09,492
1981-82	1,96,107	1994-95	8,40,211
1982-83	2,98,454	1995-96	8,18,639
1983-84	3,30,829	1996-97	10,31,298
1984-85	-	1997-98	10,23,714
1985-86	2,69,895	1998-99	10,45,092
1986-87	3,27,302	1999-2000	13,01,536
1987-88	3,21,116	2000-2001	-
1988-89	2,05,113	2001-2002	10,84,308
1989-90	3,81,090	2002-2003	10,99,008
1990-91	-	2003-2004	10,61,375

CHARTS SHOWING PROFIT ON NEXT PAGE :

It can be seen that Surat Zari Producers' Co-operative Society has played an important role in providing the credit facility to the manufacturers, Akhlededars / Artisans. The economical data of providing the advance shows the manner in which the Surat Zari Producers Co-operative Society has played an important role.

Still it requires to see that more advance facility is given to the specific section of the zari industry. New entrants should be helped more. Their problem is that they encourage only those who have already progressed. Special schemes and facilities should be provided to uplift the market. The institution has not laid stress on marketing. So marketing should also be a matter of concern for the society.

Chart 2.5.3.6 (A)

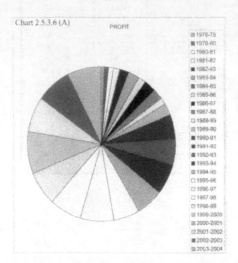

Chart 2.5.3.6 (B)

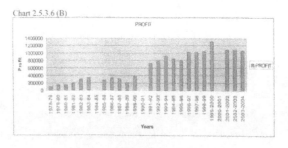

(244)

2.5.4 ROLE OF MUNICIPAL CORPORATION:

Surat Municipal Corporation has given remarkable support to the zari industry by licensing it. The simple and smooth process of licenses is extended by corporation. Corporation has also provided water facility.

2.6 NEED OF MARKETING CO-OPERATIVE SOCIETY:-

Zari Co-operative Goods' Credit Society has played an important role in providing the raw materials for the zari industry, but there is a need for monopoly marketing system through proper coding standardization and measurement tools. There should be an extension of the ZCGCS related to its original function in the sector of marketing. Otherwise, Marketing Co-operative Society separately could be formed to look after the specific functions of marketing research and development as well as distribution and sales.

2.7 ENVIRONMENTAL ASPECTS:

Environmental aspects have a profound impact on business. It is very well indicated by the fact that environmental analysis and diagnosis are among the first steps in the strategic management process. Business dynamics is in fact, a dependant factor, it depends on the environmental dynamics. Hence, the importance of environmental analysis and diagnosis.

Environmental analysis is defined as "the process by which strategists monitor the economic governmental / legal market/competitive, supplier/technological, geographic, and social settings to determine opportunities and threats to their firms."

"Environmental diagnosis consists of managerial decisions made by analysis the significance of the data (opportunities and threats) of the environmental analysis."

Environmental analysis today is an essential prerequisite for strategic management decision making. For instance, in his recent editions of Marketing Management, Philip Kotter, the world renowned professor and author, describes "Marketing Environment Audit" as the first component of marketing audit; whereas in the earlier editions of this book, the marketing audit does not have any reference to the environment.

It is now unquestionably accepted that the prospects of a business depends not only on its resources but also on the environment. Every business enterprise, thus, consists of a set of internal factors and is confronted with a set of external factors.

The internal factors are generally regarded as controllable factors because the company has control over these factors, it can alter or modify such factors as its personnel, physical facilities organization and functional means, such as the marketing mix, to suit the environment.

The external factors, on the other hand, are by and large beyond the control of a company. The external or environmental factors such as the economic factors, social-cultural factors, geo-physical factors etc. are therefore, generally regarded as uncontrollable factors.

As the environmental factors are beyond the control of a firm, its success will depend to a very large extent on its acceptability with the environment, i.e., its ability to properly design and adjust the internal factors (the controllable) variables to take advantage of the opportunities and to combat the threats in the environment.

"The micro environment consists factors in the company's immediate environment" that effect the performance of the company. This includes the suppliers, marketing immediaries, competitors, *customers and the public*. The macro environment consists of the larger societal forces that effect all the factors in the company's micro environment-namely the demographic, economic, natural, technological, political and cultural factors.

It is quite obvious that the micro environmental factors are more intimately linked with the company than the macro factors.

An important force in micro environment of zari industry is the suppliers, i.e. those who supply the inputs like raw materials and components of the firms. The importance of reliable source/sources of supply to the smooth functioning of zari business is obvious. Here it has been observed that uncertainty regarding the supply constraints often compel industry to maintain high inventories causing increase in the cost.

Zari industry faces the problem related to sensitivity of supply, high importance to vendor development, vertical integration.

Customers:-

As it is often exhorted, the major task of a business is to create and sustain customers. A business exists only because of its customers.

In zari industry what has been observed is the absence of monitoring the customer sensitivity. What is actually observed is that there is a *dependency* on a single customer which is often too risky, which has placed the industry in a poor bargaining position. Today what we find is that apart from the risk of losing business the risk of winding up of business by the customers and risk of the customers switching over to the competitors of the company is more.

Competitors:

Zari industry has competitors not only from firms which market the same or similar products but also from those who compete for the discretionary income of consumers, i.e. ready garments developed through other items of production like zari.

Marketing Intermediaries:

This is an important environmental affected factor. Because of this, industry has suffered a lot and has reached the stage of a damaged industry. It has led to a dislocation or disturbance in link between the industry and final customers and it has been observed that wrong choice of link has led the industry to collapse. The marketing intermediaries include middiment warehouses, transportation and marketing agencies. Here in this industry, there is no application of advertising agencies, marketing research firms, media firms and consulting firms.

Publicity :

An industry requires publicity which is lacking in the zari sector. Media, public citizens and local public are some of the examples. Zari *industry* has never tried to focus on the growth of consumers and therefore has failed in making the public aware of its utility.

Macro environment:

An industry operates in a larger macro environment that shapes and poses threats to the company. The macro forces are generally more uncontrollable than the micro forces.

Economic environment:

Economic conditions, economic policies and economic systems are the important external factors which constitute the economic environment of a business.

The nature of economy, the stage of development of economy, economy resources, the level of income, the distribution of income and assets found in this zari industry are important determinants. In this zari sector our observation has been that low income probably is the reason for the low demand of product. The sale of product for which the demand is income elastic naturally increases with an increase in income. The sector has been unable to increase the purchasing power of the people to generate a higher demand of its product.

Hence, it has to reduce the price of the product to increase the sales. The reductions in cost of production has to be affected to facilitate price reduction.

The economic policy of the government, needless to say, has a great impact on business. Government policy is neutral in respect of other industries, but government has not separately framed any policy for zari. The state government has also not promoted the industry in relation to other industries. There is a requirement of a restrictive import policy, a policy of protecting the home industries. Liberalization of the import policy has led to a difficulty for this industry.

Another important suggestion is that the industry should be kept within the priority sector, so that number of incentives and positive support could be taken from the government.

There is a need to declare it as a core sector. The monetary and fiscal policies, incentives should be framed neutrally. The state government should play a dominant role. Co-operative enterprise, joint sector enterprises and small scale units should be developed through preferential treatment by the government.

Political and governmental environment:

Political and governmental environment has a close relationship with economic system and economic policy. There are a host of statutory controls on business in India. Many countries today have laws to regulate competition in the interest of public. Elimination of unfair competition and dilution of monopoly power are important objectives of the regulations. In India the monopolistic undertakings, dominant undertakings and large industries are subject to a number of regulations which prevent the concentration of economic power to consumer determinant.

Some regulations brighten the prospects of small and new firms which are required for the zari sector. The special privileges available to the small sectors have also contributed to phenomenal success of zari.

Certain changes in government policies such as special industrial policy, fiscal policy, tariff policy etc. are required to be reframed.

Socio-Cultural environment:

Socio-cultural fabric is an important factor that should be analysed while formulating business strategies which has not been applied yet to the zari industry. Ignorance of customs, traditions, tastes and preferences of people has led to a high loss which is obviously reflected in the profit scale.

The factors like the buying and consumption habits of the people, their language, beliefs and values, customs and traditions, tastes and preferences, education are some of the important factors which have not been taken into consideration.

Zari industry requires to deal with social environment which encompasses its social responsibility and the alertness or vigilance of the consumers and society at large.

Demographic factors:

Size of population, population growth, growth rate, age composition, life expectancy, family size, spatial dispersal, occupation status, employment pattern, etc. affect the demand of zari goods. Markets with growing population and income are growth markets. In the zari industry, labour is highly heterogeneous in respect of language, caste and religion, ethnicity, etc. which makes the personnel management a more complex task. The heterogeneous population with its varied tastes, preferences, beliefs, temperaments, etc gives rise to differing demand patterns and calls for different marketing strategies.

Natural environment:

Geographical and ecological factors such as natural resource endowments, weather, climatic conditions, topographical factors, locational aspects in the global context, port facilities, etc. are all relevant to business. Due to the increase in pollution the climate of Surat has changed which is not very conducive for zari.

Physical and technological environment:

Weather and climatic conditions have affected the products of zari. Even technological factors have highly affected the zari industry but the zari industry has not been able to cope up with the changed scenario of technological changes in relation to other products.

International Market:

International market is important for the zari industry. The import export policies developed by Indian government has also affected the development of zari industry. Government of India has developed Exim policies on the basis of handicrafts. Zari is only a part of it. There is a need to frame a separate policy for zari industry.

CHAPTER 3 :

RESEARCH METHODOLOGY

		Page No.
3.1	SCOPES	256
3.2	OBJECTIVES	260
3.3	SAMPLING PLAN	263
3.4	METHOD OF DATA COLLECTION	264
3.5	LIMITATIONS	268

CHAPTER 3 : SALIENT FEATURES OF THE STUDY UNDERTAKEN

3.1 SCOPE:-

1. Extension of domestic market:-

Zari industry is today faced with recession. Because of dependency on distant market, marketing has decreased. Domestic market is required to be developed fast because it has a lot of scope. Zari as an antique product requires to be utilised maximum by producers, traders, Akhadedars, artisans themselves. In Surat there is a lot of scope for advancement because a large population wears ready-made garments, to which no attention has been given. Proper marketing of zari needs to be done throughout the country. Domestic market should become a source of supply for others. If proper attention is paid to the domestic market the problems of supply would be solved easily in the Indian market. Sometimes looking to the foreign demands one may forget local market, which has a lot of scope. Therefore, extension of domestic network requires to be developed through marketing utility of zari products.

2. Maximisation of more foreign exchange:-

As per the government records, export of handicrafts inclusive of zari and zari goods shows 2% share of zari only. It earns 142.32 crores of rupees of foreign exchange. If state and central government support and encourage separately and provide more infrastructure facilities to this industry, there is no doubt that more foreign exchange could be earned. If proper research and development is done more foreign exchange could definitely be earned.

3. Development of Byproducts:-

There is a greater scope of development of byproducts through zari/zardosi. Lack of proper attention on byproducts has ultimately led to recession. Unprofessionalised approach of zari traders, manufacturers and others is the reason for this recession. Zari is a product through which maximum byproducts can be developed by the artisans. Enough scope is there to enrich the domestic and foreign market through byproducts.

4. Generate more employment:-

Zari industry has generated maximum employment but still there is lack of education, training as well as skill development. Zari industry has its own reputation as it is an antique industry. If industry is properly developed there is no doubt that it would be able to generate maximum employment.

5. Technical Upgradation:-

The industry can cope with the downfall by going in for technical upgradation. Technically this industry lags behind in comparison to other industries. This industry has focused only on earning money but has not tried to focus on earning more foreign exchange and generating more employment, etc. It is totally based on thumb rule and has a traditional approach. Lack of modern management and non-professionalism has ultimately given a set back to the industry. If technically upgraded, the scope of expansion would widen.

6. Standardisation of costing:-

What we find in this industry is that, there is no standardisation of cost. There is a large variation in the cost of product, which varies from trader to trader and region to region. There is a gambling in costing. Cheating is also prevalent. Lack of professionalism, management application, is evident. There is a wide scope for standardisation of cost for each and every product of zari. Variation of cost is the basic reason for the decline of zari industry.

7. Pricing method:-

Prices of different products are not properly calculated, managed and standardised. Pricing method should be uniformly planned through associations, societies or any binding authorities.

8. Quality:-

Total dependency of this industry is on quality. As it requires specific skill there is need of maintaining quality as well as to develop quality measurement tools. There is no tool to measure quality. Every one tries to justify the quality on traditional approach. There is a lot of scope for gradation of products as well as standardisation. Quality thrust needs a lot of research and development. It also needs to acquire knowledge of foreign skill to develop the industry.

9. Adequate supply related to product:-

There is a gap between the two processes of each product. There is lack of proper management. Supply of adequate material should be made for every process.

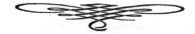

3.2 OBJECTIVES :-

The aim of study has been to analyse the pattern of manufacturing, managing and distribution pattern in Zari industry in South Gujarat. This study is likely to help the small scale sector to renovate its manufacturing, managing and distribution network. Another justification behind this research could be to open the avenues of study which is likely to get attention by the industrialists and the academicians as well. The present study incorporates the activities of Pawtha, Tania, Flattening machine, winding machine, gliding machines etc. In addition to this the study also intends to include the study of existing marketing pattern of Zari in Surat, to analyse the socio economic dimensions, to assess the potential markets of Zari and evolve suitable policy recommendations, to organize zari markets for commissioning small zari enterprises with the financial and technical support of the Government of India. Since the study of universe is unmanageably large, it was decided that representative sample and study would be undertaken for the purpose of drawing inference about the universe. As secondary data becomes easily obsolete with the passage of time, more and more reliance was laid on primary data generated during the course of the study. Further due to unavoidable reasons South Gujarat region viz. Surat was selected for the purpose of present study. However Surat remained the best option as it is very popular and could be called the originator of Zari industry. The following are the basic objectives of the undertaken study :

1. To study past and present prospects of Zari product in [Surat] South Gujarat, in India and abroad.

2. To study the pattern and depth of the problem faced by Zari manufacturers / Artisans /Contractors / Akhadedars particularly in the industry.

3. To study the concurrent policy measures and related environment which has been deciding the dynamics of development of Zari manufacturers/ artisians / contractors/ akhadedars of different varities of Zari.

4. To study the degree of intermediation of [Zari traders] and the impact of such intermediation on prospects of manufacturers.

5. To study the scope for managing , reorganising , rechannelising or upgrading from the view of manufacturers/ Artisians/ Contractors/ Akhadedars.

6. To study the scope for an alternative distribution and marketing strategy from the view of Manufacturers /Artisians / Contractors/ Akhadedars.

7. To evaluate the plans and programs of the Manufacturers in terms of their future course of development and/ or expansion.

8. To study the level of satisfaction and motivation of unit holders and efforts put forth by them.

9. To evaluate the view of financial institutions towards the marketing problems faced by manufacturing units.

10. To study the quality measures and standards affecting the prospect of manufacturers.

11. To study invisible loss in manufacturing process [wastage at all stages].

3.3 SAMPLING PLAN:

The researcher has covered the entire India but practical emphasis is given to Surat district. All zari manufacturing units and processing units in the Surat district was the subject matter of study. The sample of 100 units was drawn from district that represents the total population of approximate 1200 zari units.

3.4 METHODS OF DATA COLLECTION:

3.4.1 PRIMARY DATA COLLECTION :-

Regarding the study of this sector of handicraft specifically due to lack of research, various methods of collecting the primary data were applied. The data collected is the first of its kind and is an original compilation. Different methods were used to collect primary data, particularly in surveys which are as follows :-

1. Observation:

In this method, the information was collected by observing the process at work place. The investigator himself visited different units of real zari, imitation zari as well as metallic zari processes. The responses of the manufacturers, artisans, workers, was studied and their state of minds was analyzed and the investigator even tried to eliminate bias responses.

Through this method, I mingled with the group and actively the participated in the activities of the group, for example, I visited their social functions, Annual General Meetings of Zari Producing Co-operative Societies, Varanasi Zari Association, South India Zari Merchant and Manufacturers Association, Andhra-Karnataka Zari Manufacturing Association, Varanasi Zari Mandal, Chamber of Commerce. I gained more insight into understanding the manufacturers group, Akhadedars groups, employees groups, customers groups, Socio-economic life and tried to cover up real feelings and methods of different group members.

As a member of social organization of Rana community and also as a president of Akhil Bharatiya Rana Yuva firm, I was able to get a real picture of different groups through relationships.

Under this method of observation, I felt that observation can take place in natural settings, which is uncontrolled. Things when observed naturally reflected a spontaneous picture of life and persons in the sector of zari. I also used a technique of self photography to collect data as well as analyse data successfully.

2. Interview method:-

This method of data collection was used to understand the behaviour of the people. Under this method, unstructured interview method was applied. More freedom is given to choose the form depending on the specific situation.

Under this method, I used another method for collecting information through respondents on telephone itself.

3. Questionnaire method:-

I used questionnaire for data collection which is printed and compiled to gather data from large, diverse, varied and scattered groups in zari industry. This tool proved to be objective and qualitative in *obtaining data*. I prepared structured questionnaire to collect data which is a closed form of questionnaire. The objective of questionnaire is to secure uniformity of responses as well as to get more truthful and real picture.

4. Experimentation method:

The investigator has applied this method through observation, by surveying the presence of traders, manufacturers as well as experts in the era of production market. It also studied competitors action, weather changes in co-operative dealers which are called environmental factors. This helped to know the attitudes as well as the behaviours of all the segments including the product market, etc.

5. Previewing:

The researcher quantified response in the line for the research object by structured frame work of interviewing through samples. In this method by taking interviews of groups and by asking different questions I tried to get the response from different segments like manufacturers, traders as well as artisans and also the labourers.

The interviews taken have been recorded personally through writing.

3.4.2 SECONDARY DATA COLLECTION:

In this sector, no research is available in published form either by central, state or local government, therefore the data was collected from publication of societies, other bodies like IRMA(Institute of Rural Management of Anand), Export Promotion Council for Handicrafts, RBI bulletin, Surat Zari Merchant Association, Zari Manufacturers association. Their reports helped to collect the secondary data. The reality, suitability and adequacy has been totally checked by the researcher.

3.5 LIMITATIONS:-

1. Inability to provide information:-

The questionnaire technique used was found inadequate by the researchers because of inability of respondents to provide information. This was due to lack of knowledge, laps of memory and inability to identify their notions and their inibition in asking "Why" and lack of faith in responding to the questions.

This is a traditional business industry. It has progressed from generation to generation but has failed to progress with the need of time. Some respondents even did not know the history of their forefather's business nor did they have any idea of how it evolved.

2. Human biases of respondants:

A frequently observed tendency on the part of respondents was human bias. Ego and widespread jealousy is rampant in the community. Respondents responded strangely whenever they were asked. Some respondents were not ready to talk because of others. Some respondants preferred to keep it as a secret.

3. Semantic difficulties:-

It is difficult, if not impossible to state a given question in such a way that it will mean exactly the same thing to every respondant. Similarly, two different wordings of the same question generated quite different results.

4. Non-visionary approach of respondents:-

Lack of vision to develop the business is a problem. There was no enthusiasm on part of respondents to provide information.

5. Unavailability of past data:-

The major problematic area in this research was that there is no records of data available. The total industry is unorganised. Due to unorganisation of sectors, difficulty arose in approaching and locating the people connected with this industry.

CHAPTER 4 :

ANALYSIS AND OUTCOME

		Page No.
4.1	CHARACTERISTICS OF RESPONDENTS	270
4.2	ANALYSIS	272
4.3	DATA ANALYSIS	284
4.4	SUMMARIZED FINDINGS	316

CHAPTER 4 : ANALYSIS AND OUTCOME

4.1 CHARACTERISTICS OF RESPONDENTS:-

Zari industry is an unorganized sector which lacks knowledge, technical upgradation, intellectuality, modernization, management, professionalisation. There are different groups like manufacturers, traders, akhadedars, labourers which are the respondents.

As it is an antique sector, traditionalism has flourished naturally. The respondents were found to be not knowledgable, uneducated as well as biased. Some respondents had no interest in answering the questions as their only aim was to get their wages. Some respondents did not understand the objective of research and illiteracy on their part proved to be an obstacle for us. Since the zari sector has an interrelated process, the respondents are also biased. Some respondent did not wanted to know or interact with others. Some respondents feared that the information would be used against him/her or would become an invasion of their privacy. These types of respondents omitted sensitive questions. Some respondents answered in a very normative way i.e. the way he/she thinks.

It was also observed that respondents were even afraid that his/her responses would reveal their lack of education and that he/she would appear stupid. Some respondents behaved as if their time was too valuable to waste on study which was not applicable to him/her. Their argument was that there is no need for such a study..

A common observation amongst respondents was that they lack vision, understanding, capability to understand others, social awareness, etc. It was also observed that the disappointment due to continuous fall of business which had made a psychological effect on them.

4.2 ANALYSIS

Zari manufacturing is a traditional craft of Surat. Entrepreneurs and workers, predominantly of Rana community, had helped in the smooth functioning of Zari industry. In the changing industrial scene of Surat, the existence of Zari industry needs to be protected both in terms of historical importance and the size of employment. The database of industry needs to be strengthened. With the change in economic policy, the export of Zari needs to be encouraged. The prices of raw materials not only need to be monitored but also their regular supply to the manufacturers should be ensured for the survival and growth of the industry.

Although the development of small-scale enterprises has received increasing attention as an element of industrial policy in many developing countries, India is unique in both the extent and duration of its efforts to promote and protect small-scale firms. The rhetoric of industrial policy toward small-scale firms in India, as in other countries, tends to stress their role in the de-concentration of economic power as well as creation of employment. The history of and the present state of affairs in the industrial countries may provide a glimpse of what is in store for developing countries. In manufacturing, the very small enterprises (fewer than ten employees) are destined to near extinction unless they become a protected species. In this aspect, India is trying to *swim* against the tide of history. In many other developing countries, relative or even absolute decline is in evidence. In services, very small enterprises also suffer relative decline but are nevertheless likely to survive in large numbers.

An interesting typology of business-persons has been proposed by Smith (1967). He distinguishes two polar types, craft-entrepreneurs and opportunist-entrepreneurs. The craft-entrepreneurs have a narrow, mainly technical, education and little social awareness and involvement. They are not very good at delegation, hire on a personal basis, and have limited horizons in the realm of finance and marketing. They have no long-range plans that might involve a change in the character of the business. Opportunist-entrepreneurs are of course just the reverses. They build more adaptable firms, and success stories mostly concern such entrepreneurs and their firms. Artisans in zari industry are craft entrepreneurs rather than opportunist-entrepreneurs. On the other hand, zari trader-manufacturers are opportunist-entrepreneurs capable of making investments if favourable policy environment is created. As of now, they are not making these investments because of inadequate policy support and discouraging trends in fiscal and labour policies. One must clearly distinguish the nature of small firm economies in the zari industry and should not subject them to general industrial, labour and fiscal policies without exercising discretion. Supply constraint in the zari industry is not low productivity of small units but the difficulties encountered by many small production units in acquiring the necessary intermediate inputs and raw materials of right quality. The over all productivity of small production units is a function of the following: adopted production technique, labour productivity, adopted organisation of production and managerial skills. As far as zari industry is concerned, the adopted production technique is alright, even though there is scope for improvement. Labour productivity seems to be low in comparison with other countries but the capital intensity is also low. Production organisation in the form of merchants-job contractors-artisans is far too advantageous to the merchants and very disadvantageous to others; and lastly, the industry does not seem to suffer from lack of managerial skills, even though there are very few trained professionals working.

Contrary to popular notion, these small manufacturing firms can not succeed if they are highly dispersed. On the other hand, they require what are referred to as economies of agglomeration to supply themselves with components and services or even attract potential customers including exporters. The fact that not only Zari production but its subsequent use in other industries like textiles is also confined to certain demand centres makes it all the more clear that there are economies of agglomeration in this industry. We will gain by strengthening this process by evolving a suitable policy framework. A new approach was outlined by Hubert Schmitz (1995) that distinguishes between:

- **Geographically and sectorally dispersed producers. Most rural small industry falls into this category. The village blacksmith and carpenter are the archetypal examples. Their growth prospects essentially depend on demand from local**

agriculture. The scope for division of labour and hence for economies of scale is small.
- Clusters of small enterprises. Clustering is meant here to embrace both geographical and sectoral concentration. In contrast to the previous case, there is wide scope for division of labour between enterprises and hence for specialisation and innovation, essential for competing beyond local markets.

Clustering opens up efficiency gains which individual producers can rarely attain. A group of producers making the same or similar things in close vicinity to each other constitute a cluster, but such geographical and sectoral concentration in itself brings few benefits. It is, however, a major facilitating factor, if not a necessary condition. A number of subsequent developments are possible (some of which may or may not occur). These developments are as follows:

- division of labour and specialisation amongst small producers;
- the provision of their specialised products at short notice and at great speed;
- the emergence of suppliers who provide raw materials or components, new and second-hand machinery, and spare parts;
- the emergence of agents who sell to distant national and international markets; the emergence of specialised services in technical, financial, and accounting matters; the emergence of a pool of wage workers with sector specific skills;

- the formation of consortia for specific tasks and of associations providing services and lobbying for its members.

Most of these are present in Surat giving scope for realising collective efficiency. Even where a collective capacity to compete, adapt and innovate has emerged, it is important not to expect an island of unity and solidarity. Collective efficiency is the outcome of an internal process in which some enterprises grow and others decline. In order to understand this process, it is useful to distinguish between vertical and horizontal inter-firm relations. As regards the former, firms buy products and services either through the market or subcontracting arrangements.

In Surat, it is largely done through subcontracting arrangements. The nature of the relationship can range from exploitation to strategic collaboration. The scope for conflict is greatest at the horizontal level, because producers often compete for orders. However, competition does not exclude joint action for solving specific problems, particularly in pre-competitive areas such as the provision of services, infrastructure, or training. Thus, the notion of collective efficiency neither denies conflict nor competition amongst enterprises in the cluster. On the contrary, clustering makes the market more transparent and induces local rivalry. Equally important, it facilitates collective action to tackle common problems, either directly through self-help institutions or indirectly through local government.

Single small manufacturers can cater for local demand in non-trading goods, but when it comes to competing for distant markets they can rarely do so without being part of a local network in which firms specialise and complement each other. As stressed by Sengenberger and Pyke (1991), the problem of many small manufacturers is not their size but being isolated. Indeed, it could be argued that clustering raises the capacity to respond to crisis and opportunity since the capabilities of specialised clustering firms can be combined in many different ways; and the mastery of one process or product can lay the basis for shifting into new lines of production.

Clustering also has a **dampening effect on wages** because of abundance of labour. This large labour surplus induces competition based on low wages rather than innovation and quality improvements. This is what happened and is currently happening in Surat's Zari industry.

The idea that there are gains in clustering is an old concept in industrial economics. It can be traced back to Alfred Marshall's analysis of industrial districts in Britain. In his Principles of Economics (1st edition, 1890), Marshall stressed the economies which "can often be secured by the concentration of many small businesses of a similar character in particular localities" (8th edition, 1920:221). He refers to such gains as 'external economies' and sees them as particularly relevant to small firms. This section draws together briefly what we can learn from

Marshall for our enquiry and why his concepts are insufficient to explain the competitive advantage that some industrial districts have demonstrated in recent history. One of Marshall's most lasting contributions to economic science is the distinction between internal and external economies. The former 'are dependent on the resources of the individual houses or businesses engaged in it, on their organisation and the efficiency of their management'; the latter 'are dependent on the general development of the industry' [1920:221]. While only providing this loose definition, Marshall leaves it sufficiently clear that the concept of external economies is not tied to geographical proximity. There are external economies that can be reaped in far-away places. This is also reflected in the way contemporary economics defines external economies or diseconomies: they occur where market-priced transactions do not fully incorporate the costs and benefits to economic agents.

However, external economies are particularly significant when specialised industries concentrate in particular localities. Indeed, the concept of external economies is introduced by Marshall in order to draw out (a) why and how the location of industry matters and (b) why and how small firms can be efficient and competitive. In his own words, 'we now proceed to examine those very important external economies which can often be secured by the concentration of many small businesses of a similar character in particular localities' [1920:221]. He refers to such *localities* as 'localised industry' or 'industrial districts'. He does not provide a definition for either, but his examples make it clear that he meant a cluster with a deep inter-firm division of labour like what is obtained in Surat.

To make the point more forcefully, the notion of external economies has come to be associated with gains (or losses) arising from the operations of firms which are connected through an anonymous market and whose behaviour is determined merely by price and cost signals. This tends to conceal essential traits of firms in a well developed cluster: namely the boundaries between firms are often flexible, the relationship between them is characterised by both competition and co-operation, and trust and reciprocity are important to understand the density of transactions and the incidence of joint action in the cluster [Becattini, 1990; Harrison, 1992].

The first questions addressed were where industrial clusters can be found and how common they are in developing countries. Statistics are not available for this purpose, but an overview was pieced together on the basis of examples found in the recent literature. The main conclusion was that clustering seems common in a wide range of countries and sectors. Some clusters in Latin America and Asia have acquired great depth in terms of the concentration of specialised suppliers and support bodies. Among these are the metalworking and textile industries of Ludhiana in the Indian Punjab [Tewari, 1990; 1992]; the cotton-knitwear industry of Tiruppur in Tamil Nadu [Cawthorne,

1990; 1995]; the diamond industry of Surat in Gujarat [Kashyap, 1992]; the engineering and electronics cluster of Bangalore in Karnataka [Holmstrom, 1994]; the footwear clusters of Agra in Uttar Pradesh [Knorringa, 1994], Trujilio in Peru [Tavara, 1993; San Martin Baldwin et al., 1994], and Leon and Guadalajara in Mexico [Rabellotti, 1993]; the Korean textile cluster in Daegu [Cho, 1994]; sports goods and surgical equipment in Sialkot and cutlery in Wazirabad in Pakistan [Nadvi, 1992a]. In African clusters, the inter-firm division of labour and institutional support tend to be less developed, as observed in the metalworking, furniture making and other clusters in Kenya, Zimbabwe and Tanzania [Rasmussen, 1991; Sverrisson, 1993].

While primarily an urban phenomenon, clustering can also be a feature of rural industrialisation, as in Indonesia where one can find the specialisation of entire villages [Weijland, 1994], for example, the manufacture of roof tiles [Sandee, 1994] or rattan furniture in Java [Smyth, 1992]. Within the urban arena, clusters located in intermediate towns seem to have been particularly successful, as indicated by their growth records and ability to compete in export markets. In contrast to clusters in small and medium-sized towns, those in major cities tend to be less well-rooted and have sometimes emerged from informal self-employment coping strategies of the poor. Despite that, many such clusters display a growth potential that goes beyond informal survival strategies and indicates localised competitiveness based on increasing *specialisation* amongst small firms; examples are the metal and repair workshops in the Takora district of Lima. Peru [Villaran, 1993], and Suame, the industrial shanty suburb of Kumasi, Ghana [Dawson, 1992]. These are just some examples which suggest that clustering is of significance to the industrial organisation of small-scale manufacturing in developing countries [For details and further references see Nadvi and Schmitz, 1994].

The way clusters are organised varies a great deal. Vertical relationships range from large firms orchestrating the division of labour amongst small firms to ever-changing permutations of small firms complementing each other; and from casual exchanges of information and tools to close inter-firm collaboration. Horizontal relationships are marked by intense rivalry but evidence of inter-firm co-operation is more varied. Socio-cultural ties - where they were studied - seem to heighten economic performance, but there are exceptions. These inter-firm relationships are hard to summarise and some aspects deserve elaboration.

The sharing of knowledge of new products or processes, labour availability, reliability of suppliers and traders, featured in most surveyed studies; lending each other tools and machinery was also common. Closer forms of inter-firm co-operation were found where extensive vertical production chains had developed, both in arrangements between large and small enterprises and amongst process-*specialised* small units. Such co-operation often resulted in improvements in technological standards and skill levels, but rarely produced major innovations. Improvements in processes and products were typically of an incremental kind. Inter-firm co-operation in Surat seems to be very low. Horizontal co-operation through sectoral associations existed in a number of clusters although with varying degrees of strength and effectiveness. Not all associations served the collective interest of the cluster, some were the preserve of more powerful elements within the cluster. A few, however, stood out either for their role in providing, what Brusco [1990] terms as 'real services', or as a lobbying body articulating the cluster's collective interests. Zari merchants' Association in Surat leaves us with mixed feelings.

Clusters in developing countries tend to be associated with some form of common socio-cultural identity. Shared identity often plays an active part in providing the basis for trust and reciprocity, and for providing social sanctions that limit the boundaries of unaccepted competitive behaviour. This is true in case of Surat as well. Our understanding of how social networks actually function and influence economic relations within clusters continues to remain rather inadequate. There are indications that where over-arching social networks are weak, inter-firm co-operation is limited. There are also signs, however, that social identities can have a negative influence on inter-firm relations - as with the caste divisions in the Agra shoe cluster [Knorringa, 1994J.

The case studies from developing countries suggest that clustering has not been the outcome of a planned intervention by the state but has emerged from within. Zari industry in Surat is a case like this. This lends credence to the view that, as in the European industrial districts, collective efficiency based on the economic and social activities of a community is difficult to create from above, and develops best as an endogenous process. Nevertheless, the state, particularly at the regional level, can play an important facilitative role for small firm clusters, as shown by the example of the state administration of the Indian Punjab [Tewari, 1992; Kashyap, 1992]. Another example comes from the Brazilian Northeast where the state government of Ceara, through its procurement policy, transformed a dormant cluster into a growing one [Amorim, 1994; Tendler, forthcoming].

4.2 DATA ANALYSIS :

Table 4.2.1. TYPES OF FIRMS :

No.	Types of Firms	No. of Units	%
1	Sole Proprietorship	10	12.80
2	Partnership	46	59.00
3	Private Ltd.	21	27.00

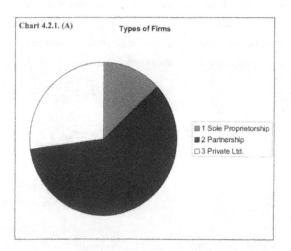

Chart 4.2.1. (A) Types of Firms

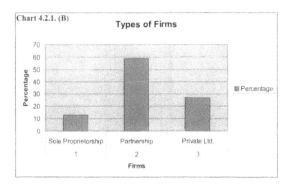

Chart 4.2.1. (B) Types of Firms

ANALYSIS:

It appears from the above table that more than half of the units belong to Partnership firm and only 10% belongs to Sole-proprietorship. Less than 25% belongs to Private Ltd. Co.

CONCLUSION:

We can conclude from the above analysis that people prefer to do their business in partnership only, because it is a business inherited from their forefathers.. They divide the profit only for the purpose of tax burden. They do not expect any benefits accept profit division amongst the family members.

Table 4.2.2. TYPES OF ZARI PRODUCT :

No.	Types of Product	No. of Units	%
1	Real	32	33.3
2	Imitation	50	52.8
3	Metallic	14	14.58

Chart 4.2.2. (A)

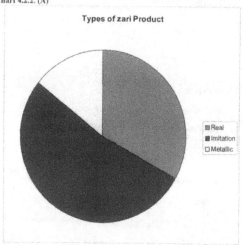

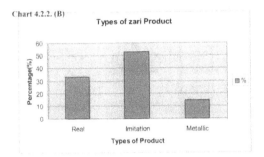

Chart 4.2.2. (B) Types of zari Product

ANALYSIS:

There are mainly three types of products in zari, i.e: Real, Imitation and Metallic. It appears from the above table that half of the units belongs to imitation zari. 30% of the units belong to real zari. But it is also seen that metallic zari trend has started and 14% of units have entered in the latest zari.

CONCLUSION:

We can conclude from the above analysis that people prefer to enter in the area which is current or upcoming in the market. It is also observed that the production of real zari has decreased. Imitation zari still is being produced. But metallic zari is in the developing stage, which has a lot of scope due to less weight and cost. Some of the manufacturers today produce all types of zari. Some of them have stopped producing real jari, due to high cost of gold and silver. Imitation zari requires copper which has also becomes highly costly these days because of which the manufacturers find it difficult to survive.

Table 4.2.3. TENURE OF PRODUCTION:

No.	Tenure of Production (Years)	No. of Units	%
1	0-5	3	3.8
2	5-10	9	11.4
3	10-15	3	3.8
4	15-20	20	25.3
5	20-30	10	12.6
6	30-40	12	15.2
7	40-50	14	17.7
8	50-60	6	7.6
9	60-70	2	2.5

Chart 4.2.3. (A)

Tenure of Production

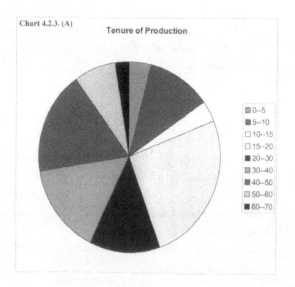

Chart 4.2.3. (B)

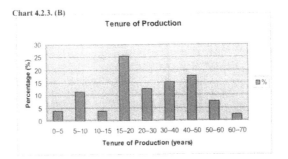

ANALYSIS:

It appears from the above table that 25% of the units started producing 20 years back, 27% of the units started producing 50 years back and only 3 to 4% units have started functioning in less than 5 years. Maximum units had setup their own business 10 years back.

CONCLUSION:

We can conclude from the above analysis that the zari industry has its own reputation and that too from long time. It is a hereditary profession. Many people have specified that their choice of joining the industry was compulsory and there is a desire hesitation on the part of their parents to keep this business alive. It is the oldest profession continuing from five decades. This shows that Rana community has its own hereditary business. It is an old and a traditional business.

Table 4.2.4. INVESTMENT :

No.	Capital Invested	No. of Units	%
1	0 - 10,000	1	1.3
2	10,000 - 50,000	10	13.2
3	50,000 - 1,00,000	23	30.2
4	1,00,000 - 2,00,000	6	7.8
5	2,00,000 - 3,00,000	2	2.6
6	3,00,000 - 4,00,000	2	2.6
7	4,00,000 - 5,00,000	6	7.8
8	5,00,000 - 10,00,000	5	6.5
9	10,00,000 - 20,00,000	18	23.7
10	20,00,000 - 50,00,000	1	1.3
11	50,00,000 - 1,00,00,000	2	2.6

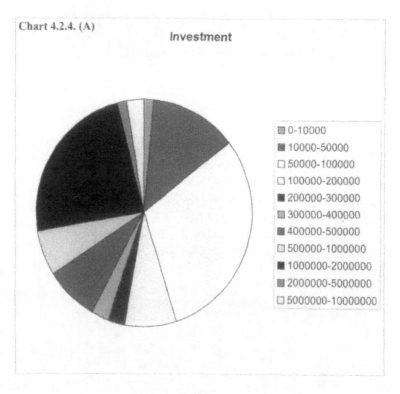

Chart 4.2.4. (A) Investment

Chart 4.2.4. (B)

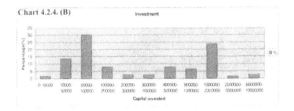

ANALYSIS:

It appears from the above table that 25% of the units have invested in more than 10 lacs of rupees. 30% of units have invested between 5 lacs to 10 lacs of rupees. 25% of the units have invested 1 lac to 5 lacs of rupees. 3% of the units have invested upto 1 crore rupees. The ratio of investment is not very high.

CONCLUSION:

We can conclude from the above analysis that investment done by manufacturers/traders is for a long period of time. It is an old industry but the investment is not much in proportion to the development. Development always shows more investment but whatever is shown is not on a wider scale. Size and nature of business is always related to the investment, but in this industry expansion is not visible.

Table 4.2.5. HOW MANY MACHINES UTILISED IN PRODUCTION :

No.	No. of machines	No. of Units	%
1	0-5	44	57.14
2	5-10	12	15.58
3	10-15	3	3.9
4	15-20	15	19.5
5	20-25	3	3.9

Chart 4.2.5. (A)

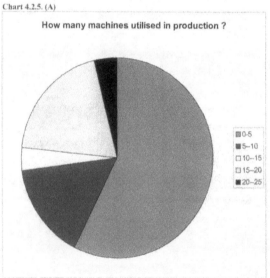

Chart 4.2.5. (B)

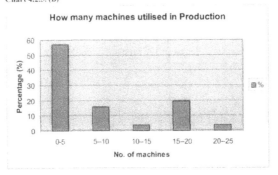

ANALYSIS:

It appears from the above table that according to the nature of business, the number of machines utilized by the manufacturers and others have not properly increased. The quantum of machines always speaks about the size of business. Only 18% manufacturers have more than 15 machines. Half of the manufacturers/traders have less than five machines. This shows that the number of machines have not increased in relation with the development of industry.

Table 4.2.6. ANY TECHNICAL CHANGE HAS BEEN DONE OR NOT :

No.	Types of Product	No. of Units	%
1	Yes	28	35.89
2	No	37	47.43
3	Not answered	13	16.66

Chart 4.2.6. (A)

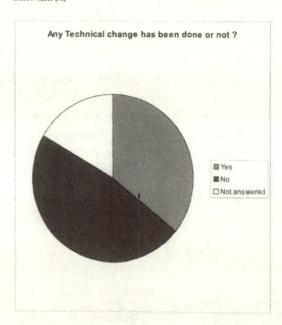

Any Technical change has been done or not ?

Chart 4.2.6. (B)

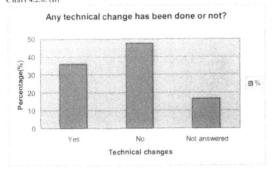

ANALYSIS:

From the above analytical table, it can be seen that people are not interested for a change in technical matters. 37% respondants were found to be disinterested in a change in the technical field. 13% respondants were even interested in the questions posed. They were not even aware of technical change. Whenever the question on technical change was asked, the respondants asked in detail about it and were not able to answer properly. 37% respondants did respond properly. What they quoted as change could be called a minor change. The technical change has been less. Whatever change has come has come in only six to seven years.

CONCLUSION:

As the analytical table shows, the technical change has not been properly understood by the manufacturers/traders. Even what has been reported as a change, that too is quite minor. Minimum changes in the

Table 4.2.7. SUPPLY OF FINISHED GOODS :

No.	Market	No. of Units	% of Units
1	Local (Domestic)	41	35.04
2	Outside within country	68	58.11
3	Not decided	3	2.56
4	Outside country	4	3.41

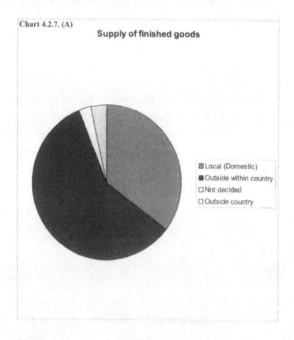

Chart 4.2.7. (A) Supply of finished goods

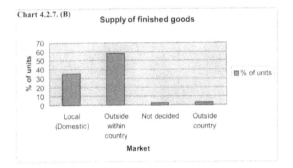

Chart 4.2.7. (B) Supply of finished goods

ANALYSIS:

From the above analytical table, it can be seen that market i.e. supply of finished goods at local level is 35%, whereas, outside and within India, it is 58.11%. The trend of local market shows that it is an interrelated process. Outside the country, it is only 3.45% which shows that no more export is there. Even 2.56% people don't want to take any decision.

CONCLUSION:

It can be observed through the analysis that market is very much expected. Maximum part of the zari has local market and maximum part of the process related to zari is interdependent. Processed zari does not have a full market at domestic level. The last product of zari has an outside market only. Maximum part of that market is at a distant. The domestic market of ready made goods prepared through the use of zari has not yet been developed. The market for end product has been developed only in southern part of India.

Table 4.2.8. AVAILABILITY OF RAW MATERIAL :

No.	Market	No. of Units	%
1	Local	75	94.9
2	Outside	4	5.06

Chart 4.2.8. (A)

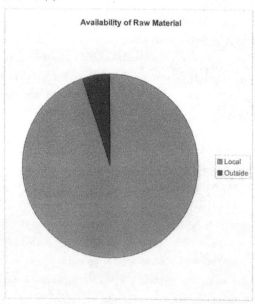

Chart 4.2.8. (B)

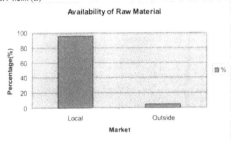

ANALYSIS:

Analytical table shows that 95% people of zari industry get the raw material the local market. This shows that the material is not being bargained with different types of suppliers from other areas. Only local level suppliers transact. There is no commercial aspect in purchasing raw material.

CONCLUSION:

From the above analysis, it can be seen that maximum people purchase the raw material from local area. Only 5% people purchase it from other than local. This shows that there is lack of professionalism. It shows that material management which is an important part of manufacturing concern is not there. There is no inventory control or supervision for material. Due to this the quality of product is not maintained. Deterioration of material is found at each and every process. Planning of purchasing-unnecessary investment-short supply.

Table 4.2.9. TRAINING RECEIVED OR NOT :

No.	Training	No. of Units	%
1	Training taken	35	22.58
2	Not taken	43	27.74
3	Needed to take training	35	22.58
4	No need to take training	42	27.09

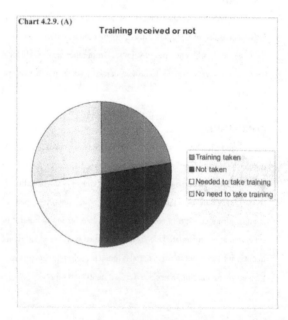

Chart 4.2.9. (A) Training received or not

Chart 4.2.9. (B)

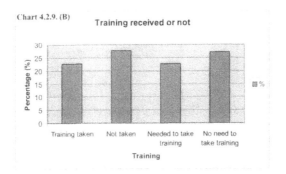

Training received or not

ANALYSIS:

It can be observed from the table that 27% people have not taken any type of training and 27% people do not agree to undertake training or require training. Only 22% people have undergone training but that also is not proper. Only minor training has been taken by them in some process of zari. 27% people are in favour of training.

This shows that training aspect has not been properly attended by the owners, manufacturers and labourers.

CONCLUSION:

It is observed from the analysis that no formal training has been taken by any employee, manufacturer, artisan or any other segment of zari industry. There is no desired requirement felt by the industry. The analysis and observation also focus on the matter that people are not aware of this aspect which is required for developing the industry.

Table 4.2.10. FINANCE FOR BUSINESS :

No.	Types of Finance	No. of Units	%
1	Family	45	51.13
2	Society	0	0
3	Govt. Loan	10	11.36
4	Supplier advance	0	0
5	Private finance	19	21.59
6	Govt. grant	0	0
7	Banks	3	3.4
8	No response	11	12.5

Chart 4.2.10. (A)

Finance for business

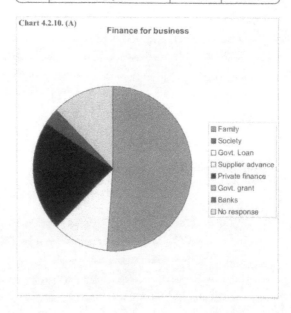

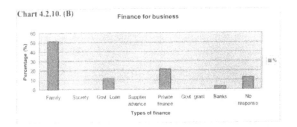

Chart 4.2.10. (B) Finance for business

ANALYSIS:

The financial source of this industry is from family background. Only 20% of the total units borrowed money from govt. agencies, private sources. The table shows that 45% of the total units employ the fund from their hereditary family backgrounds. Not much finance has been acquired from outside.

CONCLUSION:

The above analysis shows that maximum fund is not from outside. Family is the source for finance. Only 20% money is borrowed from private organisations and others. This finance is not sufficient for the industry to survive. Financial management is not there in the industry. Good knowledge is required to manage the finance.

RECOMMENDATIONS:

Financial management required to be develop:

In zari industry, there is no management regarding the collection of the finance. There is an urgent need to develop financial

Table 4.2.11. MANAGEMENT APPLIED IN BUSINESS :

No.	Education	No. of Units	%
1	X	4	5.12
2	XII	14	17.94
3	Graduation	27	34.01
4	Post graduate	2	2.56
5	Uneducated	31	39.74

Chart 4.2.11. (A)

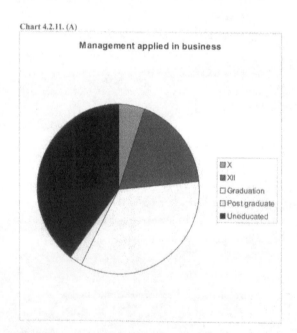

Chart 4.2.11. (B)

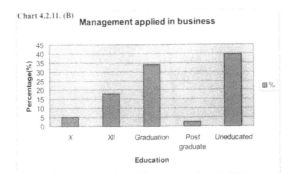

Management applied in business

ANALYSIS:

The table shows analytical approach. Specific management is lacking and there is non-professionalism of business. Specific person is not appointed for the management purpose. Education ratio also shows that 35% people related with business are graduates, only 25% are post graduates where as 23% are only H.S.C. pass and 30% people engaged are uneducated.

CONCLUSION:

Zari industry seems to be totally unmanaged. There is no management concept amongst the manufacturers, traders and akhadedars. Simple business is going on. No professional education is there in the industry. Industry lacks knowledge of management. In each and every concept management should be implemented. Management of labour, finance, personnel, market, distribution system, etc.

Table 4.2.12. ANY REASONABLE RESEARCH HAS BEEN DONE FOR THE BUSINESS :

No.	Researchable or not	No. of Units	%
1	Research has been done	47	60.25
2	Research has not been done	31	39.74

Table 4.2.13. OFFERING STUDY OR NOT :

No.	Offering for study or not	No. of Units	%
1	Offering	7	8.97
2	Not offer	71	91.025

Chart 4.2.12. (A)

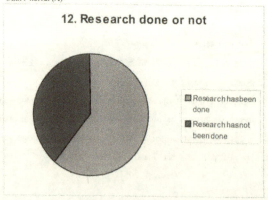

12. Research done or not

Chart 4.2.12. (B)

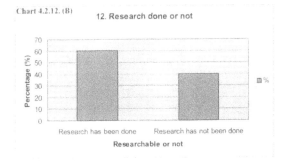

Chart 4.2.13. (A)

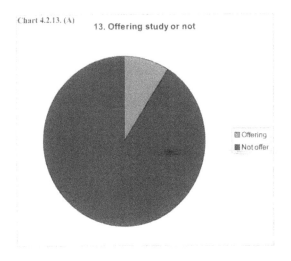

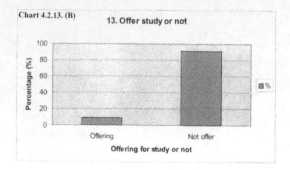

Chart 4.2.13. (B)

12. and 13. (combined)

ANALYSIS:

The analysis table consists of two concepts i.e. research has to be done or not? and whether the respondent offers to study or not?

60% people favoured the research, whereas 31% people did not respond to the study. This shows that the people those who are interested in the concept, even they have not offered for study in any organization/profession, which can be seen from the table that 2. 91% people have never offered for study. Only 8% got the chance but that was also not proper..

CONCLUSION:

This analysis shows that the industry only at the time of crisis strives for research. This also implies that people do not have any knowledge of research. People only favour the wind of short term gains. They are not

4.4 SUMMARIZED FINDINGS / OUTCOMES OF STUDY:

MANAGEMENT:

In zari industry, there seems a lack of management. There is no management in market, human resource management, production, finance and accounting, information technology, material planning and production control, purchasing function, advertising and sales promotion function, social function, which enables an industry to fulfill its social responsibility.

No financial management is there in the zari industry. There is no planning for ratio-analysis. Ratio analysis helps to understand the requirement of resources. Rationing of resources means optimum utilization of different funds available for industry. Cost of capital is not calculated. Manufacturers/traders are only using capital, but they do not have any calculation of the cost of capital. They don't have a knowledge of liquidity constraint, like whatever the surplus money or profit that is invested in fixed assets like big houses or property.

It has also been noted by observation & by talking with the people that the industry has not been able to maintain the required liquidity level for ensuring the requirement of the working capital. So industry is bound to suffer from operational problems which in the long run affects profitability.

Apart from this, the non-availability of working capital in time, and holding of excess liquidity again affects the company's profitability. So there is no assurance of the minimum & optimum holding of the liquid assets of the company.

As we know that in any organization, profitability largely depends on the efficient handling of financial resources but what we find in zari industry is lack of management of assets and financial market analysis.

A major portion of working capital in this industry is invested in the purchase of raw materials and inventories alone, business houses unnecessarily hold capital in excess of requirement, and thereby strain their profitability. A major problem according to me is the problem of excess storage cost for finished product. When there is more production without taking cognizance of the market potentialities, the industry faces the problem of storing finished products which occupies maximum space and involves a lot of cost. Not only this at a lower cost the traders are compelled to sell the product.

In this industry, the major problem of lack of management of funds, assets as well as lack of analyzing the financial market. There is dearth of planning of borrowing long term, short term, and medium term loans. The industry has some traditional ways of borrowings, borrowings from societies, banks, private financers. There is no method of issuing shares/debentures. There is a need of choosing the alternative which should be analyzed and kept most effective to ensure maximum profitability.

Similarly financial management, production management is vitally important for the same industry especially because it is engaged in manufacturing operation. Goods or products should manufactured in time. If it is not done the industry can lose its market stake or the market share. What I found in the industry is that there is no assurance about manufacturing of goods and products in the right quantity and to make it available in the market for the ultimate users. There is no effort made for cost minimization, work simplification, inventory control, product design, process improvement, quality control, etc.

The need of the industry is to use the suitable capital budgeting and to make the machines and equipments right in time and even replaced the machines with the modern available technology.

Product development and product design is also equally important as far as the management is concerned. The changing demand of the consumers heavily influences the product design and product innovation.

Nowadays the industry is suffering because they have not produced the right quantity or right product for the consumers as per their changing requirement. Free market or free competition today to a great extent exerts pressure on the industry. So industry should keep in mind that unless a product is developed suitably, based on consumer requirements, the production in the long run is bound to suffer. Similarly, product development and product innovation with work simplification and performance improving approaches ensure cost minimization also.

Industry has never seen cost efficiency, work simplification, work measurement with the help of industrial engineering, which can enable the industry to find out the exact work unit required for doing a job which in long run can help to decide wage rate more scientifically. In this industry today the major absorption of laborers/workers is there, and so whatever the efficiency industry acquires, it looses.

The major problem today is due to inventory control because unless inventory is controlled rightly or the optimum utilization of inventory resource is ensured, the production operation will definitely suffer in the long run and ultimately it will affect the company's profitability.

In this industry, there is a big lapse of market survey. There is no survey for any product market or the product value. Actually the preference of consumer has not been taken into account. "Packaging" is based on traditional system. The market potentiality has not been created by this industry. Economic and sales forecast has not been there. The Marketing research has not been done by the industry.

Nowadays the things created in the industry are produced in a static quantity, keeping in view the market stake that they having for this much quantity. Today the industry finds itself out of place because of competitors who may gradually grab the increased market potentiality for the product or products.

Suitable expansion programmes have not been undertaken from the cost point of view. No manufacturer has achieved production efficiency. Cost efficiency is only possible when a company enjoys the benefit of producing an economically run quantity and developing by products.

So in this industry, there is lack of proper development of byproducts because there is no suitable marketing research. An important part of this industry is distribution channel. In this industry, manufacturers or traders have not developed the distribution channels properly. This situation has arised due to the improper distribution of channels. Products may not reach the ultimate consumers and users for reasons of inefficient channels of distribution. This industry needs to ensure that its products reach the ultimate users in time. It requires or needs to ensure development of further marketing potential.

Apart from this, advertising as well as sales promotion is important in marketing. The Zari industry is today facing a serious and sensitive problem and there is a fear of closure due to lacking of proper distribution channels. This industry has not tried to promote the sales.

CHAPTER 5 :

RECOMMENDATIONS AND SUGGESSTIONS

	Page No.
5.1. CHALLENGES IN TIMES TO COME	322
5.2 RECOMMENDATIONS	325
5.3 FURTHER RESEARCH AVENUES	333

5.1 CHALLENGES IN TIME TO COME

(1) With the growing competition, product differentiation and positioning will become more important. Due to globalization, liberalization and the changing scenario of competititiveness and product differentiation, zari indstry is faced with a bigger challenge ahead. Zari industry requires to produce different products. Nowadays, France is competing with Indian zari market. The product differentiation as well as positioning is also required to be undertaken.

(2) Class marketing/niche marketing will grow in importance and there will be a decline in the relative importance of mass marketing, barring certain exceptions. This is a challenge to be faced by the zari industry. Due to the absence of class marketing such a situation has arisen. Mass marketing today is a problem in the zari sector.

(3) The growing competition will also increase very considerably the importance of augmented product. Levitz's comment that " the new competition is not between what companies produce in their factories but between what they add to their factory output in the form of packaging, service, advertising, customer advice, financing, delivery arrangements, warehousing and other things that people value" will become very relevant in India.

(4) Zari industry will be required to pay more attention to quality and price to survive in this competitive market.

(5) The variety of products and product forms available in the market will significantly and substantially increase the consumer choice. The zari industry requires to think and work keeping in mind the above considerations.

(6) Yet another challenge is posed by the factors which have become more popular viz. licensing, franchising and multi-level marketing.

(7) The social marketing concept will gain more acceptance.

(8) Direct marketing will gain more importance in future than today.

(9) People with technical expertise and enterprise will have enormous opportunities. It is pointed out that in future "Industries would be neither capital intensive but skill or enthusiasm intensive."

(10) Abundant entrepreneurial chances will be provided by the fast growing service sector.

(11) Personal rewards, particularly at the managerial level, will be linked to the results, much more than today. Even the tenure of employ will tend to be so linked in many companies.

(12) Companies will tend to adopt a lean structure and cut the extra flap.

(13) Global economic boom:

Naisbitt and Aburdence point out that in the decade of the 1990's the world is entering a period of economic prosperity. There is no single factor behind the economic boom, but instead an extraordinary confluence of factors the economic forces of the world are surging across national borders, resulting in more democracy, more freedom, more trade, more opportunity and greater prosperity. The growing population, the rising income and new conducive policy environment will attract more investment into the developing countries. This also will pose a challenge for the zari industry.

(14) Global strategy:

As Porter argues that a company must move towards a global strategy as soon as its resources and competitive position allow. If it is competing in global industry. A high domestic cost of capital, high domestic factors and strong currency are no excuse in global competition. Yet competing internationally is not a substitute for improvement and innovation at home. This also is a challenge for zari industry.

5.2 RECOMMENDATIONS:

1. Inputs to be declined through assessment:

Recommendations about supply of raw materials through Producers' Co-operative Society and about giving concessions, subsidies to be limited to raw materials but to abolish multiple point purchase tax on raw materials should be adopted.

The zari industry suffers from fluctuation in prices and availability of quality raw materials like gold, silver, copper, silk yarn, film and other chemicals. I also recommend to abolish multiple point purchase tax on raw materials.

2. Labour laws required to be restructured or amended:

Advantages of small firms are there in higher productivity and absentism from strikes, child labour should be stopped. The enforcement of Minimum Wages Act for the employment in zari industry should be strictly followed.

Government of Gujarat enforces "Minimum Wages Act" for the employment in zari industry. This is necessary in my opinion, to counter the dampening effect on wages due to the phenomenon of clustering, but its extension making it applicable to job contractors (Akhadedars) who are running their job work units supposedly registered under Shops and Establishment Act and who work for more than one principle is not warranted. I recommend to think on it.

3. To uplift the end product producer:

There is a necessity to uplift the end product producers, as it consumes the intermediate product totally.

4. To overcome the unorganized groups of different products:

Since there is over production, it is important to make formal groups of zari manufacturers, akhadedars and others. Z.M.A. should organise common services to those in membership and as self-help organisation, to set up the institution and service the business community requires. The separate and independent promotion of zari goods producers' co-operative society in my opinion has divided the leadership and led to unnecessary antagonistic and competitive posters they can think of sorting out problems by providing half of the positions in their respective boards for the representative of others. This way, they may be able to work with cohesion and synergy. They should not function in isolation, as they tend to do today. I recommend ZMA should not only undertake organising tours at regular intervals but should study different changes in technology, distribution and sales, advertising and also professionalism. ZMA should organise annual exhibitions and promote export market pro-actively. ZMA must be the body to expertise to undertake studies forward for organising market services including exports. ZMA must be grievance ventilating body by conducting regular meetings.

5. To upgrade the technology and research and development management :

There is a requirement for upgradation in technology as well as there should be a centre of research and development in the field of zari. For this there is need for developing 'Zari Park' in surat and adjoining areas.

The main competition comes from import. In terms of quality and price, imported zari seems to be genuinely competitive. One must raise the competitiveness of industry. It is necessary to formulate an overall development plan for zari industry. Direct assistance in form of supplying credit, raw materials, equipments, dissemination of technology information research and market development. Enumerating the characteristics of this zari industry can better do this.

An important distinguishing feature is that the units covered utilised low level traditional technologies that are characterised by manual operations most of the time employ less than 10% and do not keep any systematic record. Most of these operate either as individual units or firm part of household. Enumeration of these units causes the problem of identifying units which operates mostly inside the home or in other scheduled areas of the house hold. Out of traditional technologies may combine the largest amount of labour with unit of capital and yeild the highest value of output per unit of capital, it may not necessarily mean that these technologies optimize on the use of available resources. Technologies that are neither most labour intensive nor most capital intensive have to be thought over to avoid drudgery and / or possible exposure to hazardous condition. The role of woman in small enterprises in zari industry constitutes another difficulty on the basis of available evidents, it would seem that women make an important contribution in this industry. I do not visualise improvements in technology been feasible until zari industry moves from the status of cottage industry. Craft enterpreneurs neither have capital to invest nor have the vision and abilities to manage the zari industry at above current level of technology. The industry will continue to stagnant and may disappear under the onslaught of better and cheaper zari imports.

I recommend that government should insist on bringing zari producing firms under small scale industry category and not under category of cottage industry. Production process involving power and chemicals should not be allowed to continue in dwelling houses. Government should bring suitable legislation to shift these production activities to a carefully plant Zari Industrial Estate in consultation with The Chamber Of Commerce and Industry , Zari Merchants' Association, persons involved in zari production and Surat Municipal Corporation.

6. Substantial Reinvestment :

It is very difficult to isolate the savings and reinvestment rates for these enterprises that are components of a more complex household. Reinvestment capacity of these small entrepreneurs in the zari industry *either out of profits or institutional credit is not very substantial.*

The ability of small production units to save out their profits and reinvest such saving in their activities is essential for their growth. In many cases, their current dwelling is quite unsuitable and far too small to do these and it may not be desirable to let these units expand in the residential areas where they are currently located. Available evidence shows that very small entrepreneurs do not have access to institutional credit facilities provided by banks and other agencies. Thus, the reinvestment capacity of many of these small entrepreneurs in zari industry either out of profits or by raising institutional credit is not very substantial. In these units, the majority of which are family owned enterprises, the profits from the enterprises are often mixed with saving and expenditures from other household activities. Thus, it becomes to isolate the savings and reinvestment rates for this enterprises that are a component of more complex household.

I recommend working out long term institutional credit arrangement with S. I. D. B. I. and our commercial banks for mobilising necessary investment and working capital for transforming cottage based zari industry into a well organised small scale industry with an exclusively established zari industrial estate in Surat.

7. Suitable structure of employees/intermediary persons :

In this industry, there is no guarantee for steady employment. So there should be a proper structure of employment. Schemes like subsistence allowance, unemployment insurance can also be thought of.

As many of job work units, the availabilities of raw material is an important factor for their survival and development. In this regard, the way the production and marketing of zari goods in Surat is organised in such a manner that the entire risk are shifted on to these units. If the market is flourishing, they are flooded with orders or otherwise, they are forced to eke-out some living at the mercy of Akhadedars or Merchant Manufacturers the raw materials are very costly and long operational cycle of production and marketing in distant markets on credit leaves very little hope for these units to take up this task independently. Inspite of tax like minimum wages, child labour, etc. there is no guarantee for steady employment opportunities and stable income. When the market is not in boom, the Merchant Manufacturers minimise or completely stop their activities. Many a times, the wage rate (job work rates) are squeezed to cut short losses or avoid reduction in profit. Due to nature and structure of these job contractors in the best of times, these units survive providing subsistence and in the worst of times, they force the persons dependent on them to seek out other avenues of livelihood. In short, in the best of the times the merchants makes the best of profits and in the worst of times the merchants suffers the minimum, as he has no obligations to workers. In order to minimise the losses, he withdraws from the business for a while or shifts the burden of losses, partially if not fully, to workers by making them accept to work for less rewards. This gives the merchant an opportunity to corner most of the benefit in the *best of times* and suffer the least either withdrawing or shifting most of losses to workers by resorting to wage cuts in the worst of times.

8. To create monopoly market is an urgent need:

Bulk of output in zari industry gets saturated and is dumped same. If there is a marketing facility, it can develop new products based on marketing intelligence.

9. To fix the standards of quality:

Globalisation entails the enforcement of stringent standards of zari products of small units. Enforcement of stringent standards for zari products of small units may also have both positive and negative impacts. While such measures could contribute to high quality and therefore render them competitive, as well as safe guard public health and safety they could be inconsistent with both types of technologies used within industry and skill availability. Ultimately these policies may constitute a cause of attention for units already operating for barriers to entry of new ones.

10. To develop the infrastructure:

The provision of infrastructure, primarily in the form of industrial estates, marketing services including export marketing and other industrial services including technology development, extension and training is required.

In addition to the financial incentives offered, both central and state governments offer a broad range of services. In broad terms, these consist of the provision of infrastructure, primarily in the from of industrial estates, marketing services including export mak\rketing and other industrial services including technology development, extension and training. Co-ordination is lacking between the promotional agencies and financial intermediaries entrusted with the administration of small enterprise lending schemes. In many instances, small firms are expected to come to the organisations that provide technical and financial assistance rather than other way organisation seeking them out.

11. Promoting zari industrial estate :

The zari industry requires to have a separate industrial estate with the help of government of states and centre.

12. A separate policy should be framed :

No specific policy is there regarding zari but it is a part of handicraft. It should be advisable that proper policy may be framed for the development and upliftment of industry.

5.3 FURTHER RESEARCH AVENUES :

Research, unless it is understood in its right spirit, cannot be undertaken with success. What is important for researchers is to take research more as a passion than for career progress.

There are so many areas in zari industry for further research. Marketing of zari is one of the area where zari industry could be explored. We have different areas of research like marketing policy which involves pricing, advertising service, channels of distribution, product research, etc. Marketing research, as we all know is primarily interested in finding out the market potentiality.

A prospective researcher on management will get immense scope to investigate into these three core functional areas of management i.e. finance, production and marketing.

Research competency development is another important aspect. It focusses on integration of business plan of the company by selecting the right individual for the job. Competence is defined as the smallest unit of on-the job behaviour that is observable, measurable and changes overtime. Innovation and creativity, supply chain management knowledge, management issues, customer relationship, management (CRM), etc. are areas of researcher's interest.

One such area of interest is the financial management research. Research on financial managemnt includes different operations like: Financial Analysis, Capital Structure, Ratio Analysis, etc. Capital structure and ratio analysis enable a company to ration the requirement of resources. Rationing of resources means optimum utilization of different funds available for a company. Unless the resources available in a company are utilized we may need to find out various sources of funds and costs of capital, liquidity constraint, for a more clear understanding. Unless a company is able to maintain the required liquidity level for ensuring the requirements of the working capital, the company is bound to suffer from operational problems which in the long run may affect profitability.

Apart from such an affect, the non-availability of working capital in time, and holding of excess liquidity again affects the company's profitability. So what is needed is to ensure the minimum or the optimum holding of the liquid assets of the company. Other areas of financial management research may be the management of different funds, management of assets and financial market analysis, etc. Now we all know that in any company, profitability largely depends on the efficient handling of financial resources. Financial management research enables us to compare the operation of different companies with the help of financial analysis. If a major portion of the working capital is invested for purchase of raw materials and inventories alone, companies will unnecessarily hold capital in excess of requirements and thereby strain their profitability.

Apart from holding of raw materials and inventories which need to be controlled, companies may have the problem of excess storage costs for finished products. When we produce more without taking in to cognizance the market potentialities, we face the problem of storing finished products, which occupy maximum godown space and involve a lot of costs.

Although rationing of resources is primarily a concern for the cost management function, with the help of financial management research, using different cost indicators or using different ratios, we may find out what exactly is the optimum resource holding and in what way a company is able to hold that optimum level of the resources. Management of funds and assets and analyzing the financial market are also equally important for the financial management research.

Management of funds require an efficient planning of borrowing long term, short term and medium term loans as per the requirements. When to borrow, how to borrow and from whom to borrow is important for the company to understand in the context of different data of the company itself. The company may have some traditional ways of borrowing, like, borrowing from banks, borrowing from other financial agencies like different development banks or they may borrow by issuing debentures in the market or they may raise their capital by issuing shares, etc. All these alternatives need to be compared and anlaysed and the most cost effective one needs to be chosen to ensure maximum profitability.

Similarly, production research is vitally important for a company which is engaged in the manufacturing opertion. Unless goods or products are manufactured right in time or made available in time in the market, the company may loose the market stake or the market share.

Thus, what is primarily important for a production department is to ensure manufacturing of the right goods and products in the right quantity and to make it available in the market for the ultimate users. Thus there is a need for the development of different cost minimization alternatives, work simplification, inventory control, product design, process improvement, quality control, etc. With the help of suitable capital budgeting unless the required machines and equipments are made available right in time or unless the available machines are replaced with the modern available technology right in time, the production process will itself suffer.

Product development and product design research is also equally important. A good number of companies gradually find themselves out of market simply because they are not able to produce the right quantity or the right product for the consumers as per their changing requirements. Free market or free competition to a great extent exerts pressure on the company. Thus unless a product is developed suitably, based on consumer requirements the production in the long run is bound to suffer. Similarly, product development and product innovation with work simplification and performance improving approaches ensure cost minimization also. With the help of industrial engineering, development of the product with simultaneous reduction of the total costs is possible. Cost efficiency, work simplification, work measurement with the help of industrial engineering, development of the product with the value engineering approach, among other things, enable us to find out the excess work unit required for doing a job which in the long run helps us to decide wage rate scientifically. Unless inventory is controlled rightly or the optimum utilization of inventory resources is ensured, the production operation will definitely suffer in the long run and ultimately affect the company's profitability.

While surveying the market we found different areas of research like marketing policy which involves pricing, advertising service, channels of distribution product research, etc. Product research helps us to find out the changing consumers' requirements by carrying out survey. Improvement and use value of the present product may be carried out, as also in packaging based on consumers' preferences.

Marketing research as we all know is primarily initiated to find out the market potentiality of a particular company. With the help of economic analysis and forecasts with the help of survey of consumers or the potential consumers of the society, a company can take suitable decisions on expansion or design or outline their product process exactly coping with the requirements.

Unless a company is undertaking suitable marketing research it will definitely suffer in the long run. As we all know, no company can afford to remain in a static product or system indefinitely. To clarify this point further, company remains in producing a static quantity of some products keeping in view the market stake that they are having for this much quantity alone, in future the company may find themselves out of place because of their competitors who may gradually grab the increased market potentiality for that particular product or products.

Moreover unless suitable expansion programmes are undertaken, from costing point of view, no company can achieve production efficiency. Cost efficiency is only possible when a company enjoys the benefit of producing an economically run quantity and developing by-products. So, undertaking suitable marketing research is of utmost importance for a company.

Apart from all these things, there are other areas of research on marketing like, research on channels of distribution, etc. A company sends its products to the ultimate consumers through different channels of distributions. Products may not reach the ultimate consumer and users for reasons of inefficient channels of distribution. Thus, a company needs to ensure that its products reach the ultimate users on time. Efficient channels of distribution also ensure development of further marketing potential.

Apart from the channels of distribution, advertising as well as sales promotion research are important areas of marketing.

Thus, a prospective researcher on management gets immense scope to investigate into these three core functional areas of management, i.e., finance, production and marketing.

I : REFERENCES

SELECTED REFERENCES

1. Gujarat State Gazetteers, Surat District (1962); Directorate of government Printing, Stationery Publications, Gujarat State, Ahmedabad.

2. Zari Industry of Surat (1971), Silver Jubilee Issue, The Surat Zari Merchant's Association, Surat.

3. Desai, Rohit D (1992), "The Problems of Household Sector: A Study of Zari Industry in Surat", Monograph 17, Sardar Patel Institute of Economic and Social Research, Ahmedabad.

4. Report on Economic Census 1980 - Gujarat, Vol 1 & 2 (1992), Directorate of Economics and Statistics, Gandhinagar.

5. Monthly Statistics of Foreign Trade of India (1972), Department of Commercial Intelligence & Statistics, Government of India, Vol. 1, March, Calcutta.

6. Schmitz, Hubert (1995), "Collective Efficiency: Growth Path for Small-Scale Industry", The Journal of Development Studies, Vol. 31, No. 4, Frank Cass, London, April.

7. Knorringa, P (1994), "Lack of Interaction between Traders and Producers in the Agra Footwear Cluster", in Pedersen et al. (eds.)

8. Knorringa P. and H. Weijland (1993), "Subcontracting - The Incorporation of Small Producers in Dynamic Industrial Networks", in I.S.A. Baud and G.A Bruijne (eds.), Gender, Small Scale Industry and Development Policy, London: Intermediate Technology Publications.

9. Krugman P. (1991), Geography and Trade, Cambridge M.A : MIT Press.

10. Marshall, A. (1920), Principles of Economics, 8th Edition, London: Macmillan.

11. Rasmussen, J (1991), The Local Interpreneurial Milieu: Linkages and Specialisation among Small Town Enterprises in Zimbabwe, Research Report No. 79, Copenhagen : Dept. of Geography, Roskilde University with Centre for Development Research.

12. Rasmussen, J ., Van Dijk, M.P. and H. Schmitz, (1992), "Exploring a New Approach to Small-Scale Industry", IDS Bulletin, Vol. 23, No. 3

13. Schmitz, H. (1982), "Growth Constraints on Small-scale Manufacturing in Developing Countries: A Critical Review", World Development, Vol. 10, No. 6

14. Schmitz, H. (1992), "On the Clustering of Small Firms", IDS

Bulletin, Vol. 23, No. 3, July.

15. Schmitz, H. and B. Musyck (1994), "Industrial Districts in Europe: Policy Lessons for Developing Countries ?", World Development, Vol. 22, No. 6.

16. Gopal Lal Jain (1998) "Research Methodology" - Methods, Tools & Techniques.

17. D. K. Bhattacharya (2003) "Research Methodology".

18. N. Thanulingon (2000), "Research Methodology".

19. Abdel Baset I. M. Hasouneh (2003), "Research Methodology".

20. Charu Smita Gupta (1996), "ZARDOZI" Glittering Gold Embroidery.

II : BIBLIOGRAPHY

BIBLIOGRAPHY

1. **Abdul Haqa Dehlavi** — Akhbarul Akhiar, Delhi, 1889.
2. **Abraham T. M.** — Handicrafts in India, New Delhi, 1964.
3. **Abul Fazl Allami:** — The Ain-i-Akbari, Translated by H. Blochmann, 2nd Edition, New Imperial Book Depot, New Delhi, 1965.
4. **Academy of Fine Arts:** — Old Textiles of India, Academy of fine Arts, New Delhi
5. **"Acharanga Sutra"** — Tr. By H. Jacobi, Sacred Books of the East, Vol. XXII, Oxford, 1884.
6. **Ackermann, Phyllis:** — "Indian Embroidery", Embroidery, Vol. 3 No. 1, London, 1934, 4-10. "Textiles of the Islamic Periods – A History", in A Survey of Persian Arts, A. V. Pope (ed.), Vol. 3, Oxford University press, London, 1939, pp. 1995-2162.
7. **Alif, Shams Siraj** — Tarikh-i-Firoz shahi, Calcutta, 1890.
8. **Agrawal S. N.** — "Textile". Craft Horizon, Vol. XIX, No. 4, July-August 1959.
9. **Agrawal V. S.** — Harsha Charita-Ek Samskritika Adhyayana, 1953. "Reference to Textiles in Bana's Harshacharita", J. I. T. H., No. IV, 1959, pp. 65-68, India as known to panini, Varanasi, 1963.

10	**Ahmad, I**	"Economic and Social changes", in Jafar Imam (ed.), Muslims in India, Orient Longman, New Delhi, 1975.
11	**Ahmed, Ali**	Twilight in Delhi, Champak Library, New Delhi
12	**"Aiteraya Brahmana"**	Ed. By Th. Aufrechi, Bonn, 1879. Ed. By K. S. Agashe, Poona, 1896. tr. By Keith, HOS, Vol. XXV, Cambridge, Mass., 1920.
13	**Aiyangar, R. K. V.**	Some aspects of the Hindu view of Life according to Dharmashstra, Baroda, 1952.
14	**Al-Beruni**	Al-Beruni's India, Ed. With notes and Indices by E. C. Sachau, S. Chand, Delhi, 1964.
15	**Al-Umari**	Masalik al absar, 1838.
16	**Ali, A. Yusuf**	"A monograph on silk fabrics produced in the North Western Provinces and Oudh", Allahabad, 1900, Calico Museum of Textiles, Reprint 1974.
17	**Ali, Athar**	The Mughal Nobility under Aurangzeb, Asia Publishing House, 1966.
18	**Alkazi, Roshan**	Ancient Indian Costumes, Art Heritage Boks, 1983.
19	**Anonymous**	Travels of Sebastian Manrique, Vol. 1 and Vol. 2, New Delhi.

20	**Anonymous**	"Embroideries", The imperial gazetteer of India, Oxford, Vol. IV, 1908, pp. 218-222.
21	**Anonymous**	"Embroidered Vestments", Census of India, Vol VII, vii(a),, Census of India, Vol. VIII. vii(a) I, 1961.
22	**Anonymous**	"Catalogue of embroidered and Woven Indian Shawls and Historic Textiles from the Victoria and Albert Museum, Exhibited in the Department of Textile Industries", University of Leeds, 1st-15th May, 1970.
23	**Anonymous**	"The Zari Industry of Surat", I.E.T.J. (Handicrafts Supplement), Sept.-Oct. 1970. p. 10.
24	**Anonymous**	"Embroidery", J.I.A., Vol. II, No. 18, 1880.
25	**Ansari G.**	Muslim Castes in Uttar Pradesh, Lucknow, E.F.C.S., 1960.
26	**Archer, M.**	"Lockwood Kipling: Champions of Indian Arts and Crafts", in Dimensions of Indian Arts and Crafts: Pupul Jayakar Seventy, L. Chandra and J. Jain (Ed.), Agam Kala Prakashan, 1986, pp. 7-12.
27	**Ashraf, K. M.**	Life and conditions of People of Hindustan 1200-1550, Delhi, 1970.

28	Ashton, Leigh	"The Art of India and Pakistan: A Commemorative Catalogue of exhibition held at the Royal Academy of Arts", London, Faber and Faber Ltd., London, 1947-1948.
29	Atkinson, J.	Customs and Manners of the Women of Persia and their domestic Superstitions, London, 1832.
30	Auboyer, Jeannine	Daily Life in Ancient India (200 B.C. 700 A.D.), France, 1965.
31	Aziz, Abdul	The Imperial Treasury of the Indian Mughals, Lahore, 1942.
32	Baden Powell, B. H.	Handbook of the Manufacturers and Arts of the Punjab, 8 Vols. Lahore, 1872.
33	Bahadur, K. D.	A history of Indian Civilisaton, Ess Ess Publications, 1980.
34	Baihaqi Abdul Fazal	"Tarikh-i-Baihaqi", Ed. W. H. Morley, Calcutta, 1862.
35	Banabhatta	"Harshacharita", Ed. By K. P. Parab, Bombay, 1925. English Trans. By E. B. Cowell and F. W. Thomas, London, 1897.
36	Bandopadhyaya, N. C.	"Economic Life and Progress in Ancient India, Calcutta, 1945.

37	**Barani, Ziyauddin**	"Tarikh Firuzshahi", Calcutta, 1862, ed. Saiyid Ahmed Khan, 1888-91.
38	**Barth, Frederick**	Indus and Swat Kohistan: an Ethnographic survey, Oslo, 1956.
39	**Barua, B. M.**	Barhut, Parts I, II and III, Indian Research Institute, Calcutta, 1934, Reprint 1979.
40	**Barve, V. R.**	Complete Textile Encyclopaedia, D. B. Taraporevala Sons & Co., Bombay, 1967.
41	**Basham, A. L.**	The wonder that was India, London, 1954.
42	**Basham, R.**	Urban Anthropology, The Cross Cultural Study of Complex Societies, 1978.
43	**Batuta, Ibn**	"Travels in Asia and Africa", 1325-1354, Trans. By H. A. R. Gibb, Inst. Ed. London, 1929.
44	**Behrua, N. K.**	Peasant Potters of Orissa: A Sociological Study, Sterling Publishers Pvt. Ltd., New Delhi, 1978.
45	**Belshaw, C. S.**	Traditional Exchange and Modern Marets, Prentice Hall, Eaglewood Cliffs, 1965.
46	**Belshaw, M.**	A Village economy: Land and People of Huecoria, Columbia University, New York, 1967.
47	**Beni Prasad**	History of Jahangir, Indian Press, Allahabad, 1930

48 Bernier, Francois   Travels in the Mughal Empire (1656-1668 A.D.), Ed. By A. Constable, 1891, Reprint S. Chand and Co., New Delhi, 1972.

49 Bhatnagar, I. K.   Brocaded Textiles and their conservation, C.C.P.I. Part I and Part II, Vol. VIII, Vol. IX, 1975, pp. 41-45. 73-75.

50 Bhatt, G. S.   "Trends and measures of status mobility among the chamars of Dehradun", in Tribe, Caste and Peasantry, K. S. Mathur and B. C. Agrawal (Ed.), E.F.C.S., 1974

51 Bhushan, Jamila Brij The Costumes and Textiles of India", D. B. Taraporevala Sons and Co. Ltd., Bombay, 1959.

52 Bhushan Kavi   Bhushan Granthavali, Hindi Bhavan of allahabad, Allahabad.

53 Birdwood George   Industrial Arts of India, Chapman and Hall, London, 1880

54 Birrell, Verla   The Textile Arts, New York, 1959.

55 Blat, Solvyns   Costume of Hindustan, 1807

56 Blau, Peter   On the nature of organization, John Wiley and Sons, New York, 1974.

57 Blunt, E. A. H.   The Caste system of Northern India, S. Chand and Company, 1969.

58	**Bopegamage, A.**	Delhi: A study of Urban Sociology, University of Bombay, Bombay, 1957.
59	**Bott, Elizabeth**	"Family and Social Network roles, Norms and External relationships in Ordinary Urban Families", Tavistock, London, 1971.
60	**Braun-Ronsdorf, M.**	"Gold and Textiles, Gold and Silver Fabrics from Medieval to Modern Times", CIBA review, Vol. 3, 1961, pp. 2-16.
61	**Breese, Gerald**	Urbanization in Newly Developing Countries, Prentice Hall Inc., Delhi, 1966.
62	**Budauni, Abdul Malik**	"Muntakhabut-twarikh", English trans. By Ranking, Lowe and Haig, 3 Vols., Calcutta, 1889-1925.
63	**Bunt, Cyril G. E.**	"An Indo-Portuguese Embroidery in the Bargello", B. M., London, 1942.
64	**Burdon, E.**	"Monograph on the wire and Tinsel Industry in the Punjab", Authority Civil and Military Gazette Press, Lahore, 1909.
65	**Burgess, Robert G.**	In the Field: An introduction to Field Research, George, Allen and Unwin, London, 1984.
66	**Cable, V., Weston, A. and Jain, L. C.**	"The commerce of culture: experience of Indian Handicrafts", Lancer International, 1985.

67	Caine, W. S.	Picturesque India: A handbook for European travelers, George Routledge and Sons Ltd., 1891.
68	Carori, John Francis Gemelli	"A voyage round the world", 6 Parts, Part III dealing with India, 1704.
69	Cecil, B.	India, Thacker and Co. Ltd., Bombay, New Delhi.
70	Chakledar, H. C.	Social life in ancient India, Calcutta, 1929.
71	Chandra L. and J. Jain	Dimensions of Indian Art, Pupul Jayakar Seventy, 2 Vols. Agam Kala Prakashan, 1986.
72	Channa, Subhadra	Tradition and Rationality in Economic behaviour, Cosmo Publications, New Delhi, 1985.
73	Channa, V. C	Caste: Identity and Continuity, B. R. Publishing Corp., Delhi, 1979.
74	Chatterjee, A. C.	"Notes on the industries of the United Provinces", Supdt. Govt. Press, Allahabad, 1908.
75	Chatterjee, C. K.	"Bibliography of Small Scale and cottage Industries and Handicrafts", Vol. I, Part XI (i) Census of India, 1961.
76	Chattopadhyaya, Kamla Devi	Indian Embroidery, Wiley Eastern Limited, New Delhi, 1977.

77	**Claemer, John(Ed.)**	The new economic Anthropology, The McMillan Press Ltd., 1978.
78	**Clark, G. S.**	Indo-Dutch Embroideries of the 17th Century, Vol. I, London, 1914.
79	**Cole, A.S**	"Ornament in European Silks", Encyclopaedia Britannica, London, 1899.
80	**Collman, Jeff**	Handbook of Social and Cultural Anthropology, 1973.
81	**Cowell, E. B**	The Jatakas or stories of Buddha's former Births, Tr. By Francis H. T., Vols. I to VII, 1973.
82	**Creswell, K. A.**	A bibliography of the Architecture, Arts and Crafts of Islam to 1st January 1960, The American University at Cairo Press, 1961.
83	**Crill, Rosemary**	"Hats from India", Victoria and Albert Museum, London, 1985.
84	**Dalton, George**	"Economic Theory and primitive society", A. A., Vol. 63, 1961, pp. 1-25.
85	**Dar, S. N.**	Costumes of India and Pakistan, Taraporevala Sons and Co., Bombay, 1969.
86	**Das, S. K.**	Economic history of ancient India, Calcutta, 1925.

87	**Das, Sukla**	Socio-economic life in Northern India (A.D. 550 to A. D. 650), Abhinav Publications, New Delhi, 1980.
88	**Dayal, M.**	"Rediscovering Delhi", Hindustan Times, Sunday, World, 7th January, 1973.
89	**De, B. N.**	"A monograph on the wire and tinsel industry in the central provinces", Govt. Press, Nagpur, 1910.
90	**Desai, V. N.**	Life at court: art for Inida's rulers, 16th - 19th century, museum of fine arts, Boston, 1985.
91	**Dey, N. L.**	The geographical dictionary of ancient and medieval India, London, 1927.
92	**Dhamija, J.**	The survey of embroidery traditions, Marg. Vol. XVII, No. 2, Embroidery, Bombay, March, 1964.
93	**Dimand, M. S.**	A handbook of Muham-madan art, 2nd edn., New York Metropolitan museum of art.
94	**Dixit, P. K**	"Zari embroidery and Batwa making of Bhopal, Madhya Pradesh", Handicrafts survey monographs, Vol. VIII, Part VII-A, 1965, No. 1, Census of India, 1961, New Delhi, 1965.

95	**Doctor, B.C**	"Contemporary costumes and ornaments as reflected in bharut sculpture, J.M.S.U.B, 1997, pp. 143-151.
96	**Doshi, Harish**	Traditional neighbourhood in a modern city, Abhinav publications, New Delhi, 1974.
97	**Dozy, R.P.A**	Dictionnarie detaille des norms des vetemensts chezles arabs, Amsterdam, 1845.
98	**Dutt, M.N.**	"The Mahabharata: Adi parva", English prose translation (Ed.), 1895.
99	**Edel, Mathew**	Economic analysis in an anthropological setting: Some methodological considerations, A.A., 71, pp. 421-433.
100	**Elliot, H.M and Dowson J.**	The history of India as told b its own historians (the muhammadan period), vol. I, New Delhi.
101	**Elphinstone**	History of India, 2nd edition, P. 599.
102	**Emery, Irene**	The primary structures of fabrics, Washington, D.C. 1966.
103	**Estrade, C.**	Broideries Hindories, Paris, 1926.
104	**Etizioni, Amitai**	Modern Organization, Prentice Hall of India, New Delhi, 1965.

105	**Fabri, C.L**	Ballet costumes in Akbar's times, Marg. Bombay, Vol. VII, No. 1, 1953.
106	**Fakhruddin, M.**	"Tarikh-i-Fakhruddin Mubarakshah", Ed. E. D. Ross, London, 1927.
107	**Fanshawe, H.C**	Delhi past and present, johm murray, London, 1902.
108	**Fergusson**	Tree and Serpent Worship, Pt. LXXXVI, p. 206, 1971.
109	**Firth, Raymond**	Elements of Social Organisatin, Tavistock Publications, London, 1969.
110	**Fisher, B.A**	Small group decision making, McGraw-Hill, New York, 1974.
111	**Flangan, J.F**	The earliest dated Islamic textiles, B.M., L.X, 1932, pp. 313-314.
112	**Flemming, E.**	An encyclopaedia of textiles, New York, 1927.
113	**Folcker, E.G**	A silk and gold carpet in the national museum, Stockholm, B.M., XXX, New Delhi.
114	**Foster, William (Ed.)**	Early travels in India, 1583-1619, London, 1921.
115	**Fryer, John**	A new account of east India and Persia, London, 1898.

116	**Garner, Julian**	Indian embroideries of the Mughal period, International studies, June, 1927.
117	**Ghurye, G. S**	Indian costumes (Bharatiya Vesabhusa), Popular Book Depot, Bombay, 1951.
118	**Goetz, H**	Indian costumes of the 18th and early 19th century in the Indian Museum,, London, N.S., II, No. 6, 1927, pp. 140-147.
119	**Golombek, L. and V. Gervers**	Tiraz fabrics in the royal Ontario museum, in studies in textile history, V. Gervers (Ed.), royal ontario museum, Toronto, 1977, pp. 82-125.
120	**Goswamy, B. N**	A jainesque sultanate shahnamah and the content of the pre-mughal painting in India, Zurich, 1988.
121	**Gould, H.A**	Lucknow rickshawallah, the social organization of an occupational category, I.J.C.S, pp. 24-24, 1965.
122	**Green, L.B**	Gold and Silver lace thread industry, Census of India, Vol. XIV, Madras, Part I report, 1932, Appendix II, P. 249.
123	**Gupta, B.A**	Embroidery, J.I.A.I, Vol. II, No. 18, London, 1888, pp. 9-16.
124	**Gupta, Charu S.**	The gilded thread, India magazine, Anniversary issue on gold, December 1991.

125	Gupta, Raghuraj	Caste ranking and intercaste relations among the muslims of a village in North-western U.P., in Tribe, Caste and Peasantry, K.S. Mathur and B.C. Agrawal (Ed.), E.F.C.S., 1974.
126	Habibullah, A.B.M	The foundation of muslim rule in India, central book depot, Allahabad, 1961.
127	Hadaway, W.S	Monograph on tinsel and wire in the madras presidency, Supdt. Govt. Press, Madras, 1909.
128	Hall, Richard H.	Occupations and the social structure, Prentice Hall Inc., New Jersey, 1975.
129	Hammel E. and Lasbett, P	Comparing household structure over time and between cultures, Comparative studies in society and history, Vol. 18, 1974, pp. 73-109.
130	Hammersley, Martyn and Atkinson, Paul	Ethnography principles in practice, Tavistock publications, London, 1983.
131	Havell, E.B	The industries of madras(Embroidery), J.I.A.I., Vol. III, 1890, p. 114.
132	Hendley, T.H	Embroidery, J.I.A.I., Vol. IV, 1891, p. 5
133	Herringham,	Ajanta Frescoes, London, O.U.P., 1915.

134	**Herskovits, M.J**	Economic anthropology, Knopf, New York, 1952.
135	**Hopkins, E. W**	India, Old and New, New York, 1902.
136	**Howell-Smith, A.P**	Indian embroidery, J.E.G., Vol. 3. No. 3, 1935.
137	**Hughes, Thomas**	Dictionary of Islam (Reprint)
138	**Hunter, George Leland**	Decorative textiles, Lippincott, Philadelphia and London, 1918.
139	**Hunter, W.W**	The Indian Mussalman, 3rd Ed., London, 1858.
140	**Irwin, J.C**	Embroidery, Asia, Encyclopaedia Britannica, William Benton, Vol. 8, 1965, p. 316.
141	**Irwin J. and Hall Margaret**	Indian embroideries, Vol. II, historic textiles of India at the Calico Museum, Calico museum of textiles, Ahmedabad, 1973.
142	**Irwin, John**	Indian embroider, His majesty's stationary office, London, a publication of the Victoria and Albert museum, No. 7, 1951.
143	**Iyengar, H.K. Rama**	Gold Lace, Census of India, Vol. XXV, Mysore, Part I, report, Appendix IV, 1931, pp. 343-344.
144	**Jaffar, S.M**	Education in Muslim India, 1936
145	**Jagmohan**	Rebuilding Shahjahanabad, the walled city of Delhi, Vikas, 1975.

146	**Jahangir**	Tuzuk-i-Jahangir (Trans. By A. Rogers and H. Beveridge), Delhi, 1968.
147	**Jacobi, H**	Jain Sutras, tr. From Prakrit, Motilal Banarasidas, 1964.
148	**Jain, J.C**	Life in ancient India as depicted in the jain canon and commentaries: 6th century B.C. to 17th century A.D., Munshiram Manoharlal, 1984.
149	**Jeannine, Auboyer**	Daily life in ancient India (from 200 B.C. to 700 A.D.), translated from the French by Simon Watson Taylor, 1965.
150	**Jinavijaya(Ed.)**	Puratana Prabandha Sangraha, Calcutta, 1936, p. 39.
151	**Johnson, Allen W.**	Research methods in social anthropology, 1978.
152	**Johnson A.W. and George, C. B**	Kinship, friendship and exchange in two communities: A comparative analysis of norms and behaviour, J.A.R., 30, 1974, pp. 55-68.
153	**Joy, Leonard**	One economist's view of the relationship between economics and anthropology, Raymond Firth (Ed.), Tavistock, London, 1967.
154	**Kaegi, Adolf**	Life in ancient India, Calcutta, 1950.

155	**Kalhana**	Rajataranginin, Ed. And Trans. By M.A.Stein, London, 1900, 2 Vols.
156	**Karsten, D.**	The economics of handicrafts in traditional societies (an investigation in Sidamo and Gemu Goffa province of southern Ethiopia), Weltforven Verlag: Munchen, 1972.
157	**Keay, f.E and Karve, D.D**	A history of education in India and Pakistan, Calcutta, 1964.
158	**Keith A.B and Macdonell, A.**	A vedic index, 2 Vols., London, 1912.
159	**Kendrick, A.F and Cole, A.S**	Embroidery, in encyclopaedia Britannica, 11th ed., 1911.
160	**Kipling, J.J**	Industries of the Punjab gold and silver embroidery, J.I.A.I., Vol. II, Nos. 20, 23, 24, Oct 1988, pp. 30-32.
161	**Kluckhon, Clyde**	Culture and behaviour, the free press of Glencoe, 1962.
162	**Knight, F. H**	The economic organisaton, Harper Torch Books, New York, 1965, originally published, 1931.
163	**Krishna A. and Krishna V.**	Banaras brocades, edited by Ajit Mukherjee, Crafts museum, New Delhi, 1966.
164	**Kulshreshtha, S.S**	The development of trade and industry under the mughals (1526-1707 A.D), 1964.

165	Kuznets, S.	Economic change, Sprengler, J.J. (Ed.), New York, 1953.
166	Lancaster, C.S	The econmics of social organization in an ethnic border zone: the gold (Northern Shena) of the Zobegi valley, Ethnology, 10, pp. 445, 1971.
167	Lane, Poole	Medieval India under Mohammadan rule, 1917.
168	Laslett, P. and Wall, R.	Household and family in past time, Cambridge Univ. Press, Cambridge, 1972.
169	Latifi, A.	The industrial Punjab, 8 Vols., Longmans, London, 1911.
170	Leach, E.R (Ed.)	Aspects of Caste in south Inida, Ceylon and North-West Pakistan Cambridge papers in social anthropology, No. 2, Cambridge, Cambridge University press, 1960.
171	Leclair, E.E(Jr.)	Economic theory and economic anthropology, A.A., 64, pp. 1179-1203, 1962.
172	Levine, G. Harold	Scientists and culture heroes in ethnographic method, in reviews in anthropology, Vol. 12, No. 4, 1985, pp. 338-345.
173	Maity, S.K	The economic life of Northern India (300-500 A.D), Calcutta, 1957.

174	**Majumdar, R.C**	Classical accounts of India, the greek and roman accounts of ancient India, Firma K.L.M. Pvt. Ltd., 1989.
175	**Majumdar, R.C (Ed.)**	The Delhi sultanate, Vol. VI, Bombay, 1967.
176	**Manucci, Niccolao**	Storia de moguls, Trans. with introduction and notes by William Irvine, 3 vols., Calcutta, 1965-66.
177	**Markrish, Lilo**	The myth of the improving Westerner, in civilization on loan by Hernz Edgar Kroine, Oxford, 1973
178	**Marshall, Shalins**	Stone age economics, Tavistock, 1974.
179	**Martin, F. R**	The miniature painting and painters of Persia, India and Turkey, 2 vols., 8th to 18th century, reprint, B.R. Pub., 1985.
180	**Mathur, N.L**	Red fort and Mughal life, New Delhi, Pub. by the Author, 1964.
181	**Maurice, T**	History of Hindustan: Its arts and its sciences, Navrang, New Delhi, Vols, I and II, 1974.
182	**Mehta, R.J**	The handicrafts and industrial arts of India, Bombay, 1960.
183	**Mehta, R.N**	The historical evidence for two Jaina Velvets, J.I.T.H., No. 2, 1956, pp. 53-55.
184	**Merutunga**	Prabandha Cintamani, 14th century, 1932.

185	**Mirza, M.W**	Life and works of amir khusro, Punjab university, 1935.
186	**Mishra, J.S**	Ancient Inidan Textile designs, Part one, Prithvi prakashan, 1981.
187	**Mitchell, G**	Social networks in urban situation, 1975.
188	**Mitra, R.L**	Lalita Vistara, Calcutta, 1877.
189	**Mohanty, B.C**	Brocaded fabrics of India, Alfred Buhler (Ed.), 2 Vols., Calico museum of textiles, Ahmedabad, 1984.
190	**Monier-Williams**	A Sanskrit English dictionary, Oxford, 1956. Modern India and Indians, Kegan Paul, London, 1891.
191	**Monserrate, Antonia**	The commentary of father Monserrate, S.J. on his journey to the court of Akbar, Tr. By J.S.Hoylard, London, 1922.
192	**Moorcroft W. and Trebeck, G.**	Travels in the Himalayan provinces of Hindustan and the Punjab: in ladakh and Kashmir, 1819-25, patiala, 1970.
193	**Mukherjee, R.K**	The economic history of India (1600-1800), J.U.P.H.S., Vol. XV, pt. I, p. 91.
194	**Mukherjee, T.N**	Art manufactures of India, 8 Vols. Supdt. Govt. printing press, Calcutta, 1888.
195	**Nainar, M.H**	Arab geographer's knowledge of south India, Madras, 1942.

196	**Nissim, Ezekiel**	Calico museum of textiles, Ahmedabad, J.I.T.H., nos. 2.3.4.5 and 6, 1956,1957,1959,1960 and 1961.
197	**Nissim J. A**	Portfolio of Indian Art, London, 1881-1886.
198	**Oaten, Edward Farley**	Travel and Travellers in India (1400-1700 A.D.), London, 1909.
199	**Opler, M.E and R.D.Singh**	Economic, Political and social change in a village of central India, Human organization, 2, 1952.
200	**Oppert, G**	On the ancient commerce of India, Madras, 1879.
201	**Ovington, J**	A voyage to surat in the year 1689, London, Oxford Univ. press, 1929.
202	**Panikkar, K.M**	A survey of Indian history, Bombay, 1956.
203	**Paul Stephens C**	Persian-English-Urdu dictionary, deep pubication, 1989, pp. 309,271.
204	**Prithviraj**	Prithi Chandra Charita, prachin Gujarat kavya samagama, baroda, 1920
205	**Pope, A.U. (Ed.)**	A survey of Persian art, Vol. 3, Oxford Univ. Press, London and New York, 1939.
206	**Pope, A.U and P. Ackermann (Ed.)**	A survey of persian art, Oxford Univ. press, London and New York, Vol. XIV, 1967.
207	**Quluqshandi**	Al-Subhul Asha, Darul Kutub kadiviah, cairo, Vols. 83 and 84, 1913.

208	**Rao, V.L.S. Prakasa and K. V. Sundaram**	Delhi, encyclopaedia Britannica, revised edition, 1974.
209	**Ray, Mallinath**	A monograph on the wire and tinsel industry in Bengal, Bengal secretariat book depot, Calcutta, 1910.
210	**Riefstani, R. M**	Persian and Indian textiles from the 16th to the early 19th century, New York, 1923.
211	**Rizvi, S.M.A**	Some aspects of industry and social change among the muslim karkhanedars, Doctor of Philosophy, University of Delhi, 1981.
212	**Robert, Layton**	The anthropology of art, New York, Columbia university press, 1981.
213	**Rose, A.**	Glossary of the tribes and castes of the Punjab and N.W.F.P., Vol. 1, p. 489, 1911.
214	**Rose, H.A**	Rites and ceremonies of hindus and muslims (reprint), Amar prakashan, New Delhi, 1983.
215	**Roy, Shibani**	Status of muslim women in North India, B.R. Pubishing, Delhi, 1979.
216	**Salar Jung**	Munaga-i-Delhi, 1739.
217	**Saletore, R.N**	Life in the Gupta age, Bombay, 1943.
218	**Saraf, D.N**	Indian Crafts: Development and potential, Vikas Publishers, New Delhi, 1982.
219	**Saraswati, S.K**	Indian textiles, the publication division, 1961.

220	**Sarkar, Jadunath**	The India of Aurangzeb, Calcutta, 1901.
221	**Sarkar, S.C**	Some aspects of the earliest social history of India, p. 63, (fn. 120, New Delhi.
222	**Saxena, B. P**	History of Shahjahan of Delhi, Allahabad, 1932.
223	**Schneider, H.K**	Economic development and economic change: The caste of East African cattle, C.A., 15, pp. 259-277, 1974.
224	**Schoff, W.H.(Ed.)**	The periplus of the erythream sea, London, 1912.
225	**Sen, Geeti**	Paintings from the Akbarnama, Rupa and Co., 1984.
226	**Serjeant, R. B.**	Islamic textiles, material for a history of Islamic textiles upto the Mongol conquest, Ars Islamica, Vols. XI-XII, Ann arbor, University of Michigan press, 1946, pp. 98-145.
227	**Sewell, Robert**	A forgotten empire, London, 1924.
228	**Shanti Swarup**	The arts and crafts of India and Pakistan, Bombay, 1957.
229	**Singh, C.**	Textiles and Costumes from the Maharaja Savai Maan Singh II Museum, MSMS II Trust, City Palace, Jaipur, 1979.

230	**Singh C. and Ahiuasi, P.**	Woollen textiles and costumes from Bharat Kala Bhavan, Banaras Hindu University, 1981.
231	**Sinha, Bipin K.**	The beauties of Indian embroideries, American Magazine of Art, XVII, 1926, pp. 586-587.
232	**Smith, M.G**	The economy of the Hausa communities of Zaria, London, H. M. Stationery office, 1955.
233	**Smith, V.A**	The treasure of Akbar, J.R.A.S., 1915, pp. 231-242.
234	**Spear, P.**	The twilight of the Moghuls, Cambridge University press, p. 140.
235	**Spies, O.**	An Arab account of India in the 14th century, translated from Persian and Arabic, the Muslim University jounal, 1935, pp. 69-70.
236	**Strong, Roy**	The Indian heritage, Court life and arts under Mughal rule, V. and A. museum and the Herbert press, 65, Belsize law, 1982.
237	**Stuers Vreeda de**	Purdah among muslim women, 1971.
238	**Sykes, Sire Percy**	A history of Persia, 2nd edition, 2 Vols., London, 1921.
239	**Tann, E. H.**	Notes on eastern embroideries, Art worker's quarterly, III, pp. 147-150., with 1 coloured plate, 5 examples and 4 figures.

240	**Tansukhram (Ed.)**	Kuttanimatam, Bombay, 1923.
241	**Tavernier, Jean Baptiste,**	Travels in India, translated from the original French edititon of 1676 by V. Ball, 2 Vols., 1889.
242	**Terry, Edward**	A voyage to East India, London, 1777.
243	**Tilke, Max**	Oriental costumes-their designs and colours, translated by C. Hamilton (German).
244	**Vasu, S.C**	Astadhyayi of Panini, 1962.
245	**Veblen, T.**	Theory of leisure class: An economic study of institutions, Unwin books, London, 1912.
246	**Vyas, S. N**	Ramayan Kalin Sanskriti, Satsahitya prakashan, Delhi, 1958.
247	**Warmingtin, E.H**	Commerce between the roman empire and India, Cambridge, 1928.
248	**Watson, John Forbes**	Indian costumes and textile fabrics, Edinburgh review, Vol. 126, 1867.
249	**Watt, George**	J.I.A.I., Vol. II, Nos. 17-24, Oct 1858.
250	**Weber, M.**	The theory of social and economic organizations, New York, translated by A.M. Henderson and Talcott Parsons(Ed.), The Free press of Glencoe, 1947.
251	**Wehr, Hans**	A dictionary of modern written Arabic, ed. By J. Milton Cornon, Wiesbaden, 1979.

252	Weibel. A.E	Two thousand years of textiles, New York, 1952.
253	Welch, S.C	Indian art and culture 1300-1900, Mapin publishing, 1986.
254	Wheeler, J.T	India, Vedic and Post vedic, Calcutta, 1952.
255	Williamson, Thos	The costumes and customs of modern India, London, 1813.
256	Wilson, H.H.	The Persian Gulf, Oxford, 1928.
257	Wingate, B. Isabel	Textile fabrics and their selection, Prentice Hall Inc., Eaglewood Cliffs, New jersey, 1976.
258	Yasin, Mohammad	A social history of Islamic India, Munshiram Manoharlal Publishers Pvt. Ltd., New Delhi, 1971.
259	Yates, J.	Textrinum Antiquorum, London, 1843, Bk. III, Ch. II.
260	Yule, H. (Ed.)	The book of sir Marco Polo, third edition revised by H. Cordier, 2 Vols., p.304, London, 1903.
261	Zahida, Amjad Ali	Embroidery in Pakistan, Pakistan quarterly, VI, No. 1, 1956, pp. 51-56.
262	Zahiruddin, Faruki	Aurangzeb and his times. Zari the golden thread of India, A.I.H.B., New Delhi.

CPSIA information can be obtained
at www.ICGtesting.com
Printed in the USA
BVHW061525170223
658735BV00006B/207